DATE DUE

DUE. ○ '00			
DE ○ '00			
DE 20 '00			

DEMCO 38-296

COMPARATIVE COMPETITION POLICY

R

Comparative Competition Policy

NATIONAL INSTITUTIONS IN A GLOBAL MARKET

Edited by

G. BRUCE DOERN

and

STEPHEN WILKS

CLARENDON PRESS · OXFORD

D

RESS
Oxford OX2 6DP

t of the University of Oxford
ellence in research, scholarship,
and education by publishing worldwide in

Oxford New York

Athens Auckland Bangkok Bogotá Buenos Aires Calcutta
Cape Town Chennai Dar es Salaam Delhi Florence Hong Kong Istanbul
Karachi Kuala Lumpur Madrid Melbourne Mexico City Mumbai
Nairobi Paris São Paulo Singapore Taipei Tokyo Toronto Warsaw
with associated companies in Berlin Ibadan

Oxford is a registered trade mark of Oxford University Press
in the UK and in certain other countries

Published in the United States
by Oxford University Press Inc., New York

ISBN 0-19-828062-9

Printed in Great Britain
on acid-free paper by
Biddles Short Run Books
King's Lynn

PREFACE

The original inspiration for this collection was a research project on Comparative Competition Policy funded by the British Economic and Social Research Council (ESRC). The project involved the creation of a loose international network of collaborators which has proved most productive and has taken on a life of its own. The collaborators came together to discuss preliminary papers at a Workshop held at the University of Exeter in February 1993. The involvement of invited academics and British government officials added depth to the discussion and set the scene for a major conference held in Ottawa in May 1994, sponsored by the School of Public Administration at Carleton University. By then Bruce Doern had become a co-organizer of the research and our original collaborators, Roland Sturm and Kenji Sanekata, had been supplemented by the welcome presence of Guy Peters.

The papers presented at the Ottawa Conference have been extensively revised in the light of a most productive exchange of views, and they have been updated to reflect events up to late 1994. Three additional chapters have been added to provide context and comparison, and we believe that the volume now approaches the ideal of an integrated comparative treatment of the political economy of competition policy and competition policy institutions.

Each of the authors established close and productive working relationships with the national competition authorities in his respective country. We have been struck by the way in which at least one of the analytical concepts which we employ in later pages has come alive before our eyes. There *is* an international competition policy community. We have observed it at work and, in a fashion, we have become a satellite within its gravitational field.

Among the many contributors to the research undertaking whom we would like to thank are the officials and politicians who are often the subjects of political science research. Some are mentioned by name in the following chapters, others are thanked by individual authors. We must, however, express our appreciation of their co-operation. The enterprise has also benefited from extensive financial support and we should like to record our thanks to the ESRC under award R000232903; the Social Science and Humanities Research Council of Canada; the Daiwa Anglo-Japanese Foundation; the British Council (Tokyo); and the Research Funds of the University of Exeter and Carleton University. We would like particularly to record our thanks to the Canadian Bureau of Competition Policy, which helped fund our Ottawa meeting and which managed to persuade no less than three of its present and past Directors to contribute their experience to the debates. Among the many academics who attended the Conference, commented on papers, or generally enhanced the calibre of our work, we should particularly like to thank Michael Atkinson (McMaster), Simon Bulmer (Manchester), John Usher (Exeter and Edinburgh), and Richard Whish (Kings College London). Conventions of confidentiality do not allow us properly to thank the many individual officials and private-sector practitioners who have contributed to our work, but we feel that we should record our appreciation of some of the exceptionally helpful experts who attended the Ottawa Conference. We should like to thank the following, while exempting them from any responsibility from the inevitable inaccuracies or misunderstandings which may mar the following pages: Val Traversy and Rob Anderson (Canadian Bureau of Competition Policy), Lawson Hunter (former Director of the Canadian Bureau), Martin Howe (Office of Fair Trading), Eric Lacey (OECD), and Akinori Uesugi (Japan Fair Trade Commission).

B. D.
S. W.

Exeter
May 1995

CONTENTS

LIST OF TABLES

LIST OF FIGURES

ABBREVIATIONS

ABA	American Bar Association
ACCJ	American Chamber of Commerce Japan
AML	Antimonopoly Law (Japan)
ANZCERTA	Australian–New Zealand Closer Economic Relations Trade Agreement
APEC	Asia Pacific Economic Conference
BCP	Bureau of Competition Policy (Canada)
BEUC	European Bureau of Consumers' Unions
BKA	Bundeskartellamt (Germany)
CA	Consumers Association (UK)
CAP	Common Agricultural Policy (Europe)
CFI	Court of First Instance (European court)
CBI	Confederation of British Industry
DG IV	Directorate General IV (of the European Commission)
DGFT	Director General of Fair Trading (UK)
DIR	Director of Investigation and Research (Canada)
DOJ	Department of Justice (USA)
DTI	Department of Trade and Industry (UK)
EC	European Community
ECO	European Cartel Office (proposed)
EP	European Parliament
ERM	Exchange Rate Mechanism (Europe)
ERT	European Round Table of Industrialists
EU	European Union
FTC	Federal Trade Commission (USA)
GATT	General Agreement on Tariffs and Trade
JFTC	Japan Fair Trade Commission
LDP	Liberal Democratic Party (Japan)
MITI	Ministry of International Trade and Industry (Japan)
MMC	Monopolies and Mergers Commission (UK)
MOF	Ministry of Finance (Japan)
MOFA	Ministry of Foreign Affairs (Japan)
MTF	Merger Task Force (Europe)
NAFTA	North American Free Trade Agreement
OECD	Organization for Economic Co-operation and Development

OFT	Office of Fair Trading (UK)
OFGAS	Office of Gas Supply (UK)
OFFER	Office of Electricity Regulation (UK)
OFTEL	Office of Telecommunications (UK)
OFWAT	Office of Water Services (UK)
RPC	Restrictive Practices Court (UK)
RTPA	Restrictive Trade Practices Act (UK)
SII	Structural Impediments Initiative (Talks)
UNCTAD	United Nations Conference on Trade and Development
UNICE	Union of Industrial and Employers' Associations
VER	Voluntary Export Restraint
WTO	World Trade Organization

NOTES ON CONTRIBUTORS

G. Bruce Doern is a Professor in the School of Public Administration, Carleton University, Ottawa and is a Joint Professor in the Department of Politics, University of Exeter. His recent books include *Fairer Play: Canadian Competition Policy Institutions in a Global Market* (1995), and *The Greening of Canada: Federal Institutions and Decisions* (1994, co-authored with Tom Conway).

Lee McGowan is a Lecturer in the School of Public Policy at the University of Ulster. His previous publications include *The Evolution of German Competition Policy* (1993).

B. Guy Peters is Maurice Falk Professor of American Government in the Department of Political Science, University of Pittsburg. His recent books include *The Politics of Taxation: A Comparative Perspective* (1991), and *The Politics of Bureaucracy* (1988).

Kenji Sanekata is Professor of Law at Hokkaido University. He is a long-standing adviser to the Japan Fair Trade Commission. His recent publications include *Antimonopoly Law* (1993), and *Economic Regulation and Competition Law* (1983).

Roland Sturm is Professor of Political Science at the University of Tübingen. His recent publications include *Federalism, Unification and European Integration* (co-editor with Charlie Jeffery, 1993), and *Die Industriepolitik der Bundesländer und die Europäische Integration* (1991).

Michael J. Trebilcock is Professor of Law and Director of the Law and Economics Program at the University of Toronto. His recent publications include *Unfinished Business: Reforming Trade Remedy Laws in North America* (1993), and *Trade and Transitions: A Comparative Analysis of Adjustment Policies* (1990).

Stephen Wilks is Professor of Politics at the University of Exeter. His recent publications include *Comparative Government–Industry Relations* (with Maurice Wright, 1987); *The Promotion and Regulation of Industry in Japan* (with Maurice Wright, 1991), and *The Office of Fair Trading in Administrative Context* (1994).

1

Introduction

G. BRUCE DOERN AND STEPHEN WILKS

Competition is a ubiquitous feature of society, and economic competition is the pre-eminent dynamic force within capitalist market economies. Neither competition nor the market is inevitable or natural. Markets have to be created through processes of social change and public regulation, a genesis both historical and contemporary as we observe markets being created in the former Communist states. Equally, the extent of competition within markets is extremely variable and is conditioned by regulatory frameworks as well as by market structure, technology, and economic behaviour.

At the risk of stating the obvious, economic theory is far from united on how competition should be conceptualized, and how far competition can be taken as the main explanation of behaviour in the market. It follows that economic prescription offers varied recommendations on the extent and nature of competition that should be pursued within the market, and on the balance between competition and co-operation. Despite these ambiguities it is universally accepted that competition is essential in order to deliver the benefits available from the market. The general presumption is that competition is necessary, that it should be encouraged, and that the virtues of competition should be embodied in legal safeguards.

The presumption in favour of competition is, however, relatively recent, and derives from political as well as economic rationales. A number of European states had common-law or statute provisions against restrictive practices prior to the Second World War, but the United States was, of course, the home of 'antitrust', with the Sherman Antitrust Act of 1890. The rich traditions of American antitrust are grounded in political arguments and political pressures based on the defence of the 'little man' against the undoubted abuses of the monopolies and the trusts. Competition policy really came into its own, however, in the post-war period. Early legislation in the major capitalist economies began to be enforced effectively from the mid-1950s but, although important then, competition policy has become more prominent in parallel with the rise of economic liberalism in the 1970s. In all countries market ideologies and market solutions have entailed a reduced faith in the ability of public authorities to secure common goals through state action and, instead, governments have stressed a resort to the market and to the private sector. In turn this has required increased regulation and an enhanced competition policy, both to create markets where none existed before, and to ensure that markets operate competitively. Thus competition policy regimes have been created in the ex-Communist states and in the economies of southern Europe. They have been strengthened in Japan, in France, and in the European Union. The European case has been especially impressive and influential, and takes competition policy into confrontation with its current challenge, the creation of a competitive global market.

In several countries competition policy has taken on the status almost of an economic constitution, comparable in legal terms to the protection of private property or the freedom to contract. This has been the case in economies marked historically by monopolistic excesses, so that in countries such as the United States, Japan, and Germany; in the European Union; and in the emergent economies of Eastern Europe, competition regimes are constitutive of a competitive capitalist economy and have a symbolic value well beyond the technical considerations of economic efficiency. The pressing international debate concerns whether a competition regime can perform a similar function for the global economy.

The globalization of economic activity is creating an urgent need to create global economic institutions. The OECD has long worked to stimulate national competition policies, to encourage their convergence, and to foster mechanisms for co-operation. These attempts to create an international competition policy regime are now focused on the new World Trade Organization (WTO) which is placing competition policy questions high on its agenda. It is still too early to speculate on whether the WTO will create new policy instruments, new modes of co-operation, or new international institutions; and certainly too early to evaluate their likely impact. What we can do, however, is to provide thorough analyses of national and regional competition policy regimes which constitute the foundations on which an international regime will be erected. We can also outline some of the avenues of debate and review the options under discussion.

Competition policy is centred on law and the main areas of activity are conventionally reviewed in terms of the targets of legal action. The main issue areas are therefore cartels, restrictive practices, monopoly, and mergers. In each of these areas the extent of legal powers is important, but of at least equal importance is the stringency with which those provisions are enforced. Effective competition policy puts a premium on deterrence and seeks to encourage uncoerced compliance with the law on the part of business enterprises. By its nature competition policy provides a regulatory framework within which competition can operate unconstrained. The tendency is therefore to control potential restrictions on competition rather than actively to encourage competitive behaviour. Targets for control show some variation across the various regimes. Thus Japanese competition policy pays particular attention to trade associations and holding companies. European policy includes measures to control subsidies (state aid) and government-sanctioned monopoly; British policy is replete with sectorally specific provisions; and American policy is given vitality by the availability of private damage suits.

The administration of competition policy draws heavily on the skills of lawyers and economists. These two disciplines also dominate academic enquiry into this policy area. The core discipline is law, and there is a formidable body of legal literature and specialist journals, and a legal community which centres on 'antitrust'. Lawyers are, of course, concerned primarily with the law, with the principles built into law, with the procedures of enforcement, and with the substantive outcome of cases. Lawyers tend to be concerned with transparancy, predictability, consistency, procedural equity, and compliance with a series of concerns which they share with their client community. The influence of economists is similarly substantial but has been more variable. At some time periods (for example, during the 1980s in the USA), or over some sub-areas (as with European monopoly control), economics has been exceedingly influential. Economics inevitably provides the intellectual context of ideas, and tools with which to analyse markets and competition within them. The major concerns of economists have, naturally enough, been with consumer welfare and economic efficiency.

If the law has been concerned mainly with equity, and economics with efficiency, there remains a third intellectual strand within competition policy which is less systematically analysed: that strand can be labelled democracy. The creation and reinforcement of a competition policy regime requires a major political initiative. Behind the development of each regime has lain a strong concern with the economic and political power embodied in cartels and monopolies, and a recognition that workable political democracy is empty without a guarantee of economic democracy. These influences have been particularly strong in the United States, Japan, and Germany, but we would maintain that in every competition policy system a significant justification is the actual and symbolic protection of consumers, small businesses, competitors, and political opponents from the excessive concentration of economic power. If political ideas are important in the creation of competition policy regimes, politics is also important in interpreting their operations. The administration of competition policy involves the exercise of bureaucratic politics, whilst the priorities and importance attached to competition policy enforcement is dependent on political choices made by ministers and officials. An adequate understanding of competition policy therefore requires insights from political science and public administration to complement the legal and the economic perspectives.

This book stresses a political science and public-administrative approach, and in doing so has some claim to originality. In particular, we have chosen to take an approach which stresses the importance of institutions, including the way in which policy processes are structured by institutions, and the way in which policy actors interact in an institutional setting. The stress on institutions reflects both our choice of a particular methodology within political science and public administration,[1] and our sense of the importance of institutional endowments in assessing the comparative performance of political economies.[2] At each level within the study of competition policy, politics and public administration provide an essential component of understanding. This applies to the choice of regime, the commitment to enforcement, and the discretionary elements which determine the processing of substantive cases (especially in the area of merger control). It should be unnecessary to have to make such an obvious argument, but the fact remains that political scientists themselves have been slow to undertake systematic work on competition policy and have tended to leave the field to lawyers and economists. For their part, both of these latter disciplines will periodically concede the importance of politics and of institutions,[3] but will tend to proceed to analyse legal principles, economic models, and individual cases as in a vacuum, innocent of any systematic recognition of political acceptability or political bargaining. As in other areas of economic law, a full understanding requires a tripartite, multi-disciplinary approach which deals with the law, the economics, and the politics. Our contention is that this volume contributes a multi-disciplinary approach, but in emphasizing political science and public administration helps to redress an existing imbalance.

A further important element of the approach taken in this volume is its explicitly comparative focus. Each author was asked to address broadly similar issues, including the historical construction of the regime, the main powers, core actors and institutions, policy processes, and major substantive cases. Furthermore, the two conferences which brought the contributors together provided an awareness of the comparator cases and allowed a degree of implicit comparison within each country chapter in terms of the questions posed and the distinctive features stressed. Our aim is to stress and to explore the very considerable national variability in competition regimes. As with much comparative method this is useful in its own right, but it also serves to underline the difficulties and the potentialities for achieving policy convergence and institutional building at the regional and global levels. There are several competition models available and in Chapters 2 and 11 we point to the main features of comparison.

The structure of the book reflects the key analytical steps required. Chapter 2 sets out important conceptual issues involved in comparative policy studies, including the definition of the boundaries of competition policy across national jurisdictions and the identification of key macro-, meso-, micro-, and international levels of analysis. Chapters 3 to 8 examine each of the jurisdictions studied, the United States, Canada, Japan, the United Kingdom, Germany, and the European Union. Each chapter explores the historical context of competition policy, the basic legislation involved, the major institutions and their changing prestige and influence; the interplay of ideas, business power, and bureaucratic influence; and the basic nature of decision processes, institutional and legal cultures, and scope for discretion.

Chapters 9, 10, and 11 deal with various aspects of the international dimensions of competition policy, including their growing links with trade, investment, and environmental policy, the pressures for convergence including the potential establishment of new international institutions; and the combined effects of domestic and international pressures on the reform of international and national competition policy institutions.

Accordingly, the book strives to be one of the first volumes in the overall study of comparative public policy fields both to compare countries at the policy and institutional levels and to deal simultaneously with the internationalization of public policy, an increasingly vital requirement for full-scale policy analysis of virtually every policy field functioning in the global markets of the 1990s. Our goal is that the book be of equal interest to persons interested in and involved with competition policy in OECD countries, and to students of comparative public policy and business–government relations more generally.

NOTES

1. Intellectual currents within the study of public policy have given a more systematic prominence in recent years to the role of institutions and organizations. We wholly endorse this bias without necessarily becoming committed to any one approach. Writers working within the three schools of policy networks, bureau-shaping models, and the new institutionalism all have much to offer.

2. A rich vein of work within comparative political economy has begun to address the way in which institutional configurations affect relative economic performance and, in turn, how those institutions are embedded within distinctive national social relations. The literature is substantial, but we would cite as examples Douglass North, *Institutions, Institutional Change and Economic Performance* (Cambridge: Cambridge University Press, 1990); and Mark Granovetter, 'Economic Action and Social Structure: The Problem of Embeddedness', in M. Granovetter and R. Swedberg (eds.), *The Sociology of Economic Life* (Oxford: Westview, 1992; first pub. 1985).

3. We do not intend these observations to be dismissive of these essential disciplines, or to suggest that academic lawyers or economists invariably overlook political factors. Our argument stresses a systematic bias and an understandable, if regrettable, narrowness of viewpoint.

2

Comparative Competition Policy: Boundaries and Levels of Political Analysis

G. BRUCE DOERN

The analysis of comparative competition policy and competition policy institutions has not been a central concern of political scientists or of scholars in public administration and public policy who focus on institutions and policy formation. Political scientists are certainly involved in the study of business power, government–business relations, and industrial policy, but, with the exception of some work on the US Federal Trade Commission, they have generally not focused on the study of anti-competitive business practices as a regulatory terrain.[1] Accordingly, the purpose of this book is to bring a concerted political and institutional perspective to bear by examining comparatively the competition policies and institutions of six jurisdictions: the United States, Canada, Japan, the United Kingdom, Germany, and the European Union.

In this chapter the focus is on competition policy. The analytical focus on the institutions of competition policy comes later, once some of the problems of studying the field have been examined. At first glance, a comprehensive definition of competition policy is not difficult to construct.

Competition policy consists of those policies and actions of the state intended to prevent certain restraints of trade by private firms. Stated more positively, it is policy intended to promote rivalry among firms, buyers, and sellers through actions in areas of activity such as mergers, abuse of dominance, cartels, conspiracies in restraint of trade, misleading advertising, and related criminal and economic offences that are held to be anti-competitive.[2] For mainstream economists, the overall purpose of competition policy is to protect competition as a means of allocating scarce resources and thus of producing allocative and other types of efficiency. At the same time, competitive markets also tend to be less concentrated and thus economic power is also diffused. Allocative efficiency in turn maximizes economic welfare. And social welfare, in the final extension of this logic, depends upon the larger economic welfare. For political scientists, even if the above analytical logic is accepted, there is also an interest in how antitrust policy is forged out of the ideologies and pressures of big business and organized capitalism, and in how the state enacts measures to reassure small businesses and consumers.

The competition policy and decision process pursues these goals through interactions among interests and institutions that lead to the formulation of the main statements and statutes of competition policy and the deciding of individual case decisions by competition policy authorities.

The above definitions are sensible in their own right, but they merely get us to the analytical starting line. It will be evident in the chapters that follow that there is considerable divergence among countries in what competition policy is and how it is made. But an equally important factor in the complexity of competition policy is its growing international nature. With the falling from favour of industrial policy in the 1980s, and the reduction of trade barriers in the early 1990s, global economic policy attention has begun to focus on competition policy. Linked to concerns about effective market access once goods and services have crossed borders, competition policies and institutions dealing with restrictive business practices are being made subject to close international scrutiny.[3]

To set a conceptual context for the chapters on the six jurisdictions, and for the book as a whole, this chapter proceeds through three essential analytical stages. First, it deals concretely with the issues of defining the dependent variable, competition policy. It is from within that definition that one can then compare countries and jurisdictions and attempt to locate and identify core and tangential competition policy institutions as well as plausible sets of explanatory variables for policies and outcomes. Second, the chapter profiles four levels or aspects of the politics of competition policy analysis and previews the extent to which the chapters in the book deal with them. These analytical levels are: the macro-politics of competition policy formation; the meso-political characteristics of policy institutions and overall competition policy decision processes; the micro-politics of the policy implementation process, including the exercise of discretion and power in numerous case situations; and the internationalization of competition policy.

Finally, the chapter locates the study of competition policy within the broader terrain of comparative public policy studies. This is essential to understand not only the nature of evidence, but also the degrees of difficulty in mounting convincing efforts in comparative analysis in this policy field compared to other policy fields.

THE BOUNDARIES OF COMPETITION POLICY

Competition and competition policy are not the same thing. However, understanding the former is crucial, and it starts with economics and economists.[4] Understanding the latter means one has to deal with politics, because it is states that make public policies, and political interests and institutions that determine their implementation in practice.

Competitive markets are the idealized end product of competition policy. Whether cast as free markets or simply as competition, they require the existence of the following features:

- consumers who are able to choose and purchase both the good or service, and the provider of the good or service;
- producers of goods and services who are able to attract customers by producing what the latter want and by adjusting quality and price;
- the availability of enough information on the price, quality, and availability of the goods or service to enable the market to function;
- A sufficiently large number of producers and consumers for both to be able to choose, and for no individual consumer or producer to determine the price. This latter condition may mean that there is free entry into, and exit from, the market.

While economists concede the textbook nature of these characteristics, they also see them functioning in practice, and hence as endowing economic and political life with many desirable features, including allocative and dynamic efficiency, freedom of choice, the minimization of the coercive intrusion of the state, and the fulfilment of many wants and needs for goods and services. Hence, policies that ensure the maximized presence of these characteristics are good, whether seen as means or ends.

Debate and analysis in the economics discipline goes well beyond notions of perfect competition. For example, it embraces analysis of 'contestable markets'.[5] Unlike perfect competition, a contestable market can consist of one or a few firms which may still be efficient. This is because firms in the industry will maintain prices close to the competitive level because of the threat posed by potential entrants. This behaviour in turn is based on the characteristics of easy entrance to, and exit from, such markets. For several decades, economists have also discussed the concept of 'workable' competition. This idea, which Chapter 7 shows was influential in the formation of German competition policy, arose out of views that perfect competition did not exist. There is, however, no consensus about what workable competition is, even though all competition policy authorities undoubtedly practise some version of it.[6]

Although competition policy is concerned with many factors other than the simple competitive process, the fact remains that 'competition' and the economic understanding of competition is its dominant intellectual discourse. No study of competition policy is adequate without an understanding of the role that competition plays within the market economy and the varied interpretations which economists offer of competition and the competitive process. This volume is predominately concerned with the political, administrative, and legal dimensions of competition policy but the discussion needs to be undertaken with an awareness of the economic context.

Competition is conventionally treated as the dominant dynamic element and regulatory mechanism within the market system. It operates, in Smith's vivid image, as an 'invisible hand', surreptitiously, and ultimately benignly, co-ordinating transactions within the market economy. A basic understanding of the competitive process, the concept of perfect competition, and the outcomes in the form of consumer welfare and allocative efficiency, is common to virtually all social scientists. Indeed, the concept of competition has become something of a universal nostrum and a handmaiden to the processes of liberalization and the spread of market principles to all walks of life. In analysis of economic activity, therefore, more competition is generally thought to be desirable and impediments to competition undesirable. This provides a simple test for competition policy which is available to most laypersons. The rules of perfect competition are simple to apply, and the neo-classical analysis is seductive in its simplicity.

The neo-classical model of competition, with various adaptations, is easily accessible through standard economic textbooks.[7] Unfortunately, the advice which conventional economic analysis offers is often ambiguous and predominately case specific. Moreover, there are important (and fashionable) trends within the contemporary economic canon which offer alternative theories, some of which are sceptical as to the virtues of competition policy.

Initially it should be pointed out that competition is not the only co-ordinating force within market societies, and that its dominance within economic discourse is over-developed and displays an Anglo-American bias. Economic activity may be co-ordinated through co-operation, collectivist norms, hierarchy, and even social responsibility. The literature on these alternatives is vast but is summarized by Auerbach into two economic schools, the 'New Industrial State' and the 'Institutionalists'.[8] But the vitality of these alternative approaches is to be found in the work of sister disciplines such as sociology, economic history, and policy studies.[9] Within the economics profession concepts of competition are uppermost. It is not, therefore, surprising that support for competition policy among economists is high; indeed, 'survey results show that economists agree on the desirability of antitrust more than they concur on almost any other economic proposition' (at least in the USA).[10] Most would therefore share Donald Hay's assertion that 'a precondition for a successful market economy is the existence of an effective competition policy'.[11]

Economics indicates that the prime goal of competition and competition policy is efficiency. But it is difficult for economic analysis to offer abstract rules as to the efficiency implications of particular market structures or conducts. Sources of ambiguity are nicely reviewed by Hay.[12] They arise from the variability of firms, markets, technology, and managerial strategies, but they also arise from the fact that 'different economic approaches speak to identical issues differently'.[13] In particular, the classical dynamic view of competition associated with Schumpeter and Hayek places far less importance on competition policy and, together with theories of 'contestable markets' and the intellectual weight of Chicago School theories, has posed a striking challenge to the traditional certainties of an active competition policy, particularly in the United States.

The dynamic view of competition is counterposed to the static, equilibrium basis of neo-classical approaches. It asserts that competition is a continuing process, centred on innovation, in which present oligopolies or market-dominant advantages are likely to be the result of past efficiencies and are perpetually vulnerable to assault from innovative competitors.[14] Dynamic analysts are far more sanguine about market power and an imbalanced market structure, as are theorists of contestable markets. Contestable-market approaches[15] argue that markets may not be fully competitive, but firms will behave as if they are, as long as the market is 'contestable' through the possibility that outside firms can easily enter and begin to compete when market imperfections make it attractive to do so.

In the United States economists of the Chicago School have had a profound effect on antitrust thinking. Chicago theorists have been in the ascendant since the mid-1970s.[16] They have a basically positive attitude to antitrust, but place less emphasis on entry barriers and vertical restraints than neo-classical theorists. They view predatory pricing, vertical ties, and even resale price maintenance as fundamentally unproblematic. More recent American radical theorizing goes beyond this position to apply a hostile public-choice approach. McChesney and Shughart, for instance, have assembled a provocative set of arguments intended to 'return the attention of antitrust scholars to first principles, forcing them to consider seriously whether antitrust has any legitimate place in a market-based economy'.[17] The public-choice approach is stimulating and has at least one thing in common with the theoretical emphasis of this volume. It shares a belief in the importance of politics.

The mainstream application of economics to competition policy is, however, far more pragmatic than some of the pyrotechnic prescriptions of economic radicals. There is a familiar literature and there are widely accepted understandings about the pros and cons of agreements between firms and the workings of monopoly. Economic analysis is informed by conventional assumptions enshrined in practical administration through past reports and legal judgements. No economist seriously expects to find or to impose a market which displays all the traits of 'perfect competition'. Markets are messy, complicated, and inevitably imperfect. In practice, competition economists are mobilized by a pragmatic pressure to attack the worst abuses, to establish principles of tolerable conduct, and to pursue a goal of 'workable competition'.[18] The idea of workable competition is a norm rather than an explicit theory. It is a norm that could be expected to transmute in response to the evolution of prevailing economic theory and in response to trends in economic activity, especially globalization and technological competition.

These brief observations serve to emphasize three contextual economic factors. First, the evolution of competition policy is inextricably bound up with evaluation of various types of economic efficiency. Familiarity with the basic economic arguments is a necessity in evaluating the debates. Secondly, specific proposals for reform and change of policy inevitably mobilize economists and economic arguments. For instance, good recent studies of European merger policy illustrate the influence of economic arguments both within the process and as sources of external criticism.[19] Here, too, evaluation of the forces working for reform requires an assessment of the economic debates. Thirdly, analysis of the enforcement of policy itself requires interpretation of the influence of economists acting within the enforcement agencies and through the medium of dominant economic doctrines. Curiously, the influence of economists is modest and attenuated in Europe and Japan; but in the United States it provides the major explanatory factor in analysing the decline of antitrust enforcement throughout the 1980s, and its gradual rehabilitation in the 1990s.

The evaluation and the enforcement of competition policy are both multi-disciplinary processes. Just as students of public policy must become aware of the guidance offered by economics, so economists are unusually attuned to the importance of the design of policy and of institutions. In his recent review Hay offers as one of his key propositions, the suggestion that 'the appropriate design of policy and policy institutions is crucial to a successful competition policy'.[20] We entirely share this sentiment, and can turn to the analysis of policy in the expectation that economists will find in the following chapters a range of insights and propositions to complement their own more abstract and theoretical analyses.

Thus, when governmental policies are introduced, the analytical

Competition policy	Competition as ideal
• Core elements in descriptive terms* • Core elements in political/ statutory terms* • As reflected in exempt sectors* • As reflected in other policy fields*	• Customers able to choose goods and producers • Producer able to attract customers by changing price and quality • Adequate information on price, quality, and availability • Sufficiently large number of buyers and sellers that no individual buyer or seller can determine price

* see Figure 2.2.

FIG. 2.1 Competition policy and competition at a glance

dilemmas begin. Which of the government's policies should be called competition policy when many such policies, directly or indirectly, could affect or determine the realization of the competitive conditions listed above? All areas of industrial regulation? All social regulation, such as consumer safety and environmental policy? Only those policies which some interests choose to call competition or antitrust or anti-combines policy?

The act of 'intervening' to preserve or enhance such conditions is itself problematic. Indeed, it is puzzling why mainstream economists are disparaging of governmental efforts to practise industrial policy but much more ready to support, and even be confident about, the state's ability to practise competition policy. Industrial policy is criticized because the state, through subsidies and other policy tools, cannot possibly second-guess or be as nimble as markets. Competition policies would seem to be equally difficult of realization.[21] Indeed, because they would be more regulatory in nature, and thus less endowed with the convenient mathematics of expenditure policy, they are arguably even more difficult to practise. In short, the consequences of regulatory action show up in *private* spending and investment, and hence are even more indirect and difficult to assess. (See Figure 2.1.)

The third dilemma is the potential causal distance between competition policy (however defined) and its outcomes. The policy journey from statute to regulation to guideline, and from complaint to case to warning to enforcement to appeal to court ruling, is more akin to the Olympic policy marathon than the 100-metre policy implementation dash.

Thus the overall boundary problem of competition policy is a real one. But the starting-point is understanding what the typical elements of competition policy statutes in the six jurisdictions are. These policies seek to deal with:

- cartels, trusts, or horizontal arrangements among competitors to fix prices or allocate markets;
- abuse of dominant position or monopoly or market power;
- mergers that significantly reduce competition;
- vertical arrangements between producers and various sellers, such as resale price maintenance, exclusive dealing, exclusive territories, and tying arrangements;
- arrangements and practices that mislead consumers.

The next six chapters will show the extent to which these elements are contained within the mandate of the core competition policy institutions of each jurisdiction. Typically the first four are included, whereas consumer-related matters have often resided elsewhere. The precise mix is important, however, both for actual internal decision-making and for the politics of the lead competition policy agency and its policy community.

But these elemental groupings are in turn but a bare beginning. The politics of competition policy show up immediately in the way in which the goals of competition policy receive legal expression in the main statutes of each country or in guidelines which emanate from such laws. There are at least three modes of such political expression: the goals of the core competition policy areas; the extent and nature of non-competition policy goals that are allowed by statute to be considered in decision-making; and the provisions for exempt sectors or activities.

Consider first the core area goals. On horizontal arrangements, US antitrust law applies a *per se* prohibition backed by criminal sanctions, against such practices. Canadian law attaches the qualification that the arrangements, except for bid-rigging, must not lessen competition 'unduly'. Coming almost a century later, the laws of the European Union under article 85, as well as the post-Second World War German, British, and Japanese laws are broader still, and therefore subject to more political interpretation.

Similarly, the legal language regarding vertical arrangements also varies from the greater US use of *per se* offences, to the greater use of discretionary 'rule of reason' approaches in Canada, the EU,

Core elements in descriptive terms:

- Cartels, trusts, and horizontal agreements
- Vertical arrangements
- Mergers
- Abuse of dominant position, or 'monopoly'
- Misleading advertising and marketing, and related consumer law

Core elements as expressed in political statutory terms and language:

- *per se* prohibitions and criminal sanctions
- 'rule of reason' rationales
- qualifying phrases such as 'unduly' or 'significant lessening', etc.
- non-competition or so-called 'public-interest' provisions for goals such as regional development, employment, financial probity, and aspects of international competitiveness (e.g. fostering 'national champion' firms)

As reflected through exempt sectors:

- regulated sectors (energy, transport, telecommunications)
- export cartels
- state-owned enterprises
- banks
- R&D joint ventures
- the professions and unions

As reflected through other policy fields with impacts on competition:

- regulated sector law
- trade policy (tariffs, anti-dumping, countervail)
- intellectual property law
- environmental regulation
- foreign-investment review

FIG. 2.2 Competition policy in detail

and UK, to Japanese approaches which have often looked positively on such practices.[22] On merger law provisions and administrative guidelines, again there are divergent goals. US merger laws and guidelines apply a more precise, consumer-welfare test to mergers. Canadian law allows an 'efficiency criterion' to be used as a defence against an action by the competition agency alleging that a merger is anti-competitive.[23] (See Figure 2.2.)

Conditioning these core goals are other parts of the statutes which set out non-competition or so-called 'public-interest' criteria that regulators, ministers, and the courts may take into account in particular cases. These can vary from broad criteria and issues such as job losses, regional economic development goals, and financial probity, to the use of aspects of international competitiveness as a rationale for supporting or fostering 'national champions'. The tendency during the 1980s was generally to attempt to narrow the range of such criteria and to elevate pure competition criteria as the main focus for decision-making.[24] But as the 1990s evolve, the pressures for other factors to be taken into account, some in the name of renewed industrial policy, are certainly increasing.[25]

An example of non-competition criteria is provided by the EC article 21 provisions regarding security, financial probity, and newspaper plurality in merger cases. In fact many regimes have exceptional conditions affecting the media and 'culture industries'. Another source of extra-competition influence originates in the possibility for affected interests to cite the European Treaty preamble which enjoins all EU institutions to take into account and promote market integration as well as the social integration of the Union.[26]

The main statutory expression of the criteria to be used in competition policy in the UK is found in section 84(4) of the Fair Trading Act. It requires the Monopolies and Mergers Commission and the Director General of Fair Trading, to consider 'all matters which appear to them to be relevant' and, in particular, the desirability of the merger for:

(a) maintaining and promoting effective competition;
(b) promoting the interests of consumers, purchasers, and other users of goods and services in respect of prices, quality, and variety of goods and services supplied;
(c) promoting, through competition, reduction of costs, development and use of new techniques and new products, and facilitating the entry of new competitors into existing markets;
(d) maintaining and promoting the balanced distribution of industry and employment;
(e) maintaining and promoting competitive activity in overseas markets.[27]

While competition goals are central, there is clearly room for other criteria to be considered in the UK law (see Chapter 6). Clauses (d) and (e) imply potential job protection and regional development, and international competitiveness objectives respectively. Ministerial statements have also supplied either additional specific criteria (for example, Peter Lilley's injunctions against state ownership) or a general interpretation, seen especially in the form of the 1984 Tebbit guidelines which, although informal, are still being applied and, in effect, assert the primacy of clauses (*a*) and (*b*) above.

The issue of statutory exemptions from the law is politically important in three ways. First, it often simply represents the raw power of political interests to gain exemptions for themselves (a form of 'subsidy by statute'). Secondly, it often represents a partial overlap with economic ideas that either genuinely, or conveniently, justify an exemption. The exemption of monopoly public-utility regulated sectors were based on theories of natural monoply, but technologies soon changed to alter this 'natural' status, without altering some features of the 'exempt' status. Thirdly, it calls into question whether competition law is genuinely framework law, applying to all sectors of the economy, or merely quasi-sectoral 'industrial policy' by another name. In other words, if enough sectors are exempt, there are grounds for concern by those who are included that they are not playing by the same rules and competitive advantages.[28]

An example of the first kind of politics of exemption can be the typical exemption of export cartels from the provisions of competition law. Another is the exemption enjoyed, until very recently, by state-owned enterprises. Still others are the exemptions of labour unions, key professions, and service sectors such as banks and financial institutions.

The second tranche of exemptions (whole or partial) include many of the regulated sectors of business deemed to be characterized by natural monopolies, such as those in the fields of energy, transportation, and telecommunications. Many aspects of these fields were indeed monopolies and hence were overseen by regulatory boards and commissions (especially in the US and Canada), government departments (the preferred European model), and, a more recent model, the UK's array of one-person regulators (such as OFTEL, OFGAS, and OFFER).[29] But these exempt sectors also earned their exemptions through the appeal to other values, such as nation building (Canada), and versions of national identity and even national security (US, UK, Germany). For at least the last decade, many of these same regulated sectors have been partially deregulated. The pressure to deregulate has come partly from technological changes that undermined claims to natural monopoly status (telecommunications), and partly from economic analysis and advocacy which showed that regulated sectors were simply another name for protection and were anti-competitive in their basic nature (airlines, rail).[30]

As we move outward from core competition boundaries to exempt sectors and beyond, there are further boundary problems to deal with. Some of these we have already hinted at, namely the links to industrial policy. But of equal importance is the overspill into trade policy and investment policy. Environmental policy also looms large. While Chapters 9, 10, and 11 deal with this ultimate policy and institutional boundary problem, some basic features of it must be highlighted from the outset. The overspills deal with competition policy ideas that are in dispute. The ideas in dispute are occurring within a strong consensus that competitive market systems are still superior to any other contending approach. But despite this, there is considerable contention over what competition policy is or ought to be, especially as revealed in specific cases and situations.

The core intellectual debate about competition policy ideas is still largely confined to economists but, as we see in our final discussion of reform options in Chapter 11, law, business administration, and other disciplines are also engaged. The debate operates at several related levels, including concerns about 'system frictions', the actual versus the theoretical potential for 'managed trade' or neo-industrial policies, and the even more specific notions of policy towards strategic alliances among firms and across countries, especially in the realm of research and development (R&D), or innovation.[31]

'System friction' is an appropriate overall label for this wider array of linkages. It is the term given by economist and former OECD and Canadian senior official Sylvia Ostry to a new kind of international friction which she argued in 1990 was much broader than protectionism.[32] The term 'underlined that there were several different market models, the differences stemming from both historical and cultural legacies as well as divergence in a range of domestic policies'.[33] These system differences influenced the international competitiveness of a firm, which was essentially the product of an 'interaction between the firm's own capabilities and the broad institutional context of its home country'.[34] These frictions had to be reduced through harmonization of those policies that affected a firm's innovative capability. Ostry went on to argue that a key area of focus would have to be the issue of 'effective market access', a concept which she acknowledged to be 'soft and even slippery', and which crossed the blurred boundaries of competition, trade, investment, and 'high tech industrial policy'.

In many respects, as Michael Trebilcock shows in Chapter 9, this new tension in ideas and boundaries is the paradoxical result of policy triumph. Thus, in trade policy terms, the EU's 1992 project, the Canada–US, and later NAFTA, free-trade agreements, and key features of the GATT Uruguay Round agreement, all represent the ascendancy of free-trade views. In addition, within the realm of core competition policy, it is not inaccurate to say that policy in Western countries moved in the last decade in such a way as to leave less and less room for so-called non-economic or public-interest goals to enter into competition policy decisions.[35] Some of this change was due to the influence of the Chicago School in competition policy analysis, but it also reflected the demise of industrial policy in general.

However, like a lake that is drained, one sees below in a new, uncovered form the next layer of problems or obstacles. So it is with the new-found attention given to competition policy and its close nexus with trade, industrial, investment, and other policies.

In summary, the discussion of the boundaries of competition policy is important in the political analysis of competition policy for several reasons. There is indeed a traditional core to competition policy, largely defined by economists, which is central to what we are examining, and what we are comparing across countries. But it is difficult to compare policy outcomes, and even policy outputs, if there are quite divergent patterns of exempt sectors. The fact that policy overspills and system frictions are occurring in the nexus between competition, trade, and investment policies is also undeniably a part of the analytical challenge.

LEVELS OF ANALYSIS

The literature on both comparative public policy and competition policy suggests the need for several levels of analysis in understanding the political economy of competition policy in OECD countries. Each of four levels is profiled below: the macro-politics

Macro-politics (factors explaining outputs/current law):

- Political parties and partisan conflict
- Ideologies and ideas
- Business interests and policy community influence
- Interests and strategies of core competition agencies

Meso-politics (characteristics of institutions and overall decision process):

Comparisons made in Chapter 11:
- Jurisdiction
- Degree of autonomy
- Incorporation of economic and legal ideas and cultures
- Organizational diversity
- Theories of regulation in practice (enforcement/compliance)

Discretionary elements:
- Non-competition criteria
- Ministerial and quasi-ministerial discretion
- Intra-cabinet and intra-governmental pressures
- Hearings and direct interest representation
- Opportunities for private action
- Comfort letters and confidential guidance mechanisms
- Vehicles for study, inquiry, and media exposure
- 'One-Stop' versus multi-competition policy authorities

Micro-politics (implementation, compliance, and enforcement):

- The nature of implementation activity embedded in a mix of policy instruments
- Fairness and transparency
- The diversity of case cycles and discretion in core competition policy elements

The internationalization of competition policy (factors leading to the potential transformation of competition policy from regimes to institutions):

- Ideas about competition policy
- Political power and interests of states, blocs, and business
- International agencies and inter-agency relations within states
- Accountability, representation, and transparency

FIG. 2.3 Levels of competition policy analysis

of competition policy, or the identification of aggregate factors which help explain why overall competition policies are the way they are in each country; the meso-level of institutional politics, including overall decision-making processes; the micro-politics of policy implementation and enforcement; and the emerging dynamics concerning the internationalization of competition policy, the politics of system frictions. These levels are shown in Figure 2.3.

Macro-Politics: Explaining Core Policy Outputs

The first level of analysis is to identify the range of independent variables and their interactions that explain the presence and content of current core competition laws, most of which underwent change or amendment in the last fifteen years. As Figure 2.3 suggests, four macro-political variables require examination. First, the extent and nature of partisan conflict among a country's political parties is important. In most of the countries examined, competition policy itself has generally been on the fringes of national political struggle but, none the less, even within this marginalized role, there are varying degrees of partisan controversy.

Partisanship easily shades into the second variable, ideologies and ideas, but they are not coterminous. Ideas can also refer to more particular controversies among knowledge professions such as economists and lawyers. Hence, knowing which ideas might be emerging or dominant at the time of legislative change is important. Thus, as seen above, the Chicago School influence in the US system was crucial in the mid-1970s to late-1980s period, but may now be on the wane.[36] Vigorous waves of anti-monopoly actions in the US, including divestitures, occurred in the early part of the century, in the 1940s and early 1950s, and from the late 1960s to the early 1980s.

Especially in the post-Second World War to 1970s period, these kinds of aggressive actions were supported in economic theory by the structuralist school of industrial organization economics.[37] According to this theory, market structure, as revealed by concentration measures, was a primary determinant of economic performance, led to higher than average profits, and served as a barrier to potential new entrants.

This dominant paradigm was challenged in the 1970s and 1980s by free-market Chicago School theories which argued that the higher than average profits observed in fact were due to superior competitive performance by the firms in question.[38] The prism supplied by this alternative paradigm usually saw many particular practices as being consistent with dynamic competition in increasingly complex markets.[39] This extended to claims of efficiency being embedded in practices such as tied selling and resale price maintenance. In the USA, the influence of this approach lead to a significant reduction in federal prosecutions during the Reagan era.[40]

A partial reaction has emerged recently in response to Chicago School theories. Economic theory focuses on the potential for 'strategic entry deterrence' by monopolists, though it is a theory that has by no means supplanted the Chicago School's recent hegemony.[41] But broader ideologies are also melded into competition policy thinking and action, certainly in terms of degrees of intervention and the severity of penalties. Thus competition systems have been set in the context of views about the social market in Germany and in general views of economic integration in the EU.[42]

A third factor in the macro-politics of competition policy is the nature of business power in the context of other interest groups and elements of the policy community that are attentive to competition policy matters. These latter interests can include consumer interests (the nominal ultimate beneficiary of good competition policy), labour unions, the legal profession, and economists. But policy outputs—indeed, key clauses in the legislation—may be due to the particular interplay among business interest groups. Thus the different interests of big business versus small business, or export industries versus importers, can be important in the precise statutory expressions of policy.

Last, but hardly least, among the political variables at the macro-level are the political strategies of the core competition policy agencies themselves. As the actors with the most intimate knowledge of how competition policy laws and regulatory systems are functioning, these agencies bring their own agendas as bureaucracies to the table when laws are being forged or amended. Their own sense of aggressiveness or caution, as well as instincts for survival, are a key to understanding why laws are the way they are and how and why they change or do not change.

Meso-politics: Institutions and overall decision processes

By meso-politics, we refer to a middle-level set of factors which are necessary to appreciate how competition policy politics could potentially function once laws are in place. In short, the focus here is on what kinds of shape the overall institutions and decision processes of competition policy might take, and how they might cluster around various groups of characteristics. We take up the question of institutional comparison again in Chapter 11, after examination of the various national experiences.

One approach suggested in recent published work is an eight-point framework of middle-level elements applied to an analysis of the Canadian competition policy system.[43] The eight elements of the framework, where political behaviour is embedded or potential, are: the use of explicit non-competition criteria that can be taken into account by competition authorities; ranges of, and opportunities for, ministerial discretion; intra-cabinet and intra-governmental pressures from other ministers and departments and their political clientele interests; direct hearings or avenues for direct representation and pressure by interests; opportunities for private legal action; processes for giving comfort or guidance letters to parties; vehicles for pressure and political learning through studies, media exposure, and public persuasion; and the extent to which 'one-stop' versus multi-sector competition institutions exist and can be played off against one another.

The use of explicit non-competition policy criteria has already been referred to above. Ministerial discretion refers to the range of opportunities for ministers or quasi-ministers (for example, the EU commissioners, or the Director General of Fair Trading in the UK) to act on their view of the public interest, either through rationales related to the above-noted non-competition criteria, or simply by exercising their political judgement of the mix of facts and values before them.

Political pressures can be brought to bear on competition policy decisions through the actions and arguments of other ministers and their departments and officials. These often reflect the interests of the agencies themselves, or they may be a surrogate arena for these departments' industrial interest groups or key firms. Particular competition policy cases, even though these are usually firm specific, often raise issues of principle for larger competition policy concerns or for sectoral policy and legislation in the jurisdiction of these ministers and departments. Interests (such as firms and interest groups) have opportunities in most competition policy regimes to defend their positions directly through hearings and other direct modes of contact and pressure. Since the competition regulatory process is largely case and complaint driven, it is usually particular companies and legal practitioners that are the main parties of interest. Moreover, firms are also the main source for the provision of specialist information, a fact which also gives considerable scope to bias or change the character of official governmental consideration. Competition policy regimes vary in the extent to which they allow enforcement through direct private legal action. Without doubt, however, it is the US system which stands out in this regard.[44] For every single action pursued by US competition authorities, there are ten pursued by private firms and citizens. Under section 4 of the Clayton Act, 'any person who shall be injured in his business or property by reason of anything forbidden in the antitrust laws may sue therefor'. The law also provides for treble damages plus costs, including legal fees. The opportunity to obtain treble damages is intended to be an incentive to plaintiffs to identify uncompetitive acts and to take the time and risk involved in bringing a case to court. Class action suits can also be brought by otherwise dispersed and risk-averse consumers.

A further element of competition policy highlighted in this eight-point framework is the use by competition authorities of comfort letters and confidential guidance mechanisms. These are granted to parties who are seeking greater certainty as to how a particular authority might view a given commercial practice, merger, or deal. Such mechanisms can, on the one hand, be considered to be in the public interest if they do foster greater economic certainty and compliance with the law. But, on the other hand, they are usually secretly derived and perhaps negotiated, and thus raise issues about whether other procedural notions of the public interest are being violated.

Competition regimes as a whole can seek to promote both core competition policy goals and larger non-competition criteria through the tactical use of studies, inquiries, and media exposure. Special studies can be launched, either when they arise out of a case or a complaint, or when the competition authority seeks to advance its agenda or concerns. Sectors such as autos or beer have long histories of study and inquiry, either to expose industry practices or to help postpone action through yet another inquiry. Well-timed speeches by the heads of competition policy agencies or by ministers can 'trial balloon', through media exposure, policy concerns and put pressure on an industry or a key firm.

The extent to which a given country's competition authorities are one-stop versus multi-sector oriented is also of importance to political dynamics. Each country has a core competition regulatory regime which in principle covers all sectors. As Chapters 3 to 8 below show, this core regime may contain separate agencies so as to separate advisory, investigatory, decision-making, and enforcement functions. However, as stressed above, there are usually other sectoral regulators who have significant amounts of the competition regulatory mandate. In each of the above sets of meso-level factors, the analytical concern focuses on institutional relations and characteristics, rather than on how the current policies, as expressed in statute form, were enacted. While there is some overlap between this level of analysis and the micro-politics examined below, the latter involves ultimately an even finer conceptual lens and focus.

Micro-politics: Implementation, compliance, and enforcement

The micro-politics of competition policy involves a conceptual awareness of three linked features of the overall world of implementation, compliance, and enforcement: the nature of implementation activity embedded in a mix of policy instruments; fairness and transparency; and the diverse nature of case cycles and discretion among the core elements of competition policy.

Consider first the general pattern of theories of implementation and related notions of a policy instrument spectrum or mix. In the evolution of public policy theory as a whole, a focus on the issues of implementation has been a relatively late starter. Some attribute its birth to concerns in the early 1970s that followed in the wake of disappointment with the results of social policy initiatives launched with great optimism in the mid-1960s.[45] Thus early 'top-down' studies of implementation, such as that by Pressman and Wildavsky, focused on why things went wrong in practice and how such occurrences might be avoided in future. But even earlier empirical work had certainly warned against the temptation to think of implementation in simplistic terms. Policy implementation, in a word, was complex.[46] It was usually not the natural or inevitable unfolding of the hierarchical troops doing the precise bidding of the administrative and political generals at the top.

A series of subsequent, more 'bottom-up' studies and conceptualizations of implementation emerged from the mid-1970s to the mid-1980s and visualized a series of essentially more relational characteristics.[47] Some stressed the human and even psychological factors, such as found in the inherent disposition of implementing officials and in patterns of inter-organizational communication. Others portrayed implementation as mutual adaptation, and gamesmanship, or sought to link the legal and rational-bureaucratic imperatives of Weberian bureaucracy with an equally compelling 'consensual' imperative.

There is a necessary overlap between those who study 'implementation' directly and those who examine, separately, or in combination, the main policy or governing instruments available to the state.[48] Such instruments are variously categorized and subcategorized, but usually in the aggregate include: outright state ownership, regulation, taxation, spending, and persuasion. Clearly, implementation depends in part upon how agencies and their programmes are nested amidst an array of instruments.

For example, in an excellent study of implementation and compliance, Clifford and Webb initially leave aside what they explicitly call 'service' policies, which are mainly expenditure or grant programmes. This is so that they can demarcate the 'compliance' realm of implementation. Compliance, in their definition, 'refers to a measure of private action or inaction, insofar as it conforms to a standard of conduct requested or commanded by government'.[49] Thus compliance implies more direct coercion but, the rest of the study then goes on to show how within the compliance spectrum of activities, there are many softer policy instruments used, simply because persuasion, education, and information gathering are so central to what is involved in the compliance implementation process.[50]

Indeed, the implementation framework developed in the Clifford and Webb study was formulated to show a readership of lawyers that the real nature of implementation is 'relational' and thus 'stands in sharp contrast to the discrete isolated incident approach to law'.[51] A three-part framework is then developed consisting of: relations, instruments, and activities. Compliance implementation is relational because the parties involved include administrators, 'administrees', and third parties. Instruments refer to the basic command/penalty, incentives, and persuasion choices already noted above. Activities refers to an even finer set of actions and processes that concretely occur in compliance situations. These include inspecting, investigating, negotiating, observing, information gathering, coaxing, cajoling, warning, and the like. This dense compliance world, along with enforcement, is clearly a part of competition policy.

A second, more normative aspect of the micro-politics of competition policy is that of transparency and fairness. Competition policy bureaucracies must constantly balance the requisites of transparency in decision-making against fair protection of commercial secrets and proprietary information. They must be continually conscious of the 'demonstration effect' of case decisions and precedents in general, including those concerning such commercial practices. Not only are these choices complex and continuous but they affect how we interpret data about cases and decisions when we seek to evaluate the entire organization. Hence, an emphasis on enforcement could mean that hundreds of prosecuted cases displayed in an annual report would be an indicator of success in implementation. On the other hand, if a compliance approach is used, focusing on education and a variety of so-called softer instruments, then having only a few cases may be an indicator of success. These and other related measurement and interpretative issues will be evident in some of the country chapters.

Political and administrative discretion in competition policy decision-making is obviously crucial, in part because political interests want it that way and in part because it is impossible to express rules with sufficient precision to meet the circumstances of all cases.[52] In this last sense, the relevant basis of comparision is not just other countries but also other administrative-discretionary realms affecting business and citizens, such as tax administration, foreign-investment review, or environmental regulation. In short, the relevant comparison centres on analogous areas where policy implementation involves discretionary choices between enforcement versus compliance approaches.[53]

The day-to-day reality of competition policy is overwhelmingly case and complaint driven. However, it is equally essential to appreciate that the basic rhythm of cases varies across the functional elements of competition policy. For example, in dealing with mergers, there are very short time periods allowed for notifiable merger reviews, with only limited extensions possible.[54] Moreover, the nature of mergers is that they involve prospective rather than past behaviour. Thus, there is an even more difficult burden of proof placed upon the competition regulator if it wishes to challenge a merger. Finally, there is a presumption among competition regulators that most mergers are healthy for the economy.

In contrast, elements of the competition agency dealing with offences involving vertical arrangements or abuse-of-dominant position function in a different cycle of cases. First, they have a wider range of types of cases from fairly small vertical restraint and refusal to supply cases to large and often complex abuse-of-dominant-position cases. At any given time, there are typically many dozens of routine complaints that have to be investigated by case officers, but only two or three bigger cases ready for action. There are also no compelling statutory deadlines as there are in mergers. When large abuse-of-dominant-position cases occur, they can require a large team of officers and may take years to develop.

Last but not least, there are the cases involving *per se* offences and related criminal sanctions. The case process is different simply because criminal sanctions and standards of investigation and proof are typically involved. It is, in short, more enforcement oriented than other civil areas of regulation, although it too involves alternative case resolution methods, such as the use of prohibition orders and investigation visits. The case process is again complaint driven but standards of evidence are more difficult than for other sectors in that an offence must be proven beyond a reasonable doubt. Search and seizure powers are more likely to be used since the key evidence of covert behaviour is in corporate or business documents. In recent years, in several jurisdictions, more attention has also been placed on the evidence of corporate whistle-blowers and hence on the potential need to offer immunity. These issues, in turn, require delicate and precise rules.

Indeed, when looking at the detailed and complex vortex of cases one is forced to realize a compelling overall point about the micro-politics of competition policy. This is that such regulatory systems are constructed on the basic political-economic premiss that market systems are more or less working well. Almost by definition, the systems seek to work the outer edges of commercial activity. They practise the art of management by exception in order to ensure that the norms of behaviour remain reasonable.

Moreover, there is a practical political-administrative realization in the construction of such case-handling processes that there are absolute physical and judgemental limits as to how much competition policy authorities can and should substitute their judgement for the judgement of others closer to market realities. Competition authorities thus share limitations recognized in many areas of micro-economic governance by other regulators and investigative arms of the state. Thus, the relevant point of comparison for the adequacy of competition law is not just how other countries do it, but also how other areas of public administration inherently function under roughly similar circumstances, facing analogous policy and implementation puzzles.

The internationalization of competition policy: the politics of system frictions

The brief discussion above of 'system frictions' may suggest that international issues in competition policy are a new phenomenon. As Chapters 9 and 10 show, they are not. The original Havana Charter that led to the formation of the GATT contained an explicit set of rules on business practices that was intended to be administered by the then proposed International Trade Organization. But this package of international competition policy rules never saw the light of day. International competition policy issues have, however, been discussed, and arrangements have evolved since at least the early 1960s, when the OECD's work on this policy field formally began, as did that of UNCTAD.

However, what makes the internationalization of competition policy relatively more compelling in the 1990s is the fact that key political interests and knowledgeable experts clearly see it, along with trade, investment, and environment issues, as being part of the likely conjoined agenda for the next round of post-GATT talks. Indeed, somewhat ironically, one hears the new jargon of the need to 'Gatt-ify competition policy' at the very moment when the Uruguay Round agreement has signalled the end of GATT as a nominal organization, and the birth, long delayed, of the World Trade Organization (WTO).

The notion of 'internationalizing' competition policy is intended in this book to evoke a process that goes beyond globalization.[55] The latter is usually seen as a technological-economic phenomenon, but internationalizing processes, for our purposes, refer to the actual penetration of international regimes and institutions into the concrete functioning of heretofore relatively free-standing domestic or national governmental institutions. While this implies a one-way set of interventions from the international realm to the domestic one, it may also include the reverse, the need to accommodate many more domestic interests and decision processes into how new international institutions are designed and politically justified.[56]

While, analytically speaking, it would make sense to regard international pressures as simply another factor in the macro-politics of contemporary competition policy, there are also good reasons for dealing with it as a distinct level of analysis. Thus, Michael Trebilcock's assessment in Chapter 9 traces the substantive economic reasons for the internationalizing pressures. The more explicit political factors are analysed in a two-stage manner in Chapters 10 and 11, where four variables in total are examined (see Figure 2.3 above). In Chapter 10 the focus is on the political power of individual countries and states, trading or regional blocs, and business, and on the role of international agencies and inter-agency relations within states. In Chapter 11, the focus is on the aforementioned nexus of new or reshaped competition policy ideas as such (system friction, managed trade, co-operation in competition, and strategic alliances and co-operative R&D), and on the international aspects of institutional accountability, representation, and transparency.

To begin to approach the study of competition policy with a complementary political set of lenses to those supplied by economists and lawyers, it is essential to think through each of the above levels of analysis. However, the four-level approach to the politics of competition policy and to the study of competition policy institutions constitutes a formidable agenda. We make no claims that the book can deliver fully and evenly on all four levels or supply a full account of the current interplay among them. The first, second, and fourth levels are reasonably well examined, whereas the level of implementation and micro-politics is only hinted at in some of the country chapters.

COMPETITION POLICY AND THE STUDY OF COMPARATIVE PUBLIC POLICY

While the audience for this book is primarily persons interested in competition policy as such, the book is also directed at persons who will seek to locate it in the broader literature on comparative public policy.[57] Since this volume is the first attempt at an integrated comparative study of the politics of competition policy, it is instructive to make several initial observations about the study of comparative competition policy in relation to other fields with a longer comparative lineage. These observations deal mainly with issues of evidence, problems of comparability, and degrees of difficulty inherent in different policy fields.

In one sense, the problems of comparison are similar to other well-examined policy fields, such as social welfare policy, macro-economic policy, and industrial policy.[58] In simple terms, the dependent variable and independent variables can be fashioned and studied, and stylised levels of analysis can be differentiated. The dependent variable and its boundaries can be given a focal core definition even while recognizing that wider definitions are possible. Indeed, a part of the politics of any policy field is that interests will not agree on boundaries or will seek to broaden or narrow them in their own interests. At this level other policy fields face similar problems. Does macro-policy include or exclude monetary policy and exchange rate policy or confine comparison to aggregates of taxing and spending? Does industrial policy focus on policies directed at sectors or firms or at all policies that directly influence the productivity of industry? Does social policy include or exclude health or education?

With regard to expected independent variables that explain policy, or to classifications of variables for understanding institutional behaviour, competition policy again faces similar problems to other policy fields. Is the study of the field a true comparative one or is it engaged in aspects of comparableness? In the former, common variables are explored in several countries from the outset and in a systematic way. In the latter, one or more authors base a study on one country which they know well and then make suggested links with other countries which they know less well.[59] Again, in many respects, competition policy presents similar problems to other fields in constructing a fully comparative study. The independent variables at the macro-politics level can be broadly similar in nominal definitions, but they also exhibit a denseness, subtlety, and cultural embeddedness that allows full comparison and explanation to be carried only so far. Studies of comparative social policy, education policy, and industrial policy suggest similar dilemmas and limits in other policy fields. The disciplines of social science analysis compel the need for precision, but common-sense and national politics suggest the counter-need for caution and a subtle appreciation of soft and difficult variables such as cultures, history, and particular institutional mixes.

In other respects, the comparative study of competition policy arguably faces even greater degrees of difficulty than other policy fields. This may be true in four ways. First, there are greater problems in the inherent capacity to quantify policy outputs and outcomes. This is certainly true in comparison with studies of social welfare, or even macro tax and expenditure policy where the common denominator of public dollars is available. In this sense, competition policy shares the dilemmas of many studies of regulation where costs and benefits accrue through effects on the private budgets of citizens and firms, and hence quantification is more indirect and less easily measured.

Secondly, competition policy faces some special problems of scope and scale which arise from the fact that it seeks to be a form of framework or horizontal law covering all sectors of the economy. We have seen above in our discussion of boundaries that this full horizontal spread is not quite true but, to the extent that it is true, it does present formidable analytical problems. Again these problems may be shared with other horizontal fields, such as environmental policy, which is why in that field full comparison is also more problematical. Competition policy is also simply a less mature field of study at the comparative level among students of policy and politics.

Thirdly, competition policy, in part because of its lateness on the comparative agenda, must simultaneously be examined through the prism of the internationalization of a policy field. There is no period of basic comparative learning that has occurred before looking at internationalizing pressures, as is the case in some other fields. The 'comparing' and 'internationalizing' enterprises are simultaneously at hand for the political study of competition policy. But most comparative policy studies have typically in fact not included much of an internationalizing focus or element. As Chapter 10 shows, this is partly a function of the separation within political science between international relations and domestic politics and policy as fields of specialization. Moreover, internationalizing forces are not the same as comparative forces. They slice through policy fields in different ways. Other policy fields also now face internationalizing pressures, and thus this aspect of policy studies is growing for these fields as well.

Last but not least, competition policy arguably faces special problems simply because 'competition', and hence competition policy, goes to the heart of defining key features about what capitalism is and means in various parts of the world.[60] Paradoxically, competition policy is emerging from its relative domestic doldrums in most countries precisely because globalization is making the definition of markets more and more difficult and contentious.

CONCLUSIONS

Competition policy needs to be examined through political and institutional lenses as well as through those supplied by the disciplines of economics and law. The chapter has sketched key features of the basic analytical challenge in the comparative study of competition policy. The boundaries of the field have been examined descriptively in nominal terms and as reflected in the political language of the law. Boundaries have also been related to the twin issues of exempt sectors and linked notions of competition when other policy fields are added to the definitional realm.

The chapter has also outlined the four levels of analysis needed for a full appreciation of the politics of competition policy: macro, meso, micro, and international. Each level, while never fully distinct, involves different sets of variables and degrees of difficulty in evidence gathering and interpretation, and each is variously present in the country and jurisdictional chapters. While contributing authors have considered the wide agenda of analytical possibilities they have been asked to concentrate on the core institutions and policy processes. Other macro-or international factors have entered the discussion, but in a less systematic fashion. To this extent the challenges of analysis in competition policy share problems of comparativeness and comparability faced by students of other comparative public policy fields.

NOTES

1. See Marc Allen Eisner, *Antitrust and the Triumph of Economics: Institutions, Expertise and Policy Change* (Chapel Hill: University of

North Carolina Press, 1993), and Robert Katzman, *Regulatory Bureaucracy: The Federal Trade Commission and Antitrust Policy* (Cambridge, Mass.: MIT Press, 1980).

2. See R. S. Khemani and W. Stanbury (eds.), *Canadian Competition Policy at the Centenary* (Halifax: Institute for Research on Public Policy, 1991), and William S. Comanor, *et al.*, *Competition Policy in Europe and North America* (London: Harwood, 1990).

3. See Michael Porter, *The Competitive Advantage of Nations* (New York: Free Press, 1992), and Sylvia Ostry, *Governments and Corporations in a Shrinking World: Trade and Innovation Policies in the United States, Europe and Japan* (New York: Council on Foreign Relations, 1990).

4. See Michael Best, *The New Competition: Institutions of Industrial Restructuring* (Cambridge: Polity Press, 1990), and Terry A. Burke, A. Genn-Bash, and B. Haines, *Competition in Theory and Practice* (London: Routledge, 1991).

5. See W. J. Baumol, J. C. Panzar, and R. D. Willig, *Contestable Markets and the Theory of Industry Structure* (New York: Harcourt, Brace, Jovanovitch, 1988).

6. See G. Reid, *Theories of Industrial Organization* (Oxford: Blackwell, 1987), ch. 7.

7. See e.g. D. Hay and D. Morris, *Industrial Economics, Theory and Evidence* (2nd edn., Oxford: Oxford University Press, 1991); F. M. Scherer and D. Ross, *Industrial Market Structure and Economic Performance* (3rd edn., Boston: Houghton Mifflin, 1990); J. Kwoka and L. J. White (eds.), *The Antitrust Revolution* (New York: Harper Collins, 1989; 2nd edn. 1994).

8. P. Auerbach, *Competition: The Economics of Industrial Change* (Oxford: Blackwell, 1988), ch. 2; see also the excellent critical study, Geoffrey Hodgson, *Economics and Institutions* (Cambridge: Polity, 1988).

9. A most productive review of these alternatives can be found in J. Campbell, J. R. Hollingsworth, and L. Lindberg, *The Governance of the American Economy* (Cambridge: Cambridge University Press, 1991); and J. R. Hollingsworth, P. Schmitter, and W. Streeck (eds.), *Governing Capitalist Economies* (Oxford: Oxford University Press, 1994), esp. the introductory and concluding chapters.

10. F. McChesney, 'In Search of the Public Interest Model of Antitrust', in F. McChesney and W. Shughart (eds.), *The Causes and Consequences of Antitrust: The Public Choice Perspective* (Chicago: University of Chicago Press, 1995), 25–32, 27.

11. D. Hay, 'The Assessment: Competition Policy', *Oxford Review of Economic Policy*, 9/2 (summer 1993), 1–26.

12. Ibid. 6–12.

13. Oliver Williamson, *Antitrust Economics* (Oxford: Blackwell, 1987), 315.
14. See Auerbach, *Competition*, 22–7.
15. See Baumol, Panzar, and Willig, *Contestable Markets and the Theory of Industrial Structure.*
16. See the review of the theoretical influence in W. Shughart, 'Be True to Your School: Chicago's Contradictory Views of Antitrust and Regulation' in McChesney and Shughart (eds.), *The Causes and Consequences of Antitrust*, 323–40 (first pub. 1991).
17. Ibid. preface, p. ix.
18. See R. Whish, *Competition Law* (3rd edn., London: Butterworths, 1993), who undertakes a review of theory on pp. 1–12. On pp. 10–11 he comments on the concept of 'workable competition' and underlines its attractions to pragmatic lawyers, as well as economists.
19. The economic analysis of mergers, the market for corporate control, and the presumptive efficiency gains from merger have emerged as among the most important and productive areas for analysis. In the European setting, see D. Neven, R. Nuttall, and P. Seabright, *Merger in Daylight* (London: Centre for Economic Policy Research, 1993), ch. 2; and M. Bishop and J. Kay (eds.), *European Mergers and Merger Policy* (Oxford: Oxford University Press, 1993).
20. Hay, 'The Assessment: Competition Policy', 12.
21. This is belatedly receiving recognition among economists. In their application of a public choice perspective to US antitrust regulation, McChesney and Shughart focus on the contradictions between the Chicago School's theories of antitrust and regulation, and theories of the latter suggesting that the former would be fraught with political distortions. See McChesney and Shughart, *The Causes and Consequences of Antitrust*, ch. 1.
22. See Thomas M. Jorde and David J. Teece, 'Rule of Reason Analysis of Horizontal Arrangements: Agreements Designed to Advance Innovation and Commercialize Technology', *Antitrust Law Journal*, 61/2 (1992), 579–620.
23. See Comanor *et al.*, *Competition Policy in Europe and North America.*
24. See Michael Trebilcock, 'The Evolution of Competition Policy: A Comparative Perspective', in Frank Matheson (ed.), *The Law and Economics of Competition Policy* (Vancouver: The Fraser Institute, 1990), 1–26.
25. See K. Cowling and Horst Tomann (eds.), *Industrial Policy After 1992: An Anglo-German Perspective* (London: Anglo-German Foundation, 1990), and Robert D. Anderson and Dev Khosla, *Competition Policy as a Dimension of Economic Policy: A Comparative Dimension* (Ottawa: Bureau of Competition Policy, 1993); see also ch. 8 for developments in Europe.
26. See David J. Gerber, 'The Transformation of European Community

Competition Law', *Harvard International Law Journal*, 35 (winter 1994), 97–147.

27. See Sir Gordon Borrie, 'Merger Policy: Current Policy Concerns', in James Fairburn and John Kay (eds.), *Mergers and Merger Policy* (Oxford: Oxford University Press, 1989), 246–63, 257.
28. See Richard H. K. Vietor, *Contrived Competition: Regulation and Deregulation in America* (Cambridge, Mass.: Harvard University Press, 1994).
29. See Giandomenico Majone, 'Paradoxes of Privatization and Deregulation', *Journal of European Public Policy*, 1/1 (June 1994), 53–69.
30. See Vietor, *Contrived Competition*, 13–15.
31. See Best, *The New Competition*; Michael Gerlach, *Alliance Capitalism: The Social Organization of Japanese Business* (Berkeley: University of California Press, 1992); and F. M. Scherer, *Competition Policies for an Integrated World Economy* (Washington, DC: the Brookings Institution, 1994).
32. Ostry, *Governments and Corporations in a Shrinking World*. See also Ostry, 'Globalization, Domestic Policies and the Need For Harmonization', paper presented to a Workshop on Competition Policy in a Global Economy, University of California, Jan. 1993.
33. Ibid. 2.
34. Ibid. 2.
35. See G. Bruce Doern, *Competition Policy Decision Processes in the European Community and United Kingdom: Politics, Public Interest and Discretion* (Ottawa: Bureau of Competition Policy, 1992).
36. See Christopher Green, *Canadian Industrial Organization and Policy* (Toronto: McGraw-Hill Ryerson, 1985).
37. See Scherer and Ross, *Industrial Market Structure and Economic Performance*.
38. See D. W. Carleton and J. M. Perloff, *Modern Industrial Organization* (Glenview, Ill.: Scott, Foresman and Co., 1990), and McChesney and Shughart, *The Causes and Consequences of Antitrust*.
39. See McChesney and Shughart, *The Causes and Consequences of Antitrust*, ch. 1.
40. See Thomas M. Jorde and David J. Teece (eds.), *Antitrust, Innovation and Competitiveness* (Oxford: Oxford University Press, 1992).
41. See Dev Khosla, Robert Anderson, R. Hughes, and J. Monteiro, *Reference Document on Abuse of Dominance* (Ottawa: Bureau of Competition Policy, 1991), introd.
42. See Gerber, 'The Transformation of European Community Competition Law'.
43. See G. Bruce Doern, *Dealing With World Capitalism: Canadian Competition Policy Institutions in a Global Market* (Toronto: C. D. Howe Institute, 1995), ch. 7.

44. See L. J. White, *Private Antitrust Litigation: New Evidence, New Learning* (New York: Free Press, 1988).
45. See J. Pressman and Aaron Wildavsky, *Implementation* (3rd edn., Berkeley: University of California Press, 1984).
46. See Robert T. Nakamura and Frank Smallwood, *The Politics of Policy Implementation* (New York: St Martin's, 1980), 1–28.
47. See Paul Sabatier, 'Top-down and Bottom-up Approaches to Implementation Research', in Michael Hill (ed.), *The Policy Process: A Reader* (London: Harvester Wheatsheaf, 1992), 266–96.
48. See G. Bruce Doern and Richard Phidd, *Canadian Public Policy: Ideas, Structure, Process* (2nd edn., Toronto: Nelson Canada, 1992), chs. 7 and 12.
49. See Law Reform Commission of Canada, *Policy Implementation, Compliance, and Administrative Law* (Ottawa: Law Reform Commission of Canada, 1986), 10. See also Ian Ayres and John Braithwaite, *Responsive Regulation* (Oxford: Oxford University Press, 1992).
50. See Christopher Hood, *Administrative Analysis* (London: Harvester Wheatsheaf, 1986), 46–86.
51. Ibid. 6.
52. See Joel F. Handler, *The Conditions of Discretion: Autonomy, Community, Bureaucracy* (New York: Russel Sage, 1986); and S. Wilks and L. McGowan, 'Discretion in European Merger Control: The German Regime in Context', *Journal of European Public Policy*, 2/1 (1995), 41–67.
53. See Hood, *Administrative Analysis*, ch. 3; G. Bruce Doern, *The Road to Better Public Services: Progress and Constraints in Five Federal Agencies* (Montreal: Institute for Research on Public Policy, 1994); and Malcolm K. Sparrow, *Disposing Duties: Government's Changing Approach to Compliance* (London: Praeger, 1994).
54. See Bishop and Kay (eds.), *European Mergers and Merger Policy*.
55. See David Held and Anthony McGrew, 'Globalization and the Liberal Democratic State', *Government and Opposition*, 28/2 (spring 1993), 261–88.
56. See Joseph Camilleri and Jim Falk, *The End of Sovereignty?* (Aldershot: Edward Elgar, 1992), chs. 4 and 5; Susan Strange and John Stopford, *Rival States, Rival Firms: Competition For World Market Shares* (Cambridge: Cambridge University Press, 1991).
57. See Arnold J. Heidenheimer, H. Heclo, and C. Teich Adams, *Comparative Public Policy* (3rd edn., New York: St Martins Press, 1990), and Jurgen Feick, 'Comparative Policy Studies: A Path Towards Integration', *Journal of Public Policy*, 12/3 (July–Sept. 1992), 257–85.
58. See C. Jones, *Patterns of Social Policy* (London: Tavistock, 1985); Meinolf Dierkes, H. Weller, and A. Berthoin Antal (eds.), *Comparative Policy Research* (Aldershot: Gower, 1987); and Wyn Grant, *Government*

and Industry: A Comparative Analysis of the US, Canada and the UK (Aldershot: Edward Elgar, 1989).

59. See Jones, *Patterns of Social Policy*, ch. 1.
60. See Best, *The New Competition*; Michel Albert, *Capitalism Against Capitalism* (London: Whurr Publishers, 1993); and Hollingsworth, Schmitter, and Streeck, *Governing Capitalist Economies.*

3

United States Competition Policy Institutions: Structural Constraints and Opportunities

B. GUY PETERS

To speak about the institutions of competition policy in the United States definitely requires the use of the plural. Even if the term 'competition policy' is conceptualized very narrowly, there are several organizational actors involved. When this policy area is conceptualized more broadly, as it must be in the contemporary political economy, then the number of actors increases dramatically. Further, the positive and negative interactions among those numerous actors become all the more important in determining policy outcomes.

Thus, competition policy like all other policy domains in the United States is often dominated by questions of co-ordination and control. A president, or the Congress, if it can act collectively, may have a vision of an integrated policy, but almost never will that outcome be possible in practice. This is a function of the complexity of the institutional arrangements and the differing political and economic values embedded within the total array of actors involved. Furthermore, the federal governmental structure of the United States brings several other sets of actors into the policy-making arena for these issues, so that even greater problems of co-ordination can arise over some issues. Finally, the litigious nature of American society and the openness of the court system mean that private individuals also become involved as plaintiffs in antitrust proceedings, especially when the formal institutions of government are not inclined to pursue vigorous enforcement.

Competition policy in the United States grew out of the populist movement of the nineteenth century.[1] This movement was a reaction to many of the problems produced by early, 'robber-baron' capitalism. There was a feeling among many farmers, small businessmen, and a nascent labour movement that big business was running roughshod over the interests of 'the little man'. In particular, the creation of large trusts and near monopolies in industries such as sugar, steel, petroleum, and transportation imposed substantial costs on society. This created a fertile ground for political appeals by 'trust busters'. These included figures such as William Jennings Bryan, Senator John Sherman (Republican, Ohio), and later President Theodore Roosevelt.

The case of competition policy in the USA is especially interesting, given that it has gone from being largely a domestic policy concern to being a policy area that has pronounced foreign as well as domestic concerns. In particular, traditional competition policy has become, at least in part, linked with competitiveness policy and, like many other economic concerns in the public sector, has become heavily impacted by international trade considerations. Policies that once were very acceptable for preserving a 'free market' within a single country have become suspect as almost all countries find their domestic economies more subject to foreign penetration. International agreements and practical economic considerations do make protectionist policies difficult to implement, but neither is a country required to have internal economic policies that undermine the capacity of its industries to compete in the global market.

Thus, just as the Clayton Act was passed and the Federal Trade Commission was created to cope with problems arising from the implementation of the earlier Sherman Act,[2] there may now be a need for rethinking the existing antitrust policy and its relationship with other economic policies. One of the impacts of globalization, and even of the creation of regional trading blocs such as the European Union and NAFTA, is that the global market imposes a set of constraints that national regulatory policies would have difficulty overcoming, even if they wanted to do so.[3] One of those emerging economic constraints appears to be that higher levels of market concentration are increasingly important for success in many industries.

Another perspective on the issues of competition policy can be gained by looking at the role of patent and intellectual property laws and their increasing importance for the economic progress of a country. A patent is one mechanism for creating a monopoly legally, at least for a time, for the individual or firm holding the patent. Governments are responsible for establishing the legal

G. Guy Peters

regimes granting those rights, and increasingly also are supporting the research and technology that creates patents. Even if the right to manufacture products under the patent is franchised internationally, the methods used to control that process may be formally anti-competitive, but also can generate major economic gains for the country of the developer and owner of the patent. How then can the element of economic policy promoting competition be reconciled with the competitiveness elements, and with research and development policies designed to foster greater investment in R&D activities? Further, a vigorous antitrust policy may conflict with the increasing need for an effective policy regime protecting intellectual property rights of all types.[4]

This chapter will attempt to do three things. Its first task is to provide a general description of the legal and institutional frameworks within which competition policy is made and implemented in the United States. The political systems of all countries are complex, but that of the United States is exceptionally complex and poses several special challenges to any advocates of well-integrated public policies. At the same time, however, that unstructured morass of government organizations also presents opportunities for aggressive policy entrepreneurs. The second section of the paper will discuss several alternative versions of institutional theory that might be employed to provide a description and explanation for the behaviour of the organizations within the broad organizational framework. The final task to be undertaken is to put the two preceding segments together and to think about the issues of competition policy in the United States in those analytic terms. This analysis will not provide definitive answers to questions of competition policy, but it should provide a foundation for understanding that is more useful than that obtained from thinking about the policy in strictly legalistic terms.

THE LEGAL FRAMEWORK

Antitrust policy in the United States has a strong legal basis in two major acts, the Sherman and Clayton Acts, and a series of subsequent pieces of legislation that have attempted to refine that defining legislation. The most important of those is the Antitrust Improvements Act of 1976. These pieces of legislation are implemented by several institutions, the most important being the Antitrust Division of the Department of Justice, the Federal Trade Commission, and the court system.

The Sherman Antitrust Act was passed in 1890. It granted the federal government seemingly sweeping powers to prosecute 'Every contract, combination in the form of trust or otherwise, or conspiracy in restraint of trade or commerce among the several States, or with foreign nations.' The individuals responsible for these acts were guilty of a misdemeanour (raised to a felony in 1974), and were subject to fines and imprisonment. Individuals who were damaged by monopolistic practices were entitled to treble damages.

Although this act appears to be an extensive grant of authority to the federal government to regulate American business, it was in practice not a particularly effective piece of legislation. The language of the act was incredibly vague and the courts almost immediately began to specify the meanings of the sweeping terms used.[5] Further, as these interpretations were being made by a conservative court, the act became applicable only to glaring abuses of corporate power, and it was not well-suited to the complexities of the economy even in the early 1900s. For example, in the E. C. Knight Case (1895), the Supreme Court refused to enforce the Sherman Act against the sugar trust because its refining activities (covering 98 per cent of the market) all occurred within individual states, and hence not in interstate commerce (according to the interpretation at the time).

The problems with the Sherman Act became evident very quickly after its enactment. With the narrow interpretations of interstate commerce then in use by the court, the criminal nature of the sanctions in the Act, the style of enforcement, and the absence of resources from Congress to enforce the law,[6] the law appeared to do little to alter the trend toward concentration in US business. In fact, because there were so many clear loopholes in the act and in its enforcement, business could ensure itself of legal ways in which to increase the level of concentration and monopoly powers.[7]

The Standard Oil case (1911) was a major spur to rethinking the Sherman Act and attempting to develop new legislation for competition policy. In that case the court argued that since any commercial action established some restraint on trade, the court would use a 'rule of reason' to determine whether any particular action was legal under the Sherman Act. Under that rule an action that has an ancillary consequence of reducing competition would be permissible, while one that had as its principal reason reducing competition would likely not be allowed. Again, with the nature of the Supreme Court of that time there was a tendency to regard most anti-competitive consequences to be ancillary to legitimate business purposes.

Although interpretations of the rule of reason generally benefited business, reliance on this vague standard, and the equally vague Sherman Act created a very uncertain climate for business. This was particularly true given that the courts were responsible for enforcing this law. The legal doctrines in the United States prohibited the courts from issuing advisory rulings on actions before they were taken, and businesses could undertake what they thought were permissible actions only to find later that they were wrong. Other forms of regulatory intervention, whether through independent commissions or executive branch agencies, would permit prior discussions and negotiations about proposed actions.

The principal response to the weaknesses of the Sherman Act was the Clayton Antitrust Act, passed in 1914 along with the act creating the Federal Trade Commission. The Clayton Act was an attempt to specify the types of activities that would be illegal restraints on trade. These included price discrimination, exclusive dealing relationships, the acquisition of competing companies, and certain interlocking directorates. Further, the Act also specifically excluded labour unions as a 'combination in restraint of trade'. Labour obviously liked the Clayton Act, but it was also widely supported by business because it clarified their previously ambiguous legal environment. Further, with the Federal Trade Commission to enforce the law there was now an administrative agency with which they could negotiate prior to taking actions that might be excluded under the law.

One important feature of the Sherman and Clayton Acts, often overlooked when concentrating on the role of government agencies in enforcing anti-competitive practices, is that they make explicit mention of the role of private antitrust suits. Not only did the law permit those suits, but it provided for treble damages and the recovery of legal fees if the plaintiffs were successful. This provision opened a significant avenue of legal action against anti-competitive practices that tends to distinguish the legal regulation of business in the United States from that found in most other countries.

Antitrust legislation has been reformed through a number of laws since the passage of the Clayton Act. In particular, the Cellar–Kefauver Act (1950) sought to specify actions that would constitute anti-competitive behaviour. In particular, this act sought to fill in an apparent loophole in chapter 7 of the Clayton Act and to control more directly mergers and acquisitions of firms in the same market. As the Clayton Act in 1914 was an attempt to respond to changes in corporate structure and organization, the 1950 act attempted to cope with the changing economic conditions of the post-war world. The Antitrust Improvements Act of 1976 sought to exert even stronger controls over mergers. This act required companies planning a merger to notify the antitrust agencies in advance and to supply a large range of economic information for scrutiny. This allowed the administrative agencies to prevent illegal mergers, rather than having to rely upon the courts to void them after the fact.

The tendency in drafting legislation, and in administrative enforcement, has been to specify more clearly the actions that are forbidden and to create *per se* rules that define an action as being almost inherently in contradiction to the law. This attempt at specification has not, however, prevented the courts from continuing to exercise their own judgement about the appropriateness of certain actions. For example, mechanisms such as 'tie-ins' and other forms of price discrimination which had been thought to be patently illegal were to some extent revived under an economic 'rule of reason'.[8] Much of this shift in discretion occurred under the Reagan administration, but then persisted during the Bush administration.[9]

The importance of declining certainty in the enforcement of antitrust is not primarily a function of the cases that the FTC or the Antitrust Division may lose in court. The real importance is in the impact on the behaviour of firms. Like tax law and many other aspects of public policy, antitrust depends largely upon self-enforcement.[10] The existing enforcement apparatus would have a difficult time monitoring and enforcing the law against businesses that were willing to take their chances with an interpretation from the courts. Thus, everything else being equal, the clearer the meaning of the law, the less the need for extensive enforcement activity.

Although we will focus on the role of the public sector in antitrust policy, the economy itself has a important structural impact on the nature of that policy. Again, the increasing importance of international competition is crucial for understanding this impact. On the one hand, international competition may drive American firms to attempt to consolidate their market positions and survive in that more hostile environment. Those firms may perceive themselves being at a substantial disadvantage if US regulatory agencies impose too stringent a set of antitrust policies on them. Although large firms are the usual target of antitrust regulators, smaller firms are becoming increasingly important in economic growth in the United States.

In areas such as biotechnology and computer technology those small firms have the opportunity to become large and even dominant firms, such as Microsoft, and then to attract the attention of the regulators.[11] These changes in the economy may also mean that the targets and strategies of the two main regulators also will have to be changed. For example, the criterion for when a merger is likely to inhibit competition is now reasonably permissive,[12] but with an economy based more on knowledge and rapid exploitation of technological advances those thresholds may have to be raised even more in order to create sufficient critical mass in the industry and to provide adequate incentives for research.[13] On the other hand, the decline in defence spending and with it the push toward consolidation of aircraft and weapons companies may mean that in some industries extremely high levels of concentration will be required so that the United States can be self-sufficient in this field.[14] The United States may have to go in the direction of many European countries and have a series of 'national champions', at least within this limited area of production.

INSTITUTIONS IN THE PUBLIC SECTOR

The public sector in US government is fragmented along a number of dimensions. If we begin at the level of the federal government, we first find the now infamous institutions of 'divided government',[15] with the Congress and the President established constitutionally as political checks on one another. The problems have only begun, however, because neither of these two branches of government is itself an integrated entity marching to a single drummer. Rather, they are divided internally, with each component attempting to hold onto its own powers within the institution, as much as the institution as a whole may attempt to preserve its own powers. Finally, the courts are independent players of some substantial power in this policy arena. Both the FTC and the Antitrust Division rely ultimately on decisions of the federal courts to substantiate their views about antitrust policy; without the courts they can only hope to persuade firms to behave in the desired ways.

In the area of competition policy, as conventionally defined, the Antitrust Division of the Department of Justice is the principal executive branch agency. This organization was created soon after the First World War to be a principal means of implementing the Sherman and Clayton Antitrust legislation. It followed on earlier, less formal, organizational structures within the Department of Justice focusing on an Assistant Attorney General responsible for antitrust enforcement. The Antitrust Division is now headed by a politically appointed Assistant Attorney General, directly respons- ible to the Attorney General, and as such is an integral component of the legal arm of the federal government. The Division has over 440 employees, with the number projected to increase as the Clinton administration places more emphasis on antitrust policy. How- ever, the Antitrust Division is not alone within the Justice Depart- ment, and certainly not within the federal government as a whole, in its involvement with competition policy.

The Antitrust Division can bring both civil and criminal pro- ceedings against alleged violators of the antitrust laws. It frequently files both actions simultaneously in the hope of being able to win one or the other. Further, if the government loses the criminal case they cannot appeal, but they can appeal a lost civil case. However, as noted above, the Division hopes to be able to avoid litigation altogether and gain compliance without going into the courts. Further, the vast majority of the cases they file are settled by *nolo contendere* pleas, with the businesses accepting the wishes of the government without admitting legal culpability.

In the policy area of economic regulation American government is populated by a number of independent regulatory commissions as well as by several executive agencies.[16] These commissions are often the central players in their one area of regulation, and col- lectively have a significant impact on total governmental action in the economy. These organizations are not technically executive- branch agencies but rather are manifestations of the 'progressive' model established in the late nineteenth century by being—or so it is argued—depoliticized and autonomous. The political appointees who comprise these commissions are presidential appointees (with Senate approval), but are appointed for long terms with relative independence once in office. There has been a long political and constitutional battle over the right of a President to remove commissioners. This has generally been resolved in favour of the commissioners.

The conception underlying the independent-commission form of governance is that the commissions should be able to make decisions 'in the public interest' without the interference of partisan political influences. As Theodore Lowi and other scholars have pointed out, however, this institutional design may have eliminated (or at least reduced) partisan political influences, but it has not eliminated other forms of politics.[17] Those alternative forms of politics may be, if anything, more threatening to the public interest than partisanship. In particular, the danger of 'capture' by the very interests the commission was designed to regulate is a persistent problem in organizations of this type.[18]

In the traditional arena of competition policy the principal actor among the independent commissions has been the Federal Trade Commission (FTC). This organization was established in 1914 as a result of the passage of the Clayton Antitrust Act and its companion the Federal Trade Commission Act. Unlike the Antitrust Division, headed by a single individual who is both a policy leader and a manager, the commission structure of the FTC contains five commissioners who must collectively decide on the basic policy directions of the organization. Given that the appointments to the Commission are staggered there are usually members appointed by several presidents, and with that having several ideological perspectives on competition policy. The change from twelve years of Republican control in 1993 caused a certain amount of trepidation in the business community, which feared more activist appointees to the FTC and other regulatory commissions, but for the time being the Commission remains in the hands of Republican appointees.[19] The commissioners head an organization with just under 1,000 employees, with approximately 40 per cent of them working on antitrust issues.

The FTC functions as an administrative organization rather than a legal organization. One of the major advantages this organizational format produces is its capacity to issue binding regulations as secondary legislation. The Antitrust Division issues guidelines that are important guideposts for firms, but they remain just guidelines and do not have the legal force of the FTC regulations. Also, the FTC can issue advisory opinions to a firm, stating whether it considers a proposed action in violation of the existing laws. These opinions are then binding on the Commission. When the FTC does bring a case against an alleged anti-competitive action, the case is first heard by an administrative law judge within the Commission, and can then be appealed to the whole Commission. Only when these administrative remedies are exhausted can the case be appealed into the regular court system. The hearings within the FTC have many of the trappings of a formal court proceeding, but still can use somewhat more informal means of settling the disputes.

Given that the commissioners may also have a variety of professional backgrounds (usually economics and law), they often express different views about policy related to those academic backgrounds.[20] These differences are in addition to any that may arise from their political and ideological allegiances. In addition, within each profession or discipline there may be pronounced differences in prevailing doctrine about antitrust and competition policy. For example, Eisner points to the pronounced differences in the dominant economic theory used within the FTC across time, and the impact that these theoretical differences have had on antitrust policy.[21]

In particular, there has been a shift from the market-structure perspective on antitrust to the Chicago School, more concerned with welfare effects, and that shift has had a profound influence on the number and type of antitrust cases brought by the commission.[22] These differences also have had some ideological dimension, but the more important considerations appear to have been theoretical and professional ones. The market-structure approach, or the 'structure–conduct–performance' paradigm is concerned with the formal structure of production within an industry, and uses concentration as almost *prima facie* evidence that there has been a wrongful concentration of economic power. There was no need in this paradigm for direct collusive activity in order for there to be a combination in restraint of trade; the behaviour of a leading firm designed to maintain or enhance its market position appeared to be sufficient.[23]

While the 'structure–conduct–performance' paradigm assumed that any significant concentration of market power was inherently inimical to the public interest and economic performance, as the recruitment of Commission economists shifted toward the Chicago School, very different assumptions came into play in decisions. This school of thought assumes that big businesses and concentration of economic power are not necessarily bad in themselves.[24] Indeed, advocates of this approach argue that if a large firm is created and survives, its survival is *prima facie* evidence that the size is appropriate and efficient. In other words, if it has worked well for business then it must be good for the public. Clearly in this perspective there would have to be some overt anti-competitive activity in order to justify a claim that the regulators should intervene.

As I have already noted, the FTC may be the lead among the independent regulatory commissions in its impact on competition policy, but it is not alone in the field. Other regulatory commissions responsible for a particular economic domain will have something to say about the way in which the FTC treats 'their' firms on issues of monopoly and merger policy. For example, the Federal Communications Commission will take a strong interest in any mergers involving the electronic media, and has its own regulations about permissible levels of concentration in the communications industry.[25] The Interstate Commerce Commission may play a similar role in the transportation industry. The International Trade Commission can become a player when the role of foreign firms becomes a part of the competition question. These potential conflicts among the existing regulatory organizations point to the important differences that exist between commissions responsible for a single industry and those responsible for almost the entire range of industries.[26] The possibilities of capture are substantially greater with the single-industry agencies, and broader agencies are, everything else being equal, likely to be harder on industry. It should be pointed out that the Antitrust Division has made something of the same shift in its economic perspective, although its greater domination by lawyers has made the shift less pronounced.[27]

Internal Structure

Although the two major actors in competition policy may have certain tendencies and dominant professional groups, their internal structuring also may have some significant impacts on the ways in which they make policy. For example, the Federal Trade Commission allows a somewhat stronger role for economists in constructing policy than does the Antitrust Division of Justice. On the other hand, however, it cannot really do its work without the involvement of lawyers. In the FTC there is an internal division, with most lawyers located in the Bureau of Competition, which has a Division of General Litigation that is responsible for most of the legal action. This structure replaced a highly subdivided structure, within the earlier Bureau of Restraint of Trade, that made internal co-ordination of policy and strategy very difficult.[28] The activities of this litigation bureau must be co-ordinated with the economic analysis of the Bureau of Economics. That task is performed primarily through the Office of Policy Planning and Evaluation.

The Antitrust Division has the internal structural problem of getting sufficient economic analytical input into what might otherwise be a highly legalistic organization. This is especially true since it tends to be a hierarchical organization, with the Assistant Attorney General playing a dominant role in decisions about litigation. This economic expertise was to some extent institutionalized under the leadership of Thomas Kauper during the 1970s, when he created the Economic Policy Office within the Division.[29] Indeed, gradually the Economic Policy Office came to dominate the affairs of the Division, and had economists serving all the various litigating groups within the Bureau.

We will be concentrating on the formal role of the Antitrust Division and the Federal Trade Commission in enforcing competition law, but there is an important informal element as well. Most issues in competition policy never reach the courts or these agencies, but are instead self-enforced through corporate attorneys who advise their clients what is possible under law and practice and what is not. Therefore, the signals that the two government institutions send to the corporate and legal communities are important for determining what will happen. For example, the 'non-enforcement rhetoric' during the 1980s was important in defining how the corporate community would proceed with its merger and pricing activities.[30] Further, the use of guidelines and formal rules from the FTC can give to private attorneys additional guidance concerning what actions are likely to trigger the interests of regulators.

As noted above, the federal nature of US politics brings into play other actors concerned with competition policy. In some ways this statement may appear unlikely, given the apparent federal monopoly over the regulation of interstate commerce. The federal government certainly does have a dominant position in this area, but the states have managed to act also. In fact, the level of state activity in antitrust has been increasing. This is in part a function of the populist appeal of this activity and the political capital it can build for state attorneys general (elective officials in almost all states). These public officials have begun to file cases of potential national significance in state courts, a practice that could fragment national policy and make the environment of business very uncertain.

The states have been acting to limit competition at least as often as they have acted to promote it. For example, states (and counties and cities) often have laws requiring giving preference on public contracts to vendors coming from inside their political unit. It is not uncommon for these policies to create local monopolies or oligopolies, and perhaps also to create higher costs for the government imposing the policy. These policies do, of course, preserve local employment opportunities. Businesses can also gain protection from federal antitrust competition by accepting more friendly state regulation. On the other hand, through state corporation commissions and similar regulatory bodies, state governments also exercise some sub-national control over concentrations of commercial power, although in a limited geographical area and subject to local pressures that are often not as pro-competitive as national policies tend to be.[31]

The above discussion of local preferences points to the increasing conflicts between competition policy and a host of other economic policy considerations that focus on reducing unemployment and increasing economic growth. If we extend our concern with competition to include at least in part its interface with the emerging national concern over competitiveness policy, we can identify a number of other organizational actors of significance in this policy area. All the federal departments concerned with microeconomic policy issues—Labor, Commerce, and Agriculture in particular—become players under this broader approach. Each of those departments has a number of agencies that will themselves have a perspective on policy, and may conflict with other agencies—even those within their own department. In addition, independent executive agencies (in contrast to independent regulatory commissions) such as the Small Business Administration also have something to say about economic issues and competition policy. For example, if the Clinton administration wants to implement a more activist antitrust policy it will be confronted by a number of conservative judges appointed by the Reagan and Bush administrations. Even if ideology were not a barrier to policy change, the bench is only rarely equipped by academic training to cope with the complex economic issues now arising in antitrust proceedings, and the regulators therefore may face significant difficulties in winning certain types of complex antitrust cases.[32]

In summary, the structure of American government constitutes a major institutional impediment to establishing a coherent and integrated competition policy. At the federal level there are two agencies with primary responsibility for the policy, and they do not always agree on what constitutes the best approach to the issues. While some scholars might argue that this redundancy is beneficial and may reduce possibilities for both under-regulation and over-regulation, there are also problems of inconsistency and uncertainty that may plague businesses in dealing with these two institutional actors.[33] In addition, there are a number of other federal and sub-national actors involved. These actors are even less likely to agree about good policy, and may create even greater problems for businesses attempting to decide about mergers and other actions that may be perceived as reducing competition.

INSTITUTIONAL THEORY AND POLICY

The re-emergence of institutional theory in the study of government and public policy can make a contribution to understanding this policy area, just as it has in the case of a number of others. This body of theory comes in a variety of forms, but they share a common emphasis on the role of institutions, both as formal structures[34] and as sets of rules and values,[35] in determining the shape of policy. If we begin with the structuralist conceptualization of institutions and their influence, we find several points of relevance for US competition policy. The most important of these is the 'veto-points' argument.[36] The concept here is that different political systems have different numbers of points at which action can be curtailed. For example, everything else being equal, parliamentary regimes have fewer independent veto points than do presidential regimes. Further, in the case of countries such as Switzerland, which requires citizen referenda for approval of important policies, the significance of veto points increases dramatically.

In general the United States falls toward the extreme in terms of the number of independent veto points. As noted, the US presidential regime and independent legislature provide one barrier to any streamlined version of decision-making. The now infamous characterization of 'divided government' in the United States has indeed pointed to a barrier to rapid decision-making, but the system ultimately has been able to respond, and at times even to respond creatively to its policy challenges. On the other hand, seemingly more streamlined systems of policy-making often have been unable to respond to the challenges they face.

The other way to think about political institutions is to think of them as collections of rules, or as collections of values. In either case policy-making is structured by the internal constraints of the organizations, and policy-makers are not writing on a *tabula rasa*. Indeed, in this view (and especially in the 'historical institutionalism' school), policies are path dependent, with the choices made early in the formation of policy, and institutions having a continuing and pervasive influence over subsequent policy decisions. This observation does not mean that organizations cannot change their values and internal cultures; there are too many examples to the contrary to argue that. What it does mean is that there will be some institutional inertia that any individual or group interested in policy change will have to overcome in order to be successful.

American public organizations are no different from public organizations elsewhere in reflecting values and sets of internal rules, and in having their contemporary policy choices to some degree constrained by history. It could be argued that US organizations may be particularly subject to this historical determinacy. This is true because of the relative autonomy of individual organizations from hierarchical control, their ability to mobilize support within the public and in Congress, and the tendency of civil servants to spend most of their career within a single organization. These organizations have a greater opportunity to recreate themselves than would public organizations in most other policy systems. As professional training becomes a more important criterion for recruitment into public organizations, the tendency toward organizational separatism and self-definition may become even more pronounced. The basic idea is that any reality that surrounds a policy is a product of a social process, rather than any objective conditions. Even the initial definition of the problem is the product of such processes, and agenda-setting is perhaps the most important aspect of policy.[37] In the institutional perspective the organizations involved create the knowledge base and the ideology that supports a policy framework. Given that there may be a number of organizations that have something to say about any one policy, they are likely to be in competition and conflict over control, using their ideas and their knowledge bases as principal components of their armamentarium in the struggle.[38]

Although discussed here as being roughly compatible, there are some interesting and important differences between the rule-based version of institutionalism and the cultural version. Perhaps the most important distinction is that the rule-based version assumes that the constraints on behaviour within the organization are more visible than does the alternative version. This to some degree produces a tautology—a rule is something that is obeyed because it is a rule. Even with that, however, there is an advantage that the rules can be taught more readily to an outsider or to a newcomer. The more cultural version of institutionalism, on the other hand, is less transparent and depends more upon individuals developing an almost intuitive sense of the rules, or more precisely of the organizational culture.

The value-based strand of institutional thinking poses some interesting problems for understanding public policy. In particular, if values are so important for understanding organizational behaviour, then how can organizations with different values co-operate effectively as is required within almost all policy areas? The implementation literature has argued for some time that there is no such thing as the single organization and that point also is true for a variety of other aspects of behaviour within the complex web of government, especially one as complex as that of the United States.[39] Strong organizational value systems may be crucial for the success of individual organizations but may limit the effectiveness of groups of organizations that must co-operate and co-ordinate their actions around a policy.

Institutional analysis and antitrust policy

We have argued that the institutions of government in the United States are highly fragmented and also are characterized by apparent overlap and duplication of policies. Also, because of the relative autonomy of organizations within cabinet departments, as well as of the greater autonomy of free-standing executive agencies and regulatory commissions, the organizations within government are able to advance their own viewpoints about policy to a greater extent than would be the case in other countries. These characteristics have been identified in a number of policy areas, including some such as defence that are generally considered to be more linear and unified. There is little reason to expect that the same characteristics would not be important in competition policy.

If we begin with the division between the two principal agencies responsible for competition policy in the United States there are already some interesting differentiations in the institutional influences on policy. In the first place, the very fact that there are two organizations rather than only one operating in this area is important. Given that the target organizations of government activities in this policy area generally are not seeking benefits, but rather are being regulated, this duplication places them at greater potential jeopardy. Although co-ordinative mechanisms exist, an action that one of the two agencies regards as perfectly acceptable may not be acceptable to the second, and the business in question ultimately may find itself under investigation or in court.[40] Therefore, if we conceptualize the public at large as the principal client of antitrust agencies, then the public is, in a sense, doubly protected against uncompetitive practices by this structural arrangement.

If we look at the two organizations there are differences in their orientation to antitrust policy and to the means for enforcing that policy. For example, the Federal Trade Commission is a major player in antitrust policy, but the commission is also a major consumer protection agency responsible in particular for protection against fraudulent advertising and other deceptive practices affecting the public.[41] Thus, even internally the FTC has to reconcile, if not contradictory policies, then at least the possibility for differential emphasis on one policy thrust of the organization or another. Furthermore it faces potential competitors on consumer protection policy (the Consumer Product Safety Commission, the Postal Inspector, and increasingly numerous state-level agencies such as state attorneys general), just as it does in competition policy, and so has to guard its flanks in the power and policy game. It appears that the FTC as currently constituted has been placing an increasing amount of its effort into enforcing consumer protection legislation, therefore leaving more of the antitrust arena to the Antitrust Division.

On the other hand, the Antitrust Division is embedded within a much larger organization which has a variety of policy concerns. It has the advantage of having a somewhat more integrated vision internally than does perhaps the FTC, but by contrast has to compete with other concerns for the attention of the Associate Attorney General for the Civil Division, the Attorney General, and the rest of the leadership of the Department. The extent to which antitrust policy is a priority may depend upon the political values and the political strategies of the administration, and of the Attorney General in office. For example, the Clinton administration appears to be embarking on an activist antitrust policy after over a decade of a more *laissez-faire* approach to these issues. Even at that, the administration's priorities in the Department of Justice appear to be more on civil rights and fighting violent crime, so its profile on antitrust policy may not be as high as might be expected. On the other hand, a vigorous litigator, Anne K. Bingaman, was appointed as head of the Division and was expected to manage her own active agenda.

Eisner points out the need to understand not only the location of these organizations within the total matrix of government organizations, but also to understand their internal structuring and dynamics.[42] For example, there has been a shift in the proportion of economists to lawyers employed within the FTC, with economists becoming much more important participants in an agency formerly dominated by attorneys. This shifting in recruitment and concern within the agency was reflected in the strengthening of the Bureau of Economic Analysis and the creation of an Office of Policy Planning and Evaluation. The latter organization was particularly important in changing the focus of the FTC's attention to big issues in antitrust enforcement rather than a number of smaller cases.

The small antitrust cases had been favoured in the Commission when it was dominated by lawyers passing through the Commission for a short time. The numerous small cases gave the young attorneys a great deal of practice in actual litigation, practice useful for their careers when they went back to the private sector. The shift to a more powerful economist's perspective in the FTC was important in understanding its shift of focus to major causes and principles behaviour. It is also important to note, however, that this has been offset somewhat by pressures on the FTC to pay more attention to its role in consumer protection and fraudulent advertising. It also has been offset somewhat by the conservative appointees from the Reagan and Bush administrations who have sought to minimize restraints on business. Further, given the nature of FTC appointments, this influence will persist longer than in the Department of Justice.

In the late 1980s and in the 1990s the emphasis within the FTC has been shifting back toward smaller cases. This could be explained by the relative disinterest of Republican administrations in major attacks on big business, as well as the low probability of winning such cases with an increasingly Republican bench for most of this time. In addition there was a great deal of political and bureaucratic capital to be made by prosecuting consumer fraud cases. These gained headlines while not really affecting more legitimate businesses.

One of the most important questions in the analysis of the FTC, the Antitrust Division, and other regulatory bodies is the extent to which they are influenced by political pressures. This question is to some degree a restatement of the fundamental assumptions of the progressive movement that sought to ensure that political pressures would not dominate decisions by these bodies. The conventional wisdom in political science has become that the progressives failed and that there is a great deal of political control of regulatory agencies of all types—independent commissions such as the FTC and those within cabinet departments (Occupational Safety and Health Administration in the Department of Labor, for example). The counter-argument, however, is that the increasing professionalism of these organizations makes such control more difficult and that the organizations are more bureaucratically than politically dominated.[43]

Organizational styles and culture

To this point we have been looking at making competition policy in the United States largely from a structural viewpoint. If we are to explore the alternative, value-based conception of institutionalism we must also look at the internal values of the organizations making the policies. Attempting to characterize whole organizations in this way involves many of the same risks encountered when attempting to characterize the political culture of an entire nation. There may well be organizational subcultures acting in opposition to the dominant culture. Those subcultures may, however, actually be useful for the organization, providing it with an internal source of change and perhaps greater capacity to interact effectively with other organizations. Despite those difficulties, it still appears useful to attempt to gain some conception of the collective 'thinking' of the organizations as they confront the need to act in this policy area.

There are several apparent patterns of interest in the behaviour of the FTC and the Antitrust Division. They may have rather similar missions (at least in antitrust), but they have somewhat dissimilar approaches to the policy questions for which they are responsible. One thing that stands out is the extent to which the FTC has become more the preserve of economists, of whatever theoretical or ideological stripe, while the Antitrust Division remains more the province of the lawyer. Of course, neither organization can survive without some members of both professions, but it is also clear that one or the other does tend to dominate. Further, lawyers may be more conservative in their approach to policy, looking for precedent and clear legal guidance, while non-lawyers may be more willing to innovate and take risks.[44]

The relative powers of the two professions within the two organizations are to some degree demonstrated by the procedures by which cases are selected for pursuit and possible prosecution by the two organizations. On the one hand, in the FTC the preliminary investigatory work is done largely by economists who use their dominant paradigm to determine if there has been any harm done to the public interest (within the bounds of the logic of that paradigm). If the economists find instances that they believe are worthy of being pursued then they will bring in the lawyers to see what sort of legal case may exist. Most cases are settled without having to go to court (see above), but there is little sense in starting a case if there is no real hope of winning in the event that it goes to court.

Another important institutional contrast of these two organizations is their relative responsiveness to changes in political direction in the federal government. As noted above, the Federal Trade Commission is likely to have a very long response time to political changes, given that the commissioners are appointed for staggered terms of seven years, so that on average a one-term president can replace only one commissioner. It may therefore require a long reign by a party to be able to place its stamp on the FTC, even if we assume that the preferences about antitrust are uniform within the party. Further, the law mandates that no more than three members can be members of the same political party, and this makes balance all the more likely. Thus, even with the long Republican reign of the Reagan and Bush administrations, only a limited partisan stamp could be put on the FTC. However, given the variations in ideology within both parties, a stamp of some sort could be made.

The Antitrust Division in Justice, on the other hand, may be capable of responding relatively quickly to partisan priorities. For example, the Clinton appointment of Anne Bingaman as Assistant Attorney General in charge of this division appears to have produced some trepidation in the ranks of American business.[45] The shift to more stringent enforcement has already been manifested in the development of new strategies for pressing claims of attempts to inhibit competition and of collusive behaviour, especially vertical restraints.[46] We should not, however, be too quick in assuming that the Antitrust Division will respond immediately and willingly to all changes advocated by its nominal political masters. The Division is composed of professional attorneys who are likely to have their own conceptions of what constitutes appropriate policy in the area, and they may be capable of maintaining some of their own priorities about the policy even in the face of political pressures. Further, the large number of Reagan and Bush appointees still on the federal bench may prevent rapid changes in federal antitrust policy.

The existence of these two organizations, while appearing redundant and wasteful, may actually be functional for the society. As noted above, the redundancy is almost certainly functional for citizens who want protection from abuses by big business. Citizens (and their agents) have two options for having their interests advocated, and, equally important, there are two optional organizations which may have different perspectives on the relevant-competition issues. On the other hand, businesses may benefit from having one regulatory organization that remains relatively stable and is more likely to have consistent policies than the other organizations that respond to political changes. Further, as Eisner argued, there is a tendency to create multiple organizations so that government can fulfil both its instrumental and ideological functions. It appears that all sides may gain politically from having multiple organizations in a single policy area.

The rise of economic analysis in antitrust proceedings has tended to weaken another institution involved in this field—private litigation. When the courts applied *per se* rules that made certain actions clearly illegal under the law, it was relatively easy for a private attorney to proceed for a client who had been injured. With the more complex economic analysis now required for proving that an action violates the 'rule of reason', and the consequent need for substantial economic literacy, the private litigator is at somewhat of a disadvantage. This appears to have two implications for competition policy. One is the development of something of a return to the lack of clarity under the Sherman Act that helped produce the Clayton Act. Second, this change in the style of enforcement will tend to make competition policy more subject to the whims of political change and political appointees.

PRIVATE ANTITRUST ENFORCEMENT

The United States differs from most other countries in having provision for private antitrust actions. As noted, the framework legislation for antitrust makes specific reference to the possibilities of such suits, and establishes the principle that treble damages will be paid to successful plaintiffs. The existence of this private mechanism for enforcement presents both costs and benefits for competition policy in the United States. The most obvious benefits are, if one believes in the efficacy of competition, that there is somewhat greater probability that corporate attempts to restrain market competition will be identified and punished. As with public enforcement, just the knowledge that these punitive legal actions are possible may be sufficient to restrain many would-be monopolizers. Further, the provision for treble damages allows firms that have been harmed by the actions to regain some of their lost economic ground. If promoting competition is important, then the alternative private system of enforcement is a significant economic advantage.

The disadvantages of these provisions in antitrust law are also rather obvious. Given the abundance of attorneys in the United States and their ability to take cases on a contingent basis, there is, in this sense, little to restrain the filing of suits. The courts over time have limited the ability to sue to individuals and firms that have sustained a direct harm from the anti-competitive actions of another, but even with that restraint there are many opportunities to enter the legal arena. It should also be noted that antitrust actions can be used for anti-competitive purposes. When a merger would produce substantial reductions in production costs for some firms, a successful antitrust suit may allow less efficient firms to remain in business, thus producing higher costs for consumers.[47] We should also remember that litigation is not the only way to resolve a suit, and settlement without trial can save costs for both sides. A defendant therefore may choose to settle—even if they would probably win in court—simply because it is easier and surer.

The two decades from 1960 to 1980 were the heyday of private antitrust litigation. Although the legal provisions supporting those suits were in place from 1890 onward, almost no private cases were brought prior to 1960. During the two decades in question, however, hundreds of cases were brought each year. The reasons for the shifting role of private enforcement are not clear. The courts did open the door for more class-action suits, but these have a rather small part of the total activity. Some of the increase in private activity may have been pure opportunism, with litigants seeking to capitalize on cases that the government has already proven, while others may be attempts to use antitrust actions to prevent more efficient firms from exploiting their efficiency fully.[48] Further, the reasons for the (relative) decline of private antitrust actions is not entirely clear. In part, the courts began to define standing to sue somewhat more conservatively than they had previously. Further, with the change in the bench during the Reagan and then Bush administrations, antitrust actions were less likely to be successful, whether brought by government agencies or private individuals. Finally, the decline is relative, and there are still many more private antitrust actions than there are public actions of all types combined.

CONCLUSIONS

This chapter has attempted to describe the institutional forces at play in making antitrust policy in the United States. One of the most important of these forces arises from the internal divisions and redundancy characteristic of US government. Although this is not a policy area that presently depends upon a great deal of new legislation, the principal administrative actors do depend upon budgetary support and are subject to legislative oversight. In addition, the existence of several actors with important responsibility in antitrust enforcement means that there are at once several options for ensuring that antitrust violators are prosecuted, as well as possible confusion about the real meaning of the law. Further, the courts have not always been clear about their own interpretation of the laws, especially given that a number of different district courts are involved in making rulings in antitrust cases.

The ambiguity sometimes surrounding antitrust policy in the United States is reinforced by the increasing linkage of all economic policy issues with issues of global competitiveness. So long as the US economy was relatively independent in the world, then a stringent enforcement of laws against 'combinations in restraint of trade' appeared to make good economic sense. Once it becomes clear that the United States is engaged in a major battle for jobs and profits with other countries, then the role of antitrust becomes more difficult to sustain. This is true even though the two organizations responsible for this policy continue to exist and continue to be committed to their own policies. This then becomes a question of setting priorities for economic policy and co-ordinating a number of different policy initiatives. Few governments are really good at this task, and the United States is perhaps worse than most. There are also important questions about the extent to which politics can, and should, dominate antitrust policy-making. On the normative side of the argument there is a fundamental tenet of democracy which demands that policy should follow the outcomes of elections. On the other hand, business interests feel that they should be able to expect some certainty about the rules that are being applied so that they can plan their corporate business strategies. Empirically, although there is some support for the proposition of political control over antitrust and other regulatory policies, there is also some evidence to support the proposition of professional dominance. Both normatively and empirically there appears to be a need to strike some balance between stability and political control, as well as between business and consumer interests. This entire analysis then points to the existence of a number of veto points in US politics and the need to get a number of actors moving in the same direction if any significant policy-making is to occur. Because of the reliance on administrative rule-making and rule-making through the courts, this characteristic is less significant for antitrust policy than it is for many others, but it is still important. The existence of those veto points may become all the more important as traditional competition policy must confront demands for enhanced integration with competitiveness and other forms of economic policy.

NOTES

1. See R. C. McMath, *American Populism: A Social History, 1877–1898* (New York: Hill and Wang, 1993), and Fred S. McChesney and William F. Shughart (eds.), *The Causes and Consequences of Antitrust: The Public Choice Perspective* (Chicago: University of Chicago Press, 1995).
2. See T. C. Blaisdell, *The Federal Trade Commission: An Experiment in The Regulation of Business* (New York: Columbia University Press, 1932).
3. For a conservative view, see G. R. Saxenhouse, 'Sony Side Up: Japan's Contributions to the US Economy', *Policy Review*, 56 (1991), 60–4.
4. See I. K. Gotts, 'Regulators Focusing on Antitrust Issues', *National Law Review*, 16/21 (1994), s12–s14.
5. See H. Thorelli, *Federal Antitrust Policy* (Baltimore: Johns Hopkins University Press, 1954).
6. Prior to the Budget Act of 1921 the federal budget was an almost entirely legislative document, with the President having little control over its formation and limited power to manipulate funds at the execution stage.
7. See T. K. McCaw, 'Mercantilism and the Market: Antecedents of American Industrial Policy', in C. E. Barfield and W. A. Schambra (eds.), *The Politics of Industrial Policy* (Washington, DC: American Enterprise Institute, 1986).
8. See H. M. Reasoner, 'Antitrust Policy', in Martin Feldstein (ed.), *American Economic Policy in the 1980s* (Chicago: University of Chicago Press, 1994).

9. See H. M. Reasoner, 'The State of Antitrust', *Antitrust Law Journal*, 58 (1990), 63–70.

10. See J. S. Naguin, 'Policy Options for Combatting Tax Noncompliance', *Journal of Policy Analysis and Management*, 9 (1990), 7–22.

11. See J. E. Schwartz, *America's Hidden Successes* (New York: Norton, 1988).

12. As we note below, the criteria for selecting anti-competitive cases is still to some degree dominated by 'Chicago School' economics.

13. See B. Guy Peters, 'Policy Making for Technology: Picking Winners', *Bestuurskunde*, 3 (1993), 147–51.

14. See C. Yank, 'Lock and Load: The Pentagon vs. the Trustbusters', *Business Week*, 3556 (1994), 41.

15. See M. P. Fiorina, 'Coalition Governments, Divided Governments and Electoral Theory', *Governance*, 4 (1991), 236–49.

16. See K. J. Meier, *Regulation: Politics, Bureaucracy, Economics* (New York: St Martins, 1985).

17. See T. J. Lowi, *The End of Liberalism* (2nd edn., New York: Norton, 1979).

18. See R. L. Calvert, M. J. Moran, and B. Weingast, 'A Theory of Political Control and Agency Discretion', *American Journal of Political Science*, 33 (1989), 588–611; and J. R. Mezey, 'Organizational Design and Political Control of Administrative Agencies', *Journal of Law, Economics and Organization*, 8 (1992), 93–110.

19. See K. Barrett and R. Greene, 'Federal Trade Commission', *Financial World*, 26 Oct. 1993, 42–4.

20. See W. T. Gormley, *The Politics of Public Utility Regulation* (Pittsburgh: University of Pittsburgh Press, 1983); and R. Bell, 'Professional Values and Organizational Decisionmaking', *Administration and Society*, 17 (1985), 21–60.

21. See M. A. Eisner, *Antitrust and the Triumph of Economics* (Chapel Hill: University of North Carolina Press, 1991).

22. See D. I. Baker and W. Blumenthal, 'Ideological Cycles and Unstable Antitrust Rules', *Antitrust Bulletin*, 31 (1986), 323–39.

23. See J. Weiss, 'The Structure–Conduct–Performance Paradigm and Antitrust', *University of Pennsylvania Law Review*, 27 (1979), 1104–40.

24. See R. A. Posner, 'The Chicago School of Antitrust Analysis', *University of Pennsylvania Law Review*, 127 (1979), 925–48.

25. See M. Lewyn, 'The FCC Attempts to Reverse some Overseas Charges', *Business Week*, 18 Feb. 1991, 26–8.

26. See R. A. Harris and S. M. Milkis, *The Politics of Regulatory Change* (New York: Oxford University Press, 1989).

27. See D. R. Bickel, 'The Antitrust Division's Adoption of the Chicago School', *Houston Law Review*, 20 (1982), 1083–127.

28. See R. A. Katzmann, *Regulatory Bureaucracy: The Federal Trade Commission and Antitrust Policy* (Cambridge, Mass.: MIT Press, 1980).

29. See T. E. Kauper, 'The Role of Economic Analysis in the Antitrust Division Before and After the Establishment of the Economic Policy Office', *Antitrust Bulletin*, 29 (1984), 111–32.

30. American Bar Association, *Report of the American Bar Association Section of the Antitrust Law Task Force on the Antitrust Division of the US Department of Justice* (Chicago: American Bar Association, 1989), p. viii.

31. See G. D. Sesser, 'Unnecessary Ingredient in Antitrust Enforcement', *National Law Journal*, 15/31 (1993), 17–28.

32. See D. J. Ravenscraft and C. L. Wagner, 'The Role of the FTC's Line of Business Data in Testing and Expanding the Theory of the Firm', *Journal of Law and Economics*, 34 (1991), 703–19.

33. See J. B. Bender, *Parallel Systems: Redundancy in Government* (Berkeley: University of California Press, 1985).

34. See R. K. Weaver and B. A. Rockman (eds.), *Do Institutions Matter? Government Capabilities in the United States and Abroad* (Washington, DC: The Brookings Institution, 1993).

35. See Elinor Ostrom, 'Rational Choice Theory and Institutional Analysis', *American Political Science Review*, 85 (1991), 237–43; and J. G. March and J. P. Olsen, *Rediscovering Institutions* (New York: Free Press, 1989).

36. See Ellen Immergut, *Health Care Politics: Interests and Institutions in Western Europe* (Cambridge: Cambridge University Press, 1992); and Sven Steinmo, Kathleen Thelen, and Frank Longstreth (eds.), *Structuring Politics: Historical Institutionalism in Comparative Analysis* (Cambridge: Cambridge University Press, 1992).

37. See F. R. Baumgartner and B. D. Jones, *Agendas and Instability in American Politics* (Chicago: University of Chicago Press, 1993).

38. See P. Sabatier, 'An Advocacy-Coalition Model of Policy Change', *Policy Sciences*, 21 (1988), 129–68.

39. See B. Hjern and D. O. Porter, 'Implementation Structures: A New Unit of Administrative Analysis', *Organization Studies*, 2 (1981), 211–34.

40. See J. Johnssons and B. McCormick, 'Mixed Merger Message from Government Rankles Hospitals', *American Medical News*, 37/7 (1994), 24–6.

41. Harris and Milkis, *The Politics of Regulatory Change*.

42. See M. A. Eisner, 'Bureaucratic Professionalism and the Limits of the Political Control Thesis: The Case of the Federal Trade Commission', *Governance*, 6 (1993), 236–49.

43. Ibid.

44. K. Donovan, 'FTC Uses Novel Theory in Lawsuit: Others May Follow', *National Law Journal*, 14/52 (1992), 13–18.
45. See K. Silber, 'Monopoly is No Game to Clinton's Trustbusters', *Insight on The News*, 9/44, 12–16.
46. See C. James and J. Sims, 'Antitrust in the Bingaman Era', *Regulation*, 15 (1993), 9–12.
47. See W. F. Shughart, 'Private Antitrust Enforcement: Compensation, Deterrence or Extortion', *Regulation*, 13 (fall 1990), 53–61.
48. See S. C. Salop and L. J. White, 'Private Antitrust Litigation: Introduction and Framework for Analysis', in L. J. White (ed.), *Private Antitrust Litigation* (Cambridge, Mass.: MIT Press, 1988).

4

Canadian Competition Policy Institutions and Decision Processes

G. BRUCE DOERN

This chapter examines the politics of Canada's competition policy institutions and the Canadian competition policy-making and decision-making process. The focus is primarily on political and institutional developments over the last decade centred on the forging of the 1986 Competition Act. Accordingly, it deals with both the macro-political forces, including the interest-group politics that resulted in the major changes to the law in the mid-1980s, and the general features of internal decision processes.[1]

The chapter is organized into four parts. The first section briefly locates the Canadian competition policy system in its continental and national political-economic context and history. In the second section, the main areas of the statutory mandate are set out along with the core competition institutions and structures. A set of non-core governmental competition policy players are also profiled briefly. The third part of the chapter profiles the interest group and policy community that both pressures and supports the competition policy system in Canada. The fourth section examines the institutional traditions and changing organizational culture of the Bureau of Competition Policy (BCP). Brief conclusions round out the analysis.

THE CONTINENTAL AND HISTORICAL CONTEXT

It is essential first to highlight several aspects of the influence of the United States competition policy system and the contrasting development of the Canadian system.[2] While the institutions are quite different, both countries obviously share a close set of continental economic linkages.

As Chapter 3 has shown, the American competition policy institutional regime is characterized by six key features: the more extensive identification in law of *per se* anti-competition offences rather than offences conditioned by phrases such as 'unduly'; the application of a stronger consumer-welfare test; the vigilant pursuit of cases by both the Federal Trade Commission and the Antitrust Division of the Department of Justice; the competitive enforcement of antitrust matters through the availability of both private actions and actions by state attorneys general; and the pressure supplied by an active competition legal community which benefits from legal provisions which confer treble damages and from the availability of contingency fees.[3]

Canadian competition law predates the US Sherman Act by a year. But this early lead at the legislative starting gate over a century ago was quickly eclipsed by decades of US antitrust speed and aggressiveness that have lapped the Canadian competition horse several times over.[4] Indeed, some accounts saw the initial Canadian law as being merely a symbolic response to those interests which, at the time, opposed the then ten-year-old National Policy of 1879. The National Policy was the economic policy of Prime Minister Sir John A. Macdonald and centred on the erection of high tariffs to help develop manufacturing industry in central Canada. The initial Canadian competition (anti-combines) legislation in 1889 was seen, from this perspective, as a tactical manœuvre to deflect criticism of economic concentration that had occurred partly because of the high-tariff policy.[5] The 1889 legislation can be said to be largely symbolic because its impact until the mid-1980s, with the exception of one or two areas, was insignificant. Since 1986, however, when Canadian legislation was significantly changed, and in the wake of the Canada–US and North American Free Trade Agreements (FTA and NAFTA), pressure for greater convergence between the Canadian and US systems has increased.[6]

Despite these divergent paths in the law, another key aspect of the continental competition policy relationship is that the US antitrust system has often served as the beacon and standard for reform, especially among those economists who would like to see stronger Canadian competition law and policy.

But it is the underlying realities of the Canadian political economy that have prevented the adoption of anything like the US model. These realities are essentially fourfold in nature. First, the Canadian economy has always been and remains to this day a more trade-dependent economy than the US, with a much smaller internal market and far fewer firms competing in any given industry. As a small, open trading economy whose trade is now over 70 per cent with the US, Canada has had to craft its competition policies accordingly. For a long part of the past century, this has meant crafting it behind high, but declining, tariff walls.

Second, the Canadian economy has an industrial structure which is essentially oligopolistic in many key sectors. Four or fewer firms account for 60 per cent or more of total sales in over 90 per cent of the standard classification commodities in manufacturing.[7] This creates, in a small economy in particular, problems of distinguishing in competition policy terms, between conspiracy and parallel behaviour. For small economies it is also problematical as to how to respond in competition policy terms, because such an industrial structure is unlikely to have exploited all the economies of scale and scope available. For this reason, Canada's 1986 competition law has an efficiency defence in its merger provisions. This truncated nature of Canadian industrial production (oligopolistic, short production runs, and significant branch plant foreign ownership of key sectors) was increasingly seen as a dead end for Canadian productivity, and prosperity, and was among the reasons why the Mulroney government aggressively sought and achieved a free-trade agreement with the United States.[8]

Third, there has never been any Canadian equivalent to the populist basis of US antitrust law and actions. A free-enterprise myth has never been as entrenched as it is south of the 49th parallel. Canadians support a market economy but they and their business class have not looked to competition policy for salvation or solutions. The business community, moreover, has not been cohesive. Indeed, strong mutual suspicions within the business community have developed historically, and often regionally, between manufacturing capital and financial capital, between Toronto and Montreal as the lead commercial centres, and between resource-based capital in the western and Atlantic regions and central Canadian manufacturing and banking.

Fourth, key sectors of the Canadian economy have until very recently been structured through nation-building and nation-binding regulatory regimes for key sectors such as energy, telecommunications, and transportation.[9] For example, from the late 1960s until the mid-1980s, Canadian transport regulations were based on the stated purpose of encouraging competition 'among modes' of transport (rail, air, and trucking) rather than within and among these modes. This changed during the Mulroney era, but even recent deregulation initiatives in all of these sectors still raise important problems for the exercise of discretion in general competition regulation.

To sum up the continental connection, it can be said that Canadian competition policy, like so much else in the country's make-up, has essentially seen an ambivalent relationship with the USA. On the one hand, it has studiously avoided the US antitrust model or its zeal of application. On the other hand, its competitive existence is increasingly dependent upon ever more open access to the US market, and on the need to restructure its industrial heartland in the wake of the FTA, and later NAFTA.

THE COMPETITION ACT AND COMPETITION POLICY INSTITUTIONS

The Competition Act of 1986 was forged after ninety years of frustration with a weak and essentially criminal-law-based statute, and after fifteen years of previous failed efforts to obtain a business consensus on a new and modern statute.[10] The 1986 Act proclaims its purpose to be that of maintaining and encouraging competition in Canada in order to:

- promote the efficiency and adaptability of the Canadian economy;
- expand opportunities for Canadian participation in world markets while at the same time recognizing the role of foreign competition in Canada;
- ensure that small and medium-sized enterprises have an equitable opportunity to participate in the Canadian economy;
- provide customers with competitive prices and product choices.[11]

The legislation is framework law and thus applies in principle to all sectors of the Canadian economy with the exception of sectors or aspects such as amateur sport, collective bargaining, and regulated industries subject to other regulation (see more below). Government-owned enterprises are also covered by the legislation.

The policy behind the legislation sees competition not as an end in itself but rather as a means to the ends listed above. While there are few overt public interest or industrial policy goals stated in the statute, there can be little doubt that there is considerable room for manœuvre, including implications that Canadian firms must be able to restructure to meet continental and globalizing pressures.

A vital underpinning to the Competition Act has come from recent constitutional decisions of the Supreme Court of Canada. These decisions dealt with both the federal trade and commerce power and the Charter of Rights and Freedoms. In the 1980s, the Supreme Court clarified and broadened federal powers over competition policy matters by holding in the City National Leasing and Rocois Construction cases that competition law is supportable under the general branch of the federal trade and commerce power. This reversed a long tradition of emphasizing the criminal-law power as the basis of support, and thus facilitated greater reliance on the non-criminal sections of the Competition Act and its remedies.[12] For the most part, the courts have also found that the Competition Act does not run afoul of the Charter of Rights and Freedoms on issues such as the acceptability of the merger and conspiracy provisions as well as the composition of the Competition Tribunal.

Core statutory functions

As Figure 4.1 suggests, the various core components of the legislation can be visualized as a series of concentric circles radiating outward, with the centre point being traditional criminal law offences and misleading advertising, and then successive wider realms embracing economic offences including civil reviewable matters and mergers. The second outermost circle encompasses a realm involving the Director of Investigation and Research's role as intervener and competition policy advocate. The outermost circle indicates the presence of emerging international and globalizing pressures including the need to relate competition policy to state aids or subsidies, anti-dumping, and inter-provincial trade barriers within Canada.

In the criminal area the legislation prohibits offences such as bid-rigging, conspiracy to lessen competition unduly, price maintenance,

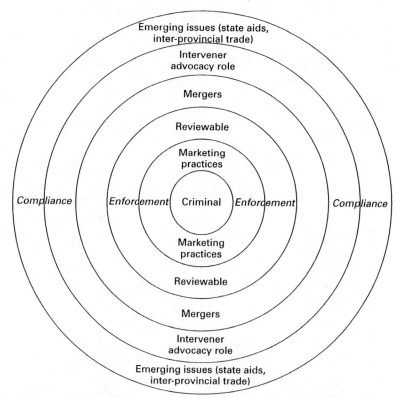

Emerging issues (state aids, inter-provincial trade)

Intervener advocacy role

Mergers

Reviewable

Marketing practices

Compliance Enforcement Criminal Enforcement Compliance

Marketing practices

Reviewable

Mergers

Intervener advocacy role

Emerging issues (state aids, inter-provincial trade)

Fig. 4.1 Canadian competition policy—core mandate areas

predatory pricing, and price discrimination. The criminal area also includes offences in marketing practices (such as misleading advertising and pyramid selling), although some activities in this aspect of commerce are often thought to be better handled if they were converted to civil offences.

The civil reviewable aspects of the law include areas which previously had been treated as criminal offences but now are viewed in relation to economic criteria. Abuse of dominant position, tied selling, and exclusive dealing are among the offences covered.

Mergers are a further vital element of reviewable matters, but are different in that they deal with feared future anti-competitive behaviour which may arise from mergers. Large mergers are subject to a pre-notification process followed by a speedy review. Decision outcomes in this realm can include approvals, advisory opinions, advanced-ruling certificates, rulings, and disallowance by the independent Competition Tribunal. A 'substantial lessening of competition' test is applied, but merging firms can defend the merger on the grounds of an efficiency exemption (see more below).

The intervener and advisory role is also statutorily enshrined. The Director of Investigation and Research may make representations on competition matters before federal or provincial regulatory boards, commissions, and tribunals, in the federal realm on his own initiative, and in the provincial realm when requested by such boards or when they give their consent. A broader overall policy advisory role emerges out of the fact that the Director reports to Parliament through the Minister of Industry. This is a recent change in the reporting minister in that, for most of the period covered by this chapter, the Director reported to the Minister of Consumer and Corporate Affairs. The nature and political sensitivity of this advisory role varies with the issue and with the arena in which the advice is being tendered.

The five core competition policy institutions

There are five core institutions and structures in the Canadian competition policy system that ultimately administer the legislation and determine the meaning of competition policy in practice: the Minister and the Department of Industry (Industry Canada); the Director of Investigation and Research (DIR); the Bureau of Competition Policy (BCP); the Minister of Justice as the Attorney General of Canada; and the Competition Tribunal and the Canadian courts.

The Minister of Industry is the cabinet minister through whom the DIR reports to Parliament. The Minister makes no decisions on individual competition cases other than that of being able to order that the DIR launch a formal inquiry (a power very infrequently used) and that of informing a party that an inquiry has been discontinued. The Industry Minister, however, is responsible for the making of competition policy.[13] This includes not only any possible changes to the Competition Act itself, but also to over sixty statutes that are part of his or her mandate. These laws were transferred only recently from the now defunct Department of Consumer and Corporate Affairs (CCA). Thus Industry Canada now has jurisdiction over a host of other mini-competition statutes in fields such as bankruptcy, patents, and copyright.

One of the nominal branches of the Industry Department is the Bureau of Competition Policy (BCP). Thus the Bureau is subject to some extent to the personnel and budgetary policies, decisions, and influences of the larger department in which it is located. But the BCP enjoys extensive independence, not in its own right, but rather because it is the body that works for the DIR, who is a distinct statutorily independent official.

The Director of Investigation and Research (DIR) is an independent statutory person appointed by the Governor in Council (the Cabinet, but in reality, the Prime Minister on the recommendation of the Industry minister).[14] The DIR has wide powers to conduct inquiries if he or she believes, on reasonable grounds, that an anti-competitive offence or practice is occurring. The DIR has no adjudicative functions and cannot issue orders. On criminal matters under the Competition Act, the DIR presents a statement of evidence to the Attorney General, but it is the Attorney General's decision to prosecute or not to prosecute. On civil reviewable matters, including mergers, it is only the DIR who can bring applications to the Competition Tribunal. Because of its statutory independence, the DIR is best seen as a quasi-ministerial official with numerous discretionary powers to exercise.

The Bureau of Competition Policy (BCP) is the agency which carries out the investigatory and inquiry work on behalf of the DIR, but also is a source of policy advice for the CCA Minister. Composed of about 225 people (see more below on its professional occupational backgrounds), the BCP has recently been reorganized so that its five branches would correspond more closely to the functional breakdown of the 1986 Competition Act. Thus there are branches on: criminal matters; marketing practices; civil matters; mergers; and policy. Prior to 1990, the BCP's branch structure was organized more along industrial-sector lines (manufacturing, services, resources, etc.).

The BCP has also had to give greater organizational and operational importance to compliance activities as distinct from enforcement activities.[15] Thus there is now a Director General for Compliance and Operations precisely because policies about compliance have had to be devised and training programmes instituted to ensure that BCP staff understand and support this approach. The different dynamics of these various branches will be highlighted in the next two sections.

The Minister of Justice (who is the Attorney General of Canada) and the Department of Justice lawyers are also pivotal. In the criminal law aspects of the Competition Act, it is the Attorney General who prosecutes. It is Justice Department lawyers who take the cases to court. These lawyers also normally take the DIR's applications to the Competition Tribunal on civil reviewable matters, including mergers. Several Justice Department lawyers are located in each federal government department, but they report to the Justice Department, not, in this case, to the Department of Industry. Thus for the lawyers, the Department of Industry and the BCP are their clients but not their bosses. Co-operative working relationships have developed but clearly there can be matters of discretion and timing as case loads build up and particular decisions arise. Cases that go to court must compete for both the timing of court schedules and the locales for court hearings with all other potential trial matters in the federal judicial system. These matters are decided by the Department of Justice and the courts. The courts are important players not only in the above sense, but also, as we have seen, in the decisions they have made about the constitutional underpinnings to the Competition Act, both with regard to the trade and commerce power and the Charter of Rights and Freedoms.

Last, but not least, among the core competition policy agencies is the Competition Tribunal (the Tribunal). The Tribunal consists of not more than four judges of the Federal Court—Trial Division and not more than eight lay members appointed by the Governor-in-Council for a term not exceeding seven years.[16] At present, there are four judicial members and three lay members, one of whom is a professional economist. One of the judicial members is designated the Chairman of the Tribunal by the Governor-in-Council.

The Tribunal is a new body created in 1986 with the intent that it would be a specialized court, hopefully combining the procedural fairness of the courts with the business and economic expertise needed to deal with complicated competition matters. The Tribunal is strictly an adjudicative body to review and decide matters submitted to it by the DIR under part VIII of the Competition Act. As mentioned above, only the DIR can initiate legal proceedings before the Tribunal, except in the case of specialization agreements. The Tribunal may make various types of orders intended to ensure a prohibition of the anti-competitive conduct in question. After the DIR has brought a matter before the Tribunal, interested parties may apply for intervener status, to give evidence on a given case before the Tribunal.

The Tribunal process has not functioned in the manner initially hoped for in two senses. First, not as many cases as expected have actually been brought to the Tribunal by the DIR (in part through a preference for compliance rather than enforcement approaches by both the DIR and the business firms involved). Second, the Tribunal in those cases brought to it still seems to many to be dominated by the judicial members, and thus it is not functioning as a procedurally more informal specialized court. There are different processes in contested versus consent-order cases.

Non-core governmental competition policy players

In addition to the core institutions sketched out above, the Canadian competition policy system also involves a set of other players both within the structure of the federal government and among provincial governments. These include: finance and industry departments; regulatory agencies; international trade and investment review agencies; and provincial governments, especially where key regionally vital industries are at stake. These players are identified in Figure 4.2. In many respects, the more that competition cases potentially involve these players, the more that non-core competition policy criteria are likely to be at stake.[17]

The Department of Finance (Finance) and the Department of Industry have all been broadly supportive of the federal government's policy of focusing on the development of competitive markets and international competitiveness for Canadian firms. But their specific mandates and programme structures, not to mention the political base of their incumbent ministers, do not always put them in full harmony with the DIR and BCP decisions and advice.[18] Moreover, there is some concern in other federal agencies at the inability of the DIR to share vital information on some key decisions.

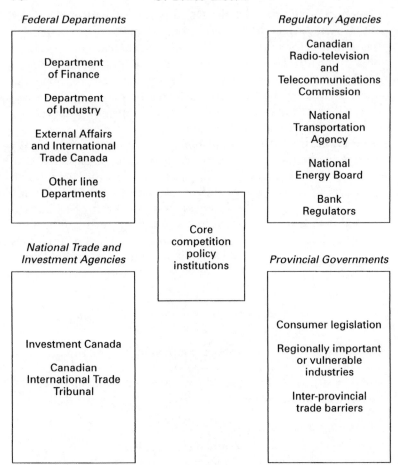

FIG. 4.2 The non-core Canadian competition policy players

The DIR's rejoinder is not only to cite the statute but also to stress practically that firms would never talk to him if he could not protect their confidential data and proprietary information.

Consider first the role of the Department of Finance. It has a major jurisdictional role (in concert with the Bank of Canada) over the banking system. Finance seeks a competitive banking and financial services sector (more competition among the four pillars of banking, insurance, securities, and trusts), but is extremely jealous of its purview over the competitive aspects of this sector. The Competition Act applies to banking and financial services but there is some jurisdictional uncertainty. The recently enlarged Department of Industry not only has a direct framework regulatory role in areas such as copyright and patents, but also has a series of sector branches that are encouraging and facilitating industrial restructuring.

It is important to note that, unlike the EU and UK, the Canadian system has no formal interdepartmental panel or committee process for the regular tendering of other department's views of particular mergers or other reviewable competition cases. Other departments and their ministers are very conscious of the legal independence of the DIR. This does not mean that they have no ways of making their views known. For example, on airline mergers, the Minister of Transport and his officials have voiced opposition to, or fears about, actual or potential decisions that the DIR might make.

Regulatory agencies such as the National Transportation Agency (NTA), the Canadian Radio and Telecommunications Commission (CRTC), and National Energy Board (NEB) are factors in the inter-agency equation in three ways. First, they invariably have a mini-competition policy role in their regulatory realms. Second, firms can use a regulated conduct defence to exempt them from some possible offences under the Competition Act. On the other hand, the mere fact of being regulated does not provide blanket exemption. Third, the DIR can, at his choice, intervene and appear by right at any federal regulatory agency's hearings or special commission hearings.[19]

In contrast to the above regulators, which tend to be sectoral, there are also other horizontal economic regulators, whose roles have been or are becoming more germane to, and potentially conflictual with, the DIR and BCP. One such body is Investment Canada, which has the dual mandate of encouraging foreign investment but also screening and approving foreign takeovers above a minimum threshold level to determine if the investment is of net benefit to Canada.[20] Procedural and substantive policy differences can arise in particular cases because of differences in thresholds at which review occurs, periods allowed for decisions, and perceptions of what is the relevant market (global, North American, or Canadian).

Trade remedy institutions such as the Canadian International Trade Tribunal (CITT) and departments with roles or interests in dealing with subsidies or state aids (the Department of Industry, External Affairs, and International Trade Canada) are arguably the new frontier areas of potential intersection with the core competition agencies. Canada has no institutional equivalent to the EU's DG IV Directorate, in which subsidies are controlled by one agency.[21] But this issue is emerging not only in an FTA, NAFTA, and GATT context, but also with respect to trade and competitive barriers within Canada among provincial and regional markets.[22]

To this list of federal players one can add the role of provincial governments whose influence shows up in various ways. The provinces in general do not have competition laws and bureaux of their own (another contrast with US state governments which do). Recent court cases have confirmed and strengthened federal jurisdiction over competition policy under the trade and commerce clause (as opposed to only the criminal law powers) of the Canadian Constitution. But the provinces, through various departments in their executive structure, can apply political pressure on cases vital to them. This pressure can affect the climate of the DIR's decision network. It must, however, be exercised by the provinces with considerable discretion.

The provinces also have some parallel consumer legislation which can overlap with the marketing practices aspects of the Competition Act. Indeed, as we will see more clearly below, the Marketing Practices Branch of the BCP is essentially a regionally based organization and hence has to establish close links with the provincial governments.

INTEREST GROUPS AND THE COMPETITION POLICY COMMUNITY

The making and implementation of Canadian competition policy clearly is influenced by a diverse set of interest groups which, in their relations with the government of the day, help set the climate of pressures within which discretion and political judgement are exercised. In mapping these interests in Canada, it is essential to distinguish between those interests activated when competition policy is being made or changed, and those involved when individual case decisions are at stake. In the former situation, an array of macro or 'peak' business associations, consumer groups, and sectoral business lobbies are involved. In the latter situation, particular firms, practising lawyers, and economists, emerge as both rent seekers and value articulators.

Interests and the making of competition policy

One cannot understand the political nature of Canadian competition policy without appreciating the interplay of interests (mainly business) in the shaping of the compromise inherent in the 1986 Competition Act. As mentioned above, there had been several abortive efforts to change the law. Five initiatives over fifteen years had been taken by the Minister of Consumer and Corporate Affairs (CCA) (who then had jurisdiction over competition policy) involving various consultative and tactical approaches to business.[23]

A 1971 draft bill set out three key features to overcome the weakness of the old statute. First, a proposal to end exclusive reliance on the criminal courts by establishing an independent tribunal to rule on economic and business matters. Second, a listing (as in US antitrust law) of practices that would be subject to outright prohibition; these *per se* offences would arguably be the toughest among OECD countries. Third, determination by an expert body of the relative advantages and disadvantages of mergers and a capacity by such a body to rule on the acceptability of specialization and export agreements, trade practices, and other aspects of competition policy in accordance with criteria established in the new law.

The proposal was not preceded by much consultation and was overwhelmingly rejected by the business community. Indeed business pressure was so decisive that the minister who introduced the bill, who was seen by business interests as being too pro-consumer, was replaced. The new minister introduced only a part of the measures dealing with issues such as misleading advertising. The key items were left for another day.

In the late 1970s another approach was tried. A major study was commissioned, followed by a 1977 draft bill, followed by its withdrawal, and followed by a 1979 discussion paper. Throughout this period, business interests opposed the package, each element of which was revisiting the 1971 proposals. The basis for the opposition was often expressed in terms of the department being too 'structuralist'. In short, CCA was viewed as being driven by an excessive zeal to establish a priori criteria of appropriate market structure to be enforced eventually by a tribunal. Business opposition during these exercises was also related to the rest of the political and economic agenda of the mid- to late 1970s, which included wage and price controls in the 1975 to 1978 period and the first energy crisis in 1979. The business community, in short, was in no mood for competition policy adventurism in the midst of other pressing national priorities.

Yet another unsuccessful effort was launched in a 1981 framework discussion document. By 1982, however, in the midst of the 1982 recession, the business community began to change its approach. Some of the reasons for this had nothing to do with competition policy itself. Rather a more proactive business approach emerged because of its reaction to two early 1980–1 Liberal government initiatives (on energy policy and tax reform) which had been both highly interventionist and unilateral in nature. It also emerged because the structure of the Canadian business lobby had changed markedly.

In the 1970s, the principal national business lobby organizations were the Canadian Manufacturing Association (CMA) and the Canadian Chamber of Commerce (CCC). By 1980, however, two new macro-groups had emerged on the scene, the Business Council on National Issues (BCNI) and the Canadian Federation of Independent Business (CFIB).[24] BCNI was especially significant because it consisted not of member companies as such but rather of the Chief Executive Officers of Canada's biggest firms, including most of the large foreign-owned sector of the Canadian economy. These CEO's in the BCNI could act more decisively and quickly than other interest groups and began an active approach which, in competition policy matters, extended to their drafting their own bill. The CFIB was not as significant in the immediate competition policy story, but its aggressive public approach to lobbying, including criticism of big business, was creating a significant political constituency for small business. As we will see below, future Mulroney Conservative ministers were especially anxious to please this small business constituency and eventually included a clause in the legislation supporting an equal opportunity for small business to compete in the Canadian economy.

During the many previous approaches, CCA ministers and officials were becoming increasingly frustrated at just how to achieve a breakthrough and a workable consensus. In 1982–3, CCA's approach was to work directly and continuously with the 'gang of three', in this case BCNI, CCC, and CMA. For its part, the gang of three set out two requirements for its participation. First, business wanted to get the policy right. Second they wanted to see the legislation in detail.

The desire to get the policy right meant primarily that business interests had to become more structuralist than they wanted to be and had to deal with matters such as threshold levels and criteria. The desire for legislative detail meant that CCA had to tilt more strongly to a case-by-case and clause-by-clause negotiation of the statute than they really wanted. Three business representatives and two CCA officials became the *de facto* negotiating group and met many times over several months.

A new 1983 bill was tabled but it too languished, in part because the Liberal government was on its last electoral legs, but also because of some opposition from the business community, including some business groups left out of the gang of three.

The newly elected Mulroney Conservative government handed the competition policy hot potato to a minister who himself had experience of small business. To finally get a new bill in place, the new minister insisted on three changes in process and tactics. First, he wanted the gang of three changed to a gang of five. The two additions were the Grocery Products Manufacturing Association of Canada, whose leader had been especially vocal about being left out of the previous process, and the Canadian Bar Association, which brought both expertise and prestige. Second, he wanted a more visible mode of consultation. This was achieved through the work of the Minister's Advisory Committee on the Competition Bill. Third, he insisted on the need to package the essence of the bill so as to give it a more saleable public image. This was done by selling it as a measure that would be fair to small business and help small and medium-sized businesses adapt to the competitive realities of the international economy. The Conservative bill also assuaged business fears about the independent tribunal by tying it more closely to the courts. Finally, US-style *per se* offences were kept to a minimum.

Throughout the above process, the consumer lobby, mainly

represented by the Consumers Association of Canada, had become an increasingly marginalized player. Other regulated sectoral groups, such as bankers, energy interests, and telecommunications companies, saw some of their interests reflected through the BCNI. The new law was to be a general law, but there were still protections afforded by regulated industry defence provisions.

A new competition deal also congealed in the mid-1980s because, by this time, key parts of the business community saw the new Mulroney government's overall pro-market agenda as being favourable to its overall view of the world. This had certainly not been the view business held of the previous Trudeau Liberal governments.

Cases and the competition policy community

When one shifts from the making of competition policy to its implementation, the structure of interests and their mode of expression and action changes. In the Canadian situation the role of lawyers, individual firms, and economists (the competition policy community) becomes important, in part because it is through concrete cases that decisions are being made. Each player in this community is both a rent seeker and a value articulator with regard to how competition policy decision-making ought to occur. Each is a rent seeker in that each has a financial stake in the outcomes and in the process. Lawyers make large amounts of money from both firms and the BCP. Economists profit as key advisers and expert witnesses. Firms have a financial stake whether they are the object of charges or the party that triggers action against another firm.

The values that each brings to judging the process and the outcomes are also important. Lawyers, especially in an era of Charter rights, bring continuous concern over procedural fairness, especially but not exclusively with regard to criminal aspects of the law. As fellow white-collar middle-class professionals, judges are also not well disposed to impose imprisonment and harsh penalties on individual white-collar business-persons, as distinct from penalties on corporations.[25]

Economists of course vary in their detailed opinions, but the small group of active independent Canadian competition policy economists tend to favour a more open set of clear economic competition criteria (without industrial policy hedges), specific *per se* offences, and the use of strong court case precedents to ensure that competition is expanded.[26] In short, they tend to have an intellectual preference for US-style antitrust laws.

Business firms bring quite practical and ambivalent values to the competition policy procedural table. Somewhat suspicious of legal and economic criteria, they tend to favour competition in general but not necessarily in specific cases. Above all, they agree on the fact that they do not want politicians meddling in specific decisions. They seek room for manœuvre along the discretion–certainty continuum, seeking transparency in the process on some occasions and confidentiality to protect commercial privilege on other occasions.

Small and big business firms also have different approaches in many substantive aspects of the legislation, from the definition of relevant markets, to the relative likely incidence of offences (such as misleading advertising), and to the likelihood that they will complain to the DIR and BCP about other firms' transgressions under the legislation.

In the 1990s, the competition policy community has also come to include officials, experts, and agencies concerned with international trade. Much of this small but growing part of the community resides inside the government or in international or foreign agencies. For example, within the BCP the economics branch contains several officers whose full-time responsibility is international competition policy matters. Three years ago, only one such officer was so engaged. In the NAFTA free-trade negotiations, it was the Canadian trade negotiators, in concert with the BCP, who suggested that the agreement would have to have a competition policy chapter. Thus the BCP has found itself dealing increasingly with the incursions of trade rules and decision processes.[27]

THE CHANGING ORGANIZATIONAL CULTURE OF THE BUREAU OF COMPETITION POLICY

As we move from the macro-political realm to the micro-realm of cases and discretion, it is essential to highlight broadly how the organizational culture of the BCP, headed by the DIR, has evolved and been changed by the 1986 Competition Act and its politics.

The more particular dynamics of each branch within the BCP is left for more specific commentary below.

The criminal law/economic law enforcement and compliance balance

The dominant feature of the BCP's organizational culture has been the need to change from an overwhelmingly legal and criminal law oriented agency to a micro-economic and mixed criminal and administrative law agency. Simultaneously, while shifting its focus and organizational personality, the BCP has also had to alter its criminal law approaches because of changes exacted in the mid-1980s by the 1982 Charter of Rights and Freedoms.[28] The DIR's approaches to investigation and enforcement had to be made 'Charter proof': in short, carried out in such a way as to ensure that actions would not be nullified on the grounds that they violated the Charter.

The BCP, moreover, approached its new mandate after it had endured many years of frustration as an agency several steps removed from national priorities or concern. The reasons for this political isolation are not hard to find. First, antitrust issues had never acquired a broad or populist base of political support.[29] Second, until 1986, federal powers were based on the criminal law provisions of the Canadian Constitution, but these in turn required that criminal conspiracy and intent be proved and that competition was lessened unduly. The result was an historical record of almost no convictions, low penalties, and little fear by business of the central provisions of the law.[30] This is not to suggest that other elements of the law, such as misleading advertising, resale price maintenance, and regulatory interventions, were not successfully pursued. But the core functions were in the doldrums. Third, competition law and other business framework law is technically complex, imposing to lay-ministers or politicians, and not the first choice as an area on which to build a career by changing the laws.[31]

DIR approaches, priorities, and circumstances

The above points must also be linked to the approaches, priorities, and circumstances of the recent DIRs. For example, Lawson Hunter, the DIR in the early 1980s, focused to a significant extent on his policy advice and intervener role in part out of frustration with the lack of success with major cases. A lawyer, but with considerable policy experience in the federal government, he sought to promote competition goals in heavily regulated sectors such as transportation and telecommunications at a time when few players were interested in deregulation. In the 1981 to 1986 period, Hunter was also able to secure a consensus for the new Competition Act through the difficult negotiations already sketched out above.

Michael O'Farrell became Acting DIR for a few months in the interregnum between Hunter and his ultimate successor, Cal Goldman. O'Farrell was a career BCP official whose short tenure as an Acting DIR scarcely allowed him to make a major leadership imprint on the organization. None the less, his efforts helped pave the way for the new legislation while still keeping the BCP focused on its crucial daily operations.

Cal Goldman assumed the position of DIR in 1986. Unlike his predecessors and his successor (Howard Wetston)—whose careers were in public regulatory law, including extensive governmental experience—Goldman was a young aggressive lawyer fresh out of Toronto's Bay Street business district. His appointment was part of the overall political compromise surrounding the statute. The new law would be tougher than its predecessors and would contain economic criteria for judgements. For key business interests (see more below) this was an acceptable but also fearful and uncertain prospect. But the first DIR to fully preside over the new legislation would himself come from the heart of the Bay Street business-law community. Goldman was seen by both business and by key ministers as someone who was not an interventionist.

Goldman's approach to altering the culture of the BCP was not, of course, only a function of his Bay Street roots. Once in office, the requisites of the job also took hold. Thus, both of necessity and inclination, Goldman's priorities were focused on the new economic or reviewable side of the mandate, and in particular on mergers. The intervener and policy advocacy roles were reduced considerably. He also placed emphasis on a guidelines or compliance approach to carrying out the provisions of the legislation. This meant a relatively new emphasis on the education of the business and legal community and on the use of instruments that were seen as an alternative to more draconian enforcement. These alternatives included oral and written advisory opinions, advanced ruling certificates, and visits.[32]

Within the BCP, these overall priorities were occurring at a time of significant budgetary restraint. Accordingly, many of the personnel resources for the new merger and compliance operations had to be found from existing branches, especially the traditional criminal sector. This in turn reduced the resources available to pursue traditional criminal offences and created some resentment from the very sector that most had to change to fit into the new legal-economic culture of the bureau.

At this point, one might surmise that the criminal area was composed of lawyers but about to be invaded by a new band of micro-economists. In fact this is not the case. The professional occupational structure of the BCP is dominated, to the extent of 66 per cent, by persons with business and economics degrees (commerce officers in the public-service personnel classification).[33] Persons with a law degree of some kind total 20 per cent of the professional staff. Both groups are spread throughout the branches. Moreover, recent data shows that at present the BCP is not an organization dominated by entrenched older staff. Over 40 per cent have been in the BCP for only one to five years, and 62 per cent for one to ten years.

None the less, it is clear in the 1986 to 1993 period that major changes in organization and standard operating habits have had to occur. Another of these was the greater formalization of the BCP's executive and priority-setting process. These developments in turn are linked to the role of the DIR.

It must be stressed that the legal decision-making powers reside with the DIR as a statutory person. The BCP is therefore almost a legal nonentity. This can create problems regarding the extent of delegation within the BCP. Throughout most of the 1980s, the BCP functioned without any elaborate executive inter-branch decision process. Branches interacted on virtually a one-to-one basis with the DIR. Two factors compelled a change. First, Cal Goldman's Bay Street private-law background forced some change. This was because Goldman had been involved in some cases as a private lawyer which were still active at the BCP when he became DIR. To keep him at arm's length from these cases, some delegation had to occur. Accordingly, a form of general *de facto* delegation was arranged by making all the branch heads deputy DIRs. Legally, all decisions remain those of the DIR, but *de facto* delegation has had to occur, and probably would have in any event because of the larger post-1986 workload.

The second factor in the need to design real executive processes was that under the post-1986 regime, the volume of cases became greater and hence there had to be a way both to keep balance among the branches and to set priorities regarding which cases to pursue. Accordingly, when Howard Wetston became DIR in 1990, a new organizational and executive structure was put in place. One part of it was the previously mentioned reorganization of the BCP into functional branches as opposed to sectoral branches. The other was to establish an executive structure composed of three committees each consisting of the same seven core executives but meeting for different purposes. The first is the Bureau Executive Committee (BXC), which meets weekly and reviews overall aspects of the bureau's policies and work. The second is BXCP, which is the BXC meeting on the review of priority cases. It meets quarterly and its case screening criteria will be examined further below. The third grouping is the Bureau Management Committee. It deals with more operational issues, but these include important and needed changes in enforcement policy and, along with the BCP Training Committee, the training and education of BCP staff to enhance the compliance approach.

The above changes to some extent also reflect the different approaches and priorities of the DIR until late 1993, Howard Wetston. He was appointed in 1990 after heading the new mergers branch for three years, but his previous legal background and experience had also been in the realm of public regulatory law. Accordingly, he sought to put in place a more even-handed approach to all parts of the statute rather than just to mergers, and, accordingly, also to establish a greater sense of perceived fairness among the new functionally organized branches.

CASES, DISCRETION, AND INTER-BRANCH VARIATIONS

My treatment of this realm is brief and illustrative, and is expanded upon elsewhere.[34] The main purpose of this section is to sketch out how cases are generally handled, where the key points of discretion are, and how these vary among the main branches of the BCP. The formal structure of the BCP is set out in Figure 4.3.

The general case review process

Cases are usually triggered by a complaint from a customer or supplier, except in the mergers field where a pre-notification requirement exists and where the Mergers Branch itself scans the financial press for cases that might be of interest. Case officers are assigned to do initial investigative work, initially by telephone contacts. If a case officer decides at this point that an issue is not worth pursuing as an anti-competitive offence under the act, it is highly unlikely that it will be acted upon further up the organizational line. In short, this is a key point in the discretionary chain.

A complaint may lead to an inquiry. Inquiries require that the DIR have a reasonable basis for determining that the actions in question may be lessening competition unduly, or substantially lessening competition, depending on the section of the act invoked. It is at this point that the project may require a team of officers. Since this is very resource intensive, however, it is more typical for cases to continue to be handled by a single officer, albeit one who is frequently in touch with his or her branch chief. The case assessment process is not one which begins, as in the US model, with a built-in value-based and analytical battle between an economist and lawyer. Rather, the case officer is typically a person with an economics or business degree, augmented by experience in analysing different industrial sectors. He or she is investigating with a view to applying a particular set of facts against a potential offence under a particular part of the Competition Act. With experience, the analyst increasingly becomes a person who is part lawyer, part economist, part administrator.

The data on cases show that only a small percentage of complaints and notifications result in further substantive investigative action, and still fewer proceed to the stage where the DIR might take any one of his discretionary actions leading to court action by the Attorney General, a challenge before the Competition Tribunal, or actions involving undertakings. The internal dynamics are such that there are undoubtedly more cases that case officers

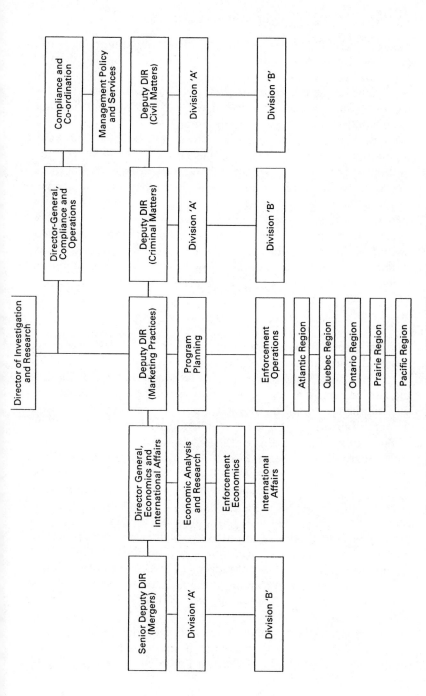

FIG. 4.3 Bureau of Competition Policy (Canada) organization

would like to act on than those which the DIR judges as worth proceeding with. Case officers, especially in the Criminal Branch, derive more satisfaction from a case that successfully goes the full route and leads to significant prevention of anti-competitive behaviour. They are far less satisfied with actions that end in some administrative compromise.

Cases that are judged to involve serious or important anti-competitive offences then move into the DIR's realm of power and discretion. It is the DIR who personally delivers the bad news to the firms of his concerns in the case of reviewable and merger offences. In the period since 1986, both DIRs have displayed a strong preference for a compliance rather than an enforcement approach. In part, this seems to be the political compromise inherent in the legislation, but it is also a part of the inherent discretionary dynamics as the complaint or case moves up the chain of command.

Setting case priorities

But discretion on cases is not just built into the typical case cycle. There is also the matter of how priorities are set among cases across the BCP. Some of this process was noted above in the discussion of executive decision-making processes. But priorities are also set through budgets, through explicit criteria applied to cases, and through other informally acknowledged factors.

Budgeting decisions affect priorities in three senses. First, absolute budgetary levels set immediate limits. If budgets were 20 per cent higher or lower, undoubtedly more or less action could be taken. Second, relative discretionary budgets among branches matter a great deal. In the interests of inter-branch (and therefore intrastatute) fairness, each branch gets a more or less equivalent discretionary budget (that is, over and above their salary or person-year budget). But extra funds over and above this base equality level are in fact subject to a kind of judgemental auction process. Third, reassigning person-years among branches, or borrowing officers for team investigations, necessarily lessens their availability in their home branch.

In addition to the budgetary effects, the BCP has begun to apply, again in the interests of inter-branch equity but also to secure more consistent rankings of cases, a formal set of weighted case-screening criteria. These are acknowledged to be an analytical aid rather than a science of priority setting. The case-screening criteria fall into three categories: economic welfare, enforcement policy, and management considerations. There is a numerical weighting scheme for each item within the three categories.

Economic welfare criteria for criminal cases include: the volume of commerce affected by the alleged conduct; market power; identification of behaviour likely to injure competition; and potential impact of remedy/deterrence. Enforcement policy criteria include: bureau priorities (such as DIR emphases in any given period for abuse-of-dominant-position cases versus cases in other parts of the statute); competitiveness considerations; probability of success; jurisprudential value; urgency; consumer or public sensitivity; repeated non-compliance; covert behaviour; and length of time of alleged conduct. Finally, the management considerations category includes: the financial resources required; and the human resources required.

Clearly the above list is the art of judgement incarnate. But it is by no means the final list of criteria. Cases will also often proceed or be held back by practical considerations, such as: the actual availability of legal counsel, and in some cases, the unavailability of particular lawyers; the availability of particular expert witnesses or of credible witnesses who do not have a conflict of interest or who are willing to help if they think it will lessen their future chances for work in the given industry; and the tenaciousness and bureaucratic skill or risk-taking of some case officers versus others. To these behavioural and procedural features of the discretionary chain one can, of course, add all the substantive terms built into the Competition Act which require discretion and judgement as to what they mean. These include terms such as 'unduly', 'lessening competition substantially', 'specialization agreements', the efficiency defence, and the regulated conduct defence.

Some aspects of these case cycles, case criteria, and discretionary terms cover the entire BCP mandate, and hence all the branches. But the variation among branches needs a closer look. So also do the branches' different rhythms and realities of decision-making.

Branch variations and constraints

The Mergers Branch became in a sense the élite branch after the 1986 changes. This is because the merger area received the largest part of the political attention. It was also the area which the DIR, Cal Goldman, gave his priority attention in the 1986 to 1990 period. Since 1986 there have been about 6,000 mergers in Canada, about 1,100 of which have been assessed (that is, been given a project number) by the BCP. Of these 12 mergers have been abandoned in the wake of the DIR's expressed concerns and about 20 have proceeded with changes (through undertakings or consent orders). Only 3 mergers have to date been challenged by the DIR before the Competition Tribunal.

The Mergers Branch decision process is characterized by several features which affect and lead to discretionary decision-making.[35] First, there are very short time periods allowed for notifiable merger reviews, with only limited extensions possible. Second, the nature of mergers is that they involve prospective behaviour. Thus, there is an even more difficult burden of proof placed upon the DIR if he wishes to challenge a merger. Third, there is a presumption that most mergers are healthy for the economy. Fourth, the assessment process begins with the need to define the relevant product and geographic market so as to determine first whether the merger will 'substantially lessen' competition. Fifth, if such a substantial lessening is found to be likely then the branch must also make the case against an efficiency defence. A merger cannot be disallowed if a successful efficiency defence is mounted by the firms. This is a feature unique to Canadian competition law and was placed in the legislation because of a view that most Canadian industries were oligopolistic, functioned in an international-trade-dependent context, and were facing rapid needs to restructure. For these reasons also the efficiency test is empirically confined to showing mainly that the production costs of the firms are being lowered by the merger, not that these cost savings are benefiting consumers as well. In the USA, mergers are assessed against consumer welfare as the main test.

These dynamics have all conspired to produce a mutual realization by firms and by the DIR, that the full route to the challenge process is costly and uncertain. As a result, there are few if any precedent-setting cases, but several cases settled by undertakings or withdrawals, and many more involving Advanced Ruling Certificates. Complex merger guidelines have also been developed. As a result, the process has attracted the expected polar opposite judgements, namely that it is pragmatically successful or that it is a form of unaccountable, excessively discretionary micro-economic governance.[36]

The Civil Matters Branch arguably has a wider range of types of cases, from fairly small vertical-restraint and refusal-to-supply cases, to large and often complex abuse-of-dominant-position cases.[37] At any given time, there are typically many dozens of routine complaints that have to be investigated by case officers, but only two or three bigger cases ready for reviewable action. There are also no compelling statutory deadlines as there are in mergers. When large abuse-of-dominant-position cases occur, they can require a large team of officers.

The case process in the Civil Affairs Branch is clearly complaint driven, the majority coming from small business. Many complainants will also complain directly to the Minister of Industry, thus requiring, not a decision from the minister, but a large volume of letter-writing in the branch. This is *de facto* a significant amount of time lost from serious case analysis.

The fact that there are only a very few large cases has resulted in pressures from DIRs that there be 'more cases'. Thus in the Civil Matters Branch too few cases could be seen by some as a sign of perceived failure, whereas in the merger area it is (arguably at least) judged a success. Of course, in practice it may not be a sign of either in either branch, since such contending 'stats' go to the very heart of how one judges competition criteria.

The Civil Matters Branch does use the case-screening criteria described above but usually more for middle- or lower-level cases or complaints. The top three or four cases are simply obvious to the key branch players. The Criminal Matters Branch operates under a case process that is different simply because criminal sanctions and standards of investigation and proof are involved. It is, in short, more enforcement oriented than other branches, although it too has, compared to the pre-1986 period, begun to resort to alternative case resolution methods, such as the use of prohibition orders and investigation visits. The Criminal Matters Branch has also been especially affected by the previously noted need to make its actions consistent with the Canadian Charter of Rights and Freedoms.

The case process is again complaint driven, but standards of evidence are more difficult than for other sectors in that an offence must be proven beyond a reasonable doubt and competition must be shown to be reduced unduly. Search and seizure powers are more likely to be used since the key evidence of covert behaviour is in corporate or business documents. In recent years more attention has also been placed on the evidence of corporate whistle-blowers and hence on the potential need to offer immunity. These in turn require delicate and precise rules.

The Criminal Matters Branch is also subject to the phenomenon of 'too few cases' referred to above. This is due to the extra standards of proof required, but it is also due to the fact that the branch is especially dependent on Justice Department lawyers and on the schedules of the courts. Cases in the criminal area also involve some judgement as to whether, in the particular circumstances at hand, the BCP and DIR should use civil provisions of the legislation. There is clearly also some room here for the DIR to use the implied threat of criminal approaches to obtain a better outcome through the eventual use of civil remedies.

The BCP's annual reports present the case data for both the Criminal and Civil branches in one table. This is partly due to recent reorganizations, but it may also be a way of avoiding having to show even lower actual case numbers if there were separate tables for each branch. Matters referred to the Attorney General, prosecutions, and applications to the Competition Tribunal are all slim and generally have declined since 1986. One can have some sympathy for the BCP when confronted by these data presentations. If real cases are too low, the Auditor General of Canada may begin to say that the BCP is inefficient. If cases are too numerous, the rumblings of the business community are bound to be heard. When a compliance-oriented approach is stressed, most such successful actions will not even show up as cases. Meanwhile, the very large volume of complaints and notifications must be assessed in keeping with the different provisions of the various sections of the statute, and in keeping with the genuine differences among the branches.

As further living proof of these diverse realities, one need look only briefly at the Marketing Practices Branch. It has complaints and cases galore. Its purview in policing misleading advertising and deceptive marketing practices results in a flood of complaints. The cases are by definition smaller and of necessity must be investigated through a system of regional offices. Moreover, its personnel have historically been primarily former police officers (though this is now changing) hired for their routine but important investigative skills. The Marketing Practices Branch has the highest volume of business and by far the highest regional political profile.

CONCLUSIONS

The above analysis of the Canadian competition policy system suggests five overall conclusions. The first is that the 1986 Competition Act, while a marked change from its predecessor legislation, is still much closer to a controlled system of discretionary case-based micro-economic governance than it is to a transparent rule-based regime for ensuring competition. Competition policy goals are central but there is considerable room for manœuvre for industrial policy goals to be addressed, provided they are cast around rationales for efficiency and restructuring to meet international competition.

Second, it is clear that the recent changes to the Canadian competition regime have required some difficult organizational cultural changes within the nexus of relationships between the DIR and BCP, within the BCP, and to some extent with the non-core competition policy players set out above. The need to strike balances between criminal and economic law and to Charter-proof both in total creates more room for discretion. New emphases on compliance rather than enforcement approaches are built into the political compromise inherent when the legislation was passed in 1986. But they are also a matter of deliberate preference by the DIR and by firms which, while longing for a more certain investment climate, also have a vested interest in well-crafted ambiguity.

Third, with respect to the interest-group structure, the analysis suggests the need to distinguish the nature of interest coalitions that form, first, when legislation is being forged; and, second, when ongoing cases are proceeding through the system. The former has been dominated by key macro business associations, but also by a recognition that it has been extremely difficult to mobilize a coalition to change legislation. In the day-to-day case situations, business associations retreat to the background and the professional competition policy community takes hold. Lawyers, economists, and individual firms and their management are the key players here both as value articulators and as immediate rent seekers in the cases that arise.

Fourth, the chapter has drawn initial attention to the ways in which the case decision process provides many points at which discretion can be and is exercised. These can be seen in the typical stages of review, in the way budgets affect case loads, in the way priorities are set among cases across and within branches, and in the way each branch of the BCP has to march to somewhat different competition, legal, and economic drummers.

Indeed, it is virtually impossible to understand the real micro-political and institutional dynamics of the DIR and BCP without disaggregating the organization. Even small organizations such as the BCP are assemblages of sub-organizations. Thus, we have seen the quite different dynamics that occur within the main mandate areas and branches of the BCP. Though there are broad similarities in the nominal stages of the case decision cycle in each branch, there are wide variations in other vital aspects of the inherent business each component is in. Thus, because of the different nature of mergers, criminal matters, reviewable matters, and marketing practices, there are wide variations in: the nature of the triggering devices that start the decision process; the volume of cases; the political and analytical meaning attached to 'too few' or 'too many' cases; the complexity of cases; criminal and non-criminal standards of proof; whether prospective or past behaviour is involved; the extent to which case law is significant or virtually non-existent; the degree to which guidelines are available; and the exact meaning of key words in particular parts of the statute which are there precisely because key players have a vital interest in their presence.

NOTES

1. For a book-length analysis of the Canadian system, including a more detailed look at cases and the Canadian international role, see G. Bruce Doern, *Fairer Play: Canadian Competition Policy Institutions in a Global Market* (Toronto: C. D. Howe Institute, 1995).
2. See William S. Comanor, 'United States Antitrust Policy: Issues and Institutions', in W. S. Comanor *et al.*, *Competition Policy in Europe and North America: Economic Issues and Institutions* (London: Harwood, 1990), 43–72.

Canadian Competition Policy Institutions

Canadian Competition Policy Institutions

Canadian Competition Policy Institutions

Canadian Competition Policy Institutions   99

On the US system, see Harry First, Eleanor Fox, and Robert Pitofsky, *Revitalizing Antitrust in its Second Century* (New York: Quorum Books, 1991); and William Shughart, *Antitrust Policy and Interest Group Politics* (New York: Quorum Books, 1990).

3. On the US system, see Harry First, Eleanor Fox, and Robert Pitofsky, *Revitalizing Antitrust in its Second Century* (New York: Quorum Books, 1991); and William Shughart, *Antitrust Policy and Interest Group Politics* (New York: Quorum Books, 1990).

3. On the US system, see Harry First, Eleanor Fox, and Robert Pitofsky, *Revitalizing Antitrust in its Second Century* (New York: Quorum Books, 1991); and William Shughart, *Antitrust Policy and Interest Group Politics* (New York: Quorum Books, 1990).
4. See R. S. Khemani and W. T. Stanbury (eds.), *Canadian Competition Law and Policy at the Centenary* (Halifax: Institute for Research on Public Policy, 1991), intro.
5. See Michael Bliss, 'Another Anti-trust Tradition: Canadian Anti-Combines Policy 1889–1910', *Business History Review*, 47/2, 177–88.
6. See Donald G. McFetridge, 'Globalization and Competition Policy', paper presented to a Conference on Canada's International Competitiveness, Queen's University, Kingston, Ont., Sept. 1992.
7. See R. S. Khemani, 'Merger Policy in Small versus Large Economies', in Khemani and Stanbury, *Canadian Competition Law and Policy*, 206–23.
8. See G. Bruce Doern and Brian W. Tomlin, *Faith and Fear: The Free Trade Story* (Toronto: Stoddart, 1991).
9. See G. Bruce Doern (ed.), *The Regulatory Process in Canada* (Toronto: Macmillan of Canada, 1978).
10. On the long struggle to change the legislation, see W. T. Stanbury, *Business Interests and the Reform of Canadian Competition Policy, 1971–1975* (Toronto: Carswell Methuen, 1977); and G. Bruce Doern, *Modernizing Economic Framework Legislation: A Discussion Paper* (Ottawa: Consumer and Corporate Affairs Canada, 1987).
11. Consumer and Corporate Affairs Canada, *Annual Report*, Director of Investigation and Research (Ottawa: Minister of Supply and Services, 1992), 1.
12. See Douglas Rutherford and J. S. Tyhurst, 'Competition Law and the Constitution: 1889–1989 and into the Twenty-first Century', in Khemani and Stanbury, *Canadian Competition Law and Policy*, 253–83.
13. See G. Bruce Doern, 'Consumer and Corporate Affairs: The Dilemmas of Influencing without Spending', in Katherine A. Graham (ed.), *How Ottawa Spends: 1988–89* (Ottawa: Carleton University Press, 1988), 233–68.
14. For one DIR's views, see Calvin S. Goldman, 'The Impact of the Competition Act of 1986', in Khemani and Stanbury, *Canadian Competition Law and Policy*, 539–60.
15. See Consumer and Corporate Affairs Canada, *Program of Compliance*, Director of Investigation and Research, Competition Act. Information Bulletin, 3 (June 1989).
16. See Competition Tribunal of Canada, *1992–93 Estimates*, Part III (Ottawa: Minister of Supply and Services, 1992).
17. See Consumer and Corporate Affairs Canada, *Canadian Competition*

Policy: Its Interface with Other Economic and Social Policies (Ottawa: Bureau of Competition Policy, 1989).

18. See G. Bruce Doern, 'The Department of Industry, Science and Technology: Is There Industrial Policy after Free Trade?', in Katherine Graham (ed.), *How Ottawa Spends: 1990–91* (Ottawa: Carleton University Press, 1990), 49–72; and Robert D. Anderson and S. Dev Khosla, *Competition Policy as a Dimension of Industrial Policy: A Comparative Dimension* (draft paper, Ottawa: Bureau of Competition Policy, 1992).

19. See, for example, Director of Investigation and Research, *Submission to the National Transportation Act Review Commission* (Ottawa: Bureau of Competition Policy, June 1992).

20. See Investment Canada, *Annual Report 1991–92* (Ottawa: Minister of Supply and Services, 1992).

21. See Stephen Wilks, *The Metamorphosis of European Competition Policy* (Exeter: RUSEL Working Paper, 1992).

22. See G. Bruce Doern and Brian W. Tomlin, 'The Free Trade Sequel: The Canada–US Subsidy Negotiations', in Frances Abele (ed.), *How Ottawa Spends: 1991–92* (Ottawa: Carleton University Press, 1991), 157–82; and International Affairs Branch, Bureau of Competition Policy, *Competition and Industrial Subsidies in Canada* (draft paper, Ottawa: Bureau of Competition Policy, Dec. 1992).

23. See Stanbury, *Business Interests and the Reform of Canadian Competition Policy*; and Doern, 'Consumer and Corporate Affairs: The Dilemmas of Influencing without Spending'.

24. On Canadian business interests, see William D. Coleman, *Business and Politics* (Montreal: McGill-Queen's University Press, 1988).

25. See W. T. Stanbury, 'Public Policy toward Individuals Involved in Competition Policy Offences in Canada', *Canadian Competition Policy Record*, 14 (1993), 57–81.

26. See e.g. Frank Matheson, M. Trebilcock, and Michael Walker (eds.), *The Law and Economics of Competition Policy* (Vancouver: Fraser Institute, 1990).

27. See Neil Campbell and M. Trebilcock, 'International Merger Review: Problems of Multi-Jurisdictional Conflict', unpublished paper, Faculty of Law, University of Toronto, 1991.

28. On the enormous impact of the Charter on Canadian politics and policy, see Alan C. Cairns, *Charter versus Federalism* (Montreal: McGill-Queens Press, 1992); and Michael Mandel, *The Charter of Rights and the Legalization of Politics in Canada* (Toronto: Thompson, 1991).

29. See Michael Bliss, 'The Yoke of the Trusts: A Comparison of Canada's Competitive Environment in 1889 and 1989', in R. S. Khemani and W. T. Stanbury (eds.), *Historical Perspectives on Canadian*

Competition Policy (Halifax: Institute for Research on Public Policy, 1991), 239–52.

30. See Stanbury, 'Public Policy toward Individuals'.
31. See Doern, *Modernizing Economic Framework Legislation: A Discussion Paper*.
32. See Consumer and Corporate Affairs Canada, *Program of Compliance*.
33. Data are estimates from the BCP.
34. Doern, *Fairer Play*.
35. See Paul S. Crampton, *Mergers and the Competition Act* (Toronto: Carswell, 1990).
36. See W. T. Stanbury, 'An Assessment of the Merger Review Process', *Canadian Business Law Journal*, 20/3 (Aug. 1992), 422–63; Roy M. Davidson, 'When Merger Guidelines Fail to Guide', *Canadian Competition Policy Record*, 12/4 (Dec. 1991), 44–51; and Warren Grover and Jack Quinn, 'Recent Developments in Canadian Merger Law', in Khemani and Stanbury (eds.), *Canadian Competition Law and Policy*, 225–42.
37. See D. Khosla, R. Anderson, P. Hughes, and J. Monteiro, *Reference Document on Abuse of Dominance* (Ottawa: Bureau of Competition Policy, 1991).

5

The Fair Trade Commission and the Enforcement of Competition Policy in Japan

KENJI SANEKATA AND STEPHEN WILKS

The Japan Fair Trade Commission (JFTC) is one of the oldest and, at least on paper, one of the most powerful competition authorities in the world. It was created in 1947 by the Antimonopoly Act,[1] which gave the agency very wide and effective powers in all the conventional areas of competition regulation. In reality, of course, the JFTC has been a unique and vulnerable agency administering deeply unpopular laws based on a widely rejected model of market competition. In an economy dominated by the 'developmental state' thinking which gave pre-eminence to industrial policy, the role of the JFTC has been ambiguous and difficult. For twenty years between 1953 and 1973 the JFTC managed only a very limited level of activity, and over the whole of its existence there has been a huge gap between the powers available to the Agency and the actual enforcement of those powers. As discussed below, that gap is closing, but the renaissance of competition policy in Japan is recent, partial, and far from fully secure.

A conjunction of influences has made competition policy much more important within the Japanese political-economy of the 1990s, and has caused it to be regarded as a legitimate and valuable tool of economic policy. Among the important domestic forces are changes in the structure of the Japanese economy; a reappraisal of the role of the Ministry of International Trade and Industry (MITI); a reappraisal of the economic theory of competition; and a popular dissatisfaction with corrupt practices within industry which have raised consumer prices and brought politicians into disrepute. It is,

Stephen Wilks acknowledges the financial assistance of the Daiwa Anglo-Japanese Foundation, and the British Council (Tokyo).

however, the international forces that have had a decisive effect on competition policy. Among business and political leaders there is widespread recognition that Japan must adopt a posture of world economic leadership, protecting free trade by opening her markets, pursuing reciprocity and harmonization with other developed countries, and conforming to global trade rules. These well-meaning sentiments have been given irresistible force by a factor which has dominated Japanese economic diplomacy for the last ten years— *gaiatsu*, or foreign pressure. In practice this, of course, means pressure from the United States.[2]

The scope and influence of Japanese competition policy is now substantial and has attracted wide attention. The standard English-language text on anti-monopoly, by Iyori and Uesugi,[3] gives a very good treatment of the scope of activities, which are also subject to detailed analysis by lawyers[4] and economists[5] and get a fair coverage in the business press.[6] This chapter presents a brief but essential historical overview in the first section, before analysing the role of trade friction. The third section deals with recent developments in enforcement, while the fourth looks at the administrative institutions and procedures. The fifth section evaluates methods of enforcement, stressing the contrast between formal and informal mechanisms, while the final section draws conclusions and relates policy to the current debate on reform and deregulation in Japan.

HISTORICAL OVERVIEW: THE ANTI-MONOPOLY REVIVAL AND THE COMPROMISE WITH INDUSTRIAL POLICY

The Antimonopoly Act reflects its origins during the US occupation, both in the content of the law and in the institution which administers it. Uniquely in Japan the JFTC exists as an independent regulatory commission modelled on the US commissions of the Progressive era.[7] As such it is independent, expert, and combines executive, legislative, and judicial functions.

The JFTC has exclusive administrative power to enforce the Antimonopoly Act. Theoretically, this independence favours vigorous enforcement. However, antitrust enforcement has been affected by several social and political factors. The Antimonopoly Act was originally passed in 1947 but, except for the period of the Allied occupation, it has been enforced actively only since the mid-1960s. Competition policy was never of serious concern to most Japanese firms until recently, when the enforcement of the Act was drastically strengthened in response to the Structural Impediments Initiative (SII) talks.

Since the oil crisis of 1973 there has been a resurgence of antitrust enforcement. This revival was a political response to discontent among consumers caused by sky-rocketing prices following the oil crisis. Widely publicized price-fixing agreements during this time provoked public concern. With the emergence of widespread expectations among consumers that anti-monopoly enforcement would act as a defence against abuses of power by big business, and serve as a means of dealing with the price problem, anti-monopoly enforcement became more active and, thus, more hazardous for big business. However, enforcement developed within the limits of overall economic policy at that time. The compromise with industrial policy was indispensable in the context of the total economic regulation system in Japan.

In the 1970s, anti-monopoly enforcement initially came into serious conflict with industrial policy. In February 1974, the JFTC filed its first criminal complaint against petroleum companies, accusing them of price-fixing and restricting output. The companies' actions in this regard had been acknowledged and even promoted through administrative guidance furnished by MITI. The outcome of this prosecution provides an illustration of compromise in Japan. In 1980, a decision by the Tokyo High Court on a production restriction cartel case declared that the production restriction cartel was illegal, despite the administrative guidance it had received. However, the defendants were acquitted on the ground that there was reasonable possibility that they may not have been aware of the illegality of the cartel due to faith in MITI's administrative guidance. The JFTC won on theory but lost on enforcement. On price-fixing cases, the Supreme Court declared in its dictum from the 1983 decision that cartels which are reasonable and necessary for the enforcement of any reasonable administrative guidances might be legal as they are acting in the public interest under the Antimonopoly Act. This applies even where the price-fixing cartel has been deemed illegal *per se*. The prison sentences against petroleum company executives were suspended on the grounds that the cartel was, in part, an implementation device for administrative guidance.[8]

In the recession following the oil crisis of 1973, the demand for protection from competition overcame, to some extent, the goals of competition policy. In June 1978, special legislation was enacted for structurally depressed industries. In June 1983, a further measure was enacted to renew and strengthen this temporary law.[9] This legislation provided an exemption for cartels from the Antimonopoly Act to facilitate disposal of their production facilities. While to some extent this is in conflict with competition policy, there was no serious objection to the 1983 legislation. In the original draft of the 1983 legislation there was an exemption for mergers and other forms of business co-ordination which were considered to be useful and necessary in effecting reorganization plans in certain depressed industries. After a sharp conflict between MITI and the JFTC the exemption clause for mergers and other forms of business co-ordination was deleted from the bill. Nevertheless, in May 1983, the JFTC did publish special, flexible guidelines on mergers in depressed industries in addition to the 1980 general guidelines on mergers. Thus, *de facto* exemption of mergers and other business arrangements was created in accordance with the 1983 legislation.

This process of compromise represents two characteristics of competition policy enforcement in the 1980s. The first is that industrial policy should, at least theoretically, be in harmony with competition policy. Thus, MITI moderated its traditional opposition to anti-monopoly policy and the JFTC, particularly in the area of cartels. The second lesson to be drawn was that compromise with industrial policy was then indispensable in order for anti-monopoly policy to survive in Japanese society. The JFTC did not object seriously to the new 1983 Act after the exemption clause on mergers was struck from the original draft. Content with their current, intimate relationship with the JFTC, senior MITI officials did not support the threat from the Liberal Democratic Party (LDP), which was contemplating the amendment of the Antimonopoly Act in order to weaken it. One MITI official declared publicly that there was no urgent need to weaken anti-monopoly enforcement. Thereafter, the LDP ceased in its efforts to constrain the JFTC's enforcement by threatening an amendment of the Act. A major factor which led MITI to adopt this favourable attitude was the criticism from abroad of Japanese industrial policies. The US government had been arguing that a protective industrial policy in Japan gave Japanese companies an unfair advantage in international trade and was a major non-tariff barrier. To MITI, the trade friction problem became of prime importance as the protection of domestic industry was no longer paramount. The fact that the JFTC was not a serious obstacle to MITI's industrial policy proposals also contributed to MITI's change in attitude to antitrust enforcement.

In the late 1980s, when trade friction with the United States and other developed countries became a serious issue, the JFTC co-operated with MITI in preparing defensive measures, urging that the alleged non-tariff barriers of restrictive distribution and trade practices, such as manufacturer-controlled distribution networks or continuing supply relations between firms enjoying *keiretsu* relations, are not exclusive but reasonable business practices that can be explained by economic rationality. Thus, no serious conflict between MITI and JFTC has existed since the late 1980s.

TRADE FRICTION AND THE RENAISSANCE OF COMPETITION POLICY IN THE 1990s

Weak enforcement of competition policy in Japan has been criticized as a practice that results in the unfair advantage of Japanese firms in competitive markets. Under relaxed competition law enforcement, Japanese firms have been accused of gaining surplus profit from restrictive practices, such as cartels and restrictive distribution practices. As a result, they have been able to subsidize their exports out of their domestic profit. On the other hand, restrictions on entry to the Japanese market imposed by government regulations or resulting from restrictive practices by private firms, have protected the Japanese market from the competition of new, foreign entrants and thus made possible domestic, surplus profit.

In the 1990s the *gaiatsu* pressure from overseas, and especially from the United States, has been one of the most influential factors to have supported the active enforcement of the Antimonopoly Act. The JFTC conducted many surveys on various fields concerning the alleged non-tariff barriers to free trade with Japan. Many of the surveys functioned as defences to criticism from overseas. However, to a certain extent, the JFTC has taken measures to improve the situation. Recently, anti-monopoly enforcement by the JFTC has been drastically stepped up, constituting an 'anti-monopoly renaissance'.

The most significant factor to have created the anti-monopoly renaissance is the SII (Structural Impediments Initiative) trade negotiations between Japan and the United States. These negotiations followed the MOSS (Market Orientated Sector Specific) negotiations from 1982–8 in which competition policy received relatively little attention. SII was very different and had a tremendous impact on the JFTC, which became a central issue and a central actor in the negotiations.

The first round of SII talks ran from September 1989 to June 1990. The Final Report declared itself to be 'a historic document' and in four of its six broad areas for action anti-monopoly policy was prominent:

- *distribution systems*: here the Guidelines on Distribution Systems, Business Practices and Competition Policy are stressed (see below).
- *exclusionary business practices*: this is the major concern of the JFTC and includes bid-rigging. The Report affirms that 'The Fair Trade Commission will strictly exclude, through resorting to more formal actions, activities violating the Anti-monopoly Act, by expanding and enhancing the investigatory function of the FTC and increasing its proof-collecting capacity against illegal activities.'[10]
- *keiretsu relationships*: the Report commits the JFTC to 'enforce the Antimonopoly Act strictly', to increase transparency, and to conduct 'close analysis' of the business groups every two years.
- *pricing mechanism*: here the stress is on consumer welfare and strengthening anti-monopoly enforcement in the areas of cartel surcharges, criminal proceedings, and facilitating private damage actions.

The negotiations were very detailed, coming down to such specifics as shop opening hours. There is no doubt that the US had ample information and understanding derived from surveys such as the study by the American Chamber of Commerce in Japan of

United States–Japan Trade,[11] but equally the level of detail in the negotiations could be construed as trespassing on domestic sovereignty. Certainly the JFTC suffered some quite critical media coverage and was called a *kokuzoku* (traitor to the country), which indicated that US pressure could be seen as a mixed blessing.

The SII agenda provided for follow-up negotiations undertaken by senior officials, on the Japanese side the Deputy Minister for Foreign Affairs and Vice-Ministers of the Ministry of Finance (MOF), MITI, and Economic Planning Agency (EPA). Thus the second Annual Report of July 1992 reports progress, new initiatives, and new commitments. It was able to report that JFTC investigatory staff had been increased by 40 per cent; that the maximum for criminal fines against Antimonopoly Act violation had been increased; and that appropriate measures had been taken to 'eliminate' bid-rigging. Some of these commitments are simply good intentions; others, such as the new commitment to eliminate all possible cartel exemption systems by 1996, indicate substantial progress. What cannot be doubted is the urgency and the importance which the Japanese bureaucracy attached to this series of negotiations. It can be startling to see to what an extent Japan is sensitive to, and responsive to, US concerns. The composition of President Clinton's trade team has been the subject of detailed analysis and front-page speculation, and an instinctive reaction at every level is to accept an agenda defined in US terms. In this setting Japanese competition policy is consistently compared with US antitrust powers and enforcement. This is a demanding yardstick and, almost despite itself, the Fair Trade Commission is being taken back to its formative principles and evangelical mission in a fashion that may make some officials uncomfortable.

This background seems to bring about the aggressive enforcement of the Antimonopoly Act against exclusive and peculiar practices. However, the actual situation is much more complicated. These practices and relations concerning distribution and *keiretsu* issues, which are alleged to be non-tariff barriers, can be justified as rational firm behaviour that result in a more efficient way of doing business. Actually, it is fashionable at this time for Japanese economists to become popular by offering a sophisticated justification of Japanese business systems and practices.[12] This is done in order to counter-attack the criticism from overseas which alleges that these business systems and practices are exclusive, peculiar, only survive in Japan, and are, therefore, unfair to foreign firms. MITI and Keidanren, the organization representing big business, agreed in principle with the reinforcement of the competition policy as a universal rule among industrialized nations, thus recognizing that interdependence among these nations and the globalization of the Japanese economy have become significant factors to be considered in policy-making. However, they have tried to mitigate the adverse effect on business activities caused by more stringent competition policy enforcement. Facing the stringent attitude of trade partners, especially the aggressiveness displayed by the United States during the SII talks, MITI and the business circle had also to reconcile themselves in practice to more rigorous competition policy enforcement. They considered this attitude to be the preferred alternative in order to avoid managed trade.

The recent record of FTC enforcement activity attests to a more activist stance from about 1990 onwards. Table 5.1 gives the statistical record which indicates a considerable increase in 'recommendations' (formal finding of violation of the act) and a sustained increase in surcharges levelled against cartels. As noted below, the formal actions of the JFTC are only the tip of the iceberg and informal activity has similarly intensified. In addition, the JFTC has begun to use the more dramatic weapons in its armoury. For the first time since the oil cartel case criminal actions were again taken in 1991 against participants in a wrapping-materials cartel (they were found guilty in 1993); and in 1992 in a bid-rigging case concerning social security stickers (the companies were convicted and fined in 1993).[13]

This increased activism is, however, regarded as fragile. The business and political forces arrayed against the JFTC are formidable and the trade talks emphasis has moved away from structural questions of the operation of the 'rules' towards more interventionist 'results-based' approaches. The implications of this for anti-monopoly are evaluated below, but the distinctive way in which the Japanese competition policy agenda has been moulded by foreign pressure deserves emphasis. The trade talks have been mobilized by questions of reciprocal market access and by the trade balance, but they have gone into quite remarkable detail on individual sectoral issues and on the detail of domestic laws. To this extent the globalization of the world economy has generated

Table 5.1. *Disposition of cases by the Japan FTC, 1979–1992*

	1979	1980	1981	1982	1983	1984	1985	1986	1987	1988	1989	1990	1991	1992	1993
Cases disposed	41	67	146	297	233	204	168	148	132	95	169	180	150	173	
Number of violations	0	13	44	78	45	36	16	19	14	8	16	16	9	42	
Caution	n.a.	n.a.	n.a.	49	60	66	62	37	28	17	28	85	88	73	
Warning (administrative guidance)	22	39	91	151	118	94	80	88	84	65	115	60	24	21	
Recommendation	16	14	11	19	10	7	10	4	6	5	10	17	27	37	
of which: complaint	1	2	2	0	0	1	0	0	0	0	1	2	3	0	
indictment	0	0	0	0	0	0	0	0	0	0	0	0	1	1	
surcharge	3	11	6	8	10	2	4	4	6	3	6	11	10	17	
Surcharge amount Y million	1,572	1,331	3,730	483	1,493	353	407	276	148	419	803	12,562	1,972	2,682	4,087
£ million	10.1	8.6	24.1	3.1	9.6	2.3	2.6	1.8	0.9	2.7	5.2	87	12.7	17.3	26.4

Source : JFTC Annual Reports, various issues.

TABLE 5.2. *Japanese trade surplus with major trading partners*
($ billons)

	1989	1990	1991	1992	1993
Overall	64	52	78	107	120
USA	45	38	38	44	50
European Union	20	18	27	31	26
UK	6	5	6	7	7
South-east Asia	21	28	37	47	57

Source: JEI Report, A, 16 Sept. 1994, table 33. The overall trade surplus for 1994 continued to rise, to $145 billion, *Financial Times*, 10 May 1995.

pressures which have shifted domestic competition policy from questions of economic regulation and towards questions of economic diplomacy. These pressures are unlikely to disappear. The trade balance with the United States remains an issue for the Clinton administration and trade negotiators. In dollar terms it shows no great improvement, as shown in Table 5.2.

As a leading economic power which derives great benefit from free trade, the reinforcement of competition policy has become for Japan a matter of principle to be respected as a common rule among industrialized nations. Nevertheless, the extent to which the JFTC could strengthen anti-monopoly enforcement has been limited within the spectrum of the reconciliation between the JFTC and the governing parties, which represent the interests of the various business groups. The Hosokawa Coalition Cabinet declared its policy to strengthen competition policy enforcement as an ingredient of its action programme in response to New US–Japan Framework Trade Talks. Thus, the situation concerning competition policy has clearly improved.

THE STRUGGLE TO STRENGTHEN COMPETITION ENFORCEMENT

The political context

Over the past twenty years competition enforcement has been strengthened, but this has happened in a delicate and controversial process which has seen setbacks as well as advances. The political background to enforcement is complex but of overwhelming importance. It has taken the normal political form of exchanges and disputes between industrialists, ministries, and LDP *zoku*[14] politicians over the desirable content of policy. It has also been tied up with the crises and intense sensitivities of election funding, corruption scandals, political manipulation, and coalition manœuvring. The most obvious example is the case of bid-rigging, especially in the construction industry, and a brief discussion of this area illustrates the precarious tightrope which the JFTC must walk.

The stringent enforcement of the Antimonopoly Act against cartels was regarded as a crucial measure to control 'exclusionary business practices' under the SII Talks. Amongst cartels, bid-rigging in public and private procurement has long been an established business practice. Known colloquially as *dango*, the practice has developed in Japan, since at least 1900, for public works projects to be offered to a limited number of designated contractors who form a cartel (often through a local trade association) and allocate a contract at a favourable and excessive price to one of their members.[15] The construction market is huge, profitable, effectively closed to foreign competition, and is cited by the USA as a prime example of unacceptable restrictive practices. Even MITI concedes that here the Americans have struck at the most vulnerable point, but the momentum for reform has also been accentuated by consumer groups protesting against high local taxes and by the whole nation protesting at political corruption. The bribes paid to LDP politicians to secure contracts were immense, notorious, and came into the open in the scandals over Shin Kanemaru, which led to the electoral downfall of the LDP. In this area, therefore, there is a national consensus in favour of reform, and the FTC has a following wind. Of the 70 cases in which recommendations were made from April 1989 to May 1992, over a third were against bid-rigging or construction-industry breaches.

Despite this recent criticism the construction industry retains great political strength. Construction companies are influential within industry and have very close connections with leading LDP politicians, who provide political protection in return for huge financial contributions and direct personal help at election time. Their political power is formalized through the Construction *zoku* of the LDP and through the Ministry of Construction. The Ministry has always been powerful, thanks to these political and financial resources, and was a vehicle for the Tanaka faction which dominated the LDP under Tanaka, Nakasone, Takeshita and, for a time, Kanemaru. In these circumstances the realists within the JFTC have been all too aware that measures against bid-rigging, against construction companies, or even against generic practices within the construction industry, can be construed as attacks on leading LDP politicians. The LDP has been able to mobilize irresistible force to curb JFTC enforcement as, for example, with the 1984 special *Antimonopoly Act Guidelines Concerning the Activities of Trade Associations of the Construction Industry in Relation to Public Works*. These were permissive guidelines, forced on the JFTC, which allowed information exchange on contract bids and effectively perpetuated bid-rigging. One of the recent triumphs of the JFTC has been to get these guidelines repealed through the 1994 *Trade Association Guidelines on Public Bids* (see below). None the less, the struggle continued. The LDP's influence was again high within the Murayama coalition and the Social Democratic Party (which took over the Construction Ministry in 1994 under Construction Minister Koken Nosaka)[16] had a long-standing reputation for relying on pork-barrel politics.

Higher profile enforcement

Among the SII commitments, the government of Japan promised to implement wide-ranging measures for the enhancement of antimonopoly enforcement. The first and most important step toward rigorous enforcement was 'resorting to more formal actions'. The JFTC has been depending mainly on informal measures, such as warnings, instead of formal actions that are automatically followed by surcharges, in the case of cartels. Rigorous anti-monopoly enforcement through formal procedure has not been accepted among business circles. Informal measures have been deemed an easier and more efficient way to enforce the Act, especially in situations where the JFTC did not have enough proof to firmly establish anti-monopoly violations. With the exception of the period from 1965 to 1974, when creeping inflation, the gradual rise in consumer price levels, and abrupt price increases at the time of the first oil crisis of 1973 were major political issues, formal actions against anti-monopoly violation were not the main measures taken. While the investigatory measures which had been taken against alleged violators had remained at a constant level, formal actions against violations declined drastically in the late 1970s and early 1980s.

Structural depression was the principal policy issue to be overcome by the restructuring of each industry through industry-wide co-operation in terms of collective disposal of surplus capacity. When the JFTC took formal measures against bid-rigging in the construction industry for the first time in 1982, the LDP reorganized its committee on the Antimonopoly Act and threatened the JFTC with a possible amendment to the Act in order to eliminate the surcharge system.

Even after 1983, when trade friction with the United States became a serious issue and the JFTC was called to prepare policy devices to eliminate non-tariff barriers in the Japanese market, the measures taken against anti-monopoly violators were mostly informal. In the 1990s, the JFTC has been strengthening the formal measures against cartels. The combined amount of surcharge orders against two cartels in the cement industry in 1990 exceeded ten billion yen—the largest surcharge ever. In the fiscal year of 1991, the formal measures taken against anti-monopoly violations reached 32, more than three times the number of formal decisions in 1989, even though informal measures are still the most important steps taken by the JFTC (see Table 5.1).

In order to ensure clarity, to enhance the deterrent effect, and to prevent similar, illegal activities from occurring, the contents of warnings, informal measures, the nature of the offence, and circumstances surrounding the violation have recently been made public. In some cases, the names of the offenders were released along with the reports. A summary of the principal warnings has been made public not only on an *ad hoc* basis but also through the JFTC annual report. The JFTC had formerly been reluctant to make public the detailed content of warnings on the basis that the warnings were given because the violations had not been clearly established, and that voluntary observance of the warnings was secured through negotiation with alleged violators in exchange for the contents not being made public. The disclosure of the content of each warning is a significant step toward more stringent enforcement of the Act.

Reinforcement of the surcharge system

In the final report of the SII the government of Japan promised to raise the surcharges against cartels so that the deterrent effect would be strengthened. In December 1990, the Consultative Group on the Amendment of the Antimonopoly Act Regarding Surcharges presented its final report that recommended a fourfold increase in the surcharge ratio.

The surcharge system against cartels affecting the price levels of the market was introduced in the 1977 amendment of the Act. The surcharge is regarded as a confiscation of excess profits rather than as a fine, and the amount of the surcharge is therefore calculated under the Act at a fixed rate against the sale of goods that were the subject of the cartel agreement during the period in which the cartel was operating. Before the 1991 amendment, the rate was 1.5 per cent, based on the principle of half the average profit of the corporate sector, which was about 3 per cent. In practice it became apparent that the surcharge was indefensibly low compared with the actual profits made by the cartels, of around 15 to 20 per cent of sales during the cartel. The low risk of being condemned made it possible for firms to calculate the risk of an antimonopoly violation, that is, the prospective amount of surcharge times the risk of condemnation. The surcharge system had been operating steadily since its introduction in 1977, and had some effect in ensuring the effectiveness of the provisions prohibiting cartels, especially the cartels among large firms. Repeat offenders seemed to be fewer than before the 1977 amendment. However, even after the introduction of the surcharge system, many cartels maintained established trade practices in many industries. A case involving the US Yokosuka Base in 1988 shows that the level of surcharge before the 1991 amendment was not enough to prevent cartels from continuing their operations. The cartel was detected by the Counter Intelligence Division (CID) of the US Navy and referred to the JFTC, who found a violation and fined one firm and the cartelized Association. About 70 entrepreneurs paid a total surcharge of around 300 million yen. The US Justice Department pursued the matter further and threatened the extra-territorial application of US antitrust. Faced with this threat about 145 member firms of the cartel association paid damages amounting to about 4,700 million yen. Here we see foreign pressure again at work. The incident illustrated the inadequate level of the Japanese fines and created strong pressure within the SII talks for upward revision.[17]

Faced with such pressure, the Final Report of the Consultative Group presented the proposal of 6 per cent as a surcharge rate. This figure was based on the average operating profits/turnover ratio of firms that have capital which exceeds 100 million yen (big business in the legislative system in Japan) in sectors other than wholesale and retailing during the period after the adoption of the surcharge system in 1977.

The declared ground for the revision of the surcharge system was that, in many cases where the surcharges were imposed, the level of the unjustifiable gain accruing from the cartel was around 15 to 20 per cent of sales and significantly higher than the former level of surcharges. International harmonization of the rules concerning competition laws, which are basic rules for business activities, was another significant reason why business circles could not object. The decisive factor was the recent trend in major developed countries toward the enhancement of deterrent measures against violations of their competition laws. This has been done mainly through legislative changes or vigorous and increased enforcement.

These changes aided the move toward the reinforcement of competition law in Japan. If the amendment to reinforce sanctions against cartels had not been achieved, Japanese firms would be criticized for having an unfair advantage because of weak competition enforcement. The report said, 'under these circumstances, it should be noted that by raising the level of surcharges, the total deterrent effect of measures against violations of the Antimonopoly Act, cartels in particular, would not be very much out of balance with those in other countries from the viewpoint of international harmony'.

In the United States, the level of the fine imposed in each case is based on the actual level of surplus profit accruing from the illegal cartel. Similarly, in the EU, the administrative fine against illegal cartels is also decided on the basis of the surplus profit accruing from each illegal cartel, although in the European case fines are intended as penalties and are increasingly set at a high level to act as a deterrent. Following its introduction by the amendment of the Antimonopoly Act in 1977, the surcharge system was identified as an 'administrative measure' designed to prohibit cartels. The aim was to secure social fairness and deter violations through collecting the 'unjustifiable gain' realized by cartels and thereby preventing it from remaining in the offender's hands. Consequently, the JFTC has no discretion in terms of imposing surcharges and deciding their amounts. Where the cartels are found to be illegal, the JFTC must impose the surcharge calculated by the fixed rate that is applied to the industry in general. The proposals from the Consultative Group were accepted, and on 26 April 1991 the Diet amended the Antimonopoly Act to provide for a 6 per cent surcharge rate for manufacturing industry (with 1 per cent for wholesale and 2 per cent for retail firms). The fixed-rate system is a better policy alternative within the Japanese political framework. It avoids discretion and secures the deterrent effect through the establishment of a clear-cut, built-in disincentive for offenders.

The level of the reinforced surcharge expected by the United States was at least 10 per cent. The United States was not satisfied by the 6 per cent level and insisted that additional measures be taken to strengthen the criminal penalty. In response to this added pressure, the Study Group on Penal Sanctions in the Antimonopoly Act was hastily established in January 1991, resulting in the amendment of the Antimonopoly Act which increased the sum of the criminal fine for corporate violators twenty times over.

The enhancement of criminal sanctions against cartels

True to its origins in US antitrust, the Antimonopoly Law includes comprehensive and severe criminal penalties against individuals and corporations that breach its provisions. Except for a very few famous incidents (such as the oil cartel case) these provisions have barely been employed. This is hardly surprising. Litigation is highly unpopular and seldom embarked upon in Japan,[18] even by public agencies, and criminal cases raise the burden of proof and controversy. Problems of liaison between the JFTC (which is more disposed to prosecute) and the Justice Ministry (which is less disposed) have raised practical difficulties, but the prevailing environment has been of a general lack of public support. Iyori and Uesugi remark that 'probably, anti-monopoly violations would be ranked by the general public in Japan slightly above traffic violations'.[19]

Despite this context, the USA pressed the question of criminal prosecution in the SII talks and, since 1990, an increased level of activism has been seen.

In April 1990, the FTC set up a liaison-co-ordination section with the Criminal Affairs Bureau of the Ministry of Justice and thereafter engaged in examining matters such as accusation procedures, so that criminal accusations and prosecutions could be adequately conducted.

The JFTC published its policy document in June 1990, stating that it would actively accuse and seek the application of criminal penalties.[20] The criterion for the JFTC to identify and pursue cases is 'vicious and serious cases which are considered to have widespread influence on people's lives', and 'violation cases involving those businesses or industries who are repeat offenders'.

Thus, the system was well prepared for the more rigorous enforcement of criminal penalties. It is typical of the method of policy enforcement in Japan where the new system is initially established for public relations, with the actual enforcement following gradually. While the establishment of the apparently efficient system to enforce sanctions may help to prevent violations to some extent, it will only serve as a scarecrow without actual, rigorous enforcement.

In November 1991, for the first time since 1974, the JFTC filed criminal accusations against cartels involved in the transparent wrapping-film industry for the business sector. They explained that the grounds for this accusation were that the materials controlled by the cartel were used within superstores and, thus, directly affected consumer interests. The offenders had also repeated the violations in the past, one offender having repeated the violation ten times. This accusation was criticized as being merely a means of preparing the record of accusation for the purpose of satisfying the United States in SII, and with the aim of reinforcing the ground for the proposal of increased criminal fines. While the cartel was a rather minor one and, in fact, unsuccessful in raising actual prices, the accusation was a milestone toward the more rigorous enforcement of criminal sanctions by the JFTC. In this case, not only were the chiefs of concerned sections accused, but also senior executives involved in the cartel. Following this accusation, the JFTC repeatedly declared its policy of actively resorting to criminal accusation whenever the aforesaid criteria were applicable to the cartel. This accusation constituted a real shock among business circles by establishing that the JFTC had real biting power for the first time. In 1993 the Tokyo High Court found all the defendants guilty. Whether the JFTC maintains its bite depends on its attitude in continuing actively to pursue violations. In a recent case of bid-rigging in Saitama prefecture the JFTC gave up its efforts in pursuit of an accusation due to the reluctant attitude on the part of the prosecuting authority. This was blamed on the lack of convincing evidence concerning the participation of three corporate individuals in the cartel's activities. This showed, in effect, the significant constraints on an aggressive policy toward criminal accusation. Continuing hesitancy from the JFTC has led observers to suggest that criminal sanctions against individuals have become an inherited treasure sword—used only for decoration.

Another step toward the reinforcement of criminal sanctions was the proposal to drastically increase the criminal fine on corporate bodies, as distinct from those imposed on individual people. The maximum fine imposed on Antimonopoly Act violators is now 5 million yen. This is small in itself and clearly incapable of acting as a deterrent to major corporate violators, although social stigma and effects on the corporation are significant deterrents. Accordingly, in 1991 the JFTC organized a task force and proposed a modification of legal doctrine. Under Japanese criminal law a company standing alone was not punishable separately from the criminal responsibility of employees. The JFTC proposed that this link be severed and that criminal fines against companies be raised to 500 million yen. The ground for this proposal was cleared by scandals in the securities industry as a result of which the MOF revised the Securities Act to allow for separate and larger fines for companies. In addition the Ministry of Justice's widely respected Legislative Council made a similar proposal in December 1991.

The final report of the JFTC Study Group was rejected by the LDP because of a rebellion by Construction *Zoku* at a session of the LDP's Special Committee on Antimonopoly Law. After negotiation with LDP leaders, the proposed sum of the criminal fine was settled at 100 million yen. The bill to amend the Antimonopoly Act to this effect was decided by the Cabinet in March 1992, and passed in December 1992.

In this area of criminal penalties Japanese enforcement has

therefore responded positively to US pressure. There is, however, some doubt among competition policy advocates about the utility of criminal penalties. Criminal actions are likely to be taken only as a last resort and are adversarial and protracted. They may begin to act as a potent deterrent but increasing attempts to use criminal sanctions may also inhibit the development of a stringent administrative surcharge. Although the US regime allows civil, criminal, and private actions most other regimes do not. The EU regime relies on heavy civil fines rather than criminal enforcement. The risk of double jeopardy, prohibited in the Japanese constitution, would make it more difficult to introduce large administrative fines, even though these might be more effective than criminal actions.

JFTC measures to reinforce damage remedies

The triple-damage remedies available to injured third parties are a distinctive and powerful element in US antitrust law. Article 25 of the AML allows for damages as does article 709 of the Civil Code. This was another area in which the USA pressed for more effective enforcement under the SII talks.

In Japan, the damage system under the Antimonopoly Act is extremely ineffective. The main reason is the negative attitude of the courts based on the rigid construction of tort law. In consumer actions, there are significant imbalances between consumer plaintiffs and corporate defendants. Court decisions concerning consumers' anti-monopoly damage actions have been extremely rigid and legalistic. From 1955 to 1992 only six claims were ever filed under article 25, and none of them was eventually successful.[21]

The first reason for this ineffectiveness is the difficulty in proving a violation of the Antimonopoly Act. Even when there is the final JFTC decision concerning the violation of the Act, the courts usually treat the JFTC's final decision as, 'one of the materials on which the courts freely find the relevant facts'. The second and most significant reason for the ineffectiveness of the damage action system is the rigid attitude of the courts in finding the causal relation between the alleged violation and the damage suffered by consumer plaintiffs. The standards of proof required by the Supreme Court have been so complex and comprehensive that in practice consumers' actions for damages have been fatally handicapped.

The Antimonopoly Act provides that the court has to allow the JFTC an *amicus curiae* brief concerning the amount of damages accruing from the violation that is found in the JFTC's final decision. Theoretically, the JFTC's *amicus curiae* brief is to be respected as the opinion of an expert agency that is primarily responsible for enforcing the Act. However, the JFTC brief was dealt with by the court as only one of the materials on which the court could independently find the causation between the violation and the actual amount of damages.

Consumer actions have been policy oriented, supported by consumer organizations, citizen volunteers, and also by volunteer lawyers and scholars. In exceptional cases, the total amount of damages awarded to consumers in the lower courts was only around 5 million yen, a negligible amount in comparison with the huge, surplus profit realized by firms from illegal cartels. In practice, however, the damage action is ineffective without introducing the class-action system, such as exists in the United States, even if the aforementioned obstruction by the conservative courts could be overcome. The adoption of the class system was one of the requests of the United States in the SII talks. Facing the request to reinforce the damage system in the Antimonopoly Act, the JFTC changed its attitude towards third-party damages. The JFTC had taken the stance that it did not support or intervene in private damage actions between private parties. The new policy was declared in June, 1991. This policy declaration made it clear that a private action for damages functions as a policy device to supplement the effectiveness of the Antimonopoly Act enforcement. The JFTC also declared that it will affirmatively support private damage actions by providing the plaintiffs with detailed opinions and by allowing access to materials obtained through its investigations and other inquiries.

This affirmative support for private damage actions represents a drastic shift in the policy of the JFTC. In support of this policy it published its criterion in July, 1991, under which it will disclose materials to the concerned parties, including consumer plaintiffs. The significant change of attitude on the part of the JFTC is that the criterion of trade secrets, which are exempt from disclosure, had been drastically tightened. The crucial criteria of the 'trade secret' had been that the concerned firm would like the material to be kept as a trade secret. However, such material would not be dealt with as trade secrets unless it is in the public interest to do so. Under the new policy the affirmative support of the private suit is in the public interest. Therefore the material would not be dealt with as a trade secret in cases where disclosure of the material would be useful and necessary to support the private damage suit. Despite these changes, consumers have been slow to take advantage of the new opportunities. They continue to be deterred by the known sceptical stance of the Supreme Court and by the inability to pursue class-action suits. The class-action system used in the United States allows one exemplary case to be used to impose the total amount of damages suffered by all victims of the violation. It makes legal cases financially viable and imposes an effective penalty on violators, but it is still not available in Japan. A study group of the Judiciary Ministry has been examining the issue for over ten years, but is very reluctant to propose such a radical change.

Very recently, however, there has been a sudden upsurge in private actions, but from companies rather than consumers. In the first ever successful damages case under the AML, the Toshiba Elevator Company was required to indemnify a company to whom it had refused to supply parts. The case was won in the Osaka High Court in July 1993 and Toshiba chose not to appeal. This was followed by two cases by discount retailers who took private action against manufacturers on the grounds of refusal to supply. In the Shiseido case the retailer won in a judgement of the Tokyo District Court in July 1993; and in the Kao case the retailer was victorious in the Tokyo District Court in July 1994. In both cases appeals are pending against decisions requiring the Shiseido Cosmetics Company, and the Kao Soap Company, to supply goods to the discount outlets. The Shiseido case has generated intense interest. Shiseido is the biggest cosmetics company in Japan, and the case has great precedent value. It is interesting that the plaintiff filed a suit with the District Court only after the JFTC had refused to act. The company, Fujiki Honten, had discounted Shiseido products by up to 20 per cent and was becoming very popular when Shiseido abruptly cancelled its supply contract in May 1990. The company complained to the JFTC but was told in July 1991 that 'we have decided not to take action in this matter'.[22]

There are several similar cases in the pipeline. They may offer up a wholly new and effective avenue in antitrust enforcement, not only through court action but also by obliging the JFTC to become more activist.

INSTITUTIONS AND PROCEDURES

The rise of the Fair Trade Commission

The Fair Trade Commission is unique in Japan as an independent regulatory body modelled on the Federal Trade Commission (FTC) of the United States. It is exclusively responsible for the enforcement of the Act. Independence in exercising its power to enforce the Act is its most significant institutional characteristic. However, the actual independence has been ambivalent and ambiguous. While the USA has a dual enforcement system, involving the Department of Justice (DOJ) and the FTC, the JFTC is the sole administrative body responsible for enforcing competition law.

The main enforcement measure is an administrative decree ordered after a quasi-adversary procedure. This quasi-judicial power of the JFTC is the basis for its independence. The JFTC has a quasi-legislative and administrative power as does the FTC in the USA. The actual difference between the JFTC and the United States FTC rests in fewer formal decisions and a heavy dependence on informal measures, such as warnings or advance consultations under published guidelines.

In evaluating enforcement the role of the JFTC is central. The way in which the institution chooses to define its role will dictate the degree to which latent powers become actual. The JFTC has become more activist, more confident, more visible, and more respected over the past ten years, but it is still a small and very cautious institution. It has enjoyed a significant increase in personnel, which contrasts starkly with the cutbacks elsewhere in the Japanese bureaucracy. It plumbed a low point of 237 staff in 1958, but had reached 461 in 1989, and its current staffing is 494, reflecting a significant increase in the Investigation Department. This compares favourably with European competition authorities if not with those of the USA. It is attached to the Prime Minister's Office but, in Japan's political system, this does not confer particular advantage. Two of its striking characteristics concern the nature of the Commissioners and the way in which it forms links with other ministries.

The Fair Trade Commissioners are not independent business people or academics but have always been appointed by the Prime Minister from the ranks of retired bureaucrats. Scrutiny of appointments by the Diet has been a formality. In a system dominated by the bureaucracy this may be advantageous, but Commissioners have brought with them the attitudes and caution generated by a successful career in the Japanese 'establishment'. More importantly, they have also brought the interests and attitudes of their former ministries. In a pattern typical of Japan, the Commissioner posts have been shared out among the leading interested ministries. The key post of chairman is the territory of the Ministry of Finance (MOF), which has provided every chairman since 1963. Setsuo Imezawa, who retired in August 1992, was former Director-General of the National Tax Administration. His successor, Masami Kogayu, was the former Vice-Minister of MOF, the fourth Vice-Minister to hold the post. As the leading official of MOF the Vice-Minister is possibly the most senior civil servant in Japan; thus Mr Kogayu comes with a formidable pedigree.

The four other Commission posts are shared out. Commissioners serve for five years, and one always comes from MITI; a second from the Ministry of Justice; while the third and fourth Commissioners will come from one of the MOF, the Ministry of Foreign Affairs (MOFA), or the JFTC itself. The denial that the Commissioners consider the interests of their parent ministries lacks plausibility. It is, for instance, frequently alleged and widely believed that the relaxed application of the anti-monopoly laws in the fields of banking and securities is due to the dominance of the MOF at the JFTC. Thus, in practice, the constitution of the JFTC has been an actual impediment to the active enforcement of the Act.

The Executive Office is composed of professional bureaucrats with very few exceptions. Most have been working exclusively for the JFTC. This exclusive membership is conducive to active enforcement and independence. However, bureaucrats from other ministries, mainly the MOF, usually occupy one of the Director of Bureau posts or several division-chief posts. The Chief of the Planning Section of the Secretariat, the General Staff for the JFTC, has been occupied exclusively and continuously by bureaucrats from the MOF. Similarly, some JFTC staff spend periods on secondment with other Ministries such as MITI and Justice. Such interface with other ministries has contributed to the establishment of

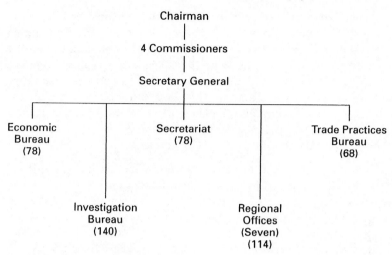

Chairman
|
4 Commissioners
|
Secretary General
|

Economic Bureau (78) | Secretariat (78) | Trade Practices Bureau (68)

Investigation Bureau (140) | Regional Offices (Seven) (114)

Note: staff numbers in parentheses.
Source: H. Iyori and A. Uesugi, *The Antimonopoly Laws and Policies of Japan* (New York: Federal Legal Publications Inc., 1994), 205. Position as at Dec. 1992.

Fɪɢ. 5.1 Organization of the Fair Trade Commission

smooth relations but has been a significant element in the constraint on active enforcement of competition policy. Figure 5.1
gives an organization chart for the JFTC. There is a substantial
framework of seven regional offices and a large secretariat to handle
the complex but crucial issues of relations with other ministries,
the LDP, and business groups. The big staff expansion has come
in the Investigation Bureau. Unlike some other competition authorities, such as DG IV and the Bundeskartellamt, the investigation staff are not organized in sectoral groupings. Instead teams
are assembled according to staff availability and may handle a
great variety of work. This could have the virtue of avoiding
sectoral capture, especially since the teams will be making recommendations about informal enforcement measures to their Bureau
Director-General and to the Commissioners.

As part of its administrative powers the JFTC has extensive
powers of investigation. In addition, it has the duty to receive and
approve various reports filed with the JFTC, to authorize depression cartels, to approve stock holdings by a financial company,
and to consult with other ministries.

The formal requirement to consult, and be consulted by, other ministries is most important. It ensures that the JFTC is integrated into the fabric of government and gives it the potential to become a core economic-policy agency. The consultation process keeps the JFTC abreast of current developments and provides a wide range of contacts and a vast amount of information. To this extent the JFTC is a highly competent player in policy-making and cannot be ignored. It is therefore useful to examine these formal inter-ministerial contacts in detail. They require:

- advance notification and consultation in cases where the JFTC takes a step against monopolistic situations;
- advance consultation with the relevant ministry on the approval of exemptions that are under the JFTC's jurisdiction;
- acceptance of advance notification or advance consultation with the relevant ministry on the approval of exemptions falling under the jurisdiction of other ministries;
- advance consultation with the relevant ministry concerning exemption clauses in any bill prepared by the ministry.

The JFTC has no authorization to participate in a regulatory process that is under the jurisdiction of other ministries. However, it has been engaging actively in the preparation and publication of recommendations on regulatory reform, an area which is earning increasing respect from other ministries. Informal adjustment with other ministries has often been resorted to concerning informal, regulatory measures taken by them, such as intervention in industries through administrative guidance. There have been several cases where MITI has withheld its administrative guidance at the request of the JFTC, especially in situations aimed at the reorganization of certain industries, such as the creation of joint selling companies. Indeed, the 1994 Administrative Procedures Act has made the job of the JFTC easier by restricting the operation of administrative guidance. Traditionally the JFTC found it difficult to act against cartels which claimed that their co-ordinated action was prompted by administrative guidance from another Ministry. This defence will now be far more difficult to use, and it has been possible for the JFTC to issue guidelines for administrative guidance, in June 1994. The guidelines confirm that actions which would normally violate the AML will still be regarded as illegal even if precipitated by administrative guidance. They give a series of illustrations which include market sharing. Interestingly, this would include imports. Thus, if a Ministry sets an import target for foreign products, this, *prima facie*, would be in breach of the Act and the Guidelines.

As a quasi-legislative agency, the FTC has rule-making power to designate commodities for which resale price maintenance is permissible, and to define unfair business practices. In fact, the whole process of defining and promulgating guidelines has a quasi-legislative tone. It also establishes the procedures for handling cases brought before it and determines the form of reports required to be filed with the JFTC. As a quasi-judicial power, the Act provides the procedures to be followed by the FTC when handling cases, and it issues decisions after a hearings procedure. Unusually, appeals against JFTC decisions go directly and exclusively to the Tokyo High Court, which provides full judicial review.

A combination of factors has raised the salience and prestige of the JFTC and has allowed it to deploy its latent powers more effectively. It has found new friends, among consumers, among internationally orientated business leaders, and within MITI itself. This has been reflected in its resources and staffing. Indeed, Mr Hashimoto, the Minister of International Trade and Industry in 1994, was actually quoted as saying that 'The FTC is too poor in both organization and staff.'[23] As we see below, however, the relative influence of the JFTC remains fragile. The move towards deregulation contains threats for regulatory agencies.

Procedural issues

The JFTC will conduct investigations, hold hearings, and issue a cease and desist order if it finds a violation of the Act. The administrative procedure is: (*a*) preliminary investigation; (*b*) compulsory investigation; (*c*) recommendation to the respondent; (*d*) if the recommendation is rejected, the issuance of a complaint; (*e*) trial-type hearing and formal decision.

(*a*) Preliminary Investigation. The Investigation Bureau engages in a preliminary investigation, either upon a complaint from entrepreneurs or other interested parties, or upon its own initiative. Any person may request the FTC to institute an investigation. Around 1,000 complaints a year are received, many trivial, some very serious. There has been no great increase in complaints and there is no significant backlog. Although a special section and procedure has been established to facilitate complaints from foreign companies it has barely been used.

(b) Compulsory Investigation. In cases where there are grounds to believe that a violation of the Act may have occurred, after a preliminary investigation, the JFTC is empowered to take compulsory measures. These include orders to give testimony, to produce documentary evidence or expert testimony, entering any place of business, and inspecting said business operations and property, financial records, documents, and other materials. Normally, it is the investigators designated by the JFTC who actually take these steps. The majority of evidence showing a violation is obtained by utilizing these investigatory powers, especially by ordering the submission of documents found at the place of inspection.

In many cases, however, inadequate proof is discovered. Table 5.1 indicates that the majority of cases are discharged through informal means. Thus in 1992 there were 143 'warnings' or 'cautions', 10 recommendations, and only one complaint leading to a hearing.

(c) Recommendation System. When the FTC finds that there exists a violation of the Act, it can recommend that the party concerned take appropriate remedial measures, as specified by the JFTC. When the recommendation is accepted, the JFTC will issue a decision of the same content as the recommendation. If rejected, or if no notice from the party has been filed, the JFTC will (d) issue a complaint against the party and open a formal hearing procedure.

(e) Formal Hearing Procedure. The JFTC may conduct a hearing, but usually hearing examiners are designated for this purpose. Normally, a tribunal of three examiners is formed for each case. The examiners hold their posts as part of their career as JFTC Staff Office bureaucrats and are not professional lawyers. This is in contrast to the hearing examiner in the FTC in the United States, who is usually selected from among professional judges. While the hearing by the JFTC Commissioners is prescribed in the Act, the JFTC usually approves the initial decision prepared by examiners and accepts it as a formal decision.

Hearings are open to the public except for cases where protection of trade secrets is necessary. The finding of fact in the formal decision should be based on substantial evidence which is examined at the hearing procedure. In this hearing procedure, designated investigators, usually members of Investigation Bureau, act like public prosecutors, and respondents are given the chance to rebut the complaint or provide a defence. Details of the hearing procedure are prescribed in the Act. They resemble adversary procedures before the court and are prescribed to ensure fairness. Such quasi-adversary procedures are one of the most important foundations for the independence of the JFTC.

These administrative procedures form the main avenues of enforcement. As noted above, both criminal and civil procedures are also available in law but, although there has been a recent surge of interest in these, they have traditionally been virtually moribund.

MEANS OF ENFORCEMENT

The jurisdiction of the JFTC is very wide, including virtually all the conventional competition policy areas. It includes control of monopolies, mergers, vertical restraints, oligopolistic structures, and retail price maintenance. In some areas Japan has distinctive provisions, especially in relation to control of abuse of subcontractors, registration and control of trade associations, and provisions to control large conglomerate groups. The most famous provision is, of course, section 9 of the AML, which exercises a permanent and absolute prohibition on holding companies.

Many of these provisions are enforced through reporting and filing requirements, and through surveys of industrial structure. The extent of filing requirements is very substantial. The JFTC receives literally thousands of reports per year in relation to areas like technology agreements, trade associations, cross-shareholdings, and treatment of subcontractors. Among these reports is a system of mandatory pre-merger notification; Japan was the first country in the world to introduce this system, in 1947. Rather than attempt a comprehensive survey here, the position regarding cartels is examined, drawing a centrally important distinction between formal and informal modes of enforcement.

Formal sanctions against cartels

The basic measure provided in the Act against violation is an elimination measure, a cease and desist order, ordered by a formal decision. In addition, the surcharge on cartel members, preventive administration through guidelines and corrective guidance, and resort to adverse publicity are characteristic methods used for antitrust enforcement in Japan. The surcharge was enacted in the 1977 amendments. Before the amendments, regulation of cartels through the Antimonopoly Act had been futile. The main measure against cartels was, and still is, a cease and desist order, even though there are still few formal actions (see Table 5.1). This order requires members of cartels to enter into an agreement to dismantle the cartel. However, this is, in effect, simply a ceremony and cartel prices seldom fall. Responding to public discontent over the ineffectiveness of this measure, the JFTC originally proposed that price roll-back orders be introduced. The roll-back order was not adopted in the 1977 bill because most economists objected to it. Instead, a surcharge was proposed as an economic disincentive to cartel members.

The Antimonopoly and Fair Trade Law also provides for other preventive sanctions against cartels, namely, criminal prosecutions and actions for civil damages. As noted above, both these measures have been ineffective in Japan. Civil actions for damages have been even less effective than criminal sanctions. Very few individuals choose to litigate because personal damages are usually nominal. Those individual cases that are brought are usually policy oriented and can only be maintained because of financial support from consumer organizations and lawyers who volunteer their services. With the exception of one unexpected victory by a consumer group in a 1985 Sendai High Court decision, most civil actions against cartels have been unsuccessful. The courts are prone to interpret the law strictly, and this is a major obstacle to litigants as it is extremely difficult conclusively to prove the necessary degree of proximate causation between illegal cartels and price levels during cartel periods.

With such ineffective sanctions, businesses readily repeated their violations of the Antimonopoly Law. From 1973 to 1975 almost half of the recommendations were against repeated violations. In two years, 1973 and 1974, one big company was the respondent in seven recommendations and two companies were the respondents in six recommendations. Thus, the surcharge system was introduced by the 1977 amendment. A surcharge was imposed to improve this situation and to provide an effective means of preventing the activities of cartels. The rate of the surcharge was, until the 1990 amendment, in principle 1.5 per cent of sales during the cartel period of items subject to the cartel. This was raised to 6 per cent in the 1990 amendment, although the new rate only applied to cartel activities effected after July 1991; the deterrent effect should be measured from fiscal 1991 onwards.

The surcharge rate was criticized as being too low in the case of aggressive cartels, but it has since proven to be effective. It sometimes results in the exaction of huge sums (see Table 5.1). The surcharges in the 1981 paper mill case were 1.17 billion yen (£7.3 million),[24] the highest levied until the 1990–1 cement cartel cases. There followed a decline in recommendations against cartels, prompted by more cautious enforcement and by difficulty in proving cases in the presence of such severe sanctions. However, the actual number of illegal cartels may also have declined. After 1977 repeated cartels were not found until the cement cartel against which swingeing fines were imposed in fiscal 1990. Eight firms in Chugoku District were surcharged 6.62 billion yen and cement companies in total paid 11.2 billion yen (approximately £70 million). The total in fiscal 1993 was 4,087 million yen, the second highest ever.

Enforcement through informal measures

The JFTC has been dealing efficiently with many investigations, but there have been relatively few formal proceedings. There have also been few recommendations, although informal warnings against violators have been issued frequently. Such warnings have been used in order to avoid the difficulty of proving violations. Alleged violators seldom dispute these warnings because of the advantage of avoiding formal sanctions such as the surcharge.

Resort to informal procedures has been one of the characteristics of Japanese antitrust enforcement. Informal enforcement is not uncommon in other countries, but the JFTC seems to resort to informal procedures much more than is the case elsewhere. One reason for this attitude has been the business community's opposition to the Antimonopoly Law. As a result, the JFTC has been careful not to resort to formal sanctions quickly.

Over the last fifteen years the JFTC has developed a sophisticated approach to informal enforcement which is adapted to the Japanese environment and may be a more effective approach than adversarial measures. It is an approach orientated towards encouraging compliance and has been called, by Iyori and Uesugi, the 'preventative law approach'. 'Under this approach, the FTC announced various guidelines and took measures to secure compliance with them, instead of stressing remedial measures against those who had violated the law.'[25] Guidelines should therefore be taken far more seriously in Japan than in Europe (or certainly the UK). The basic premiss is that if anything breaches the guidelines it is illegal, and as guidelines are developed, refined, and tightened, so the stringency of the law can be gradually increased. Guidelines are widely publicized and conscientiously observed (at least formally), so much so that the main systems encourage 'prior consultation', in which firms can apply for a negative clearance, which provides, of course, a point at which officials can use their discretion to negotiate informal compliance. Guidelines have achieved a recognizable impact on anti-monopoly enforcement only since 1980, but are now the FTC's main policy instrument.

A number of guidelines were issued between 1979 and 1981. Most of them have been reviewed and strengthened over the last five years. Several new guidelines have been issued (see list below). This very substantial area of 'soft law' is quite strictly controlled by JFTC officials, and most doubtful acts are not approved. The stringent attitude adopted by JFTC bureaucrats has been criticized as going too far. Two examples illustrate the extent of enforcement activity.

August	1979	Guideline on Trade Association Activities—revised September 1994
July	1980	Merger Guideline—revised August 1994
July	1981	Retail Merger Guideline
Sept.	1981	Stockholding Guideline—revised August 1994
April	1987	Unjust Return of Unsold Goods Guideline
Feb.	1989	Patent and Know-how Licensing Guidelines
July	1991	Distribution Systems and Business Practices Guidelines
April	1993	Joint Research and Development Guidelines
June	1994	Guidelines on Stockholding by Financial Companies

| June | 1994 | Guidelines on Administrative Guidance (supersedes Memorandum of March 1981) |
| July | 1994 | Guidelines Concerning the Activities of Firms and Trade Associations in Relation to Public Bids |

The first example concerns the area of concentration of economic powers where formal actions have been very rare. In the case of mergers the JFTC in fact has extensive informal involvement, which was defined in the 1980 Guidelines, which have just been updated and clarified. Merger activity has increased very substantially since 1989, and the new guidelines establish *de minimis* standards and indicate a market share of over 25 per cent as meriting intensive scrutiny. In all cases, however, mandatory pre-notification still applies which allows JFTC officials to require adjustments to be made as a condition for approving the merger. This process is fairly effective, as indicated in the Oji Paper case. In July 1993 the JFTC advised the Oji Paper Mill Company, the leader in the industry, to dispose of part of its capacity to certain competitors in order to reduce its market share to acceptable proportions following the proposed merger with Kanzaki Paper. There were several other suggested amendments which were accepted by the merging companies and the merger was approved.

A second example is provided by trade associations. In Japan trade associations are ubiquitous and powerful. They are often actively involved in co-ordinating the activities of member companies, with many possibilities for breach of the AML. For this reason trade associations are controlled under section 8 of the Act. They must register with the JFTC and their constitution and activities are strictly but informally controlled through the Guidelines. Thus, in 1992, the JFTC examined 808 cases in which the legality of trade association activities was called into question. It found in 34 per cent of these cases that there was a clear violation and the activities were abandoned or modified.[26] Here an intense area of enforcement exists which is not reflected in statistics of formal decisions.

Since the 1977 amendments, businesses have been more seriously concerned about antitrust enforcement than before. According to a survey, antitrust law is the second most important issue dealt with by the legal sections of big companies. Public expectations regarding the Antimonopoly and Fair Trade Law are more wide-spread than before, and there has recently been an increase in complaints of violations by the public to the JFTC. After the 1990 amendment and 1991 publication of the Distribution and Business Practices Guidelines, many firms prepared their compliance programme to avoid anti-monopoly violation. According to a 1993 survey, around 40 per cent of listed companies that answered to the survey had compliance programmes, and around 15 per cent of these companies are preparing or going to prepare compliance programmes. Thus, voluntary compliance by firms has become much more significant.

In recent antitrust history the surcharge and, increasingly, administrative guidance have been effective measures in exacting industry compliance. While the less formal approach has sometimes been necessary in the face of adverse circumstances, it has also been an effective technique in the aggressive enforcement of antitrust law.

CONCLUSION

The salience and effectiveness of competition policy in Japan has changed quite radically over the past ten years. This so-called 'renaissance' of policy has taken place in response to overseas pressure and to changes in the domestic economy. While the Fair Trade Commission was never quite as marginalized and insignificant as foreign observers suggested, it has certainly become a more prestigious actor over the recent past. It is still not an economic policy-making agency, but it is now taken seriously by the economic policy-makers in government, MITI, and business.

The increased importance of competition policy has arisen largely from *gaiatsu* from the United States, with Europe riding on American coat-tails. To this extent more active Japanese competition policy has been a reflection of economic diplomacy and has therefore been more vulnerable, more superficial, and more eccentrically biased than if pressures had come from deeper-seated domestic sources. It could, though, now be argued that foreign pressure is being replaced by a genuine domestic support for active competition law enforcement. Symbolically, the JFTC offices in Tokyo have just moved from a drab Annex of the Ministry of Foreign Affairs Building to a new, spacious government building next to the Ministry of Justice.

Of course, foreign pressure continues. The 1994 ACCJ White Paper continues to argue that 'the JFTC could play a more positive and proactive role' and, of its fourteen recurrent issues, items 1 and 2 concern the 'lack of access to *keiretsu*' and the 'failure to enforce existing anti-monopoly laws' respectively.[27] Of greater current importance, however, is the domestic debate over deregulation.

Substantial elements within internationally competitive industry have begun to argue for genuine deregulation in Japan to cut costs and liberate consumers. MITI has moved its policy stance dramatically in favour of deregulation and is now engaged in confrontation with the more traditional regulatory industries (such as Transport and Construction). Deregulation is now at the heart of the domestic Japanese debate on economic and industrial policy. This might be regarded as good news for the JFTC, which is certainly in favour of more competition, but, in fact, the portents are threatening.[28]

For parts of industry, and for MITI, 'deregulation' should include a reduction in regulation by the JFTC. It appears that no distinction is made between regulation 'to create' the market (the role of the JFTC); and regulation 'within' the market (detailed intervention by regulatory ministries). Thus the climate became more hostile to the JFTC under the coalition government of Tomiichi Murayama. In the closing days of the Hosokawa coalition, in March 1994, a Cabinet decision on External Economic Reform included very strong support for expanding and strenthening the enforcement activities of the JFTC. In contrast, the famous 279 deregulatory measures issued by the Administrative Reform Headquarters in June 1994 at the very beginning of the Murayama coalition were more threatening for the JFTC. These proposals were planned to form the basis for a five-year deregulation programme to be initiated in Spring 1995. Lip-service was paid to the 'active implementation of competition policy',[29] but the aim of the measures is to improve the environment for the restructuring of companies. As part of this there appears the following extremely unwelcome proposal: 'appropriate implementation will be pursued for the system controlling stock-holding companies . . . with a view to making the Japanese market more open as well as stimulating business activities of entrepreneurs'.[30] A literal translation of this anodyne formulation is 'we intend to abolish the prohibition on holding companies'. This would be regarded as absolutely disastrous and demoralizing by the JFTC, and to be headed off by all possible means. It is a proposal backed by many businesses who are resentful of this distinctive restriction. MITI is also in favour of the proposal which would have the knock-on effect of requiring wide changes in a number of laws (such as the commercial code and corporate tax legislation). Most dangerous, however, is that foreign business interests might support the legalization of holding companies, reasoning that this would facilitate their own market entry. The JFTC regard section 9 of the Antimonopoly Act as the core of their credibility. The threat to repeal the Act is potent, and economic policy-makers can use it to constrain JFTC activism.

Although anti-monopoly enforcement has become fairly active in Japan, its extent has always been determined by the balance struck between well-defined forces for and against it. Recently this traditional conflict has softened. Japanese industries having developed to a point where they no longer require protection, MITI now refrains from naked forms of protectionist intervention. Currently MITI explains industrial policy as being a means to promote future competitiveness. This rationale brings industrial policy and anti-monopoly enforcement into greater harmony, in theory at least. To maintain this harmony the JFTC has relaxed enforcement to a greater degree than accommodation to its opponents perhaps requires. Many cartel cases are being settled informally, without imposition of surcharges. Industrial policy and anti-monopoly enforcement have struck a new and quite different balance. It may now be said that anti-monopoly enforcement is accepted as a child of the family of economic policy in Japan.

Institutionally, the JFTC has an independent role in exercising its power to enforce the Act, but its actual value as a deterrent to restrictive practices has not been enough to prevent these illegal practices from being instituted. In reality, various factors constrain the active enforcement of the Antimonopoly Act by the JFTC. In such a tenuous position, dependence on informal measures and regulation through persuasion will prove to be better alternatives for the enforcement of competition policy.

NOTES

1. *Act Concerning Prohibition of Private Monopoly and Maintenence of Fair Trade*, Act no. 54 (Apr. 1947).

The FTC and Competition Policy in Japan   137

2. For a discussion of these factors see Stephen Wilks, *The Revival of Japanese Competition Policy and its Importance for EU–Japan Relations*, preface by Kenji Sanekata (London: Royal Institute of International Affairs; Japan Institute of International Affairs, 1994).

3. Hiroshi Iyori and Akinori Uesugi, *The Antimonopoly Laws and Policies of Japan* (New York: Federal Legal Publications Inc., 1994).

4. Mutsuo Matsushita, *International Trade and Competition Law in Japan* (Oxford: Oxford University Press, 1993).

5. See especially the work by Kotaro Suzumura, e.g. 'Exemption Systems from Antimonopoly Law and Other Anti-Competitive Measures in Japan: Overview and Evaluation', Revised Draft (Nov. 1993), Hitotsubashi University; and *Competition, Commitment and Welfare* (Oxford: Oxford University Press, 1995).

6. Tokutaro Imogawa, 'Is the Fair Trade Watchdog Finally Learning to Bite?', *Tokyo Business Today*, Apr. 1993, 22–4.

7. See e.g. Marc Eisner, *Regulatory Politics in Transition* (Baltimore: Johns Hopkins Press, 1993), ch. 2; or Iyori and Uesugi, *The Antimonopoly Laws*, 17. The classic text on origins is Eleanor Hadley, *Antitrust in Japan* (Princeton, NJ: Princeton University Press, 1970).

8. A lot of attention was attracted to the oil cartel case. See Kenji Sanekata, 'Administrative Guidance and Antimonopoly Law', *Law in Japan*, 10 (1977), and the other contributions to that volume.

9. For background see Richard Boyd and Seiichi Nagamori, 'Industrial Policy Making in Practice: Electoral, Diplomatic and Other Adjustments to Crisis in the Japanese Shipbuilding Industry', in S. Wilks and M. Wright (eds.), *The Promotion and Regulation of Industry in Japan* (London: Macmillan, 1991).

10. *Structural Impediments Initiative, Final Report*, June 1990, section 4, II, I.

11. American Chamber of Commerce in Japan, *United States–Japan Trade White Paper, 1989* (Tokyo: ACCJ, 1989). The ACCJ is a significant lobbying group and has given evidence to several JFTC specialist study groups.

12. For more measured treatments see the chapters by Aoki and by Koike in Masahiko Aoki and Ronald Dore (eds.), *The Japanese Firm: The Sources of Competitive Strength* (Oxford: Oxford University Press, 1994.

13. See the FTC English-language publication, *FTC/Japan Views*, 17 (Feb. 1994), 11–12.

14. 'Zoku' politicians are those Diet members, mainly from the LDP, who take a specialist interest in a given policy area.

15. See e.g. Robert Cutts, 'The Construction Market: Japan Slams the Door', *California Management Review*, 30/4 (summer 1988); John Macmillan, 'Dango: Japan's Price Fixing Conspiracies', *Economics*

and Politics, 3 (Nov. 1991); and the recent *Antimonopoly Act Guidelines Concerning the Activities of Firms and Trade Associations in Relation to Public Bids* (Tokyo: Fair Trade Commission, tentative trans. 5 July 1994).

16. See *Nikkei Weekly*, 7 Nov. 1994, 7.
17. For details see Iyori and Uesugi, *The Antimonopoly Laws*, 88–93.
18. See Wilks, *The Revival of Japanese Competition Policy*, 14–16.
19. See Iyori and Uesugi, *The Antimonopoly Laws*, 246.
20. Fair Trade Commission, *The FTC's policy on Criminal Accusation Regarding Antimonopoly Act Violation*, 20 June 1990.
21. J. Mark Ramseyer, 'The Costs of the Consensual Myth: Antitrust Enforcement and Institutional Barriers to Litigation in Japan', *Yale Law Journal*, 94/1–3 (1984–5), 604–45, 617.
22. Hiroshi Fukunaga and Kyoko Chinone, 'Taking on the System', *Tokyo Business Today*, May 1994, 11.
23. *Nikkei Weekly*, 1 Aug. 1994, 2; see also interview with Mr Kogayu in *Nikkei Weekly*, 7 Nov. 1994, 2.
24. Converting at Y160 = £1.
25. Iyori and Uesugi, *The Antimonopoly Laws*, 56.
26. Details from FTC Annual Reports, various issues (in Japanese).
27. American Chamber of Commerce in Japan, *United States–Japan Trade White Paper 1993: 1994 Update Working Draft* (Tokyo: ACCJ, 1994), 3, 81.
28. See Atsushi Ishinabe, 'FTC Weak but Coalition May Come Up with Help', *Nikkei Weekly*, 1 Aug. 1994, 2.
29. Administrative Reform Promotion Headquarters, *Regarding the Policy for Promoting Deregulation Hereafter* (Tokyo, provisional trans., mimeo, 28 June 1994), 4, para. 2.3.
30. Ibid., 4, para. 2.3.

6

The Prolonged Reform of United Kingdom Competition Policy

STEPHEN WILKS

INTRODUCTION

Although lawyers can happily trace common-law competition doctrines back to Magna Carta,[1] it took Britain a long time to enact specific laws and erect administrative machinery to pursue a competition policy. The first British legislation, in 1948, followed Canada (1889), the USA (1890), and Japan (1947), which none the less makes it one of the first European countries to formulate a competition policy. The responsible Minister recently observed that 'I believe the UK has a more transparent and rigorously enforced system of competition policy than countries such as Japan and France, and one which is about on a par with the USA and Germany'.[2]

Notwithstanding these ministerial beliefs, since 1948 British policy and legislation has developed in a fashion that is sporadic, haphazard, sometimes contradictory, and increasingly complex. The breadth of the legislation and the range of institutions has evolved to the point where systematic reform is well overdue. The history indicates substantial elements of continuity in British policy and institutions and therefore renders this policy area distinctive. In many other areas of industry-related policy, government initiatives have been radical, comprehensive, and short lived. One thinks of areas such as training, prices and incomes, regional policy, or industrial policy itself. Competition policy has not excited such

The author gratefully acknowledges the assistance of officials in the OFT, MMC, DTI, and CBI. The chapter has benefited materially from detailed comments by senior officials and academics, including especially Professors Richard Whish and Rob Merkin. Research for this chapter was generously supported by the Economic and Social Research Council under award R00023903.

passions. It has been bi-partisan, relatively uncontroversial, influenced by technical arguments, and incremental in its development.

Competition policy is certainly complex and by now the level of legal sophistication has reached a point which inhibits the layperson and even the non-specialist lawyer. But complexity is not a sufficient answer for low political salience: there is a more profound strain of ambiguity running through competition policy and the British reception of it. In virtually every area of industrial politics there are arguments both for and against an activist competition policy. There is not therefore the overwhelming political pressure for reform which could force ministers to act. This is despite the fact that currently every significant interest from consumers to the CBI, and including the competition authorities, accept the need for reforms. Equally they accept the government's fully formulated proposals in the White Paper on Restrictive Trade Practices,[3] and a majority accept the Green Paper Proposals on Monopoly Control.[4] The government is fully committed to the introduction of new legislation but is as yet unable or unwilling to proceed, due, allegedly, to a lack of parliamentary time. Many fear that competition policy reform has 'missed the boat', that legislation is now unlikely in this Parliament (which should run to 1996–7), and that with increased delay a further review of the proposals might introduce further uncertainty and yet another set of legislative proposals, perhaps from a future Labour government. In melodramatically purple prose *The Economist* expressed the discontent that also provides the organizing theme for this chapter. It observed that members of the Trade and Industry Committee, hearing evidence in March 1995, 'found themselves listening to one long scream of rage. Those testifying before the committee have unleashed a barrage of criticism at the country's competition laws and regulatory bodies.'[5]

The current British reluctance to legislate has serious implications for the processes of international convergence of competition policy systems. Retention of a distinctive British system perpetuates some distinct incompatibilities. Most obviously the retention of a pragmatic, politically dominated system of public-interest tests and discretionary undertakings maintains a British exceptionalism. Whether this failure to legislate heralds a laxer or a more stringent regime is another question to which we return below. Under the present government and present ministers a more permissive regime is being applied.

THE HISTORICAL LEGACY

It is an historical curiosity that the country which originated much of the practice and the theory of markets and competition should also harbour such ambivalent views of the virtues of competition. Within business, competition was long moderated and controlled through family businesses, freedom to make restrictive contracts, and norms of self-regulation. Although British business will trumpet the virtues of unfettered competition, the pursuit of market closure is equally congenial in British industrial culture. Within society at large Britain has never experienced the populism and principled criticism of big business that generated US antitrust, and which has been a constant refrain in over one hundred years of US politics. From Louis Brandeis to Ralph Nader, US corporations have had to face challenges on their own terms, from critics who accept the capitalist system, but pursue rigorous control of monopoly on the grounds that political democracy necessitates some degree of economic democracy. The British critics have not been populists, they have been socialists, and have therefore challenged the system as much as the corporations. British criticism of industrial concentration has been provoked during each merger boom, it came to dominate Labour industrial policy-making in the late sixties (with proposals for 'planning agreements'), and still has echoes in Labour policy-making.[6] For the most part, however, criticism of monopoly and 'big business' has come from outside the free-market establishment. It has been revolutionary rather than reformist and has pressed for radical solutions of nationalization, planning, and industrial democracy rather than reformist measures of an assertive competition policy. British competition policy has therefore been insulated from adversarial party-political debate and has evolved in a moderate, pragmatic fashion, relying on co-operation from industry and an administrative reasonableness rather than radicalism and an adversarial approach.

Half a century of permissive legal practice was heralded by the *Mogul Steamship* case of 1892, which limited the impact of the common-law restraint of trade doctrine and declared 'that one may do anything to get rid of a business rival provided that one does not commit a well defined tort'.[7] British business pursued methods of stable co-operation, combination and self-regulation through private coercion, negotiation, and compromise.[8] Although superficially similar to German permissiveness the British position was based on the individual's absolute right to contract, rather than the conscious suppression of competition in the national interest, and hence on a quite dissimilar conception of the public good.[9] English law remained a void on monopolistic practices until the 1940s, prompting an acidic American commentator to observe that under English Law 'Economic mayhem was tolerated if it was motivated by avarice, but not if it was motivated by spite'.[10] Against this legal background family-owned enterprises could survive in a cocoon of supportive agreements, and it is widely argued that the move to managerially dominated, multi-divisional enterprises on the US model was retarded.

The battle to reintroduce real competition into the British industrial economy was waged within government during 1943–4. The inspiration for the 1948 Monopolies Act, and the 1956 Restrictive Trade Practices Act, is widely taken to be a memorandum written by two temporary civil servants in the Board of Trade, Hugh Gaitskell and G. K. Allen, in 1943. Their paper *The Control of Monopoly* represented, says Freyer, 'a turning point in the British Government's approach to the monopoly problem'.[11] Although legislation was slow to come, elements of the memorandum featured in the 1944 White Paper on Employment and in the Beveridge Report. But curiously, the deciding factor in the move towards control of monopoly was full employment. Gaitskell and Allen 'argued that the growth of market power which had occurred was incompatible with postwar full employment because of its adverse effects on efficiency, costs, the demand for labour, new enterprise, and the distribution of income'.[12] Thus the origins of British competition policy had more to do with the pragmatic pursuit of policy goals than with the purity of economic doctrine or the righting of social injustice. The nature of the debate and the policy solutions selected are important. For the next fifty years the idiosyncratic law and pragmatic implementation of UK competition policy continued to reflect the principles of the Gaitskell/Allen memorandum.

As policy has developed over the post-war period, several key choices have been made about policy design which have influenced the way policy has operated and have become tacit, widely accepted norms which have given British policy its characteristic colouration. There have been four main areas of choice:

1. between public and private enforcement
2. between a form-based system and an effects-based system
3. between administrative action and judicial action
4. between informal and formal approaches

In the 1948 legislation the initial choice was made of an administrative system. Debate within the Board of Trade during 1944 argued that the proposed Commission should 'avoid legalistic procedure'[13] and proceed in an informal fashion to discuss the public interest. This judgemental approach, wary of law and rejecting the adversarial implications of a judicial avenue, was wholly in keeping with British practice. It envisaged a pattern of informal negotiation and self-regulation on the part of industry which Vogel's excellent study has identified as an abiding feature of British industrial regulation.[14] Consistent with this approach, the 1948 Act embodied virtually no sanctions (as can be said of current arrangements). Politicians were confident that publicity alone would induce improvement on the grounds that British industries were 'more amenable to Government persuasion than perhaps was the case in America'.[15] Initial approaches were therefore biased towards a model that was public, effects based, administrative, and informal.

The 1956 Restrictive Trade Practices Act brought a volte-face. Acting, apparently, under pressure from business, which had found the Monopolies Commission too slow and unpredictable,[16] the government made a series of alternative choices. Although it continued to opt for public action, the restrictive practices legislation was formal, with registration of agreements; took the form of a judicial system, with a new Court and procedure; and was form based, orientated towards the form of agreement rather than its effect. Although the Commission was retained it became inactive. From 1958–65 it produced only six reports,[17] and only became active again when attention turned to monopoly investigations in the mid-1960s. A major step was taken in 1965 when the Labour government introduced merger control using the same machinery and the same public-interest test as with monopolies control. By the end of the 1960s, therefore, the British 'twin' system was in place.

The early 1970s brought a greatly strengthened administrative system. The 1973 Fair Trading Act ushered in a 'silent revolution',

TABLE 6.1. *Principles of UK competition policy*

	Restrictive trade practices	Monopolies and mergers
action	public and private	public
control	form based	effects based
evaluation	judicial	administrative
mode	formal	informal
status	influential but limited activity	active and dominant
reform proposed	Cm 727; article 85-type effects-based prohibition	Cm 2100; strengthen existing legislation

a 'policy metamorphosis'.[18] The creation of an independent agency emphasized the discretion of the new DGFT (Director General of Fair Trading) and an informal process of bargaining and judgement in relation to monopoly and partially to restrictive practices. Effects were emphasized at the expense of form and the Restrictive Practices Court continued the pattern established in the early sixties of relative disuse with very few significant cases.[19] O'Brien's explanation for this change of emphasis again stresses business influence. He suggests that industrialists had become thoroughly disillusioned by the adversary legal process in the Court. That 'forensic fun', 'which to a non-lawyer looks very much like bullying and intimidation',[20] had persuaded firms to go to extreme lengths to avoid the Court. In the majority of sectors British industry extensively decartelized during the 1960s.

Current law and practice therefore embraces two sets of principles which can be outlined as in Table 6.1. This coexistence of principles has produced a complex, untidy system which is frustrating to administer and which does not lend itself to effective compliance.

GOALS, LEGISLATION, AND INSTITUTIONS

There is a recent, and not wholly facetious, definition of industrial policy in Japan as being 'whatever MITI does'.[21] There is a close and analytically important relationship between policy, institutions, and legislation which is well-illustrated by the extreme example of MITI (Ministry of International Trade and Industry). Perhaps, though, a similar argument could be made for Directorate General IV (DG IV); the Bundeskartellamt (BKA), and the OFT? Namely, that through a combination of intellectual leadership, administrative competence, political legitimacy, and longevity they have come to define the policy area, propose new policy initiatives, and sustain a particular policy stance (or regime).

In narrow and rather economistic terms the tasks of British competition policy over the post-war period have been substantial. Defining the overall goal as 'workable competition' presented the UK authorities with an economy that was far from the ideal, being extensively cartelized, highly concentrated, and extremely prone to mergers. Recent privatization policy has also presented the authorities with the task of creating actual or surrogate competition within natural monopolies. Just to summarize the present position, these problem areas are covered by legislation as shown in Table 6.2. These acts also embody substantial numbers of sectoral exemptions but are, of course, operating under a commitment to fundamental reform, as discussed below.

This picture of legislative and institutional multiplicity has provoked Whish to write of 'the bizarre and complex structure of the domestic competition law',[22] which has similarly been described by Craig as 'a web of Byzantine complexity'.[23] In addition, of course, British industry is also subject to the parallel jurisdiction of the European competition authorities. The British and European systems are based on different principles, involve different processes and different actors. Unlike most other member states the British authorities do not have the powers to apply articles 85 and 86; and in looking at the present system, reform seems absolutely essential.

The reform proposals considered below involve new law and new principles of operation but would broadly retain the existing institutions. All the major competition policy regimes share some institutional features in that they have entrusted the administration of the competition rules to an independent agency. In this way competition provisions have been at least partially insulated from politics, to take on an impartial status which could be likened to the 'economic constitution' of the state. Thus we have the Federal Trade Commission, the Fair Trade Commission, the

TABLE 6.2. *UK competition legislation and organizations*

Problem area	Legislation	Institutions
Cartels and restrictive trade	Restrictive Trade Practice Act 1976 Resale Prices Act 1976 Deregulation Act 1994	• Restrictive Practices Court • High Court • OFT (Director General of Fair Trading)
Monopoly, oligopoly, and mergers	Monopolies and Mergers Act 1965 Fair Trading Act 1973 Competition Act 1980 Companies Act 1989 Deregulation Act 1994	• MMC • OFT • MMC • DTI (Secretary of State) • OFT/DTI
Natural monopolies	Utility Acts, e.g. Electricity Act 1989 Fair Trading Act 1973 Competition Act 1980 Deregulation Act 1994	Utility regulators, e.g. • OFFER • MMC • DTI • OFT/DTI

Bundeskartellamt, and DG IV. The British equivalent came late in the day. The Office of Fair Trading was created in 1973 as an appendage of the Director General of Fair Trading, in whom are vested significant legal powers and who enjoys legal independence.

But the role of the OFT in monopolies and mergers is very substantially constrained by the Monopolies and Mergers Commission, which makes all judgements on 'the public interest', and by the DTI and the Secretary of State, who retains the right to make all final decisions.

The Monopolies and Mergers Commission (MMC)

The Commission has enjoyed remarkable longevity. It was created in 1948 to enquire into monopolies and restrictive practices, but without sanctions and without a presumption of illegality. The US system was explicitly rejected in favour of an inquiry into 'the public interest' on the presumption that the system of business self-regulation allowed a relaxed regime of control.[24] Its brief was expanded to cover mergers in 1965.

The MMC is a quintessentially 'English' body made up of a full-time Chairman, three half-time Deputy Chairmen, 27 part-time Commissioners, and 77 staff. This reflects a traditional English pattern of part-time, amateur administration by 'notables', which in this case incorporates 14 business people, 7 academics, 6 professionals, 2 public officials, and 1 each from a Union and a business interest group (the total includes 5 women).[25] The Commission has a very well-developed culture of strict impartiality, a non-adversarial courtesy, due procedure, deference to its Commissioners, and pride in the thoroughness of its investigations. It works through small teams of four to six members who undertake exhaustive investigations and produce reports which provide thorough and fascinating accounts of industrial sectors. There is wide affection for the MMC, especially from academics who benefit from its detailed analyses, but there is also widespread criticism from business, consumers, and policy reformers.

The recent Trade and Industry Select Committee report focused those criticisms and allowed outspoken attacks on the way information is gathered, the procedures of the MMC, the judgements which its Panels arrive at, and the way in which these judgements are interpreted. The Consumers Association went so far as to assert that 'the MMC has developed a reputation for quirkiness and unpredictability which is as damaging, in the long term, to business as it is to consumers'.[26] They went on to argue for the abolition of the Commission and its merger into the OFT. A more biting vein of criticism has been to suggest that the MMC has become too soft on business. Its Chairman, Graeme Odgers, is a businessman who came from a career in construction and telecommunications. The combination of a majority of business people in the Commission, together with free-market economists, may have produced a reluctance to detect breaches of the public interest. There may also be, although the MMC would stringently deny it, a sensitivity to current political imperatives which, under Michael Heseltine, put the perceived needs of industrial recovery ahead of an active competition policy.

There is plentiful opportunity to analyse the reports and recommendations of the MMC and pick out trends and inconsistencies. What is more interesting from the point of view of the overall operation of policy is the way in which the MMC neutralizes regulatory discretion as well as political bias. In considering action against a monopoly, oligopoly, or merger, both the DGFT and the Secretary of State are always aware that the case must go through the MMC machinery. This opens up debate, introduces biases, and introduces unpredictability. This separation of powers acts as a very potent constraint on the other competition policy actors, and it could be argued that it sacrifices effective policy to the demands of due process. In this context it is interesting that the November 1994 Deregulation and Contracting Out Act contains competition policy provisions which allow the Director General and Secretary of State to accept 'undertakings' in the case of mergers and of monopolies as a substitute for referral of cases to the MMC. If these powers begin to be used extensively, as is likely, then the MMC might begin to be marginalized and the discretionary power of the other actors would be substantially increased.

The Office of Fair Trading

The OFT was created in 1973 to service the responsibilities of the Director General of Fair Trading (DGFT). The first DGFT, Sir John Methven, described the OFT as 'a regulatory agency . . . in US terms it combines the functions of the Anti-Trust Division of the Justice Department and the Federal Trade Commission'.[27] It was interesting that he should have chosen a US parallel even when addressing a conference concerned mainly with EC policy.

The creation of a new regulatory agency was a pivotal development in relation to competition policy specifically, and British policy on regulation more generally. The location of regulatory authority in the hands of a named individual rather than a minister or collegiate body was similarly a momentous innovation. The legislation created a very distinctive apparatus for the deployment of administrative discretion and acted as a precursor for the more specifically focused regulatory agencies of the 1980s. Frazer has suggested that 'the practical strength of the UK's competition policy turns on the effectiveness of the incumbent of that office (DGFT) and of his staff in the OFT'.[28] The DGFT has very considerable authority as defined in the legislation. The key question is how he chooses to define and deploy it in the context of the constraints placed upon him.

In this light the debate over the creation of the OFT offers a mixed message. In his excellent discussion Ramsay points to the way in which economic analysis was upgraded and priority was placed on increasing efficiency by reinforcing the market. But he also stresses the 'consumer protection' element.[29] The abolition of the Consumer Council in 1970 generated a very adverse reaction among the public and interest groups. There was pressure within government to respond, with suggestions from the CPRS (Central Policy Review Staff) drawing on foreign models, and active leadership from Geoffrey Howe as Consumer Affairs Minister. The outcome was the deliberate creation of a new 'player' who would be independent, non-political, and would act as a vehicle for articulating consumer interests. This association of consumer protection and competition policy has been hailed as a beneficial manifestation of the philosophy of the social market economy (by Geoffrey Howe),[30] but it has also had uncomfortable aspects which have created tension throughout the life of the OFT. It has meant that the Office and the Director General has often been more concerned with consumer rights and complaints than with industrial structure and economic efficiency. Sir Gordon Borrie, for instance, had made his name as a consumer-rights campaigner and gave clear evidence of relishing that side of the job. He opened his penultimate Annual Report as Director General with the declaration that 'The fundamental aim of the Office of Fair Trading is to promote and safeguard the interests of consumers.'[31] The British institutional structure thus embraces areas of detailed contact between retailers and the public which are separately handled in other systems. This is the British eccentricity. The EC authorities deal with state aids; the Japanese with trade associations; and the British with consumer protection. Each quite properly linked but introducing distinctive national biases.

The provisions of the Fair Trading Act 1973 deserve a moment's consideration. Section 2 defines the duties of the DGFT very widely 'to keep under review the carrying on of commercial activities in the UK . . . with a view to his becoming aware of, and ascertaining the circumstances relating to, monopoly situations or uncompetitive practices'.[32] The Act defines various aspects of the relationship between the DGFT, the Secretary of State, and the MMC. They embody a considerable scope for discretion and a concern with the 'public interest'. The famous section 84 of the

Act defines the public interest very broadly. The desirability of 'promoting effective competition' features prominently, but this is only one element to be considered 'among other things'. Although public-interest judgements are largely the prerogative of the MMC, in practice both the Secretary of State and the DGFT have to formulate their own interpretations. The DGFT's ability to evolve an independent and influential view of the 'public interest' lies at the heart of his role.

The formal administrative resources available to the DGFT are substantial. The Office is divided into two divisions dealing respectively with Consumer Affairs and Competition Policy. The 1993 annual report shows a budget of £19.3 million and a staff of 428 with 71 senior staff including 12 lawyers and 16 economists. Successive reports show staff levels fluctuating between 300 and 350 from 1974 to 1990, but a recent increase is likely to take staffing up to 450. Of these, around 300 staff and at least 40 per cent of the budget goes on consumer policy and associated regulatory activity such as administering the Consumer Credit, Trade Descriptions, and Estate Agents Acts. The core of staff devoted to strict competition policy is therefore quite small at around 120.

The Secretary of State and the DTI

The Secretary of State for Trade and Industry is the sun around which British competition policy orbits. Not only is he the main policy-maker, he has extraordinary legal discretion, administrative influence, and powers of patronage. The incumbent from 1992 to 1995 was Michael Heseltine, who revived the traditional title of 'President of the Board of Trade'. Mr Heseltine has strong views on British industrial policy, and unambiguously put priority on ways in which government can help British companies to compete in international markets. A strong competition policy was not regarded as an important part of the agenda. The responsible minister was therefore strong, decisive, capable of assertive policy initiatives, and one of the most powerful ministers in John Major's Cabinet.

Day-to-day responsibility for competition policy is taken by a third-tier junior minister, in 1994–5 Jonathan Evans, a Parliamentary Under-Secretary of State. Of course ministers require a staff

TABLE 6.3. *DTI Organization for Competition Policy*

President of the Board of Trade	Michael Heseltine
Corporate Affairs Minister	Neil Hamilton*
Competition Policy Division	
• Under-Secretary (grade 3)	Arthur Pryor
• Branch 1, Mergers, 13 staff	
Assistant Secretary (5)	John Alty
• Branch 2, RTP, Monopolies, international and new legislation, 18 staff	
Assistant Secretary (5)	Alan Cooper
• Branch 3, General, utilities and transport, 14 staff	
Assistant Secretary (5)	Charles Bridge

Notes: Correct at March 1994. * resigned during 1994, replaced by Jonathan Evans.

to advise on decisions and assist with policy formulation, but the competition policy staff at the DTI has grown significantly as shown in Table 6.3. With 50 staff plus specialist economists, the DTI now has substantial administrative resources. Expansion reflects increased liaison with Europe and the preparation of new legislation, but the merger boom of the mid-1980s also had an impact. As budgets and responsibilities declined elsewhere in the DTI so competition work grew in salience, and much of the staffing increase dates from the mid-eighties. Ministers find merger work urgent, exciting, and important. In a non-interventionist era it gives ministers a delightful encounter with raw power.

The Restrictive Practices Court

The Court adjudicates on restrictive agreements between two or more parties trading in the UK. All such agreements which meet certain formal criteria must be registered with the DGFT in his role as Registrar. Nowadays virtually all agreements are carefully drafted and potential infringements are eliminated on the advice of OFT staff, so the Court now sits infrequently. It is specialist and unusual, comprising three High Court judges, a Northern

Irish and a Scottish judge, and up to ten lay-members. The Court meets in 'chambers' of one judge and two lay-members. The lay-members are selected for their industrial experience, but the Court is 'non-specialist' and depends on the economic evidence laid before it. The creation of the Court in 1956 was highly controversial and was strongly supported by industry. Over its first decade it was felt to be very successful in eliminating rampant restrictions and cartels. Rather contrary to expectation, it has found virtually all registrable agreements referred to it to be contrary to the public interest, but in a process which many observers feel makes such demands of value judgements and economic judgements that it is beyond normal judicial competence.[33]

The utility regulators

The privatized utilities are subject to specific and relatively stringent regimes of regulation operated by a utility regulator employing more extensive powers than the DGFT in respect of the sector, and typically in a more forceful and adversarial fashion. Regulation is aimed at counteracting the potentially baneful effects of monopoly but is also aimed at promoting competition within these industries. As part of a wider arsenal of weapons, the utility regulators have concurrent powers with the DGFT to make referrals to the MMC under the Fair Trading Act and the Competition Act. The utility regulators have substantial powers and substantial staff, and have taken personalized regulation to extraordinary heights of controversy (see Table 6.4).[34]

The 'Core' institutions are the triple structure of the OFT, the MMC, and the DTI. Their different competencies, biases, and priorities make the evaluation of competition policy difficult, and its administration hesitant. It is essential that these agencies co-operate but, whilst relationships are amicable, there is a strong note of tension between them. We will return to this after reviewing the wider constituency of 'non-core' players and interest groups.

'NON-CORE' PLAYERS AND INTEREST GROUPS

The range of companies and groups likely to be affected by competition policy is very wide but for most interests competition

Table 6.4. *UK utility regulators*

	Formed	Staff	Budget £m.
OFTEL—Office of Telecommunications Director General Don Cruickshank	1984	143	7.5
OFGAS—Office of Gas Supply DG Clare Spottiswoode	1986	28	1.9
OFWAT—Office of Water Services DG Ian Byatt	1989	132	6.3
OFFER—Office of Electricity Regulation DG Professor Stephen Littlechild	1990	214	10.6

Note: figures for 1992–3; incumbents at Dec. 1994.

influences are brief and episodic. Substantial oligopolists (like BAT Industries or Powergen) must retain a constant awareness of the state of play, as must business representative organizations and those interests concerned with the broad range of policy-making and enforcement.

Within government, departments interested in a particular episode of enforcement, such as a merger reference or a European hearing under article 85, will routinely be consulted by the OFT. Thus the Treasury has an interest in financial services, Transport in bus companies, and Environment in the construction industry. The responsible Cabinet Committee is 'EDI'—Ministerial Committee on Industrial, Commercial, and Consumer Affairs. In 1994 it was chaired by a non-Departmental minister, Lord Wakeham (Lord Privy Seal) and not by Michael Heseltine, and its main Departmental members include the Home Office, Agriculture, Environment, and two regional offices—Scotland and Northern Ireland. For the most part competition policy within government seems fairly well insulated within the core institutions. The main exception is the regional issue. Particularly in Scotland there has been great sensitivity to the takeover of significant Scottish companies such as the Royal Bank of Scotland and Scottish and Newcastle Breweries. The controversy surrounding these cases contributed to the mergers review of the mid-1980s and to Paul Channon's decision to embark on comprehensive policy reform.

Outside government clearly all businesses should be aware of the regulative framework of which competition law constitutes a significant part. How much that is in fact the case is contentious. In a provocative argument Robin Aaronson has suggested that 'companies pay too little attention to competition policy because the world of the competition authorities is foreign to them, they do not speak the language and thus find it hard to understand the rules'. As he argues, the implications of this are momentous, 'from a public policy point of view, this suggests that competition policy is only effective when the authorities make a direct intervention to deal with a particular case. Its deterrence effect is much weaker.'[35] To question the deterrence effect of competition policy is to strike at its very roots. By its nature competition policy is a regulative system dependent on willing compliance enforced in exceptional circumstances by law or administrative action. No constitution is effective if its every application has to be policed; compliance must become automatic, natural, taken for granted. This requires clear laws enforced with consistency and transparency. For that very reason Aaronson's criticisms have a ring of truth when applied to UK law, and he identifies an increasingly acute syndrome as British law becomes increasingly discredited by a failure of reform. His criticisms are supported in a recent cogent critique by Pratt, who quotes Aaronson with approval, observes that there is 'little evidence that the [Competition] Act has changed attitudes and indeed there is some evidence that businesses continue to disregard the Act'.[36] He quotes Lever on the 'estrangement' of the restrictive trade practices law and is generally critical of the failure to reform British law.

Aaronson's argument is less persuasive when applied to competition law in the round, including European law. Here there is widespread acceptance that the size and frequency of article 85 fines, the smooth operation of the merger regulation, and the accumulation of case law (including article 85 and 86 cases in the national courts) have greatly increased corporate awareness. Corporate compliance programmes are no longer a rarity and business has become sufficiently alerted to the profound ramifications of competition policy to be very concerned with law reform as well as enforcement.[37]

Just as many large companies and oligopolistic industrial sectors have become sensitized to competition policy, so business-related groups have begun to take a closer interest. This includes trade unions, trade associations, business policy groups (such as chambers of commerce), and, of course, the Confederation of British Industry (CBI). The CBI has a competition policy and consumer affairs division, staffed mainly by lawyers, and works through a very large competition policy committee consisting of around sixty representatives from companies, associations and professional firms. This competition policy activity has been influential, and the CBI has particularly close links with the DTI. Members of the Committee will sit on government working groups and offer advice; equally senior DTI officials attend CBI meetings and address specialist groups. It was significant that Michael Heseltine made his major competition policy speech in February 1994 to a CBI conference.

The CBI is usually, and rightly, regarded as a relatively weak representative body. It is inhibited by the sheer range and incompatibility of interests of its membership, and its leadership finds it difficult to define and mobilize in any forceful fashion. Indeed, for many academic analysts the inability of British business to define and articulate common interests is one of the curiosities of the postwar era. Most British companies exhibit attitudes of prickly independence. Collective discipline is slight and they bridle at attempted co-ordination from the CBI, just as they do at similar attempts from government. Diagnoses of British corporatism which tended to disregard these characteristics were always suspect. It is therefore interesting to see relatively strong and consensual views emerging from the CBI over the reform of competition policy. On restrictive practices the proposal to align British law with article 85 of the Rome Treaty has been 'broadly supported by the CBI', although they have some technical and policy reservations.[38] On monopolies and anti-competitive practices, however, the CBI was strongly in favour of strengthening the existing British system and avoiding alignment with article 86. Its extensive 19-page critique concluded that 'Whilst CBI is not opposed to the introduction of a well-defined UK prohibition on restrictive trade practices, we are very strongly opposed to any parallel adoption of a prohibition on abuse of market power.'[39] The theme of the CBI argument was that they liked the pragmatic, case-by-case approach of the British authorities; they approved of negotiated undertakings; were suspicious of third-party damage actions; and vastly preferred administrative action to a judicial system. 'The existing regulatory authorities have such [relevant] experience and the value of this resource should not be underestimated.'[40] The CBI view expressly embraced the opinions of its small and medium-sized member companies, but their views on the desirable development of policy were most emphatically not shared by other interested parties. An alternative analysis was put forward by consumer groups, by academics and by lawyers in academia and in professional practice. The consumer view favours a neo-classical version of competition policy which emphasizes consumer welfare and naturally also favours very vigorous enforcement. The main consumer groups are the National Consumers Council (NCC), which is funded by government but which is respected for its independent research; and the Consumer's Association (CA). The CA is wholly independent as one of the five biggest UK charities and publisher of *Which?* magazine. Its policy section is quite well resourced, and it has been a consistent and well-respected advocate of competition policy activism. Not surprisingly it lobbied for the most stringent of the monopoly reform options (option 3). A rather disparate group of academics also regularly express views on the shape and reform of policy. On the whole they are either economists or lawyers with quite close links to fellow lawyers in practice. The academic views on British policy are gradually evolving from the politely sceptical to the polemically outraged. Many academics favoured the logical neatness of aligning British monopoly policy with article 86, and virtually all want to see a strengthening of British policy which goes beyond a modest improvement on current practice.

This leaves the professional constituency of competition policy, the lawyers. Competition law has been one of the growth areas for professional lawyers over the 1980s. The big firms in London and Brussels are building lucrative practices out of EC case work, merger references, advice on strategy and on compliance. The CBI wryly observed that the total number of UK-based competition law specialists in 1973 was approximately the same as the current staffing of the competition section of a large London practice. This growth of a powerful legal community is very important indeed. It provides a vocabulary, a set of concerns and a reform agenda that significantly biases the shape of competition policy. The lawyer's concern with due process, with internal consistency, with precedent, with case-made policy, and with the ultimate decisions of the courts carries the danger of losing sight of the overall objectives of policy. At the very least it produces an opaque and insular policy community and a policy debate that is conducted in arcane terms which become divorced from the real concerns of business and government. This, arguably, is something of what has happened with the Bundeskartellamt. A good demonstration of a creeping legal imperialism is the House of Lords Report of the Select Committee on the European Communities. The Report on the *Enforcement of Community Competition Rules*[41] is most interesting, but it was an investigation led by lawyers, taking evidence from lawyers, and written for lawyers. It is useful, perhaps even important, but it is dominated by legal points and matters of technical procedure.

How, then, should we assess the varying influence of these groups on the shape of British competition policy? Most accounts of the evolution of policy affirm a pattern atypical in UK political economy, that is, the influence of the business lobby. All the major legislative changes have been associated with pressure from business and business views about how policy should be designed. If British policy is an incremental confused construction, then it reflects the changing interpretations and the confusion of business itself. If this view is correct there is no particular reason why the current period should be any different. If, in other words, there have been controversial choices about the shape of current reform; and if there is a reluctance to proceed with reforms; then both the choices and the reluctance could be expected to reflect business preferences.

This view of events is denied by most participants in the policy process. The CBI denies that it is in any way encouraging government to 'go slow' on reforms. Officials in the DTI and the OFT similarly dismiss a 'conspiracy theory' of this sort as unrealistic. They all argue that business wants law reform. It wants certainty, transparency, reduced compliance costs, and an effective regime in which to pursue efficiency and competitiveness. Allegedly the real reason for hesitancy in reform is political priorities and a simple shortage of legislative time.

In two respects, however, business influence is clear. The *Abuse of Market Power* Green Paper offered three possible choices for reform of monopoly and anti-competitive practices legislation. Crudely the choices were:

option 1, strengthen existing UK legislation;
option 2, align UK legislation with the EC article 86;
option 3, a dual system of an article 86 prohibition plus the Fair
Trading Act monopoly provisions.

Many analysts and some DTI officials would have preferred option 3. In the event the government chose option 1, the option preferred by the CBI. In making its choice the DTI conducted a consultation exercise. Among the 143 respondents, 30 per cent chose option 1, 24 per cent option 2, and 26 per cent option 3. It is very hard to believe that the government attached as much weight to this highly imbalanced consultation exercise as it professed to do, for this would have amounted to an abdication of responsibility. But assuming that consultation did have some influence, it is instructive to examine the participants in the consultative process. In fact we can cast the net a little wider to examine the interests and groups active or important enough to be involved in four recent evaluations of competition policy. The four constituencies of interests are (see also Table 6.5):

1. August 1993, DTI Consultation exercise on possible changes to competition legislation and procedures to reduce the burden on business (42 respondents)[42]
2. May–August 1993, House of Lords Select Committee on *Enforcement of the Community Competition Rules*, oral and written evidence (16 participants)[43]
3. November 1992–February 1993, DTI Consultation exercise on responses to the *Abuse of Market Power* Green Paper (143 responses)[44]
4. November–December 1990, Trade and Industry Committee Inquiry into *Takeovers and Mergers*, oral and written evidence (79 participants)[45]

Of course the results given in Table 6.5 are impressionistic and strictly incomparable, but using them in this way is no different to the DTI's own usage where it indicated that '30 per cent' were in favour of option 1. Table 6.5 indicates that the organizations sufficiently interested in competition policy to contribute to consultation exercises or parliamentary inquiries were service-industry companies, trade associations, legal firms, and manufacturing industry companies in that order. This is not perhaps particularly

TABLE 6.5. *Participants in competition policy debates*

Interests	1. DTI Consultation	2. House of Lords Consultation	3. DTI Consultation	4. Trade and Industry Select Committee	Total	Per cent
Government agencies	—	5	14	17	36	12.9
Business:	(34)	(2)	(82)	(31)	(149)	(53.2)
Associations	6	2	36	5	49	17.5
Manufacturing companies	13	—	11	12	36	12.9
Service companies	15	—	35	14	64	22.9
Advisers:						
Legal firms	8	9	22	9	48	17.1
Accountants	—	—	4	4	8	2.9
Consumer organizations	—	—	3	2	5	1.7
Labour organizations	—	—	2	7	9	3.2
Academics	—	—	16	9	25	8.9
Total	42	16	143	79	280	100

surprising, although one might have expected a more active voice from labour organizations and consumer interests.

In terms of business influence, therefore, it is evident, first, that the CBI views on legislative options accorded with those adopted and, secondly, that in considering policy options government has been informed overwhelmingly by business corporations, their representatives, and their legal advisers. It is to be hoped that the DTI was influenced by its own autonomous views and defence of the public interest. To defer to business in this area is surely like asking the poachers to arrange the gamekeeper's schedules.

ORGANIZATIONAL CULTURE AND THE COMPETITION POLICY COMMUNITY

The concepts of 'culture' and of 'community' can be helpful in evaluating the institutions involved in the formulation and enforcement of competition policy. The concept of culture is intended to capture the idea that well-established organizations develop a corporate identity and a set of standard responses that can exhibit sufficient coherence to constitute policy preferences or biases. It is a familiar observation that organizations engender sets of attitudes and expectations which are tacit and can be described as norms of behaviour. They produce a vocabulary, a set of filters, and a repertoire of preferred solutions to familiar problems. Such cultures are observable but often perverse. They cannot be manipulated in ways suggested by management gurus, but do provide an important perspective on why organizations behave as they do. It can be suggested that each of the 'core' organizations—the OFT, the MMC, and the DTI—are sufficiently large, distinctive, and well established to have developed identifiable 'cultures'. It can be suggested that the culture of the MMC is 'judicial'; that of the OFT economistic, and that of the DTI political.

The concept of 'community' extends the idea of 'culture' into an inter-organizational framework. Policy is not made by individuals or even by individual organizations but by interaction between a large and varied set of interests. The idea of a 'policy network' is useful in evaluating the individuals and organizations who are mainly and substantially concerned with the policy area. Participants in a policy network need to co-operate with one another, to exchange resources (of information, influence, personnel, and so on), and to establish good working relationships. In embarking on this necessary co-operation they develop shared norms and understandings of sufficient coherence to justify the metaphor of a 'community'.

These ideas of culture and community can be applied relatively well to the area of competition policy. The continuity remarked on above can be seen in well-established organizations such as the MMC, and a set of issues which are partially defined in law. The issue areas of monopoly, restrictive practices, and mergers have of course been expanded to cover European interactions, specialized sectors (such as broadcasting), and now utility regulation. But the issues and the principles are well-established and understood. Equally the interested parties have fairly well-defined and urgent agendas to pursue. Whether they are government agencies, law firms, or large companies they are aware of the dependencies which make co-operation essential, and the ideological confrontations typical of many policy areas are absent. Two further ingredients are supplied by the 'sociology' of the organizations and by the established processes of communication.

The sociology of the competition policy area is marked by a distinct continuity of personnel and by staff mobility between the various institutions. The OFT and the MMC are staffed largely by secondments from the DTI, and senior staff in all these institutions often have a career record of consistent involvement in the field, including spells in two or more of these agencies. This personnel network is particularly applicable to economists, who may move out of government to work on competition issues in economic management consultancies or move across to generalist administrative posts. More recently the network has begun to embrace legal specialists who can move easily between academia, legal practice, and government. Legal specialists employed in the DTI regularly come in on secondment from leading law firms, where they eventually return and are able to use their knowledge and contacts.

The processes of communication and interaction are also well established, although they are rather more formalistic than might be expected. There are a limited number of formal committees, especially DG IV's advisory group of national specialists, and the 'Merger Panel' which meets under the Chairmanship of the Director

General of Fair Trading. Otherwise, senior officials of the core institutions are in regular contact and meet relatively frequently. There is, however, a strong awareness of the independence and neutrality of the various institutions. The OFT investigates and advises; the MMC (or RPC) adjudicates; and the DTI decides. This is a quite deliberate separation of powers, and sits oddly with a British administrative tradition in which powers are often quite crudely combined. Perhaps for this very reason officials are careful and deliberate about their interactions, especially those with the DTI. At least formally, the DTI does not suggest courses of action or give guidance and direction to the OFT or the MMC. It certainly does not intervene in individual cases. Such intervention would be fiercely resisted and would also breach legal requirements. The Secretary of State and his officials should not 'fetter his discretion' by expressing views in advance and nowadays the MMC is very formalistic in its observation of due process, in order to head off applications for judicial review which, although rarely successful, are becoming almost commonplace.

The organizational culture of the OFT

The concepts of culture and community are slippery and generate a degree of uncertainty among policy analysts. None the less, applying this approach to the OFT draws attention to some features of its activities not normally stressed, and also may illustrate the utility of the approach.

Like DG IV, the OFT combines legal, economic, and administrative expertise. Unlike DG IV most of the staff are generalist civil servants, and the limited number of lawyers are segregated into a legal division (an arrangement they prefer). None the less, to an initial observer the tone and ethos of the OFT is more dominated by statute than is typical of the civil service. This general tone probably reflects the fact that the first two DGFTs were lawyers by origin. The role of economics and economists is similarly difficult to define. Economic ideas can transform competition policy, especially where they challenge existing definitions of policy design and when they are articulated at a senior level. The US experience is particularly instructive. As a participant in the debate, O. E. Williamson, notes, 'An additional contributory factor

[to the impact of Chicago School economics] was the reorganization of the economics staff of the Antitrust Division. Whereas
previously the staff economists were used almost exclusively to
support the legal staff in the preparation and litigation of cases,
they were now asked to assess the economic merits of cases before
filing.'[46] Economists are prominent within the competition policy
machinery, both in the DTI and the OFT. They are in touch with
academic research, participate freely in conferences, and debate
and publish in the field.[47] It was felt that the creation of the OFT
would increase the salience of economic analysis and, indeed, a
similar expectation might be attached to current proposals for an
'effects-based' reform of policy. But Britain has seen no victory of
economic ideas to parallel the practical influence of the Chicago
School in the United States. One conclusion might be that economists in government had been moulded to the more pragmatic and
judgemental approach typical of the civil servant. An alternative
view might be that economists have been marginalized by standard civil service procedures. Economists, like lawyers, still operate
in 'parallel hierarchies', and are consulted on decisions rather than
being actual decision-makers. Chicago School thinking would have
had a mixed effect in Britain. Competition policy economists in
the UK had always given high salience to the analysis of barriers
to entry, and would therefore argue that Chicago School-type thinking had always been a part of their basic analytical approach. On
the other hand, the permissive approach of Chicago to vertical
restraints would be rejected by many British officials.

An alleged lack of technical expertise is one of the standard
lines of criticism of the OFT. This, together with the pressure of
work, was taken up by the DGFT in his 1981 and 1986 Reports.
Writing also in the mid-1980s, Ramsay noted a concern about the
high level of turnover of senior and specialist staff, and noted that
the dominance of career civil servants might diminish the credibility of the OFT within the business community.[48] There does not
seem to have been any acceptance of this argument by the DTI.
The Deputy Secretary responsible, Robin Mountfield, told the Trade
and Industry Committee that 'I do not think there has been any
comprehensive review in the recent past of staffing resources.'[49]
None the less, the Trade and Industry Committee (TIC) relayed
quite direct criticism from the CBI and some companies, and
observed that 'we were impressed with the breadth of experience

of the senior staff of the competition authorities we met in the USA and Canada'. In a subtle word of implied criticism they went on to say that such people 'were likely to have greater abilities and a wider experience than would generally be found in the OFT and MMC in the UK'. Their conclusion was that 'unless something is done about this now, the private sector interests which come into contact with these bodies will begin to lose confidence in them'. Hence they recommended changes in recruitment practices.[50]

The nature of the staff of the OFT is important not merely in terms of competence but also in relation to how they use the powers potentially at their disposal. Are the staff of the OFT proactive or reactive? Risk-takers or risk-avoiders? Do they want to expand their jurisdiction or settle for a quiet life? As has been argued elsewhere,[51] one of the reasons that DG IV became so influential during the 1980s was due to the activism and sheer evangelism of its staff. A proactive stance by the OFT could affect its impact on industry.

A proactive stance would involve more '*ex officio*' action on the part of the OFT. Like health care, the demand for action on competition policy is almost limitless. The underlying inspiration of competition policy (perfect competition—like perfect health) is so idealistic and so intangible, and the range of breaches is so extensive, that there is a great potential for the widening of policy. The key factor is the balance between reacting to complaints on the one hand, and assertively searching out breaches and new application of law on the other. Sharpe has observed that 'as the Office lacks a large investigatory staff and wide investigatory powers, it is critically dependent on the lodging of complaints by concerned bodies'.[52] The Office receives many complaints on competition issues, although on a slightly falling trend (1,690 in 1991, 1,577 in 1993). Of those, around 200 will be investigated in depth and perhaps 25 would result in a reference to the MMC or informal assurances from the firm. But many cartels, monopolies, and new anti-competitive practices will only be identified if the Office takes the initiative, and it undoubtedly monitors firms and keeps a series of industrial sectors under review. This aspect of its activities is surprisingly low key.

The OFT recently observed that 'It is not the policy of the division to "go fishing" for subjects to investigate',[53] but in this it is making a virtue of necessity. The investigatory powers of the

OFT are woefully inadequate, and a cautious approach has been taken to developing indicators of infringement, such as measuring rates of return. The *Abuse of Market Power* Green Paper acknowledged the weakness of the OFT's investigatory powers. As regards restrictive practices, the Director General complained in 1986 that: 'my powers to investigate suspected unregistered agreements are somewhat limited (they are only exercisable when I already have reasonable grounds for believing that an unregistered and therefore unlawful agreement exists), a catch-22 situation if ever there was one, and I have long felt that there is a clear case for strengthening them. This is particularly so where our information consists of unconfirmed accounts of what may have taken place at meetings or in telephone conversations.'[54]

The OFT is therefore largely reactive and complaints-led. It is possible that staff would find a more evangelical, crusading approach more stimulating, and a small initiative was made in February 1995 when a 'Cartel Task Force' was launched to encourage complaints.[55] Realistically, however, a more proactive stance would require more adequate powers of investigation.

This brings the discussion to the final concern of this section, which is the relationship between the OFT and the other bodies within this field, particularly the DTI. Relationships with the Secretary of State (President of the Board of Trade) can be tense. Disagreements periodically emerge into the public gaze. Merger references cause particular excitement and, for instance, in 15 cases since 1979 the Secretary of State has rejected the advice of the DGFT concerning referral of a merger to the MMC. Early in 1993 Michael Heseltine reawakened controversy by overriding Sir Bryan Carsberg's recommendations twice in two weeks. The DGFT recommended referral of a merger between a defence components business of GEC and Philips; and later of the bid by Airtours for the Owners Abroad Group. The latter bid was widely seen as a clear case for MMC referral, and there was much concern about renewed politicization of the policy area.[56] A further disappointment came in February 1994, when Heseltine vetoed OFT plans for the investigation of anti-competitive practices by a bus operator on the Isle of Arran. In itself this was an insignificant case, but it was very symbolic, as it was the first time an investigation proposed by the OFT under the Competition Act had been overruled. Until the resignation of Sir Bryan Carsberg open disagreement was very much the exception, and policy in Britain has not fallen foul of doctrinaire party-political conflict.[57] Thus Sir Gordon Borrie worked amicably with a series of doctrinaire Conservative ministers, despite himself being a Labour appointee.

There is no doubt that the President of the Board of Trade has ultimate authority over competition policy matters. He has powers to override other actors in virtually all areas of competition policy. O'Brien, to take just one example, observes that 'The act of 1973 ... gives the relevant minister quite remarkable powers.'[58] The President appoints the Director General and the Chairman of the MMC, in each case for five years renewable. At the same time the DGFT has his own duties as prescribed by statute. He negotiates his budget directly with the Treasury and is a public figure. As Sir Gordon Borrie recently put it, 'The DGFT has a role independent of Government Ministers. His Office is a non-Ministerial Government Department.'[59] Despite these constitutional autonomies the DGFT has not managed to create an area of real autonomy. He has been likened, slightly unkindly, to a signalman who merely directs cases to their appropriate destination. Certainly it has become apparent that the DGFT has less real independence than do utility regulators within their sectors. This relative dependence of the OFT and the deterioration of its relations with the DTI was underlined by the resignation of Sir Bryan Carsberg.

The question of whether the DGFT should be responsible to 'the Act' or to 'the Secretary of State' poses an interesting test of relative influence. Section 84 of the Act defines a wide spread of factors which are 'relevant' to an assessment of the public interest, including quality, technology, employment, and exports. The uncertainty contingent in this range of factors was reduced by the Tebbit doctrine, which sought to restrict references to 'competition grounds'. The guidelines are of sufficient importance to quote. In an answer to a Parliamentary Question Mr Tebbit stated that 'I regard mergers policy as an important part of the Government's general policy of promoting competition within the economy in the interests of the customer and of efficiency and hence of growth and jobs. Accordingly my policy has been and will continue to be to make references primarily on competition grounds.'[60] This, then, is a statement of the Secretary of State's policy, not a statement of law. The DGFT is thus equally within his rights to continue to operate a wider definition of the public interest. Yet it is clear that

Sir Gordon Borrie regarded himself as bound by the policy of the government of the day in precedence over a literal interpretation of the Act. The Trade and Industry Committee pressed him hard and critically on this. In a highly significant conclusion they declared that: 'by accepting that he does choose to operate within stated government policy, Sir Gordon Borrie is, in our view, both limiting his independence and compromising the integrity of the advice he gives'. They went on to recommend that 'the DGFT should form his own independent policy on references taking into account all the factors in Section 84'.[61] Borrie clearly found his room for manoeuvre circumscribed, although he was, on the whole, regarded as an astute and successful Director General.

It was felt that Sir Bryan Carsberg might have adopted a more independent stance. He came to the OFT in 1992 after eight years' experience of proactive regulation in OFTEL, during which time he evolved some distinctive regulatory views. Among them was a liking for 'incentive regulation', which in the case of utilities meant using devices such as price caps and compensation schemes to encourage them to increase efficiency. Similarly Carsberg was attracted by rate-of-return analysis as a way of identifying abuse of monopoly power.[62] As an academic and accountant, rather than a lawyer, it was expected that he would stress competition over consumer policy, and his early speeches indicated that he intended to be proactive. The *Financial Times*' coverage of his first speech declared that 'Sir Bryan Carsberg . . . gave a clear warning yesterday that he would not hesitate to take tough measures to stamp out market abuse.'[63] But Sir Bryan's scope for activism was constrained. The failure to legislate is a source of intense frustration, and here the relationship with the DTI is of the essence. There has been bemusement about the relaxed pace at which the DTI is proceeding to reform and legislate on competition policy. Much of the time and effort of continuing to operate the Register of Restrictive Trade Practices is regarded as futile, and the delay in acting upon the recommendations of the July 1989 White Paper is regarded as most unfortunate. In his valedictory report Sir Gordon pointedly observed that 'my greatest disappointment with lack of legislative follow-up to an evident and widely accepted case for change is the failure of Government to strengthen the law on cartels and other restrictive trading agreements'.[64] The task of responding to this concern lies with the DTI.

Relations with the DTI

There is undeniably dupliction of activities between the OFT competition policy division and the DTI competition policy division. The DGFT advises the Secretary of State on competition policy matters and referral of mergers, while initiation of monopoly references is by convention undertaken by the DGFT. MMC references are formally made by the Secretary of State to whom the MMC addresses its reports. The President of the Board of Trade thus receives separate advice from his own officials which involves reanalysis of the facts of the case; reinterpretation in the light of political priorities and the wider picture; and recommendations which will inevitably vary in nuance if not principle from those originating with the OFT. The DTI does not undertake a fresh investigation, but it has its own staff of economists and lawyers and could be expected to introduce fresh ideas, new material, and additional consultations. As noted above, its resources are quite respectable. It might be expected that this apparent duplication of activities would cause delay, compromise, and intense frustration on both sides. The physical separation of the OFT, sited near Chancery Lane, and the DTI in Victoria Street, must accentuate a sense of divorce over some issues.

In the case of mergers the machinery is a little more open, and the decision to refer is often considered by an inter-departmental committee known as the Mergers Panel. This is chaired by the DGFT, and although Frazer describes its proceedings as 'shrouded in mystery',[65] its activities do often enter the public arena. The Secretariat of the Panel is located in the OFT and its proceedings, by all accounts, are both formal and substantive. It has a significant influence over decisions. There are indications that it may formulate a position prior to discussion with the EC, but quite how it does this, and whether it has a hand in defining necessary undertakings or divestitures, is unclear.

The DTI also limits the independence of the OFT in more structural and unavoidable ways. The Minister and his civil servants participate in the Cabinet machinery and particularly in the main Cabinet Committee (EDI). Without access to this network the DGFT has limited opportunities for appeal when his views are ignored. In the same way, input to the European Council of Ministers goes through the DTI, and the DGFT's views on the structure and substance of European competition policy must be mediated through the DTI European machinery.

When we turn to the evolution of new policy the subordinate position of the DGFT becomes even clearer. Policy is made by ministers and promulgated through ministerial speeches. The Green and White Papers on reform are written in the DTI and published by DTI ministers. The role of the OFT and the DGFT in this process, if significant, is far from evident. It might be thought that the expertise, experience, and even preferences of the OFT might feed more clearly into the process of policy development and law reform. It seems, however, that the 'independence' of the DGFT is largely limited to the interpretation and implementation of existing policy and not to the development of fresh directions in policy.

BRITISH POLICY IN TRANSITION

British competition policy is currently going through an extraordinarily long, drawn-out period of reform. A review of the law on restrictive trade practices was announced by the then Secretary of State for Trade and Industry, Paul Channon, in 1986, and we have therefore seen ten years of legislative inaction.

Competition law reform has not evidently been at the top of the political or legislative agenda since 1992. Michael Heseltine shifted the emphasis to competitiveness and the current commitment to legislate is due to the inclusion of a promise in the Conservative Party 1992 election manifesto. There was little discussion of the issue, but under the highlighted commitments (in the 'privatization' section) came the promise that 'We will tackle all anti-competitive and restrictive practices with vigour. We will introduce new legislation giving stronger powers to deal with cartels.'[66]

All the same, delays in reform are extraordinary and intolerable for the OFT. The Green and White Papers on restrictive trade practices contain a blistering indictment of current law. The Green Paper concluded, in March 1988, that 'our present system is inflexible and slow, too often concerned with cases which are obviously harmless and not directed sufficiently at anti-competitive agreements. The scope for avoidance and evasion considerably weakens any deterrent effect the system has and enforcement powers are inadequate.'[67] Such views are constantly repeated and continue

to be candidly conceded by government. The recent DTI Consultation exercise rubbed in the message. It reported that: 'Those
respondents who had regular dealings with the Restrictive Trade
Practices Act 1976 (RTPA) were almost unanimous in their view
that the RTPA should be repealed at the earliest opportunity.'[68]
Views on mergers and monopolies were less outspoken, but as
regards the Competition Act 1980, 'This was the piece of legislation which, in general, respondents either had least experience of
or, if they did, viewed as lacking any credibility.'[69] This is the
official view. This is also the system that is operating at present.
Clearly such a system lacks credibility and the standing of the
institutions operating it must be diminished.

The timetable for reform of the law on restrictive practices has
been delayed by the perceived need also to reform the law on
monopoly and abuse of monopoly power. The laudable aim is a
comprehensive act which will provide consistency and clarity.
Detailed proposals have been discussed, formulated, approved, and
incorporated in a draft bill. They take the following form.

Proposals on restrictive trade practices

The proposals in the White Paper *Opening Markets* (Cm 727)
have received wide approval. They constitute a transformation in
the principles and operation of restrictive trade practices policy.
Almost the only element of continuity will be the institutions themselves, and the OFT would become a national DG IV.

Thus the proposal is to model cartel and restrictive practices
control on article 85 of the Rome Treaty, which will involve a
prohibition on agreements, or actions which prevent, restrict, or
distort competition. In terms of the categories explored in section
2 above it will represent a move in every category:

	From	To
action	public	public and private
control	form-based	effects-based
evaluation	judicial	administrative
mode	formal	discretionary potential
status	stagnant	potentially very active

The proposals have important procedural and administrative implications. They incorporate increased powers of investigation,
provision for substantial penalties, and procedures for considering

exemptions. The work-load will come from two sources; first from applications, either for negative clearance (agreement not caught), to be dealt with by a 'comfort letter', or for exemptions; secondly, from investigations undertaken by the OFT. The EC system of compulsory notifications is being avoided, which has significant implications for administrative activism.

Equally important, the traditional 'public-interest' criterion is consciously being abandoned. It is argued that the exclusion clauses can be interpreted widely and 'will not exclude benefits not normally perceived primarily in economic terms from being taken into account'.[70] None the less, the thrust of the legislation will become significantly more economistic.

British policy is therefore to be 'aligned' with EC law, to use the phrase of the Green Paper.[71] There is considerable logic in this, but also some problems. Whish regrets the absence of any discussion of the function of competition and of competition law.[72] Competition for its own sake is an unexamined totem. On a less abstract level there are problems associated with reproducing EC legislative provisions in national law. In fact initiative is being surrendered to DG IV and the European Court. British administrative practice and judicial decision will follow European law, precedent, and jurisprudence. This is a great advantage from the point of view of consistency, but the fact remains that these are 'foreign' institutions in a different cultural and historical setting, which are not permeated with British attitudes and expectations and which have a different mix of priorities. The most obvious conflict is over aims, which in the EC setting include integration of the single market, and in the British setting have put a premium on self-regulation.

Equally the OFT is not DG IV. The consistency, complementarity, and evolution of the two parallel administrative regimes will depend heavily on the institutions involved. The Green Paper remarks that the operation of the prohibition will depend 'on two important issues: the way in which the exemption criteria are drawn up and the administrative procedure for operating the law'.[73] It would be fascinating to compare the work of the DGFT and the OFT with that of the European Commissioner and DG IV.

Proposals on monopolies and abuse of market power

The options in the *Abuse of Market Power* Green Paper have generated more controversy. There is far less general approval of the operation of article 86 and far less dissatisfaction with the operation of domestic law. It would clearly be beneficial to reform competition policy 'in one go', with consistent principles; equally it is logical to align monopoly control with article 86, just as restrictive practices is following article 85. But the benefits of monopoly reform are less clear-cut and, as Whish observes, 'there is a feeling that the proposed changes are being advanced by lawyers for the sake of neatness and consistency rather than because of any clearly identified commercial need'.[74]

Article 86 should apply directly to the great majority of UK dominant companies, and it seems redundant to reproduce it in national law. It is, in any case, flawed. The British authorities are reluctant to accept it as it stands, and advocated a retention of the monopoly provision of the 1973 Fair Trading Act to produce a dual system. This is analysed as 'option 3' in the recent Green Paper and was initially the option that officials hoped that consultation would endorse and ministers would select. In fact a strong groundswell of opinion also developed in favour of option 1— strengthening existing domestic legislation with enhanced powers of investigation and penalties. This would have the advantage of a less profound and contentious piece of legislation, and would retain the 'public-interest', case-by-case approach.

The monopoly reform proposals envisage the same institutional arrangements as those proposed in the restrictive practices White Paper. The RTP Green Paper endorsed an investigating authority very similar to DG IV or the Bundeskartellamt, which would investigate and decide.[75] In the White Paper this was adapted to propose a new collegiate body, a restrictive trade practices tribunal to operate as part of the MMC, with appeal to the High Court. Contested cases would go to the tribunal for resolution.[76]

The monopoly Green Paper envisages employing the same OFT machinery, with recourse to the MMC in the case of monopoly references if aspects of the 1973 Act are retained.

The prospects were therefore for an enhanced OFT and probably for an enhanced MMC which would also continue merger control. The DGFT would have had substantial new powers, a potentially much stronger legislative framework within which to work, and an enlarged administrative capacity. The down-playing of the 'public-interest' element in decisions and repeal of much of the existing law might well have reduced the influence of the

Secretary of State, although the influence of DG IV both directly and indirectly would have been substantially increased.

This, for the OFT at least, presented a cheerful prospect, but events moved quickly and institutional arrangements which appeared appropriate in 1989 seem less ideal in 1993. In the meantime the Trade and Industry Committee endorsed the idea of a merger of the OFT and the MMC into a single body, a 'Competition and Mergers Authority', in their Report of 1991.[77] There were also increasingly voluble demands for rationalization from the world of utility regulation, with discussion of a regulatory commission involving more formal links to the OFT and the MMC.

In April 1993 Neil Hamilton announced the proposals for new legislation on monopoly and anti-competitive behaviour. As noted above, the government opted to strengthen existing legislation, including improved investigatory powers, enforceable undertakings, and interim orders; the Minister stressed the outcome of the consultation exercise. He declared that 'it is intended to include the changes in legislation to introduce the prohibition on restrictive trade practices'.[78] But over the summer something went badly wrong. In the timetabling of new legislation the Competition Bill lost out and was not included in the November Queen's Speech for legislation in the forthcoming session. Instead, and even worse, the DTI sponsored a portmanteau 'deregulation' bill which contained six clauses dealing with competition policy. This tinkering around the edges rather than comprehensive reform was not only unsatisfactory, it implied an unwillingness to legislate at all in the Parliament, which should run to 1996/97.[79]

What went wrong? The DTI was adamant that the only blockage to legislation was a shortage of parliamentary time. As Michael Heseltine said in February 1994: 'Today's programme mentions an "unfulfilled commitment" to reform Restrictive Trade Practices (RTP) legislation. Let me stress that commitment. I recognise that the present law is unsatisfactory. I and my Government colleagues are therefore fully committed to introducing an effective (prohibition based) system as soon as Parliamentary time allows.'[80] This formulation indicated only partial reform, with no substantial amendment of monopoly provisions and no indication of when parliamentary time would allow. The considerations that might have made the Cabinet reluctant to embark upon competition legislation are opaque, but six factors can be identified. First, the bill would have been complex and in some respects (such as the prohibition, third-party action, fines, and appeals) would have been controversial. It was a major piece of legislation. Secondly, however, it is not clear that the Bill would have been a vote winner. While the intention was mentioned in the manifesto, competition policy is not a 'populist' issue; neither, curiously enough, has it become part of the Conservative pantheon. 'Deregulation' was more compatible with ministers' self-image of a radical, liberalizing government. Thirdly, lack of business enthusiasm was probably the decisive factor. The CBI and companies pay lip-service to the need for reform, but there is a wide suspicion that privately, or even schizophrenically, many business leaders are content with a weak policy laxly enforced. Fourthly, the issue should not be taken in isolation. The 'San Andreas' fault line within the Conservative Party was over attitudes to Europe. The proposed RTP reforms could have been presented as 'pro-European', adapting UK law to the Brussels model. This might in itself have been enough to make ministers shy away from it. A fifth, linked factor was the intangible atmosphere of contemporary British politics in which the government of John Major had 'lost its nerve'. From 'Black Wednesday'—16 September 1992, when Britain left the ERM—to the 1994 European elections and the disastrous 1995 local elections, the government has been on a slippery slope towards ever-lower levels of popularity, attended by a series of policy fiascos and an image of 'sleaze'. It may seem fanciful to link this to the prosaic world of competition law, but the instinct in government (or at least in the DTI) was to play safe, to keep heads below the parapet and avoid anything smacking of controversy. Sixthly, major initiatives need ministerial leadership. Michael Heseltine put 'competitiveness' ahead of 'competition', and did not see political or policy mileage in competition policy. In addition, of course, he was convalescing over the summer of 1993 following his heart attack in Venice. The DTI has been the most extraordinarily unlucky of government departments in its leadership since Mrs Thatcher took power in 1979 (consider Joseph's atheism; Tebbit and the 'Brighton bomb'; Brittan's resignation; Lord Young's public relations obsessions; and the sheer turnover of ministers). In the summer of 1993 it was unlucky again, with an absentee landlord.

Policy relaxation?

Instead of the intensification of competition policy which was widely
expected when the *Abuse of Market Power* Green Paper was issued in November 1992, the reality was instead a relaxation of
policy. This is not the official position of the government, but it
is difficult not to draw this conclusion from four recent developments. First, a series of procedural changes were put into effect
arising from the government's 'deregulation' exercise. This deregulatory preoccupation has drawn on extensive consultation with
industry, and allowed firms to create an agenda of issues which
they find onerous, time consuming, and which generally are alleged
to reduce competitiveness by increasing 'compliance costs'. Thus
the government has significantly increased the *de minimis* merger
referral threshold from assets of £30 million to £70 million. It has
also drawn up speedier timetables for dealing with monopolies,
mergers, and restrictive practices in all the competition agencies.
Deadlines are now so tight that they have become a real constraint
and are influencing how cases are evaluated and decided. This is
dangerous. We have seen with the EC merger regulation that undue
priority given to deadlines creates a bias towards superficial analysis, hasty deal-making, and approval.

Secondly, and also arising from the deregulation initiative, the
new Deregulation Bill contains provisions to abolish preliminary
investigation by the OFT under the Competition Act; it greatly
increases the discretion of the authorities to negotiate undertakings in competition and merger cases; and it creates a new power
'which would allow companies to offer enforceable undertakings
to the Secretary of State as an alternative to an MMC monopoly
reference by the DGFT'.[81] It is significant that undertakings will be
made to the Secretary of State on the advice of the DGFT or the
utility regulators, and this greatly expanded use of undertakings
removes much of the transparency that has been such a feature of
MMC investigations, to replace it with a process of opaque deal-
making. The undertakings will, however, be published and will
give rise to third-party rights to injunctions and damages if they
are breached. Existing undertakings were published in April 1994,[82]
and the Register is likely to become a very significant document
for policing and evaluating competition enforcement.

Thirdly, this increased availability of discretion greatly depends, of course, on how it is used. The feeling that Michael Heseltine regards competition policy as a residual framework which should not impede the competitive strategies of companies has been reinforced by his recent major speech on competition. In February 1994 he stressed the context of competition enforcement in three 'realities': namely, 'increasing globalisation of industry'; 'players big enough' to compete; and 'the rapid pace of technological change', which makes market power fragile. Hence, he said, 'It follows that one of the best ways in which I can help business is by ensuring that we operate an effective and realistic competition policy. *A policy that will promote competitiveness.*'[83] Mr Heseltine's preferences are seen in his recent Competitiveness White Paper, which mentions UK law reform in one paragraph of a 159-page paper.[84]

The fourth development is the early resignation of the Director General of Fair Trading. Sir Bryan Carsberg was appointed in 1992 by Michael Heseltine after distinguished service as Britain's first utility regulator, the head of OFTEL (Office of Telecommunications Regulation). He announced his resignation on 28 November 1994, without a great fanfare, giving as his reason a better job offer. His motives for going were complex and included annoyance with both the MMC and the President of the Board of Trade, frustration with his constrained role compared with freedom of manœuvre at OFTEL, and disappointment with the absence of law reform. He did not directly attack the government, but made his disillusion clear, and his departure can only be read as a condemnation of British competition policy. His resignation acted as a powerful catalyst. It prompted the parliamentary inquiry into monopoly policy which unleashed the 'scream of rage' described by *The Economist* (see above).

In his own evidence to the Trade and Industry Committee, given before his term of office ended, Sir Bryan broke with convention to criticize government policy. In a prepared statement he astonished the Committee, by observing that 'I would favour the establishment of a unitary competition authority for the UK'.[85] This was in direct contradiction to the DTI evidence to the Committee, which had described the tripartite structure of government bodies and declared that 'The Government are content with this broad structure'.[86] Sir Bryan has thus delivered the most authoritative and unimpeachable critique of current policy, and in doing so has emphasized its weakness.

The current combination of a weakly enforced competition policy, based on discredited legal and organizational structures, has fuelled a level of criticism which might be seen as irresistible. But government is under no compulsion to act, and Reports from Parliamentary Committees are regularly ignored. Many business interests, including the CBI, are opposed to a unitary competition authority. At the time of writing the outcome is very difficult to predict. The government has the ability to implement reform and Michael Heseltine has a reputation for radical moves. At the very least he has to appoint a new Director General of Fair Trading (an industrialist, Mr John Bridgeman, from British Alcan, was appointed from October 1995). In the longer term he may also wish to pre-empt Labour reforms. It is widely expected that Labour will win the 1996–7 general election. The Labour Party has turned its attention to competition policy, which fits in comfortably with its new social-democratic ideology. In a significant speech Labour's Shadow Chancellor, Gordon Brown, declared that 'Action is overdue to ensure competition is fair and open. . . . We need to replace the current confusion of laws with a coherent, pro-competition policy based on clear rules transparently applied and properly enforced by a strengthened OFT which brings the UK into line with the best European practice.'[87]

Such Labour views raise the prospect of even more radical reform than is currently waiting to be enacted. In this respect some reformers are beginning to feel that the failure to reform is 'a blessing in disguise'.[88] Many would now share the view of legal academics, such as John Pratt, recently expressed in the *European Competition Law Review* under the apt title 'UK Competition Law: A Wasted Opportunity'. In an excellent analysis he suggests that 'a golden opportunity' has been missed, that the government has been overly reliant on unsystematic business views, and that the possibility of creating 'one competition authority' should urgently be considered.[89]

CONCLUSIONS

In a chapter of this length perhaps a conciliatory gesture can be made in restricting the conclusions to a few brief points. The first is the regrettable but unavoidable conclusion that the current failure to legislate on competition law reform is calling British competition policy into disrepute. The reform proposals are being held in a state of suspended animation which perpetuates a situation universally accepted as being unsatisfactory, which creates uncertainty, and which pre-empts any constructive discussion of further developments in policy or institutional change.

Secondly, there are conclusions to be drawn about the nature of the institution of British competition policy and the organizations which administer it. Current law reform proposals do not envisage fundamental organizational reform, and if there is one positive facet of the failure to reform it is the possibility that a further appraisal will address the organizations as well as the law. The choice of institutional structure, process, personnel, and resources has potentially an equally important effect on the future of competition policy as the choice of economic theory or legal principle. Prescriptions for reform vary, although the idea of a single 'Competition Authority' embracing the OFT, MMC, most of the DTI people, and the utility regulators is becoming a common nostrum. What is clear is that the present multiplicity of institutions cannot be allowed to continue. It is not just the delay, the ambiguity, and the lack of leadership arising from multiple institutions; a more serious problem is the coexistence of three 'philosophies' of competition policy (in the DTI, OFT, MMC; and four if you count DG IV). This gives rise to inhibited enforcement, inadequate deterrence, poor compliance, and muddled reactions to new challenges and international initiatives.

Thirdly, this chapter has stressed the influence of business on the design and enforcement of British competition policy. The cooperation of business is essential, particularly in the British system, but it might be asked whether business influence has gone too far. Competition policy should protect consumers, it should protect market freedoms as well as competitiveness, and it has an important role in society as an antidote to excessive concentrations of market power. Recent reform proposals have instead focused on alleged 'burdens' on business and have given privileged attention to business viewpoints. Does this begin to look like 'capture'? Not in the crude sense of business influencing individuals or decisions, but in the more general sense of occupying the ideological terrain, tilting the agenda and the options to accommodate those who, after all, are the targets of regulation.

Fourthly, the international agenda of competition policy discussions, mediated through the OECD, talks extensively of convergence. The lack of reform in Britain together with the likely continuation of the 'public-interest' test for monopolies and mergers means that British policy is 'divergent'. The peculiar British characteristics of pragmatic administration, business co-operation, lack of sanctions, political control, and the consideration of 'non-competition' factors will all be continued. 'Convergence' is only being realized in the extent to which European law is extending its influence and jurisdiction into the domestic scene, a process as gradual as it is uncertain.

Finally, it is perhaps interesting to ask whether there is a British 'model' of competition policy which is different from the 'European (German)' and the 'American' models and which might have some attractive features. In the areas of monopolies and of mergers there is some satisfaction with the British system. It is pragmatic, flexible, relatively transparent, and capable of delivering assertive action—mergers can be banned, monopolies broken up. A strengthening of that system has much to commend it in the areas both of industry generally and of the privatized utilities. In this latter area of utility regulation the action is coming thick and fast, and it may have a demonstration effect, indicating what can be done across industry as a whole.

NOTES

1. Tim Frazer, *Monopoly, Competition and the Law: The Regulation of Business Activity in Britain, Europe and America* (Brighton: Wheatsheaf, 1988), 106.
2. Michael Heseltine, 'Competition is Good for Competitiveness', speech by President of the Board of Trade to CBI/Nabarro Nathanson Conference on Competition, 1 Feb. 1994, transcript para. 19.
3. See Department of Trade and Industry (DTI), *Opening Markets: New Policy on Restrictive Trade Practices* (London: HMSO, July 1989), Cm 727.
4. See Department of Trade and Industry, *Abuse of Market Power: A Consultative Document on Possible Legislative Options* (London: HMSO Nov. 1992), Cm 2100.
5. *The Economist*, 'Screaming at the Umpire', 1 Apr. 1995, 27.
6. For a review of Labour policy-making see Stephen Wilks, *Industrial Policy and the Motor Industry* (Manchester: Manchester University

Press, 1988), chs. 2 and 3. For current policy debate see Keith Cowling and Malcolm Sawyer, 'Merger and Monopoly Policy', in K. Cowling and M. Sawyer (eds.), *A New Economic Policy for Britain* (Manchester: Manchester University Press, 1990).

7. Quoted in T. Freyer, *Regulating Big Business: Antitrust in Great Britain and America 1880–1990* (Cambridge: Cambridge University Press, 1992), 78.

8. Ibid. 104.

9. M. Keller, 'Regulation of Large Enterprise: The United States Experience in Comparative Perspective', in A. Chandler and H. Daems (eds.), *Managerial Hierarchies* (Cambridge, Mass.: Harvard University Press, 1980), 165.

10. R. Bernhard, 'English Law and American Law on Monopolies and Restraints of Trade', *Journal of Law and Economics*, 3 (Oct. 1960), 137.

11. Freyer, *Regulating Big Business*, 244.

12. J. D. Gribbin, *The Post War Revival of Competition as Industrial Policy*, Government Economic Service, Working Paper 19 (London: Price Commission, 1978), 9.

13. Freyer, *Regulating Big Business*, 252.

14. D. Vogel, *National Styles of Regulation* (Ithaca, NY: Cornell University Press, 1985).

15. Freyer, *Regulating Big Business*, 262, 268.

16. See K. George and C. Joll (eds.), *Competition Policy in the UK and EEC* (Cambridge: Cambridge University Press, 1975), 15; and J. Jewkes, 'British Monopoly Policy 1944–56', *Journal of Law and Economics*, 3 (Oct. 1960), 4.

17. D. O'Brien, 'Competition Policy in Britain: The Silent Revolution', *The Antitrust Bulletin*, spring 1982, 218.

18. Both phrases from ibid. 218, 232.

19. Ibid. 231.

20. Ibid. 234.

21. R. Komiya, 'Introduction', in R. Komiya and K. Suzumura (eds.), *Industrial Policy of Japan* (Tokyo: Academic Press, 1988).

22. R. Whish, *Competition Law* (3rd edn., London: Butterworths, 1993), 730.

23. P. Craig, 'The Monopolies and Mergers Commission', in R. Baldwin and C. McCrudden (eds.), *Regulation and Public Law* (London: Weidenfeld and Nicholson, 1987), 202.

24. Freyer, *Regulating Big Business*, 265–8.

25. See the Monopolies and Mergers Commission, *Annual Review, 1994* (London: MMC, 1995), figures as at Dec. 1994.

26. Consumer's Association, 'Submission by Consumer's Association to the Trade and Industry Select Committee Inquiry into UK Policy on

Monopolies', copy, Feb. 1995, 13. Publication is anticipated with the Minutes of Evidence under HC 249 of 1994–5 (London: HMSO). See also *The Economist*, 1 Apr. 1995, 27–8.

27. J. Methven, 'Introductory Remarks', in George and Joll, *Competition Policy in the UK and EEC*, 3.

28. Frazer, Monopoly, *Competition and the Law*, 36.

29. I. Ramsay, 'The Office of Fair Trading', in Baldwin and McCrudden (eds.), *Regulation and Public Law*, 178–81.

30. See the speech given by Geoffrey Howe upon Sir Gordon Borrie's retirement. Lord Howe of Aberavon, 'The Birth of an Office: A Midwife's View', speech at the Café Royal (London: OFT, 29 May 1992).

31. G. Borrie, 'Serving Consumers' Best Interests', Introduction to OFT, *Annual Report of the Director General of Fair Trading, 1990* (London: HMSO, Session 1991, HC 502), 13.

32. *Fair Trading Act 1973*, section 2 (2).

33. Frazer, *Monopoly, Competition and the Law*, 136–7.

34. The four big utility regulators have become public figures. The most recent and spectacular controversy arose from the announcement on 7 March 1995 by Professor Littlechild of a review of the pricing formula of the twelve Regional Electricity Companies. This was totally unexpected and came the day after the final privatization of the two power generators. It generated something approaching hysteria in the City of London.

35. Robin Aaronson, 'Do Companies Take Any Notice of Competition Policy?', *Consumer Policy Review*, 2/3 (July 1992), 143, 141.

36. John Pratt, 'Changes in UK Competition Law: A Wasted Opportunity', *European Competition Law Review*, 2 (1994), 94.

37. Confederation of British Industry, *Refocusing the Competition Rules: Making the Single Market Work* (London: CBI, 1994).

38. Confederation of British Industry, 1989 White Paper: 'Opening Markets . . .', note CA 696.92, CBI, Feb. 1993, esp. para. 3.

39. Confederation of British Industry, Nov. 1992 Green Paper, 'Abuse of Market Power . . .', note CCL 27.93i, CBI, Feb. 1993, para. 12.7.

40. Ibid. para. 6.20; a position confirmed in written evidence to the Trade and Industry Committee in Feb. 1995, where the CBI commented that 'the current law and institutional framework is the most appropriate'. Confederation of British Industry, Memorandum to the Trade and Industry Committee, copy, 27 Feb. 1995, para. 19; publication anticipated in HC 249 of 1994–5.

41. House of Lords Select Committee on the European Communities, *Enforcement of Community Competition Rules*, Report with Evidence, Session 1993–4, HL 7 (London: HMSO, Dec. 1993).

42. Department of Trade and Industry and the Office of Fair Trading, *Consultation Exercise on Possible Changes to Competition Legislation*

and *Procedures to Reduce the Burden on Business* (London: DTI, Sept. 1993).

43. House of Lords Select Committee on the European Communities, *Enforcement of Community Competition Rules*.

44. DTI, *Abuse of Market Power Green Paper (Cm 2100): Summary of Responses* (London: DTI/Competition Policy Division, Apr. 1993).

45. Trade and Industry Committee, *Takeovers and Mergers*, Session 1991–2, HC 90 (London: HMSO, Nov. 1991); and *Memoranda of Evidence*, Session 1990–1, HC 226i (London: HMSO, Feb. 1991).

46. O. E. Williamson, 'Antitrust Enforcement: Where it Has Been: Where it is Going', in J. Craven (ed.), *Industrial Organization, Antitrust and Public Policy* (Dordrecht: Kluwer-Nijhoff, 1983); repr. in *Antitrust Economics* (Oxford: Blackwell, 1987), 324.

47. See e.g. Adrian Walker-Smith, 'Collusion: Its Detection and Investigation', *European Competition Law Review*, 12 (1991), or the work of J. Gribbin and M. Howe, both economists who took up senior administrative positions at the OFT. Also Nick Gardner, a former Senior Economic Adviser at the DTI, who has written a 'businessman's guide' to the practical operation of competition policy, *A Guide to United Kingdom and European Community Competition Policy* (London: Macmillan, 1990; 2nd edn. forthcoming).

48. Ramsay, 'The Office of Fair Trading', 182.

49. Minutes of evidence to the Trade and Industry Committee, *Takeovers and Mergers*, Session 1990–1, HC 226iii (London: HMSO, 1991), 163.

50. Trade and Industry Committee, *First Report: Takeovers and Mergers*, Session 1991–2, HC 90 (London: HMSO, 1991), paras. 105–9.

51. See Stephen Wilks, 'The Metamorphosis of European Competition Policy', Exeter, RUSEL Working Paper 9 (1992), repr. in F. Snyder (ed.), *European Law in Context: A Reader* (Aldershot: Dartmouth, 1993).

52. Tom Sharpe, 'British Competition Policy in Perspective', *Oxford Review of Economic Policy*, 1/3 (1985), 85.

53. OFT, *Fair Trading*, 3 June 1993, 9.

54. Sir Gordon Borrie, 'Restrictive Practices Control in the UK: Big Bangs and Lesser Detonations', The Travers Memorial Lecture, 11 Mar. 1986, repr. in *Journal of Business Law*, 1986, 364.

55. The small Cartel Task Force was launched on 2 Feb. 1995, mainly in response to the OFT's House of Lords legal victory in the ready-mix concrete case. It involves an information pack and a hotline, but was also associated with an appeal to the government to strengthen the law. See OFT, Cartels Task Force package.

56. This has become a widely cited statistic. Details are given in 'Supplementary notes by the DTI', published in minutes of evidence to the Trade and Industry Committee, *Takeovers and Mergers*, 1990–1, HC

226 xi (London: HMSO, 1991), 319. Five of the cases were in 1990–1. For the 1993 cases see e.g. *Financial Times*, 25 Feb. 1993. The fifteenth case took on a note of farce. In February 1995 Mr Heseltine overruled Sir Bryan's recommendation to refer the proposed takeover of the UK company Waddington by the US company Hasbro. Waddington is, of course, the maker of the famous board game 'Monopoly', and Mr Heseltine's snub came only a week after Sir Bryan's critical evidence to the Trade and Industry Committee. See N. Cope and M. Fagan, 'Heseltine Moves to Third Snub in Monopoly Game', *The Independent*, 1 Mar. 1995.

57. For an interesting American treatment of political influence, see W. Comanor, 'Antitrust in a Political Environment', *The Antitrust Bulletin*, winter 1982.

58. D. O'Brien, 'Competition Policy in Britain; The Silent Revolution', *The Antitrust Bulletin*, spring 1982, 227.

59. 'Memorandum submitted by Sir Gordon Borrie', Memoranda of evidence, Trade and Industry Committee, *Takeovers and Mergers*, 1990–1, HC 226 i (London: HMSO, 1991), 47.

60. Quoted in John Swift, 'Merger Policy: Certainty or Lottery?', in J. Fairburn and J. Kay (eds.), *Mergers and Merger Policy* (Oxford: Oxford University Press, 1989), 267.

61. Trade and Industry Committee, *First Report*, paras. 254, 256.

62. See Sir Bryan Carsberg, 'OFTEL', in C. Veljanovski (ed.), *Regulators and the Market* (London: IEA, 1991); and C. Veljanovski, *The Future of Industry Regulation* (London: European Policy Forum, 1993), 34.

63. R. Rice, 'OFT Chief May Use Price Caps Against Market Abuse', *Financial Times*, 12 Sept. 1992.

64. Sir Gordon Borrie, 'Reflections of a Retiring Director General', *Annual Report of the DGFT, 1991* (London: HMSO, 1992), 10.

65. Frazer, *Monopoly, Competition and the Law*, 77.

66. Conservative Party Manifesto, *The Right Approach*, May 1992, 10.

67. Department of Trade and Industry, *Review of Restrictive Trade Practices Policy: A Consultative Document*, Green Paper (London: HMSO, Mar. 1988), Cm 331, para. 2.8.

68. Department of Trade and Industry and OFT, *Consultation Exercise on Possible Changes*, para. 55.

69. Ibid. para. 45.

70. Department of Trade and Industry, *Opening Markets*, Cm 727, para. 3.3.

71. Department of Trade and Industry, *Review*, Cm 331, para. 1.5.

72. Whish, *Competition Law*, 761.

73. Department of Trade and Industry, *Review*, Cm 331, para. 4.6.

74. Whish, *Competition Law*, 764–5.

75. Department of Trade and Industry, *Review*, Cm 331, para. 6.17.

76. Department of Trade and Industry, *Opening Markets*, Cm 727, paras. 4.5–4.7.
77. Trade and Industry Committee, *First Report*, paras. 286–97.
78. Department of Trade and Industry, Press Release, 14 Apr. 1993.
79. This will again require Richard Whish to deal with 'Reform of domestic law' as an Appendix to a prospective fourth edition of *Competition Law*, as he has done with the second and now the third editions.
80. Michael Heseltine, 'Competition is Good for Competitiveness'.
81. Note by the DTI and the OFT, *Deregulation of Competition Law and Procedures: Proposed Changes* (London: DTI, Jan. 1994), para. 15.
82. Office of Fair Trading, *Register of Undertakings and Orders; under the Competition Act 1980 and the Monopoly Provisions of the Fair Trading Act 1973* (London: OFT, Apr. 1994).
83. Michael Heseltine, 'Competition is Good for Competitiveness'.
84. *Competitiveness: Helping Business to Win*, Cm 2563 (London: HMSO, May 1994). This was a very substantial paper running to 159 pages. It was seen as something of an unfocused jumble of ideas. The OFT were not consulted in its preparation. A second, more action-orientated version, is expected in the summer of 1995.
85. Sir Bryan Carsberg, Opening Statement to Trade and Industry Select Committee, copy, OFT, 22 Feb. 1995. Publication anticipated with Minutes of Evidence, HC 249, 1994–5.
86. Department of Trade and Industry Written Evidence to the Trade and Industry Select Committee, Jan. 1995. Publication anticipated as ibid.
87. Gordon Brown, Corporate Governance Speech, PIRC Conference, 17 Mar. 1995, transcript, 7.
88. Consumer Association, 'Submission', 13.
89. Pratt, 'Changes in UK Competition Law', 99.

7

The German Cartel Office in a Hostile Environment

ROLAND STURM

INTRODUCTION

The literature on the German Cartel Office (Bundeskartellamt) contains two extreme positions. Many publications on the German political economy simply ignore the Office as an insignificant ornament to the dynamics of the German economy. Economists and experts in competition law, however, and many politicians and business managers, praise or criticize the power of the Office for a wide range of different reasons. Such contrasts in perception of the Cartel Office and the lack of a middle ground in public opinion have a lot to do with the complicated network of environments in which the Office has to operate. From the perspective of the Office's internal institutional identity the diagnosis is unambiguous. A strong sense of mission seems to be justified and essential. One of the reasons for the feeling of institutional superiority is certainly, as will be shown, the fact that the Office functions on an organizationally sound basis. The institutionalized sense of purpose is provided to a great extent by the cartel law. The Cartel Office itself characterized the cartel law after 20 years of experience as being synonymous with the very principle of Germany's economic order, the social market economy.[1]

With regard to other institutions the greatest respect for the Office's role is to be expected from the Monopoly Commission. The Commission was created in 1973 when the original cartel law of 1957 was revised for the second time. Its task is to monitor the concentration process in industry, and to write regular biannual reports and reports on special merger cases, either initiated by the Commission or the economics minister.[2] Very important for the general climate in which the Office has to make decisions are the economic philosophy of the government of the day, the country's economic situation, and the demands of economic pressure groups. Whereas these factors may influence the general trend both of the decisions of the Office and the public-interest in its role, for specific cases, such as mergers or the abuse of dominant market positions, the efficient counterparts of the Office are the courts. In the courts firms can challenge verdicts of the Office, and by writing legal opinions the courts are not only deciding on specific cases, but are also developing the legal framework in which the Cartel Office has to operate.

Recently a new dimension has gained importance in the role of the Cartel Office and its relative strength as an institution, namely the internationalization of competition and, to some extent, competition rules. Of greatest importance in this respect is the ongoing process of European integration. Predating the Single Market are the competition rules of the EEC treaty in its articles 85 and 86, and the European merger-control regulation of 1989. Of increasing importance for the Office has been the fact that all firms, including the bigger German ones, do not regard Germany, or even Europe as the framework for their activities, but rather they use the world market. Standardization of competition rules on this level is in its infancy, although the OECD competition committee has made some progress towards this goal.

The following sections of the chapter deal in greater detail with the complicated world of external pressures the Cartel Office has to operate in, as well as with factors determining its institutional identity. The renewed interest of the social sciences in institutions advises us to focus our attention on the Office's internal consensus-building strategies. The analysis of the self-definition of the Office's role, its organizational identity, and its rules and traditions are necessary to understand the driving force behind rule-making in German competition policy. But, as has been mentioned, the Office's 'independence' is very much restricted by networks of decision-making on different levels, intra-organizational, national, European, world-wide. Those authors who see the Office overwhelmed by this mostly hostile environment doubt that today it is still a significant institution. From the Office's point of view what counts is that there is (substantial) decison-making power left, and that the task ahead is to 'transfer' and possibly extend this decision-making power in a process of internationalization of the Office's principles to the European and broader international level.

THE LEGAL FRAMEWORK AND THE OFFICE'S CORPORATE CULTURE

History

The Federal Cartel Office was established in Berlin on 1 January 1958. Until 1973 its task was restricted to the control of cartelization and to the control of abuses of dominant market positions. The definition of, and the action against, unfair trade practices are not the responsibility of the cartel office. Unfair trade is classified as a form of criminal behaviour when it violates a specific law originating from 1909 banning such behaviour (*Gesetz gegen den unlauteren Wettbewerb*), or one of a number of other special laws on fair prices and product information.

Important sectors of the economy, such as agriculture, the utilities, banking, and insurance, are still exempt from competition rules. These exemptions can be explained and to some degree justified in two ways. One explanation is that the cartel law is a political compromise. In the 1950s most of the representatives of German industry[3] opposed the idea of a cartel law, which they saw as an impediment for industrial growth and reconstruction in post-war Germany. For the political decision-makers, and above all for the then economics minister, Ludwig Erhard, who argued that a law guaranteeing competition was essential for the success of a market economy, the question was whether there would be a law at all with major exemptions, or no law. The exemptions granted were explained by traditional arguments. On the one hand, there was the need to retain some degree of national economic autarky in cases of future crises, perhaps associated with the cold war. This argument justified, for example, uncompetitive behaviour in agriculture and the utilities industries. On the other hand there was the public interest argument. This was used, for example, to justify the exemption of banking and insurance. It was said that after the German experience of two currency reforms within decades, which led to the loss of individual savings in banks or insurance companies, banking and insurance needed extra protection. Dangerous free competition, which might lead to new bankruptcies, should be avoided. It is obvious that such arguments are less convincing now. The pressure of European market integration has led to a general debate in Germany on the deregulation of many of the hitherto exempt sectors of industry. In the final consequence this will have to lead to a revision of the cartel law, and to a broadening of its brief.

The Cartel Office's task is to execute the cartel law. The 1973 reform of the cartel law gave the Office the task of merger control. In performing its functions the Cartel Office sees developments in the economy primarily in the narrow perspective defined by the law. The economics minister may correct this perspective by decisions to override the Cartel Office's conclusions in the public interest. The Monopoly Commission has a more general task of providing information on the changing ownership patterns in industry and it comments on the role the Cartel Office can fulfil. Since 1973 the cartel law has been revised five times, most recently in 1990. The federal government now believes that for the time being the cartel law should remain unchanged. Otherwise there could be a danger of over-regulation. The next revision should make the German law compatible with the changes brought about by the competition control framework of the EC.[4] The major opposition party, the Social Democrats, are, however, in favour of a general ban for mergers above a certain size.[5]

The Office is legally a part of the Economics ministry. It is a federal agency (*Bundesoberbehörde*) and has to respect the rules which apply to such agencies, for example with regard to financial control, employment, and other organizational aspects. The Office is formally independent, however, both with regard to decisions on which cases to select for an investigation, and with regard to decisions on the question of whether or not these cases violate competition rules.

The organizational framework of the Office has been fairly stable over time, without any kind of major reallocation of competences. The Office has only had three presidents: Eberhard Günther (1958–76), Wolfgang Kartte (1976–92), and Dieter Wolf (since 1992). The President is, above all, the chief communicator. By making skilful use of the media he tries to create both public attention and esteem for the work of the Office. Here personality factors matter more than any kind of legal or organizational tradition. The Office was more or less the brainchild of Eberhard Günther, who had the greatest influence on its organizational development. Because of his interest in economics he was convinced that an independent agency for safeguarding competition has to have special resources. Günther was a lawyer, but against the German civil-service monopoly of lawyers he fought for an equal role for economists in the new Office. Günther not only had a vision, he was also able to give it practical effect with far-reaching consequences.[6] His successor, Wolfgang Kartte, also became a very well-known president. He regularly gave interviews or even wrote essays for influential and widely read newspapers and journals, such as the weekly *Der Spiegel*. His successor, Dieter Wolf, seems to prefer a lower public profile and seems to be less able or willing to seek publicity. In contrast to his predecessors he has a less hostile attitude towards industrial policy. What he calls economic interventionism is a strategy he at least would be ready to discuss in detail.[7]

Organization

The most important parts of the Office are the decision-making units, *Beschlußabteilungen*, which investigate and decide on violations of the cartel law. These units are organized by sectors of industry, such as chemicals and chemical products, iron and steel, and iron and steel products (see Figure 7.1). A unit has a staff of ten to twelve people, more than half of whom do investigative work exploring the development of certain sectors of industry. The others are responsible for the unit's routine business, including the sending off, and the reporting on, several hundred long questionnaires (with an average of 80 questions) mailed to many firms when problems of competition in certain sectors of industry are investigated. In extreme cases the cartel law gives the Cartel Office, *de facto* the decision-making units, the right to initiate police raids and to search for files in firms which are under suspicion of having violated the cartel law. It may confiscate the files, but after three days it needs a court decision to support its actions.

Some organizational reforms have been made which reflect both the growing work-load and some degree of institutional learning. The Office started with five decision-making units, four of which were organized by sectors of industry. The fifth unit was supposed to act as a co-ordinating and revising chamber (*Einspruchsabteilung*), a sixth unit was planned as a second revising chamber.[8] In 1960, however, because of the quality of the daily work-load, the decision was made to opt for a fifth decision-making unit and not to

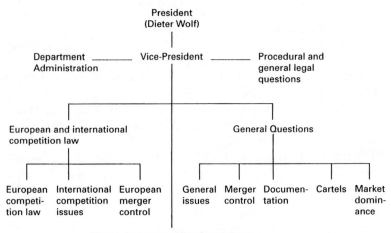

The 10 decision-making departments

organized into branches: non-metallic minerals, glassware (Dept. 1); leather goods, textiles, agriculture and forestry (2); chemical products (3); mechanical engineering products (4); Ores (5); printing, tobacco, film and advertising (6); aerospace, rail, data telecommunications (7); mining, water, energy, banking (8); consumer goods (9); paper, health, and professions (10). Exclusive responsibility for cartels lies with Dept. 2, licensing and public procurement authorities with Dept. 5.

Source: Gerd Aberle, *Wettbewerbstheorie und Wettbewerbspolitik* (Stuttgart: W. Kohlhammer, 1990), 83.

FIG. 7.1 The organizational structure of the Bundeskartellamt

create a second revising chamber. The total number of units was now six: five sectoral decision-making ones and one revising chamber. When firms complained about decisions of the Office they could approach the Einspruchsabteilung which would then reconsider the case in question. In theory this was an opportunity to get a second opinion before the case might go to the courts. In practice it soon turned out that, because if not the same people, at least the people trained in the same way of thinking, reconsidered cases in this sixth unit, decisions were usually not changed. After 1966 this sixth unit was given another task. It became responsible for the general matters of market dominance, competition rules, and fines for offenders, which were outside the responsibility of the other five decision units organized by sectors of industry.

In the early seventies the number of units responsible for general matters was increased to three, and the total number of decision-making units to eight. In 1973, when the Cartel Office was made responsible for merger control, this new task was also given to the units with broader responsibility. The principle of extension was at first that new units were simply given the new tasks. This was changed, however, in the late 1970s. What happened, and this is of great importance for the organizational cohesion of the Office, was that the existing work-load was spread out amongst all units, and the new tasks were integrated into the total work-load. With regard to merger control this meant that, at first, decision-making units responsible for sectors of industry had no responsibility for merger control. This, however, created tensions in the Office, because merger control not only grew rapidly in its importance for the Office's work, it also was seen by the staff as the most prestigious field of their work. In the late 1970s (after a first extension of merger control responsibilities from three to four units in 1977) a new rationale of reorganization, namely an equal spread of responsibilities for sectors of industry across all decision-making units, was accepted. In the early 1980s merger control responsibilities were also broadened and given to every single decision-making unit.

A further extension of the number of decison-making units occurred in 1980 when a ninth unit was added, because additional capacity was needed in the wake of the fourth revision of the cartel law. In 1990 a tenth decision-making unit was created to cope with the work-load caused by the privatization of the East German economy. As before, this was not done by creating a unit for the new special purpose, but only by a redistribution of work now between ten instead of nine units. All units have no other assignment than to monitor a certain sector of industry. At the moment there are three minor exceptions to this rule. Decision-making unit two has the general responsibility for market restrictions by cartels which define conditions of sale. A general competence for licensing and public procurement problems has been given to unit five, and for market distortions in the case of regulations of demand by trade or industry to unit nine. The Office regards these exceptions, however, as unproblematic pragmatic solutions.[9]

The decision-making units report to their organizational superiors, especially if cases are important and controversial. This does not mean, however, that the units' decisions will be or can be revised. Efficient co-ordination of the work of decision-making units is achieved through weekly meetings of their heads. During these meetings controversial cases which have come up in one unit or the other are debated, and before decisions are made the legal questions involved are considered. A special division on the principles of the Office's policy only has a service function. It was founded in 1977 by a merger of the Law and the Economics divisions. The major reason for the merger was the intention to strengthen in the Office the interdisciplinary co-operation of civil servants trained in law and civil servants trained in economics.[10] The special division on principles can be used by the units to co-ordinate their actions, and its very existence serves as a kind of institutional memory which provides information on past principles of decision-making. This kind of information is important to guarantee a certain degree of continuity in the Office's decision-making. Other special divisions cover broad fields of expertise with regard to national markets. There is know-how on cartels, dominant market positions, and merger control. With regard to international competition there are divisions on European cartel law, international competition, European merger control, and more recently on the harmonization of international competition control. The latter is used to co-ordinate the work of all other international divisions.

Community

What is striking is the non-hierarchical character of the Office's organization. This is important for the motivation of the staff, but it also contributes to a high degree of identification with the office and its task, even to the degree that the independent work in the Office is seen by some members of its staff as being preferable to a better paid job outside. Personal independence includes the possibility of publishing views on cases or principles of competition policy without asking for permission. It even includes the right to publish contradictory opinions. The latter is, however, not the rule. Staff publications usually reflect the Office's thinking in a more general way. Seen from the inside there is a pervasive élitist attitude amongst the staff, with a certain disdain for other government agencies and with little respect for advice or criticism from outside. Even lost court cases do not really matter, because courts are seen as instruments of the Office which allow the Office to test its room for manœuvre.

Important for the community feeling at the Office is its organizational stability, its small and stable size, and the organized process of intra-organizational socialization, which has been perfected over the long years of the Office's existence. The Office started with a staff of 88 in 1958, 26 of which were in the core group of decison-makers. In 1959 the office already had 137 employees, and in 1960 it had 170, with a core group of 48. It grew to a size of over 200 in the 1960s and 1970s, and had 252 employees, and 110 in the decision-making group in 1992.[11] The basic organizational principle is the co-operation of academics trained in law and economics. Though a process of mutual learning has to take place to organize work efficiently, the predominance of the legal culture, evident here as everywhere in the German civil service, cannot be avoided. When the Office started its work this was even more pronounced, because of the greater numerical strength of civil servants trained in law. This had the effect that the decision-making process was more formalized than it is now. To some extent formalization had also to do with a certain initial insecurity with regard to the Office's future role. One should not forget in this regard the long struggle it took to find a statutory base for it. During this struggle quite a number of different role models were debated.[12] Another indicator of what could be called 'initial insecurity' is the fact that the Office's first president, Eberhard Günther, from 1965 onwards, annually assembled a group of academic experts in competition law and policy, judges, and high-ranking civil servants to debate competition policy issues (*Arbeitskreis Kartellrecht*).[13] The Office's current view of this continuing annual meeting is that it should survive for nostalgic reasons, but that the work of the Office has in the meantime become so complicated and requires so much inside knowledge that experts from outside can no longer contribute anything essential to its work. In other words, from the Office's point of view, the real experts now sit in the Cartel Office, and no longer in the universities.[14]

Today one finds in the Office an almost equal proportion of economists and lawyers, even with regard to the leading positions in the decision-making units. A lawyer heading a decision-making unit has an economist as vice-chairperson and vice versa. Head counting by one profession or the other is regarded as hardly necessary, not only because, as mentioned above, there are no principal differences in their approach, but also because the decision-making process itself is non-hierarchical. Decision units are consensus-oriented bodies where arguments are heard and discussion is preferred to pressures from above. Final decisions are made in a group of three, the chairperson and two collaborators.[15] On becoming head of a decision-making unit the person in question usually has collected about twenty years experience in the work of different decision-making units. This also contributes to the standardization of organizational culture. Standardization does not, however, mean uniformity. Procedures may be stable, but this involves the danger that new aspects of new cases may be overlooked. The independent variable for every decision-unit is the possibility of new interpretations.[16] Standardization and common routine are supported by the fact that there is a non-institutionalized process of exchange of personnel between different decision-making units but, at the same time, hardly any exchange of personnel with the economics ministry or, in a broader context, with academia or the business world.

By non-institutionalized exchange it is meant that personnel move from one decision-making unit to another, not because of certain rules, but because the upper hierarchy sees pressing needs. These may arise because there are vacancies to be filled; because a decision-making unit needs additional help, because of its work-load, or expertise; or it may be the case that firms complain that they now have had to deal for a fairly long time with the same unco-operative or disliked person in the Office, and they would be grateful to see a less familiar face.

Whereas the Office's staff is moved about in the Office, there is hardly any career pattern that connects work in the Office with the outside world. Staff have to be sent on a temporary basis to Brussels to the EU or to the East German Länder, but neither industry nor the legal professions, nor other ministries, are possible alternative sources of employment. Those who actually leave the Office are very young. They leave before they reach the official status of a civil servant: for lawyers, in their first year; and for economists, in their first three years.

Independence

Independence in decision-making, organizational and geographical separation from the Economics Ministry (the Office is in Berlin, the Ministry still is in Bonn, and when the Ministry moves to Berlin it is planned to house the Office in Bonn), and an intra-agency network held together less by hierarchy and routine than by a certain sense of mission and superiority, have together given the Federal Cartel Office a great deal of institutional stability. This explains to some extent why the Office can live so easily with the fact that a great deal of its work has little effect when measured statistically. The 1980s have witnessed a constant rise in mergers. Sometimes the Office even has to admit that many of the promises firms make to justify mergers do not materialize. What really matters for the institution as such is that its point has been made, that the community within the Office has come together for the support of a certain strategy, which is based on shared values in the institution no matter what are the values of those who might disagree in the outside world. It is impossible for the Office to judge whether the rise of mergers as such is a positive or a negative development for competition in the German economy, because this implies that the cartel law would define clear criteria in this respect. The law, however, only triggers reactions of the Office to certain developments, and it is for the decision units to decide whether they should intervene or not. Often formal intervention is not necessary, because firms agree on certain standards for mergers or refrain from a planned merger once they have talked to the Office. Still, there remains a large discrepancy between the number of cases in which the Office feels justified to intervene, and the success rate of its interventions.

The main problem, or fear, the Office has, is that one day the outside world may forget about the institution or may believe it is superfluous. The anti-capitalism of important sectors of the German opinion leaders in the late 1960s and early 1970s speeded up the introduction of merger control into the German cartel law. The work of the Office was then seen as a direct contribution to the strengthening of the market economy and an important argument against all attacks on 'monopoly capitalism' from the Left.[17] In its comments on the work of the Office in the year 1969 the federal government wrote that 'political democracy and market economy are unthinkable without a decentralization of power'.[18] The Office is now aware that, in the past, political support for competition as the cornerstone of the German market economy was much more pronounced. Today the general climate for the

Office's work has become much more hostile. The economic crisis, interventionism justified in the name of a healthy environment, a weakening of competition policy rules by the EC, and the neglect of competition principles in the process of the privatization of the East German economy contribute to this new hostile environment. It is typical of the Office that it does not react to this challenge with an identity crisis, but with an effort to educate politicians and the general public. To reach the latter it briefs the press on competition control cases of local importance to attract maximum media attention. It offers opinions on controversial cases, and tries to convince the politicians that even in the European context, as we will see, the Office has a role to play. Until 1978 it published annual and since then it publishes biannual reports on its activities.

THE LOGIC OF DECISION-MAKING

Economic Theory

Decision-making in the Cartel Office is characterized by the absence of a debate on how Germany's economic order under today's economic conditions should ideally look.[19] In other words competition rules, as defined by law, are interpreted without any clarity provided by a more general framework, or any debate on economic theory.[20]

Although the Cartel Office started with a very critical attitude towards any kind of monopolistic or oligopolistic restrictions of competition,[21] the debate on competition theory in Germany brought compromises. It was soon accepted that the notion of economic competition by numerous comparably sized competitors in given markets (polypoly) was more a model than a reality. The observed reality of economic power structures in the markets was given legitimacy by a redefinition of the notion of the ideal form of competition. This redefinition was influenced by the concept of workable competition developed by, among others, the US economist J. M. Clark in 1940.[22] The most influential German economist who worked with this concept was Erhard Kantzenbach, who in 1973 became a member of the first Monopoly Commission, especially because he was well-known for his theoretical contributions. Kantzenbach, argued very much like the workable competition school.[23] He accepted the reduction of polypolies (the competition of an unrestricted number of economic actors of comparable size) to wide oligopolies as a precondition for economic innovation. Oligopolies still have a number of competitors. This factor keeps the principle of competition alive. In contrast to polypolies, the greater size (and therefore also greater resources for research work) of competitors in their markets facilitates technical innovation and modernization by making it both more profitable and more likely. For competitors in an oligopoly it is less easy than in a polypoly to react only slowly or not at all when one large competitor has an advantage in the market. In a polypoly lost income is at least in the beginning lower, and the incentive is higher to come to a gentleman's agreement with some of your competitors either to co-operate to meet the new challenge or to block the innovation.

Kantzenbach's contribution which was influential in the late 1960s and early 1970s[24] was, however, very much criticized for empirical reasons.[25] There was no evidence that the highest degree of competition was to be found in wide oligopolies, the form of competition Kantzenbach had advised the government to see as the final aim of competition policy. In addition, at least two questions remained unresolved: 1) How can the state know which market at which time is dominated by which stage of the product cycle (innovation, mass production, product becomes obsolete)? 2) What is the 'relevant' market and are there any relevant 'national' markets dominated by 'national' firms left?[26]

It was above all the neo-liberal school which argued that competition was not the problem, but the state. Instead of thinking about ideal forms of competition control the neo-liberals saw competition as an automatic result of free markets. The problem they identified was that what they regarded as creeping socialism had eroded market structures. Competition control came to be regarded as some kind of state interventionism and industrial policy. For those defending competition control in principle as a necessary tool for safeguarding competition itself, it remained difficult to refute such attacks as long as the criteria for empirically evaluating competition remained so vague and so much open to criticism. One way of getting around the problem of defining what competition really means is to simply accept the legal framework found in a given society for competition control.[27]

The situation is to some extent paradoxical. Activities of the

Cartel Office are based on the assumption that the single case of competition control can be decided on its own merits, but at the same time it is clear that such a decision implies a hidden vision of what competition actually means, even if it is never spelt out. There seem to be two dominant factors which shape the hidden vision. One is a general consensus amongst decision-makers. But even in the heyday of German Keynesianism this never meant the aceptance of industrial policy by the Cartel Office. In its 1976 report it defined 'active' competition policy as: *a*) support for the co-operation of small and medium-sized enterprises; *b*) information on and the transparency of its decison-making process; and *c*) contacts with industrialists, interest groups, and unions to help them understand the logic of and the freedom for economic activities provided by competition policy.[28] Today's expectations, shared by the federal government, of what competition policy is supposed to be all about have been labelled 'dynamic competition'.[29] This notion implies that the major task of 'intervention', in the form of competition policy, is the privatization of state-owned firms, of infrastructure and public services, and the deregulation of markets. This also implies an ideology of the minimal state.[30] The organizational culture and the traditions of the Office provide a background which gives the decision-makers security. The Office has, however, no legal right to monitor the development of competitive structures of the market economy in general. The fact that its decisions with regard to specific cases may not be accepted by the courts is seen to some extent as a test of the implied assumptions of the Office. For the Cartel Office's staff this does not mean, however, that their general understanding has to be revised. They may have lost a tactical battle, but the fight about the right approach to competition control never ends.

Merger control

Among the traditional fields of competition policy (merger control, abuse of dominant market position, and cartels), merger control has become the major battleground. This is not only because German firms, like other European firms, reacted to the prospect of a Single European Market with a greater interest in mergers, but also because merger control is also the field in which the Office sees its best chances for efficient intervention. The strategies of firms to undermine competition have changed. The national cartel of sectors of industry is dying out. The national register of cartels, which was a responsibility of the Cartel Office, was discontinued by the law on unnecessary economic regulations (*Gesetz zur Bereinigung wirtschaftlicher Vorschriften*) of 27 February 1985. Furthermore, the abuse of dominant market positions is hard to uphold. The Cartel Office is in a difficult position in the courts when it tries to argue that firms abused their market positions to impose excessive price levels on customers, and to suggest which hypothetical price of a good would be the adequate one.[31] Already in 1974 the government admitted that a clear distinction between market induced and market power induced price changes is almost impossible. Following the advice of the Monopoly Commission,[32] it then still hoped that the Office would be able to identify structural elements in markets which cause distortions even if the Office has difficulties when it comes to the question whether specific prices on markets are justified or not.[33] The following decades of practical work have shown, however, that even these limited expectations were too optimistic. As a consequence the federal government has advised the Office to concentrate on very obvious cases of abuse.[34] Even if the Office is successful in the courts, the structure of the markets remains unchanged. A certain exception has recently been developments in East Germany, where market structures are in their infancy, and the weakness of markets has led to a great number of situations of potential or real abuse of dominant market positions. At first this had to be controlled mainly by the Office alone, but after a transition period in which the new *Länder* (states) in the East established their Land cartel offices, this responsibility is now a shared one.

Merger control can influence market structures, and, in merger control, interventions of the Office have greater chances for success in the courts. In addition, the cartel law gives merger cases priority over other cases. Its article 24a(2) allows as a general rule only a period of four months for the merger decision. Moreover, in merger control, considerable media attention is guaranteed. The number of proposed mergers, which have to be controlled by the Office, is far greater than the number of cases in other fields of competition control. In 1991/2, for example, the Office had to investigate 3,778 merger cases, but only 65 cases which fell into the category 'abuse of dominant market position', and 7 cartel

TABLE 7.1. *Mergers registered by the Cartel Office (1973–1992)*

Year	Number	Year	Number
1973	34	1983	506
1974	294	1984	575
1975	445	1985	709
1976	453	1986	802
1977	554	1987	887
1978	558	1988	1,159
1979	602	1989	1,414
1980	635	1990	1,548
1981	618	1991	2,007
1982	603	1992	1,743

Note: The post-unification period after 1990 shows a big increase. Mergers with East German partners: 1990: 121; 1991: 784; 1992: 521. For comparison: from 21 Sept. 1990 when the European merger control regulation came into force, until 31 Dec. 1992, 133 mergers were registered by the Commission. Of those mergers four were withdrawn, among the remaining 129 were 35 cases in which German firms were involved, and 74 which had direct consequences for the German market.
Source: *Bundestagsdrucksäche*, 12/5200, pp. 11, 66, 147.

control cases.[35] The fifth revision of the cartel law in 1990 introduced a catch-all clause (section 23, 2(6)) for mergers below the formal levels defined in the law, to give the Office the opportunity always to veto a merger when there is a danger that the competitive situation of a third firm will be strongly affected by the merger. Critics feared that this revision would result in a total control of all mergers by the Office, but it has used these new powers infrequently.[36]

Trends in industry, especially the preference for mergers over competition (see Table 7.1), have not been greatly influenced by the Office's decisions. Between 1973 and 1992 informal testing by the Office stopped 224 mergers. A total of 16,146 mergers were registered, however. The Office vetoed 101 (0.6 per cent) of them, but won only 55 cases in the courts (0.3 per cent of total cases). In fifteen cases the firms involved asked for the special permission of the economics ministry to merge, because they claimed their merger was in the public interest. In only six cases was this permission given. Permission for mergers can be made conditional. Firms guarantee some kind of internal restructuring as a precondition for the Cartel Office's green light. When this was first put into practice in the mid-1970s parliament assumed that there was no need for legislation to stress the binding character of the guarantees given by the firms. The Cartel Office was sceptical.[37] But today it is clear that firms which ignore commitments made as preconditions for a merger risk a new confrontation and even a possible ban of the merger.

The courts

The most important counterpart of the Cartel Office are the courts specializing in cartel law. A deliberate decision was made to locate cartel cases not in administrative courts, but in the sphere of civil law, to underline that decisions about markets are not based on administrative decisions by the state. This is the same logic which guarantees the Cartel Office its relative autonomy. One of the characteristic features of the cartel law is that it provides wide room for interpretation. This interpretation refers to, as does the legal interpretation of the judges, the normal behaviour of the 'enlightened consumer'. The Cartel Office only decides cases, never principles. As a consequence it can lose court cases when the courts use other implied principles than the Office. For the Office there is no reason to despair. It tries to use up all the room for interpretation it sees, based on the Office's consensus. If it loses a case today, it may well win another case in another court and in another economic environment, which could have been vetoed for the same general reason the lost case had been vetoed. There are certainly trends in the rulings of courts, and legal advisers of firms constantly seek for general restrictions to the Office's power of intervention. In an early phase after the establishment of the Cartel Office the courts tended to look for general rules. After this initial phase the courts concentrated more on specific cases and then even tried to write their decisions in a way which could give the courts a clue how they would decide in similar cases in the future.[38] From the point of view of the Office the courts can change or restrict the legal framework the Office has to work in. Sometimes the restriction has been quite far reaching. Above all, however, there is a conflicting logic between legal guarantees of liberties for firms and the people who act in their name on the one hand; and of the structural restrictions created by economic power relations in markets on the other hand. This logical conflict has never been adressed.[39]

After the legal decision on the Coop/Wandmaker merger (food chains) in 1986, which eliminated the Office's veto against this merger, the Office came to the conclusion that in this sector of the market the only case for which it still has a right of intervention is when a firm secures itself a clear monopoly. Such a monopoly is, however, difficult to find even on the local and regional level.[40] As a result of this major court decision of the mid-1980s the Office was almost helpless when in 1993 the biggest chain store on the German market (Karstadt) and the third in size (Hertie) asked for permission to merge. The Office's former president, Kartte, had warned against this development when he said in an interview that the court decision of 1986 had eliminated merger control in one sector of industry. He characterized this decision as the biggest disappointment of his presidency and criticized the government for its resistance to a revision of the cartel law, which would have given the Office its powers back.[41]

The question of when there is enough evidence for the abuse of a firm's position on a market is an open one, just as is the more general question, should the Office intervene in the economic process, and if so, to what extent? A new conflict between the courts and the Office centres on the problem of the free flow of goods, which may be hindered when the Office asks international firms to allow competition between German branches of these firms. The courts have given preference to the free flow of goods over competition in markets.[42] The Office has respect for the courts. It admits that the judges are thorough, experienced, and fully aware of mistakes the Office might make. There is a feeling in some quarters of the Office that 80 per cent of the cases lost have been lost because the Office's arguments were too weak, and the courts were correct in deciding against the Office.[43]

THE DOMESTIC POLITICS DIMENSION

Informal pressure

In the German political arena the Office has always been confronted with an attitude which saw its existence and interventions as obstacles to economic growth. The very fight for its establish-ment as well as the fact that it took until 1973 until merger control was made its responsibility, are successes of German in-dustry, which at first argued that, for post-war economic recon-struction, competition control was unhelpful, and in the 1960s began to see growth as a precondition for German competitiveness on the world market. In the post-1973 period the Office could not completely free itself from influences which were strictly speaking outside the framework defined by the cartel law.

There have always been such 'atmospheric' elements in the Office's decisions. One problem is that those on the staff work a long time in only one decision-making unit. This means that they are responsible for the control of only one specific sector of indus-try and may start to think too much the way this sector thinks. Another problem is the general mood among economists and political opinion leaders regarding the 'adequate' size of German companies. The political decision-makers are, of course, influenced by interest groups which argue that the Office's interventions are an obstacle to foreign investments or that they cost jobs, because they have delayed or stopped potentially successful mergers. An-other argument is the old one, namely that Europe needs big firms to survive the challenge of US juggernauts on the world market. This argument won the support of the then Economics Minister of the Grand Coalition, Karl Schiller, who has remained a critic of what he sees as the market purism of the Cartel Office.[44] In its modern form the adequate-size argument is used by industrialists, for example by the Daimler chairman Edzard Reuter, to justify mergers and strategic alliances.[45]

Public interest

Public-interest criteria have always played a role in the decisions of the Office on whether or not to intervene against, or veto, specific cases. These criteria are usually not explicit, but there is no doubt that the Office has the 'whole economic picture' of the firms involved and the markets and their prospects when it de-cides. It also knows about the consequences of its decisions (at least in the short run) and tries to verify the potential economic dangers seen by the firms involved. The former President of the

Cartel Office, Wolfgang Kartte, admitted in several interviews that the question of securing jobs by mergers is a crucial one for the Office's decision (though the firms in the long run may never keep their promises, as even the federal government has officially stated).[46] When confronted with the criticism that public-interest deliberations are outside the legal framework the Office should operate in, Kartte replied: 'In strictly legal terms this is true, but we in the Office are also citizens who worry about jobs.'[47] Sometimes other aspects also play a role. A recent example is the Office's attitude towards the *Duales System Deutschland*, a recycling monopoly initiated by industry to deal with waste produced by packaging goods of all kinds. In terms of competition policy the Office should use its instruments against this new monopoly. For the new recycling industry, for the firms who have to deal with the responsibility for the 'waste' they sell as containments for their products, and possibly also for the environment an intervention of the Office at this stage would be disastrous. Consequently it has chosen a 'soft' approach, which means it watches the case, collects information, and for the first time has established contacts with the Federal Environmental Protection Agency (*Bundesumweltamt*). It has also advised local government, which is responsible for waste disposal strategies, to limit the period of time for which they hire a firm to work for it in the framework of the recycling monopoly.[48]

The important difference between the use of the public-interest argument in the German case and in other countries is that in Germany public interest arguments do not produce the legal criteria for intervention or non-intervention. The right of the Office to intervene is defined by 'neutral' criteria, such as turnover, share ownership, or the structure of markets, which are codified in the cartel law. How important and probable certain positive consequences of mergers are, and how such aspects enter into their decision-making process, is left to the discretion of the decision-making units. There are no standard rules, and above all there is no official political intervention on that level in support of one merger or the other.

German unification

A major challenge to the Office's neutral principles for intervention against mergers was certainly German unity. The official political expectations clearly favoured a rapid transformation of the East German economy. Because of its lack of competitiveness this rapid transformation seemed to be impossible without partners from the West. West German industry was, itself, very keen on mergers to eliminate possible future competitors. The Office was to some extent in a no-win situation. A lot of intervention could have meant that it obstructed the necessary transformation process, whereas less intervention could have been seen as an embarrassing departure from its past principles and could have ruined its reputation both nationally and internationally.

Before unification the Cartel Office could only react to the changes taking place in the West German markets, and it had to ignore mergers in the German Democratic Republic (GDR). After the first democratic elections in the GDR in March 1990 the new government installed a competition control agency (*Amt für Wettbewerbsschutz*). This agency, which only existed for a few months until German unification in October, was a weak copy of the Cartel Office. Its staff was trained by the Office and its legal framework was similar, but its internal organization still followed the old East German top-down pattern. It was headed by a vice-president (the president had already left, because of another responsibility found for him), who was also the head of the unit on principles of competition policy. The decision units were not autonomous, but controlled by a hierarchical order. In the eyes of the Cartel Office this East German effort was not to be taken seriously, because of its lack of expertise, and it was dangerous, because in its constitution, decisions based on the 'neutral' criteria one finds in the cartel law were not separated from public interest arguments.[49] The GDR economics minister had to be informed by the GDR competition control agency a fortnight before a merger was finally made illegal by the agency. This gave him the opportunity to override the agency's veto by reference to public-interest arguments.

Pre-unification competition control led to one major debatable decision, namely the merger of the GDR state-owned life-insurance company with the biggest private West German insurance company, Allianz, because the latter claimed that it was in the public interest to both guarantee full insurance to the insured East Germans after 2 July 1990 and to save many jobs. The standard result of merger tests by the GDR agency was, however, that GDR firms were by no means dominant in markets, and that, mostly, they were not even competitive. Mergers were planned exactly to remedy the latter problem. Western firms who were involved in mergers usually did not become dominant in markets. They only reproduced the same kind of (limited) competition (with the same Western competitors) in East Germany. This meant that the dangerous cases were those in which a West German monopoly planned to buy up an East German one, such as in the post-unification case of the planned merger of the West German airline Lufthansa and the East German airline Interflug, which was stopped by the Cartel Office.[50]

After unification the Cartel Office was at first ignored by the *Treuhand*, the federal privatization agency for the East German economy. The Office made its presence felt, however, by investigating mergers in the East with the same thoroughness as in the West. Up to the end of 1990 about 600 mergers were investigated. In 5 per cent of the cases the Office objected to the way the merger was planned.[51] The Office's major aim was to stop mergers which would have upheld the regional monopolies former East German state-owned firms frequently had. To avoid conflicts, the *Treuhand* changed its strategy and involved the Office at an early stage in its decision-making process. The Office decided faster than it normally did and, often after consultations with the economics ministry, with more 'generous' rulings. This was above all justified by the argument that the East German economy was in a transition period and thus some competition rules should be temporarily suspended.

Those supporting this argument defended market distortions, delivered through subsidies favouring East German firms, as a strategic element to create a level playing field for them in the new all-German market.[52] After all, buying up an East German firm rarely meant for investors that they bought themselves into a new market. It only meant the reduction of the number of competitors in a shrinking market. But the Office was not ready to accept the argument that merger control was in itself an obstacle to investments in the period of economic transformation.[53] It fought against a mere substitution of state monopolies by private monopolies in East Germany. It also opposed the buying up of East German firms by West German consortia of firms (in areas such as electricity, sugar, and cement), because it feared that the group effects might finally restrict competition in West Germany.

Still, the Office is less than happy with the market structures that exist in East Germany as a result of privatization policies. However, sometimes the Office had no legal justification for intervention. Thus only one merger on the print media market was actually stopped by the Office.[54] It criticized decisions of the *Treuhand*, which in the Office's opinion favoured at a very early stage certain competitors and investors instead of giving other competitors a chance. In short, it believes that a golden opportunity has been missed to revitalize competition in the whole of Germany with the help of new investments by foreign competitors in East Germany. The *Treuhand's* efforts to offer East German firms on the international markets simply came too late. The Office also disliked the *Treuhand's* attitude towards small and medium-sized firms. To involve them in the privatization process as investors is a complicated and cumbersome process, and what a single firm can buy is miniscule. But a greater role for small and medium-sized firms would have strengthened competition. The *Treuhand* preferred the easy option of selling big to big firms rather than the more important principle of promoting as much competition through privatizations as possible.[55] The Cartel Office was also unhappy with the dumping methods used by the *Treuhand* to establish its firms on the market. After all it was the taxpayers' money which was used by the *Treuhand* to subsidize East German firms heavily with the aim of beating other private competitors. The Office admits that without an intervention of this kind the East German economic situation would be even more difficult, but it strongly regrets that a result of this strategy was the elimination of a number of small and medium-sized companies from the markets. So far, only a few of the smaller firms affected have asked for the support of the Cartel Office.[56]

The internal structure of the *Treuhand* was, like the Office, organized by sectors of industry. Some decision-making units tried to teach the staff of the *Treuhand* during their mutual contacts, what a really competitive order in their sector should look like, but other decision-making units were less exposed. They simply waited to be asked by *Treuhand* divisions for their advice. The Office as a whole exerted a lot of informal pressure on the *Treuhand* to end discrimination against firms on the East German markets and to limit price dumping strategies.

The Economics Ministry

A second pillar influencing domestic decision-making on competition policy is the Economics Ministry. The Ministry has the right, defined by article 24(3) of the cartel law, to override the veto of the Cartel Office against mergers. This kind of decision is theoretically and in practice the rare exception. Firms can only hope for an override if they can convince the Ministry that it is in the public interest to restrict competition by the planned merger. So the second pillar implies a separation of responsibilities. Competition control as defined by the 'neutral' rules of the cartel law is in the Cartel Office's responsibility. The formal decision on public-interest arguments (such as positive effects on the economy or other aspects, such as jobs, an independent energy base, or technical progress) is made by the Ministry. The definition of the common good and what is a functioning economy for which the merger is needed is left to the economics minister. Her or his decision cannot be contested by the courts as long as the minister's argument is logically consistent. The law mentions that for the definition of the public interest international markets may be included. It also 'restricts' the minister's defining power by stating that whatever merger she or he allows, this cannot be one that threatens the market economy in principle. The law also gives the minister the possibility to demand a set of changes in ownership and market strength from the firms who intend to merge.

The neat separation of responsibilities between a first (Cartel Office) and a second (the Ministry) pillar of competition policy is in practice less clear-cut. The Cartel Office decides first. Its decision provides the original framework. In the Office it is often quite clear what kind of decision the Ministry would prefer. For example, in the famous Daimler/MBB merger case (1988/9)[57] the Ministry leaned heavily, but unsuccessfully, on the Office in the hope that a veto could be avoided.[58] Expectations, in other words, do not always result in obedience. In the Daimler/MBB case the Office was very happy that the formal separation between responsibilities for political decisions and competition control existed. It could argue that what in its view 'went wrong' was all the minister's fault or responsibility, and the broad public debate on the merger case, with all the embarrassing implications this had for the Ministry, again taught it the lesson that it is well advised to use its public-interest argument and its right of intervention very carefully now and in the future.[59]

The general framework the Ministry provides for the actions of its competition control agency, and the set of 'neutral' operating rules, including the cartel law, can be influenced by the Cartel Office itself, if the Ministry follows the advice the Office gives. The Office has to work within the existing legal provisions and is more aware of necessary changes than the ministry. It also sees itself as the guardian of continuity in German competition control. Governments may change, ministries have over the years had different economic philosophies, but the Office, at least in its own perception, has remained stable and reliable. It has therefore been able to influence revisions of the cartel law and rule-making by the Ministry in a way which is similar to making the rules itself. This current self-confidence provides a striking contrast to the early reactions of the Economics Ministry to the work of the Cartel Office. In these reactions the Ministry even commented and critized single decisions of the Office and stressed that it was, after all, its decision whether it would allow the Office to carry on with its work in the way it had started or to stop it by giving it new guidelines.[60] Today it is almost the other way round. The Office tries to convince the bureaucrats in the Ministry which changes of guidelines are necessary for reasons of practicability and when it is better to issue a ministerial ruling instead of taking the initiative for another revision of the cartel law. For new rules the results of the theoretical and technical debates amongst academics is only of marginal interest.

A good example for rule-making in its own interest is the Cartel Office's successful lobbying which resulted in a revision of section 47 of the cartel law and allowed the Office to use EC competition control rules (articles 85–9 of the EC treaty) in its national jurisdiction. This ruling strengthened the Office's position in the courts and with regard to firms which had argued that the Office's use of EC law was *ultra vires*. It also had the consequence that the German high court responsible for competition cases (*Bundesgerichtshof*) has in some cases asked the European Court for an opinion before its final decision.[61] The Office has also officially confirmed its role in the preparation of bills to revise the cartel law.[62] In general, the self-confidence of the Office and its interest in making its presence felt, and thereby justifying its institutional autonomy and survival, have led to the Office's greater inclination to test its powers and to challenge existing boundaries. But there are also other tendencies. The Ministry's power to restrict the Office's room for manœuvre, even if it is rarely used, is a constant threat to its autonomy. The former president of the Office, Kartte, has therefore asked for more autonomy or at least a formal process of communication between the Ministry and the Office, which could be made public, and in this process more controllable and less dominated by political power.[63]

Monopoly Commission

The Office's views usually secure the support of the Monopoly Commission. The Commission, after a brief period in the 1970s under the influence of Eberhard Kantzenbach, no longer aims at developing a more general picture of how competition in the German market economy ideally should work. Still, because the Commission is such a small body, the notion of the competitive order it prefers depends very much on personalities, and especially that of its chairperson. When Ernst-Joachim Mestmäcker and later Ulrich Immenga headed the Commission they favoured, at least in the eyes of the Office, a fairly narrow concept of competition policy. In contrast Carl-Christian von Weizsäcker's views are seen as being too vague. In general it can be said the Commission is now content to make use of the competition criteria developed by the Office. This means that in cases where the economics minister wants to override the Cartel Office's opinion with public-interest arguments, the Monopoly Commission is usually on the Office's side.[64] This is of political significance and attracts public attention, because the economics minister has to ask for the Commission's opinion before she or he overrules the Office and agrees to a merger, although the minister is not bound by the opinion. The Monopoly Commission also has the task of monitoring the work done by the Cartel Office. It has the right of access to all the Office's files, which may lead to embarrassing results in cases when in hindsight the Office had chosen the wrong alternative when dealing with competition control cases. This threat is, however, more theoretical than real. The Office is convinced that it will hardly be possible for the Commission to dig deep enough to unearth really problematic cases.[65]

Small and medium-sized enterprises

The Office finds it difficult to comment on its influence on the development of the German market economy in general. It sees some long-term trends especially in the political culture of the country, such as the consensus on the market economy, but no specific period in which its work was of critical importance. A public consensus on the principles of the market economy does not mean that in practice the Office has not experienced defeats which it sees as violations of important principles. The only aspect in which the Office is more specific with regard to initiatives to strengthen the market economy is its interest in small and medium-sized enterprises (SMEs).[66] It believes that the importance of these firms for economic growth is generally underestimated, and does its best to help them to survive. The cartel law provides opportunities for co-operation among small firms. Such co-operation is not categorized as an illegal cartel, and there is a legal justification for this routine by section 5b,c of the cartel law.[67] Since 1978 the Office even has been holding meetings at local chambers of commerce during which the special problems of small firms are discussed. As with other initiatives to help the SMEs, for example the EC's efforts to strengthen them, the result of the Office's initiative has been disappointing. Though thousands of contacts were made and information was given to a great many interested firms and individuals, in the period between 1958 and 1993 only a handful of SME co-operation projects were 'initiated' by the Cartel Office.[68]

THE INTERNATIONAL DIMENSION

European Union

The international dimension of competition control policies prompted an organizational reform in the Cartel Office as early as 1977. This dimension has gained importance in recent years both objectively and in the eyes of the Cartel Office. The European market seems to develop oligopolistic structures and has to be careful to avoid transforming itself into an economic fortress.[69] Influential interpretations of the European merger regulation have argued in this context that, especially in connection with the industry article of the Maastricht treaty, merger policy on the European level could be given the meaning of an instrument supporting European industrial competitiveness.[70] The Office sees itself in a dangerous position, which is different in quality from the previous interventions in competition policy on the European level based on articles 85 and 86 of the EEC treaty.[71] The principles of the Office may be sacrificed in the name of European unity, and its responsibilities may be completely eroded when firms can bypass the Office's jurisdiction. The European merger control provisions lack, from the Office's point of view, an autonomous, 'non-political' decision-making body. In the ideal case this would be a European Cartel Office. At the moment the Office can be quite content with the principles of European merger control.[72] What it criticizes is that the regulation weakens competition in Europe by raising the thresholds for controls.[73] A lowering of the threshold would, however, only increase the Commission's workload to unmanageable levels and would result in more cases for which both the Commission and the Office claim responsibility. What is even more worrying for the Cartel Office is the political character of merger control decisions, and the widely different notions of competition policy at the European level.[74] This implies the need for compromises between national governments, different party-political approaches, and between competition policy and an industrial policy approach,[75] which aims at influencing structural change in industry. Indeed, it may even be affected by the fear of Commissioners of endangering their personal careers if they lose votes in the Commission too often. There is also a very personal element in the decision-making process if one compares the economic policy views of Sir Leon Brittan and his successor as EC competition commissioner, Karel Van Miert. Van Miert described his task as follows: 'I'm inclined to look at the whole picture. Since I've received specific responsibility for competition I will look after that element first. But I will not lose sight of the other considerations and other interests involved.'[76] (See also the discussion of these issues in Chapter 8.)

The finding of compromises has a procedural and a material aspect. The Cartel Office criticizes European merger control decisions, because they lack transparency, and are characterized by political horse-trading behind the scenes. In one recent case (the Alcatel/AEG merger) the Commission only gave the Office 48

hours to read through the files and to write a comment. The
German government, at the last minute, decided not to challenge
this procedure in the European court.[77] The results of European
merger control are hardly seen as encouraging. It is argued that
not only have they become dependent on industrial policy deliberations, it is also obvious that only the bigger firms, especially the
state-owned ones, find support in the Commission.

The Office believes that in the area of European competition
control it would be ideal to base institutions on the German experience, because that would allow a separation of the public-
interest debate from routine controls. The latter should be the
responsibility of a European Cartel Office, and the Commission
could decide on exceptions from the rules of merger control.[78]
This demand finds the support of the federal government,[79] which
introduced this suggestion officially at the 1990 conference on a
European economic and currency union. For the near future the
Office believes that it is necessary to fight on two fronts to safeguard competition in Europe. One idea strongly supported is 'convergence', by which is meant an ever greater similarity of the
principles and practice of competition control in all EC countries.
Efforts made to achieve greater convergence in the field of competition policy can be justified by the general aims of cohesion and
harmonization in the EC, and with regard to competition policy
by the notion of fair competition in the Single Market, the level
playing field. One way to achieve convergence is for the Office to
use its influence for furthering a common approach of national
competition control agencies in the EC with regard to cases the
Commission decides. The advisory committee on cartel and competition control problems should aim at majority decisions, and
should be allowed to publish its decisions before the Commission
decides. Between 1990 and the end of 1992 the advisory committee
met 27 times and wrote 44 opinions on cases. The idea of an early
input by a common approach of all national EC competition control
agencies in the decision-making process of the Commission was
first introduced into the debate by the Cartel Office's former president Kartte. Today the opinion of the advisory committee is published only after the decision in the Commission has already been
made. The Office is also heard by the Commission at annual
meetings of Commission representatives and the heads of the
national competition control offices, when it takes part in hearings

in Brussels, and when the Commission needs support for its investigations of merger cases in Germany.

A second initiative of the Office is based on the notion of subsidiarity, and, after Maastricht officially recognized the principle, the Office felt particularly justified using the subsidiarity principle as its argument. During the debate which resulted in the European merger control regulation of 1989 this principle was less important, and all the efforts made by the German side to safeguard national responsibilities were finally institutionalized under article 9, the so-called 'German clause'. In legal terms article 9 of the regulation takes into account the wish of a national competition agency, such as the Office, for controlling national markets. The Commission may refer a case to the Cartel Office, even if its size puts it in a category which is the Commission's responsibility. Between 1990 and the end of 1992 the German Cartel Office asked the Commission four times for permission to investigate cases which were registered with the Commission. A fifth case was demanded by Britain. The Commission refused the German requests and only allowed a later case to be dealt with by the German authorities due to a mistake in calculating the time limits. This denies the Office the possibility to veto a merger. It is up to the Commission to make the final decision.

The 'German clause' is fairly immune to reform, because, although in 1989 it was agreed that it had to be reviewed after four years, unanimity in the Commission is required to change it. In 1993 the decision was made to confirm the *status quo* at least until 1996. From the German point of view the clause should not only be retained, it should be expanded to counteract the strategies of German-based firms, which prefer the Commission as merger control agency, because there they expect the least resistance. The German Federation of Industry (BDI) supports lower thresholds for the Commission's interventions in merger policy, hoping that this would facilitate mergers for German firms.[80] To some extent this expectation is justified. In the recent Mannesmann/Hoesch (steel) merger case the mere assumption that in the near future current monopolies might have to face competition was sufficient to justify a positive decision of the Commission against the wishes of the Cartel Office. What is from the Office's point of view difficult to see, is how undertakings given by firms as a condition imposed by the Commission when it permitted them to merge will actually be put into practice.[81] Even the courts have in some cases already hesitated to interpret the German cartel law very strictly, because they argued one should also take the implications of the European merger control regulation into account.[82] Developments which have a strong influence on German markets, so the Office argues, should always be its responsibility, especially if on the other hand the Office in the advisory committee has to give opinions on merger cases in other European countries, which often hardly affect German market structures.

Recently a new dimension has been added to this problem which led to a conflict between the German Economics Ministry and the Cartel Office. In the case of the merger of Kali-Salz AG, Kassel, and Mitteldeutsche Kali AG, Sondershausen, the economics minister, supported the merger which had been initiated by the Treuhand, the East German privatization agency, with the support of its ministry, the Finance Ministry. The Economics Ministry therefore did not allow the Cartel Office to ask the Commission, which has to decide on the merger, to hand the case back to the Office (German clause). Such a demand can only be made through national governments. The Cartel Office did its utmost to secure its influence and wrote, against the wishes of the Ministry, a letter to the Commission to explain its position and the problems for competition involved in the planned merger. What really has happened here, and what means a new quality of merger control, is that the Economics Ministry by blocking the Office has acted as if it was granting a special permission for the merger, because of public-interest deliberations, but without using the proper channels. In short, Europe served as a way to bypass German law.[83]

The provisions of the European merger regulation are seen by the Office as being too superficial, because they mechanically register turnover in the EC, but forget to demand a close look into the consequences of mergers for market structures of specific national markets. The federal government fears that, because of the growing workload in Brussels, the Commission may decide to loosen restrictions for mergers instead of shifting the work-load to the lower (national) level.[84] In the view of the Office the Commission is too generous with its 'comfort letters', which reduce the routine procedure of competition control to a farce and exempt whole sectors of industry from competition control.[85] On the other hand, the federal government has welcomed group exemptions from

competition rules if they create incentives for technological progress.[86] The Office has argued that 'innovation monopolies' of this
kind should be limited and should help, above all, small and
medium-sized firms.[87]

Deregulation

Where Europe is seen by the federal government and the Cartel
Office to have a positive effect on the German markets is in the
field of deregulation. The Office does not defend the exceptions
made in the cartel law for certain sectors of industry, such as the
utilities or insurance industries. It supports deregulation as a strategy to produce greater competition. This attitude is shared by the
federal government, whose Commission on Deregulation[88] has
advocated more competition in the electricity and gas industries.
An important part of the final decisions to be made in this respect
is supposed to be based on the British experience. The tendency to
privatize public monopolies, such as rail services and the post
office, has made the Office's often repeated criticism of their business behaviour obsolete. The Cartel Office had noticed the tendency of public monopolies to work together with only one big
private firm as their technology partner and supplier (e.g. the post
office with Siemens).[89] Standardization was preferred to competition by those state-owned firms. Deregulation and competition in
the European context now forces these firms to work together
with a broad spectrum of private partners.

World Market

The broader arena of the world market is also seen by the Cartel
Office from the perspective of the German national market, the
only market it is responsible for.[90] International market changes
are important if competition in Germany is affected, and the second important question would then be the intensity of the distortion. The Office supports the OECD convergence project, though
de facto convergence on the broader international level is more
difficult to achieve than on the European level. It flatly rejects the
argument that a monopoly in Germany or any other kind of
dominance on the German market should be permitted in cases

where this strengthens the competitiveness of a firm abroad. If such a case should be decided positively at all, this would have to be an exception to be made by an official decision of the economics minister. The Office does not share the opinion that merger control in Germany might make it difficult for foreign capital to invest in Germany.[91] Legal hurdles against unfriendly takeovers and the role of the big private banks are seen as being much more important.[92]

The Office has to admit, however, that world-wide strategies of firms, such as strategic alliances,[93] though not new, are ever harder to control from a national base.[94] A first profound experience in this respect has been the Office's failure to control the price policies on the German market of the multinational oil companies during and after the first international oil crisis in 1973/4.[95] The necessary legal instruments were not available.[96] The consequences of world-wide strategies for national markets are difficult to estimate. And most of the time the market shares of international firms remain below levels which would normally trigger the Cartel Office's intervention.[97] National law may stop mergers on the German markets which have a clear German dimension, though they also affect the interest of foreign countries. International law forbids, however, a German intervention if essential interests of other nations are affected. The argument that the co-operation of firms both on the national and the international level may produce synergy effects is seen by the Office as synonymous with industrial policy arguments. The Office doubts that less competition can result in greater economic potential. In the context of the OECD co-operation efforts it has also investigated non-tariff barriers and anti-dumping strategies, in other words the relationship between trade and competition policy.

CONCLUSIONS

The political environment for the Cartel Office has indeed become complex and hostile. Even in the early post-war years, when Germans still had to be convinced that the market economy was the best possible solution for organizing wealth production, the political supporters of the Office had to fight long 'wars', first to get it established, and later to broaden its competences in order to establish a role in merger control. What is more, from the start the courts have continuously reduced the Cartel Office's room for manœuvre. Sometimes even the Economics Ministry, with special permissions justifying mergers in the public interest, has publicly reduced its status. What remained was case-oriented intervention, and incremental competition policy without an overall vision and, what is equally important, without broad public support.[98]

Measured against these obstacles it is surprising that the Office survived with an intact organizational culture, a high degree of motivation and a sense of mission amongst its staff, and even a certain arrogance towards other federal institutions. The Office's intra-organizational network has been stable and there has not been a major and rapid turnover of leadership and personnel. In this community atmosphere competition policy has its attractions, even if it is to a certain degree regarded as a game to be played with partners in industry and the courts. Losses are seen by the Office mostly as lost games, not as inroads into principles of competition policy.

The Europeanization of competition policy has, however, proven a more serious threat, because it tends to reduce its status. The Office's pride in the overall fact that the European merger regulation 'follows' the German example is less important than the day-to-day fact that political decision-making is now a larger element in the shaping of merger control. The Office is not a political player and has comparatively little influence on the federal government's position in Brussels or the Commission. It has even turned out that not only the German firms, but also the Economics Ministry have supported strategies to eliminate the influence of the Cartel Office in the decision-making on merger cases. The question of what the survival of the Cartel Office under increasingly difficult conditions means for its future role in German and European competition policy will become the central one in the future. The answer to this question will decide whether the Office will hibernate as an institution which does little more than register or monitor mergers, or whether it will function as a watch-dog which can guarantee the very principles of the German-style market economy. Optimistic perceptions nurtured by the Office's institutional stability and the contemporary reality of its permanent loss of power are the contradictory elements which define today's competition policy-making.

NOTES

1. See *Bundestagsdrucksäche*, 8/1925, 6.
2. The Monopoly Commission was intended to be in competition policy what the Council of Economic Advisers (*Sachverständigenrat*) is in economic policy-making—a politically neutral institution which analyses the situation objectively and provides general guidance.
3. For background information see Roland Sturm and Edmund Ortwein, *The Normative and Legal Framework of German Competition Policy: A Political Science Perspective* (Exeter: RUSEL Working Paper 15, 1993). After the war, Allied decartelization law provided guidance and was used cautiously by the Economics Minister from 1955 until 1958. In detail, Robert Rüdiger, *Konzentrationspolitik in der Bundesrepublik Deutschland. Das Beispiel des Gesetzes gegen Wettbewerbsbeschränkungen* (Berlin: Duncker & Humblot, 1976).
4. *Bundestagsdrucksäche*, 12/848, 3.
5. *Frankfurter Rundschau*, 14 Aug. 1992, 9. In the context of the Daimler/MBB merger the then chairman of the Monopoly Commission, Ulrich Immenga, stressed that size alone in industry may be dangerous, because it means economic power can be used as political power. See 'Haussmann steht gewaltig unter Druck', interview in *Der Spiegel*, 1 May 1989, 31.
6. See Heinz Ewald, 'Eberhard Günther', in Helmut Gutzler, Wolfgang Herion, and Joseph H. Kaiser (eds.), *Wettbewerb im Wandel* (Baden-Baden: Nomos, 1976), 11–24. Eberhard Günther, 'Zehn Jahre Bundeskartellamt: Rückblick und Ausblick', in *Zehn Jahre Bundeskartellamt*, (Cologne: Carl Heymann, 1968), 11–37.
7. See *Frankfurter Rundschau*, 4 July 1992, 9.
8. The Monopoly Commission in its sixth report of 1986 (*Gesamtwirtschaftliche Chancen und Risiken wachsender Unternehmensgrößen* (Baden-Baden: Nomos, 1986)) (unsuccessfully) favoured a similar institution to co-ordinate the work of the Cartel Office which it called a 'Grand Senate'. The decision-making units did not like the idea of a committee restricting their autonomy.
9. Interviews, Oct. 1993.
10. See *Bundestagsdrucksäche*, 8/1925, 9.
11. In 1992 the Office spent 20.06 million DM and had an income from fees for services and fines of 21.25 million DM. Source: K. Pressestelle, *Das Bundeskartellamt* (Berlin, 1993, unpub. manuscript). Source for data: various reports of the Bundeskartellamt.
12. Rüdiger, *Konzentrationspolitik*.
13. Fritz Rittner, *Wettbewerbs- und Kartellrecht* (3rd edn., Heidelberg: C. F. Müller, 1989), 435.

220   *Roland Sturm*

14. The *Arbeitskreis* was last mentioned in polite words in the Office's
    1978 report.
15. See *Gesetz gegen Wettbewerbsbeschränkungen*, sect. 48
16. Interviews, Oct. 1993.
17. See *Stellungnahme der Bundesregierung zum Kartellamtsbericht 1971*,
    Drs. VI/3570, p. IV.
18. *Bundestagsdrucksäche*, VI/950, 3.
19. Norbert Eickhof, 'Wettbewerb, Wettbewerbsfreiheit und Wettbewerbs-
    beschränkungen', in *Hamburger Jahrbuch für Wirtschafts- und
    Gesellschaftspolitik*, 35 (1990), S.225–38.
20. For an overview of theoretical efforts see Carl Wolfgang Neumann,
    Historische Entwicklung und heutiger Stand der Wettbewerbstheorie
    (Frankfurt am Main: Campus 1982); Ingo Schmidt, *Wettbewerbspolitik
    und Kartellrecht* (3rd edn., Stuttgart: Fischer, 1990). The diagnosis
    that science has not yet produced a convincing definition of compe-
    tition is shared by the influential legal text: Volker Emmerich,
    Kartellrecht (6th edn., Munich: Beck, 1991), 17.
21. See *Bundestagsdrucksäche*, 3/1795, 8.
22. J. M. Clark, 'Towards a Concept of Workable Competition', *Ameri-
    can Economic Review*, 30 (1940).
23. Erhard Kantzenbach, *Die Funktionsfähigkeit des Wettbewerbs*
    (Göttingen: Vandenhoek, 1966).
24. See the federal government's arguments in *Stellungnahme zum Bericht
    des Bundeskartellamtes 1970*, Drs. VI/2380, 4. Also *Stellungnahme
    zum Bericht des Bundeskartellamtes 1966*, Drs. V/1950, 2. And, most
    explicitly with a reference to Kantzenbach's book, the Cartel Office's
    arguments in *Bundestagsdrucksäche* V/530, 8 ff.
25. Dieter Grosser, 'Wettbewerbspolitik', in Dieter Grosser (ed.), *Der
    Staat in der Wirtschaft der Bundesrepublik* (Opladen: Leske, 1985),
    87 ff.
26. For background information see Elke van Arnheim, *Der räumlich
    relevante Markt im Rahmen der Fusionskontrolle* (Cologne: Carl
    Heymanns Verlag, 1991).
27. See Dieter Schmidtchen, *Property Rights, Freiheit und Wettbewerb-
    spolitik* (Tübingen: J. C. B. Mohr, 1983).
28. See *Bundestagsdrucksäche*, 8/704, 7 ff.
29. See *Stellungnahme der Bundesregierung zum Kartellamtsbericht 1987/
    88*, Drs. 11/4611, I.
30. See *Stellungnahme der Bundesregierung zum Kartellamtsbericht 1991/
    92*, Drs. 12/5200, II.
31. Central to this debate has been the special report of the Monopoly
    Commission No. 1, *Anwendung und Möglichkeiten der Mißbrauch-
    saufsicht über marktbeherrschende Unternehmen seit Inkrafttreten
    der Kartellgesetznovelle* (Baden-Baden: Nomos, 1975). See also the

comments of the Cartel Office in: *Bundestagsdrucksäche*, 7/5390, 7 ff.

32. Ibid.
33. *Stellungnahme der Bundesregierung zum Kartellamtsbericht 1974*, *Bundestagsdrucksäche*, 7/3791, II.
34. *Stellungnahme der Bundesregierung zum Sechsten Hauptgutachten der Monopolkommission 1984/85*, Drs. 11/555, 2.
35. *Bundestagsdrucksäche*, 12/5200.
36. *Bundestagsdrucksäche*, 12/5200, 23.
37. See *Bundestagsdrucksäche*, 7/5390, 20.
38. Siegried Klaue, 'Die bisherige Rechtsprechung zum Gesetz gegen Wettbewerbsbeschränkungen', in *Zehn Jahre*, 253 ff.
39. Ibid. 260.
40. *Bundestagsdrucksache*, 11/554, 9.
41. 'Wir sind doch nicht blind', interview in *Der Spiegel*, 6 Apr. 1992, 151.
42. *Bundestagsdrucksäche*, 12/5200, 25.
43. Interviews, Oct. 1993.
44. The negative reaction of the Cartel Office to the argument that the world market is the relevant market and that this implies that German merger control is superfluous, is to be found in its 1968 report, *Bundestagsdrucksäche*, V/4236, 8 f.
45. On strategic alliances, see Edzard Reuter, 'Ein neues Netz für den Frieden. Plädoyer für mehr Partnerschaft', *Die Zeit*, 16 July 1990, 41 ff.
46. *Stellungnahme der Bundesregierung zum Kartellamtsbericht 1985/86*, Drs. 11/554, p. iv.
47. 'Wir stehen häufig unter Zwängen'. Kartellamtspräsident Wolfgang Kartte über die Konzentration in der Wirtschaft, interview in *Der Spiegel*, 4 Dec. 1978, 98.
48. *Bundestagsdrucksäche*, 12/5200, 21.
49. This view is supported by academic research. See Hans-Hagen Härtel and Reinald Krüger, 'Aktuelle Entwicklungen von Marktstrukturen in den neuen Bundesländern', in *Aus Politik und Zeitgeschichte*, 29 (1991), 25.
50. *Bundestagsdrucksäche*, 12/847, 7 f.
51. *Bundestagsdrucksäche*, 12/847, II.
52. *Bundestagsdrucksäche*, 12/5200, 4 f.
53. *Bundestagsdrucksäche*, 12/5200, 11.
54. The merger Axel Springer publishers/Leipziger Stadt-Anzeiger, because Springer already had a dominant position in the Leipzig newspaper market. *Bundestagsdrucksäche*, 12/5200, 12.
55. *Bundestagsdrucksäche*, 12/5200, 14 f.
56. *Bundestagsdrucksäche*, 12/5200, 32 f.

222   *Roland Sturm*

57. For an overview see Roland Sturm and Edmund Ortwein, *The Normative and Legal Framework*, 11 ff. The decision of the Cartel Office is to be found in *Wirtschaft und Wettbewerb*, BKartA 7 und 8, (1989), 233 ff. The permission by the minister for the merger is to be found in *Wirtschaft und Wettbewerb*, BMW 11 (1989), 191 ff.
58. Interviews, Oct. 1993.
59. See *Bundestagsdrucksäche*, 12/847, 18.
60. See *Stellungnahme der Bundesregierung zum Kartellamtsbericht 1959*, Drs. 3/1795, 2 ff.
61. See *Bundestagsdrucksäche*, 12/5200, 31.
62. For the fourth revision see *Bundestagsdrucksäche*, 8/2980, 26. For the first revision see *Bundestagsdrucksäche*, IV/1220, 7 and *Bundestagsdrucksäche*, IV/378, 11.
63. See Wolfgang Kartte, 'Wettbewerbspolitik im Spannungsfeld zwischen Bundeswirtschaftsministerium und Bundeskartellamt', in Gutzler *et al.*, *Wettbewerb im Wandel*, 55 f.
64. This was not so in the Daimler–MBB merger case. This case led to heavy controversies in the Commission, and later to the resignation of its chairman Ulrich Immenga.
65. Interviews, Oct. 1993.
66. For a more detailed account of the historical relationship between competition policy and the support of SMEs see Ursula Beyenburg-Weidenfeld, *Wettbewerbstheorie, Wirtschaftspolitik und Mittelstandsförderung 1948–1963* (Stuttgart: Franz Steiner, 1992).
67. *Bundestagsdrucksäche*, 12/847, 32. In the late seventies there was still the rule that the market share of the SMEs involved should not exceed 5%. See *Bundestagsdrucksäche*, 9/565, 8. In detail, see Erwin Herresthal, *Die Praxis der Mittelstandskooperationen nach 5b GWB* (Berlin: Duncker & Humblot, 1983.)
68. Interviews, Oct. 1993.
69. *Bundestagsdrucksäche*, 11/4611, 5.
70. Ulrich Immenga, *Die europäische Fusionskontrolle im wettbewerbspolitischen Kräftefeld* (Tübingen: Mohr, 1993), 18 ff. This is an opinion supported by Martin Bangemann, the EC's industry and internal market commissioner. See Martin Bangemann, *Mut zum Dialog. Wege zu einer europäischen Industriepolitik* (Stuttgart: Bonn aktuell, 1992).
71. For details see Josef Blank, *Europäische Fusionskontrolle im Rahmen des Artt. 85, 86 des EWG-Vertrages* (Baden-Baden: Nomos, 1991).
72. Hans-Jörg Niemeyer, *Die Europäische Fusionskontrollverordnung* (Heidelberg: Verlag Recht und Wirtschaft, 1991).
73. Heinrich Hölzler, 'Merger Control', in, Peter Montagnon (ed.), *European Competition Policy* (London: Pinter, 1990).

74. It is telling that so far only in one case has a merger been stopped, and that the debate on this decision only concentrated on political and economic arguments, but did not refer to the need for safeguarding the competitive structure of the European industry as a cornerstone of a functioning Single Market. See Roland Sturm, 'Konkurrenz oder Synergie? Nationale und europäische Industriepolitik', in Michael Kreile (ed.), *Die Integration Europas* (Opladen: Westdeutscher Verlag, 1992) (special issue PVS 23), 242 ff. See also Immenga, *Die europäische Fusionskontrolle*, 7 ff.

75. In the aftermath of the EC veto of the De Havilland/Aérospatiale/ Alenia merger, its German Liberal(!) industry and internal market commissioner Bangemann attacked the 'gurus' who staff national and Community merger control authorities. With an eye especially on the Cartel Office, he said, 'What I'm angry about is that there are some academics, mostly lawyers by profession, who have no idea of the reality of economic life. They are the experts who are taking the competition decisions, which is complete madness.' *Financial Times*, 11 Feb. 1992, 2. In his book *Mut zum Dialog*, 31, he critizes German procedures for decisions based on the public interest argument as being too open to discussion. He sees the firms involved as being in the role of poor victims, threatened by the Cartel Office's influence on public opinion.

76. *Financial Times*, 13 Jan. 1993, 1.

77. See Interview with Dieter Wolf, in *Frankfurter Rundschau*, 12 Sept. 1993, 9.

78. Critics have argued that this is not enough. Whereas the German equivalent, the economics minister, is committed to the principle of competition, the Commission will always be a political body. See Immenga, *Die europäische Fusionskontrolle*, 36.

79. *Stellungnahme der Bundesregierung zum Kartellamtsbericht 1991/92*, Drs. 12/5200, I f. Also *Stellungnahme* (1989–90), Drs. 12/847, p. iv.

80. See *Frankfurter Rundschau*, 2 Apr. 1993, 13. European merger control has already been celebrated as a success for European business; see Robert Rice, 'Marriages Made in Brussels', in *Financial Times*, 19 Jan. 1993, 13, and Rachel Brandenburger, 'EC Merger Regime Defies Expectations of Critics', in *Financial Times*, 3 Sept. 1992, 9.

81. *Bundestagsdrucksäche*, 12/5200, 28.

82. Merger case Kaufhof/Saturn, vgl. *Bundestagsdrucksäche*, 12/5200, 27. Immenga, *Die europäische Fusionskontrolle*, 16.

83. See e.g. *Der Spiegel*, 16 Aug. 1993, 91 ff.; *Frankfurter Allgemeine Zeitung*, 7 Aug. 1993, 9.

84. *Stellungnahme der Bundesregierung zum Kartellamtsbericht 1991/92*, Drs. 12/5200, VI.

85. *Bundestagsdrucksäche*, 12/5200, 7.
86. *Stellungnahme der Bundesregierung zum Kartellamtsbericht 1987/88*, Drs. 11/4611, S.VII.
87. *Bundestagsdrucksäche*, 10/350, 6.
88. Deregulierungskommission, *Marktöffnung und Wettbewerb*, 2 vols. (Bonn: photocopied, 1990 and 1991).
89. See e.g. *Bundestagsdrucksäche*, 9/565, 39 f.
90. For the European perspective see Alexis Jacquemin, 'The International Dimension of European Competition Policy', *Journal of Common Market Studies*, 31 (1993), 91–100.
91. Nor does the federal government: see *Stellungnahme der Bundesregierung zum Kartellamtsbericht 1981/82*, Drs. 10/243, II.
92. For details: Hermannus Pfeiffer, *Die Macht der Banken* (Frankfurt am Main/New York: Campus, 1993). The Monopoly Commission has suggested that a limit for the acquisition of property by the banks outside the banking sector should be introduced. See *Gesamtwirtschaftliche Chancen und Risiken wachsender Unternehmensgrößen* (Baden-Baden: Nomos, 1986).
93. For details see Jordan D. Lewis, *Partnerships for Profit* (New York: Free Press, 1990).
94. *Bundestagsdrucksache*, 12/847, 5.
95. *Stellungnahme der Bundesregierung zum Kartellamtsbericht 1973*, Drs. 7/2250, III.
96. Interviews, Oct. 1993. *Bundestagsdrucksäche*, 12/5200, 5.
97. *Bundestagsdrucksäche*, 11/554, 18.
98. Werner Zolnhöfer, 'Wettbewerbspolitik in der Demokratie', in Gutzler et al., *Wettbewerb im Wandel*, 43 ff.

8

Competition Policy in the European Union: Creating a Federal Agency?

STEPHEN WILKS WITH LEE MCGOWAN

In 1991, with Directorate General IV at the height of its powers, and he himself at the height of his prestige, Sir Leon Brittan was able to declare that 'In recent years the Commission has established for itself a reputation as one of the world's leading antitrust enforcement agencies.'[1] Many would have gone further to suggest that, at that time, with US antitrust in the doldrums, the European regime was globally pre-eminent. Its rise to prominence provides a spectacular case study in organizational success. In ten short years DG IV had transformed itself from a sleepy, ineffectual backwater of Community administration into a formidable machine for economic integration.

As we shall see below, the ingenious exploitation of legal autonomy has allowed DG IV to establish itself as a regulatory agency which enjoys a high degree of autonomy. The extent of its powers is remarkable and in some ways unique. Unlike other antitrust agencies, it exerts authority over governments as well as companies through its powers to control state aid (subsidies) and to control nationally owned or sanctioned monopolies. In this respect it is 'supranational' in the strong sense of the concept, having authority over nation-states, and, to that extent, it can be termed a 'federal agency'. DG IV is also distinctive as regards its goals. The goals which provoked the creation of antitrust and which inform its enforcement are multiple. They include the control of big business, the promotion of the free market, the pursuit of competitiveness, and the protection of the consumer. European

The authors acknowledge the support of the Economic and Social Research Council under award R000232903. Also the generous assistance of many interviewees in Brussels, Bonn, Berlin and London.

policy gives priority to none of these; instead its primary goal is 'integration'. In the words of one of the most eminent legal authorities, 'market integration has been elevated in competition cases to an end in itself'.[2] This is the basis for the crucial and under-emphasized partnership between DG IV and the prime agency of integration, the European Court of Justice.

This role of DG IV in establishing the terms under which the European economy integrates (and on which new member states join) gives it and the competition rules almost a 'constitutional' status. It is not too fanciful to suggest that European competition policy is one element determining the evolution of European capitalism, an element with a potential to take pre-eminence over other areas of Community Law.[3] Just as the prospective European Central Bank will guarantee sound money across Europe, so the Competition Authorities will guarantee a sound market. Accordingly the competition authorities have a level of policy-making discretion which is unusual in comparable national systems. DG IV has moved competition enforcement into new areas (e.g. utility regulation), has innovated in its legal powers, has focused on some sectors and issues, and has developed linkages with other policy areas. The competition commissioner makes policy as well as enforcing it, and it is therefore tempting to analyse DG IV as an autonomous institution.

There are a variety of theoretical positions which aspire to define the political dynamics of the European Union and which advance hypotheses about the nature of the regime and its degree of supranationality.[4] Stress in recent years has been put on theories of 'inter-governmentalism', the proposition that the power and policy direction of the Commission is dependent on a series of political bargains between the member states.[5] From this perspective, European competition policy could be expected to be serving the interests of some coalition of member states, and, indeed, suggestions about an Anglo-German alliance have plausibility. It is, however, intriguing to examine to what extent the Commission has managed to assert real autonomy and to escape from the confines of inter-governmental bargaining. It is suggested below that a degree of institutional autonomy has been achieved. Further, that the current debate over the reform of European policy is conditioned by a desire on the part of member states to restrict that autonomy; and a parallel desire on the part of European big business to support (and perhaps capture) autonomous European institutions.

A reappraisal of European competition policy is high on the current agenda of the European Union. The pressures for reappraisal are multiple and often incompatible. Perhaps the three major pressures can be labelled competitiveness, consumerism, and policy linkage. The competitiveness issue seeks to link competition policy to the global competitiveness of European industry. The consumerism issue seeks to retain a strong, principled, and adversarial policy in the interests of consumer choice and price discipline. The question of policy linkage is concerned with aligning competition policy with other important EU policy competencies in areas such as regional and environmental policy. Each of these perspectives mobilizes a complex coalition of interests and each would endorse a combination of specific reforms to policies and institutions. Reform options include procedural changes and increased staffing, revision of key regulations, measures to allow extensive subsidiarity (delegation to national authorities and courts), measures to strengthen DG IV, and proposals to create a new European Competition Agency—a 'European Cartel Office' (ECO).

This chapter proceeds in five sections to discuss, in the first and largest section, the functions of EU competition policy and the core actors involved. Secondly, we discuss the increased influence of this policy area in the 1980s, the 'metamorphosis' of DG IV, before going on to present, thirdly, a review of the current performance of policy. The fourth section explores the relationship between competition policy and industrial (or 'competitiveness') policy, whilst the fifth section speculates on directions for reform and offers some conclusions.

THE INSTITUTIONAL CORE: POWERS, ACTORS, AND NETWORKS

Core powers

The foundations of EU competition policy were laid in the 1950s, first within articles 65 and 66 of the European Coal and Steel Community (1951), and secondly, and more significantly, in article 3(f) of the European Economic Treaty (1957), which sought to ensure 'that competition in the Common Market is not distorted'. This aim was given expression under articles 85–94 of the Treaty, which were influenced by US antitrust law. The creation of a substantial competition policy framework heralded a decisive transformation from the pre-war regime, which had been marked by an almost complete absence of competition policy. Indeed, concentration and cartelization had been a standard feature across many branches of European industry.

The repertoire of European competition powers is now well developed and widely understood. Competition law is particularly well covered, with some quite outstanding texts, extensive case analysis, and specialist journals.[6] These powers have, however, developed in a sporadic and uncertain fashion and really only came together in an integrated whole over the past fifteen years. It is important to dwell for a moment on the nature and extent of the European competition competencies as a preface to later analysis.

The core powers are based on articles 85 and 86 of the EC Treaty. Article 85 is a powerful effects-based prohibition which prohibits agreements or concerted practices 'which have as their object or effect the prevention, restriction, or distortion of competition within the common market'. There is a very substantial article 85 case law which more recently has displayed a change of emphasis away from vertical restraints to the classic horizontal cartel restraints. Administrative fines of up to 10 per cent of turnover are permitted. Fines were unusual before the early 1980s but are now sufficiently frequent, and of such magnitude, that European companies are compelled to take notice. Recent examples are given in Table 8.1.

Article 85 deals with restrictive practices and cartels and is generally thought to be effective in concept and in application. There is less widespread approval of article 86, which controls monopolies through the prohibition of abuse of a dominant position. The test is aimed at behaviour rather than structure and relies heavily on economic analysis both of relevant markets and of abusive behaviour within them. In practice high market shares of 40 to 45 per cent tend to be looked for as a structural pointer, and several Commission decisions on article 86 cases have been extensively criticized.[7] A specific issue is the question of oligopoly, which was in practice not attacked under article 86, at least until the *Italian Flat Glass* case of 1990, which has provoked a reappraisal.

TABLE 8.1. *Recent fines under articles 85 and 86*

Date	Case	Fines	
		ECUm.	£m.
December 1990	ICI and Solvay fined for soda ash cartel	47	37
July 1991	Tetrapak fined for abuse of dominant position in liquid packaging (article 86)	75	59
February 1994	16 companies in steel beams cartel	104	81
July 1994	19 carton board producers fined for 'pernicious' cartel	132	104
December 1994	33 cement producers and associations fined for prolonged cartel	248	193

Note: As penalties escalated, each of these was 'the highest to date'.

Article 86 began to be used much more actively in the mid-1970s, after the oil shock, when the general European preference for 'national champions' became less definite and the concern with controlling inflation came to the fore. As European policy became more actively enforced, the glaring gap in European competence became steadily more apparent. For seventeen years the Commission had pressed for a competence to control mergers and acquisitions, but it was not until 1989 that Sir Leon Brittan, as Competition Commissioner, finally succeeded in persuading the European Council to pass a Merger Regulation. The Regulation came into operation in October 1990. Its passage was eased by the merger boom of the late 1980s,[8] and support from big business and from Single Market enthusiasts for a genuine 'one-stop-shop'. The powers granted by the Regulation are surprisingly 'federalist' and consistent with articles 85 and 86. The Merger Task Force in DG IV has been given extensive discretion to investigate, negotiate, and decide whether mergers 'create or strengthen a dominant position'.[9] The involvement of the member states is limited to an advisory committee, but a major constraint is the high notification thresholds, which, at a combined turnover of ECU 5 billion, cover only the very largest mergers. The member states vetoed a reduction in the thresholds during 1993.

The operation of merger control has had a radical and unanticipated effect on European competition policy. It has mobilized business, aroused disquiet among the national authorities, greatly increased the salience (and prestige) of the European institutions, and generated an intense wave of debate and criticism which promises to bring major reform of European policy.

Articles 85 and 86, together with merger control, provide the European Commission with a complete armoury of powers with which to tackle actions by private companies. Over the last ten years it has also developed potent weapons to attack restrictions on competition arising from the actions of member states. This has brought a reorientation in enforcement activity during the 1990s, which has also had a profound effect on the reception and operation of competition policy. In its 1990 Competition Report the Commission observed that 'whilst many barriers to intra-Community trade and competition are created by companies themselves . . . it is felt that at the present stage of economic integration . . . the barriers are greatest in markets subject to state regulation'.[10] These barriers have been tackled by applying article 86 to state-owned monopolies but also by activating article 90 of the EC Treaty, which allows the competition rules to be applied to public undertakings. Action has been taken furthest in the field of telecommunications, although the controversy over the Maastricht Treaty has caused the Commission to be more cautious in its enforcement of article 90.

The activities of member states have also been constrained by the application of articles 92–4, which permits the Commission to control 'state aid' (subsidies) given by states to private- or public-sector enterprises. This competence is unique to European competition policy and is often excluded from analysis of the policy area. That would be misleading. The control of state aid is a major preoccupation of DG IV and the Competition Commissioner. It interacts with other aspects of competition policy and profoundly affects the policy dynamics of the field. It is also extremely important in its own right with substantial impact on key industrial sectors and providing one of the most important parameters within which national industrial policies have to operate.

After many years of inaction in the field of state aid, the Commission began to enforce the rules forcefully in the late 1980s as part of what can only be described as a 'crusade' by the Competition Commissioner, then Sir Leon Brittan. A regime of notification and control has been established, with the development of case law and the drawing-up of various generic and sectoral frameworks for, for instance, regional aid and aid to the motor industry. The state-aid regime has involved the Commission in some dramatic confrontations with member states, particularly the French. Together with measures against national enterprises and regulation under articles 86 and 90, the net effect has, in the words of one acute recent analysis, been of 'a dramatic shift in the system's substantive focus. The Commission has shifted the emphasis in competition law away from its traditional concerns with private conduct and towards the problem of government interference with the competitive process.'[11] This shift has arguably accentuated criticism of the Commission in an era where member states are asserting their spheres of independence. In comparative terms it also underlines the distinctive mission of European competition policy, which is to pursue integration through control of states as well as of private companies.

The Treaty provisions outlined above are mere aspirations without administrative powers with which to enforce them. Although DG IV was among the first DGs to be established, in 1957, it was small and powerless. As late as 1964 it still had a staff of only 78,[12] but by that time it had acquired its key source of procedural power in the form of Regulation 17 of 1962. Regulations of the European Council are specific, immediate, and binding on all member states. Through a series of regulations the Council has granted extensive legal authority to DG IV (the other major areas being block exemptions and mergers). Regulation 17 provides a very broad base for the enforcement of articles 85 and 86. In Goyder's words, 'It gives to DG IV indeed powers probably greater than would be accorded to it were the Regulation being now debated',[13] and it is no coincidence that reform of Regulation 17 is a central element in the current reform debate.

Prior to the enactment of Regulation 17, the national authorities had begun to apply the competition law provisions. Regulation 17, based on a German model of notification, evaluation, and exemption, effectively centralized enforcement and marginalized the national authorities. It provided for jurisdictional pre-eminence (in that member states had to cease investigation if DG IV took up a case); for exclusive authority over exemptions from the application of article 85; for notification to the Commission; for a high degree of autonomy (subject only to an advisory committee); for a degree of discretion and ability to negotiate with companies; for authority to impose substantial fines of up to 10 per cent of turnover; and for extensive powers of investigation including forced entry and seizure.[14] Regulation 17 thus created a procedural machinery with the potential to enforce the competition rules forcibly and flexibly. In practice it took about twenty years before that potential became fully realized.

Core actors

To talk of 'the institution(s)' of competition policy could be construed as referring to the primary organizations responsible for its development. The usage employed here is more broad than an organizational definition, and regards competition policy as a mixture of organizations, values, and norms analogous to the way in which 'the family', 'the judiciary', or even 'the law' are termed 'an institution'. The normative basis of competition policy is especially important in such a definition. Norms are tacit, unarticulated (and not necessarily consistent), but are widely shared within the institution and provide a routine, instinctive guide to action.[15] The following five norms are prominent within European competition policy:

- a commitment to integration, used as a criteria in selecting cases and making decisions;
- an understanding of competition policy as 'law' to be settled by due process, precedent, and adjudication (rather than by political negotiation—although this norm may be in transition, see below);
- a commitment to 'competition', understood often in evangelical terms of 'competition' for its own sake and with overtones of scepticism of economic concentration, defence of individual consumers, and a sense of a moral commitment to the free market as the constitutional basis for the European economy;
- a pragmatic awareness of the importance of the competitiveness

of the European economy and therefore a willingness to compromise with corporate demands. This is seen in the choice of cases, the exercise of discretion in negotiation, and particularly in the operation of the Merger Task Force;
* a tolerance of national interests and a willingness to recognize the imperatives of national political and economic forces.

It can be argued that competition policy, often expressed as 'the competition rules', has become an institutional pillar of the EU. Snyder speculates on the extent to which competition law might become a principle standard of European economic law, and, while he is equivocal, he emphasizes the effect of competition law on other policy areas (such as the regions, the CAP, or the environment).[16] If competition policy has taken on this sort of institutional significance, it can be regarded as a constitutive element of the European polity, to be regarded as part of the 'high politics' of constitutional settlement rather than the 'low politics' of political bargaining.

To conceptualize competition policy in this fashion broadens our definition of 'core actors' beyond the central organization of DG IV to encompass others who contribute to those institutional norms and are party to the constitutional settlements involved. In this sense the 'core actors' include the competition commissioner, his *cabinet*, and DG IV itself, but also the courts, elements of the national authorities, and perhaps elements of the legal community. We proceed to analyse those actors.

The European Commission is a distinctive body of twenty independent commissioners nominated by the member states. The Commission is collegiate and indivisible, so that, although we concentrate on DG IV, it acts in the name of the Commission as a whole. The pivotal appointment is that of the commissioner responsible for competition. Commissioners in recent years have been:

1981–Jan. 1985, Frans Andriessen (Dutch)
1985–Jan. 1989, Peter Sutherland (Irish)
1989–Jan. 1993, Sir Leon Brittan (British)
1993–Jan. 1995, Karel Van Miert (Belgian)
1995–   Karel Van Miert

The commissioner is supported by a *cabinet* (private office) on the French model, which comprises up to eight members drawn typically from the national civil service and from within the

Commission. The cabinet will be headed by a *chef de cabinet*, and the system of inter-cabinet co-ordination and negotiation has become elaborate, formalized, and central to the process of EC decision-making.[17] The ability of the commissioner and his cabinet to overcome opposition in the Commission through negotiation, persuasion, and threat is central not only for the development of policy but also for its enforcement. It was thus important that 'the Brittans' (Leon Brittan's cabinet) were 'generally acknowledged to be the best staff in the Berlaymont (except for Delors's)'.[18]

All decisions must be approved by the full Commission and every *cabinet* has a competition policy specialist whose main aim is to protect the national interest of the Commissioner's home country. So important is competition policy that twice a week all the chefs de cabinet hold a special meeting devoted to competition cases (if they can agree, the Commission will accept their recommendations). In his recent study of the Delors cabinet Ross paints a quite astonishing picture of the cabinet battles over merger control. The Delors cabinet worked hard to prevent the Brittan cabinet from bringing cases forward and fought heroically against the rejection of the ATR–de Havilland merger, which was the first case turned down by the Commission. Ross graphically portrays the realities of Commission politicking when he reveals that, during the Commission vote on the merger, which went nine to eight in favour of Brittan, 'Manuel Marin, the swing vote, gave an utterly incomprehensible argument to explain himself, but seemed to have traded his vote for help from Brittan on a pending project to reorganize the European fishing fleet, an essential Spanish dossier'.[19] The Commissioner and his cabinet are surprisingly detached from DG IV, a detachment symbolized by the physical separation of the cabinet (in the Commission building) from DG IV (in Avenue Courtembourg).

The Director General of DG IV is a permanent official but participates openly in policy-making in a Franco-German manner which is very unlike the British tradition. The crucial 'German connection' has meant that all Director Generals to date have been German: up until 1990 Dr Manfred Caspari; since then Dr Claus-Dieter Ehlermann, who is retiring in 1995 to take a post at the European University Institute. His successor is Dr Alexander Schaub, also German and the former Deputy Director General of DG III. The structure of DG IV in 1994 is given in Figure 8.1.

Commissioner: Karel van Miert (Belgian)
Chef de Cabinet: Claude Chene
Cabinet (six members)

Director General: Claus Dieter Ehlermann (German)

Deputy Director General: Raymond Simmonet (French)

Directorate A—General Competition Policy and Co-ordination
(5 divisions)
Directeur: Rafael Garcia-Palencia Cebrian (Spanish)

Directorate B—Restrictive Practices, Abuse of Dominant Position; 85/86 I
(4 divisions = electrical, information technology, banking, textiles)
Directeur: Jean Dubois (French)

Directorate C—Restrictive Practices, Abuse of Dominant Position; 85/86 II
(3 divisions = energy, chemicals, non-ferrous metals)
Directeur: Gianfranco Rocca (Italian)

Directorate D—Restrictive Practices, Abuse of Dominant Position; 85/86 III
(4 divisions = coal, steel, transport, cars)
Directeur: John Temple-Lang (Irish)

Directorate E—State Aid; 92–4
(6 divisions = general, R&D, regional, two industry divisions, and inventory)
Directeur: Asger Petersen (Danish)

Merger Task Force
Directeur: Phillip Lowe (British)

FIG 8.1 The organizational structure of DG IV

There is a fairly sharp functional division between the Merger
Task Force; Directorate E, which deals with state aids; and Directorates B, C, and D, which deal with articles 85 and 86. Each of
these three subsections has built up a sub-culture of its own.
Directorates B, C, and D are organized a bit like the German
system into sectoral subdivisions. Here the majority of officials are
lawyers, they act as *rapporteurs* on individual dossiers on the
French model, and have a very heavy case load, working possibly
on up to 15 cases at one time. Directorate E employs more economists. Here cases are less legally driven and officials are dealing
mainly with government agencies; there is little interaction between these 'two sides of the House'. The Merger Task Force was
established in 1990 and quickly emerged as an élite unit. Brittan
observed that 'a Task Force has been established within DG IV
and we have recruited to it some of the very best officials within
the Commission and on secondment'.[20] The Merger Task Force
has been prestigious, even glamorous. It has enjoyed generous

resourcing, has a far lower case load and may perhaps have drained talent from elsewhere in DG IV. It has aroused some internal tensions but also generated outside criticism arising, perversely, from the sheer efficiency of its operations. The procedural aspects of merger control have been greeted with almost universal approval, especially from industry. The procedure is 'user-friendly', reasonable, and, above all, rapid. This provoked the obvious question. If DG IV can administer merger control so promptly and efficiently why can it not achieve similar standards in the rest of its work?

We come back to these criticisms below, but one obvious response concerns staffing. DG IV is quite ludicrously understaffed. Table 8.2 provides details of current staffing which show a total of 411 staff compared with around 400 for the Office of Fair Trading and 250 for the Bundeskartellamt. But DG IV deals with a market now totalling 370 million, works in eleven languages, covers state aid, and acts as a co-ordinator and international negotiator. The outcome is a process that is absurdly slow in dealing with article 85 and 86 cases and creates a resort to unsatisfactory administrative short-cuts, an inability fully to pursue some important cases, a high level of criticism of procedural inadequacies, and a lowering of morale. The chances of increased staffing are very small. This state of affairs leads to unsatisfactory enforcement and fuels the proposals on subsidiarity and an independent European Cartel Office reviewed below. The internal organization of DG IV is very important. It affects the enforcement of policy, the legitimacy of the policy, and can even affect policy-making itself. There is a longstanding criticism that DG IV operates as detective, prosecutor, judge, and jury. This criticism can be countered by emphasizing the internal procedures, the 'Chinese Walls' and the procedural safeguards (such as the Hearings Officer). But the administrative procedure does allow an individual official to have significant influence. Each case is handled by a 'rapporteur' using the French dossier system. They investigate, draft, and recommend, leading the House of Lords Committee to quote the criticism that 'the application of competition procedures appears to rely too much on the individual feelings (and abilities) of the Rapporteur'.[21]

Although there are multiple checks, this ability to initiate makes the individual rapporteur influential and puts the emphasis on

TABLE 8.2. *Staffing of DG IV*

Function	Total[a]	'A' Grade[b]
Director General's Office	6	4
Directorate A	36	23
Directorates B, C, D (articles 85, 86)	181	92
Directorate E (state aid and article 90)	98	50
Merger Task Force	49	29
Support and documents	41	12
Total	411	210

Notes: [a] Figures provided in *23rd Report on Competition Policy*, 111, as at 31 Dec. 1993.
[b] Figures are author's estimates derived from treating A-grade staff as roughly pro-rata to total staff. Note, the figure includes 24 seconded specialists from national authorities. A-grade officials engage in administrative and advisory functions and have a university education.

committed, vigorous, and well-informed officials. It also emphasizes the significance of transparency and, while the European Commission is probably the most open major administrative system in Europe, many regard DG IV procedures as unacceptably opaque.

In a related vein the nature of the staff is also important. The calibre of staff is generally felt to be high, especially the younger generation of lawyers who have entered since the early 1980s and who are confident and entrepreneurial. There is, however, unease at the legal bias within DG IV. Lawyers outnumber economists by 7 to 1 and the paucity of economic analysis has been widely criticized.[22] In assessing the norms of DG IV it is also important to note the stability of staffing. Officials tend to join early in their career and to stay within the Commission, and within DG IV. Since DG IV is a regulatory body, rather than a spending agency, the calibre of the staff and the culture of the organization are key determinants of its effectiveness. We return to these issues of culture, legitimacy, and compliance below, after extending the discussion to the other core actors.

The other core actors, in order of importance, are the Courts, the national authorities, and the European Parliament. The legal norms within DG IV have been reinforced and justified by its

close, mutually supportive relationship with the European Court
of Justice. It has become a commonplace to identify the European
Court as the main vehicle of integration in the EC, especially in
the years of stagnation between the Luxembourg Compromise of
1966 and the Single European Act of 1985.[23]

The Court had steadily endorsed the expansion of competition
law jurisdiction through, for instance, a liberal interpretation of
the 'effects on trade' doctrine, and some notably expansionist cases
such as *Continental Can* in 1973. Like DG IV its prime goal was
integration, and it was willing to embark on some formidably
teleological and imaginative decisions in ways that spoke almost
of a tacit conspiracy between DG IV and the Court.[24]

Since the late 1980s the Court has become rather more cautious
and has concentrated on refining existing doctrine rather than
looking to major jurisdictional expansion.[25] It has also begun to
stress 'effects-based' criteria which require that Commission decisions specify the effect on competition of an infraction, rather
than arguing from legal principle. This shift elevates the importance of economic analysis and the Court has been noticeably
more stringent in its review of cases, a trend consolidated by the
creation in 1989 of the Court of First Instance (CFI) which has
taken over initial responsibility for all competition cases. The CFI
has proved to be a rigorous reviewer of Commission decisions and
created a shock wave in 1992 when it concluded in the *PVC* case
that the Commission had failed to comply with its own rules of
procedure. Serious procedural shortcomings were also found in
the *PTT Post* case (February 1992), *Flatglass* (March 1992), *Danish
Furs* (July 1992), and *Wood Pulp* (March 1993).[26] The Commission is adapting to this procedural rigour and may actually be
strengthened in that it can rebut critics of procedural inadequacies
by pointing to this new and potent check.

The national competition authorities of the member states can
also be regarded as 'core actors' even though they have minimal
formal involvement in policy-making and enforcement. Regulation
17 and the Merger Regulation establish advisory committees on
Restrictive Practices and Monopolies, and on Concentrations. The
committees are made up of one representative from each member
state, in practice from the respective competition authority. The
Committees meet regularly and draw up views on each major
decision. These views are strictly advisory, there is no power of

veto (which the French advocated when Regulation 17 was being negotiated). The views of the Restrictive Practices and Monopolies Committee are appended to the decision but not published. The views of the Merger Committee can and have been published. The indications are that DG IV takes the deliberations of the Committees seriously and will not lightly dismiss a unanimous finding. It also uses the Committee meetings and network to consult over the implementation of new policy, as, for instance, with proposed regulations, notices, or block exemptions.

The involvement of the national authorities with European policy is, of course, far more intimate, intense, and influential than these bare administrative links imply. The national authorities collaborate in investigations, second staff, and exchange views on a regular and routine basis. They have routes into European policy-making through the national permanent representatives, the national *cabinets*, and the Council of Ministers, although in each case their views are selected, filtered, or sometimes plain manipulated by the responsible ministry. Thus, the two most influential national authorities, the BKartA and the Office of Fair Trading (OFT), are represented in European debate by, respectively, the Federal Economics Ministry and the Department of Trade and Industry.

The national authorities are becoming more critical and more jealous of their independence in the 1990s. There are, of course, more of them. The French system was revised and strengthened in 1986, the Italians created a new Antitrust Authority in 1990, and a 'European model' of competition policy has become accepted.[27] These reinforced national authorities want to deploy their powers and are eager for effective subsidiarity. The influence of the national authorities was all too apparent in the negotiations over the proposed reduction in the merger thresholds. The Commission's formal observation was that 'some (national) authorities believe that any extension of Community competence for mergers should be examined in the wider context of a general review of the share-out of tasks between the Commission and the Member States in the application of the Treaty articles on competition'.[28]

These neutral phrases concealed a bruising period of negotiation in which the German and British authorities (particularly the DTI) refused to sanction a reduction in thresholds. The Germans went so far as to link agreement on lowering thresholds to the creation of an independent ECO.

Notwithstanding such disagreements the European and national competition authorities have strong ideological interests and self-interests in enhancing a strong competition policy regime. They share a concern with extending jurisdiction and strengthening enforcement, and share also a common view of the importance of competition. These shared vocabulary, norms, and problem definitions reflect a 'community of interest'. While often disagreeing on detail it might, therefore, be expected that this cross-European community of interests would act to defend the structures and assumptions of competition policy. It has thus come as a profoundly worrying development for DG IV that the key national authorities, the Germans, have begun to level fundamental and bitter criticism at the European regime.

The European Parliament (EP) would not, until recently, have been regarded as a 'core actor' in virtually any area of EC policy-making. It is, however, rapidly growing in influence, and in the competition policy field is a potential ally which DG IV is keen to cultivate. Thus the relationship is undergoing continual change as the EP acquires increased powers and significance under the Single European Act (1986) and the Treaty on European Union (1992). Contact between the Commission and the Parliament is deepening rapidly and is most clearly evident in the deliberations surrounding the Commission's annual competition policy report. This is submitted to the EP's Committee on Economic, Monetary, and Industrial Affairs which in turn appoints a rapporteur (a one-year appointment) to examine the Commission's report in detail, to draft comments, and to report back to the Committee. In the discussions that follow both the Competition Commissioner and the Director General of DG IV become involved and attend the Committee's meeting to defend DG IV's actions. As this relationship matures it is to be expected that the EP's views will bear on the Commission's perspective on competition policy. Its comments are published in the Annual Competition Report and are often forceful and to the point.[29]

In recent years business has woken up to the augmented powers of the EP and is fostering ever closer dialogue with MEPs and particular parliamentary committees. Accordingly the EP's Committee for Economic, Monetary, and Industrial Affairs, and its competition policy rapporteur have become constant targets for lobbyists, who seek to influence the rapporteur's opinions when drawing up the annual EP response to EU competition policy, as the competition policy rapporteur is only too ready to affirm.[30] This growing relationship between business and the EP is stimulated by the recently enhanced powers of co-decision and the representation of business interests through the Economic and Social Committee. It is a relationship which in turn increases the weight of the EP in the Commission's eyes. DG IV is very sensitive to business views and presssures and it is aware that major business groups such as UNICE are following determined strategies to project their views through Parliamentary forums.[31]

Networks and 'non-core' actors

An orthodox and productive way of analysing policy-making is to examine policy networks. At the sectoral level the policy-network approach can be extremely useful in identifying interested actors, picking out patterns of stable relationships, and identifying the shared norms and negotiated understandings which have been built up by network participants.[32] The utility of this theoretical approach is explored further in Chapter 11, here we can examine to what extent it is helpful in the setting of European competition policy.

The three main criteria for participation of actors in a policy network are high salience, overt interdependency, and sustained involvement. In other words, for the actor or organization involved, success in the policy area must be important for goal achievement; there must be a recognition that goal achievement is dependent on co-operation with other actors; and the actor must have a long-term interest in the field. In the field of competition policy a policy network is apparent among inter-governmental actors. It could be mapped as centring on DG IV and embracing elements of other DGs and their *cabinets*, and specialists in the Council, the Parliament, and the Committee of Permanent Representatives (COREPER). The network would extend beyond the European institutions to include elements within the national competition authorities and some other international agencies such as the OECD. This network is quite self-conscious. OECD officials talk of a 'competition policy community' which has a sociological dimension, of people who know one another and meet frequently;

and a cognitive dimension of a series of norms and shared interpretations. In other settings the latter has been termed an 'epistemic
community'.[33] Curiously this network operating within government does share some of the coherence of the expenditure policy
community famously analysed by Heclo and Wildavsky in their
'Whitehall Village' image which served as a precursor to the early
policy network debate.[34]

It is far less easy to identify a policy network that stretches
outside government. Competition policy does not lend itself to the
sustenance of network relationships. By its nature it is episodic,
reacting perhaps to a cartel case or a merger. It does not involve
a regular cycle of activity and does not control a spending programme. What is more it is multi-sectoral, dealing with chemicals
at one moment, telecommunications at the next. Added to this are
the inherent difficulties of creating pan-European networks due to
differences in culture, legal systems, and language. Thus it is not
perhaps surprising that no neo-pluralist policy network seems to
have grown up in the field of competition policy. Indeed, such networks appear to be exceptional at the European level. Richardson
and Mazey observe that 'the unique structural characteristics of
the EC policy-making process do inhibit the establishment of stable
policy communities'.[35] This conclusion does not imply that lobbying on competition policy issues is either infrequent or ineffectual,
quite the contrary. Big firms are immensely influential lobbyists.
No Commission official will refuse to see the representatives of
Daimler Benz, which has a most effective Brussels lobbying operation.[36] Similarly Fiat wields more influence than many Italian
ministries and Philips has been credited with writing the briefs
with which Dutch officials negotiate.[37] In the same vein business
groupings have a powerful impact. The American Chamber of
Commerce 'is possibly the most effective lobbying organization in
Brussels', say Richardson and Mazey,[38] while Cawson *et al.* suggest that 'perhaps the most powerful supra-national lobbying organization is the European "Round Table"'.[39] For its part UNICE
(the Union of Industrial and Employers' Associations) claims that
it was 'able to influence heavily the formation of the Merger
Regulation, helping the Commission to produce a workable
policy'.[40] While the influence of business is great, it has tended to
be issue based and episodic. More recently, however, practically
all leading companies have become involved in specific product

associations; industrial groups such as the ERT (European Round Table of Industrialists), or employer associations such as UNICE who are in constant dialogue with the Commission. They regard involvement as a necessity and consequently court active participation in policy development through formal and informal contacts, the setting up of their own competition divisions and working groups, and the production of regular bulletins and responses to developments. The Commission will remain the focus of the industrial lobbyist for the immediate future and dialogue with DG IV will remain an imperative. An interesting issue is the extent to which lobbying and dialogue becomes transmuted into consultation and negotiation. Indeed, if lobbying became routinized critics would be able to talk of regulatory 'capture', an issue we return to below.

Similar conclusions about outside involvement in policy-making could be drawn in respect of consumer organizations such as BEUC (European Bureau of Consumers' Unions). The great exception to this argument is the lawyers. The dominance of lawyers over European competition policy is remarkable. It is, of course, paralleled by the legal dominance over US antitrust, although there economists have made an impact. In Germany too, competition policy is so dominated by legal specialists that the terms 'competition law' and 'competition policy' can be used almost synonymously. This legal bias deserves sustained attention.

The last three Competition Commissioners trained as lawyers and, indeed, Sutherland and Brittan both practised as barristers. The last Director General of DG IV was formerly the head of the Legal Service and lawyers predominate within the organization. The salience of competition policy in the 1980s was reflected in the rapid increase in the number of law firms establishing offices in Brussels and the vast recruitment of competition law specialists. The legal profession has proven to be one of the major beneficiaries from the impact of competition law and has increased staff to meet an ever-growing demand. Indeed, Euro-firms such as Lovell White Durrant have seen their competition law staff rise from 3 in 1975 to 35 by 1993, with the increase most actively felt in the merger division. They discern no sign that their activities in this area are going to lessen. On the contrary, the legal profession believes that their work-load will continue to increase as the EU itself expands eastwards and northwards.

The network of competition lawyers extends beyond professional firms into companies (and, of course, academia). In terms of competition policy compliance it is important with regard to whether companies 'externalize' legal advice through professional firms, or internalize compliance through in-house lawyers. In a speech to the new assembly of in-house counsels, Dr Ehlermann stressed their importance as 'one of the major links between the EC institutions and the business community [who] transmit principles developed at Community level to top management'.[41] Lawyers in private practice or in companies play a leading role in formulating business input into competition policy-making. Thus, for instance, the CBI's recent statements on competition policy were formulated via their competition law advisory group chaired by an in-house counsel and composed mainly of lawyers.[42]

This picture of competition policy as a heavily juridical process based in law, enforced by lawyers, adjudicated by the European Court, criticized on legal grounds and debated in a legal vocabulary and philosophy is nicely illustrated by the recent House of Lords report on the competition rules. This influential investigation by the Select Committee on the European Communities was chaired by a former President of the European Court, took evidence predominantly from lawyers, and concentrated on legal issues in its deliberations and in its report.[43] This was reform by lawyers for lawyers, a ubiquitous characteristic of recent reform proposals which is seen also in the German criticisms by lawyers from the BKartA.

The legal dominance of competition policy produces a network which is linked professionally (by cases, conferences, and personnnel exchanges) rather than administratively (through committees and papers). It produces some very distinctive policy dynamics in which legal ends, legal criteria, legal norms, and legal participants come together to pursue a policy that has its own logic but can be regarded by outsiders as arcane, inappropriate, and marginal. It was industrially perverse logic that prompted Martin Bangeman's famous outburst against the 'competition ayatollahs'[44] and provoked the interesting comment from Karel Van Miert that, 'Just as war is too important to be left to the generals, competition law and policy is too important to be left to the lawyers.'[45] It may be that the generals have had their day. Recent pressures and trends in competition policy have tended to play down the role of law and the courts in favour of politics and the Commission.

THE WAXING, AND WANING?
OF COMPETITION POLICY

The growth in influence of European competition policy and of DG IV up to 1990–1 was based on a complex conjunction of factors but was grounded in quite exceptional legal powers. The competition rules gain invaluable authority from their status as Treaty provisions enshrined in articles 85–94 of the Treaty of Rome (incorporated, unamended, in the Treaty on European Union—Maastricht Treaty of 1992). Reinforced by early permissive Council regulations, especially the procedural Regulation 17, and by the consistent support and incitement of the European Court of Justice, the competition rules have provided a formidable competence. At the beginning of the 1980s Jacobs observed that 'the Commission is, in effect, a federal agency, operating directly within the territory of the Member States and having exclusive competence . . . in this respect competition law is unlike any other area of EEC law'.[46]

Thus the competition authorities act directly. They have no need for the support of the Council of Ministers and there is no Competition Council; the Advisory Committee of Member States is only advisory; the European Parliament has no veto; European procedures take priority over national jurisdictions and there is no need for the complex 'comitology' of implementing arrangements that complicate so much European implementation. The main inhibitions on the activities of DG IV are the College of Commissioners itself, the European Court, the low staff numbers, and 'self-restraint', which is, perhaps, a euphemism for 'politics'.

Yet for the first twenty years of European policy these powers remained virtually unused. Actions by the Commission were partial, hesitant, and DG IV was widely regarded as ineffectual.[47] What changed in the 1980s? Three sets of factors deserve emphasis. First, there was the power of ideas. The neo-liberalism that swept across Europe in the 1980s found expression in the Single Market programme and the Single European Act. Market integration has always been the prime goal of DG IV, to have it elevated to the pre-eminent objective of the Commission raised the salience of competition policy, was good for morale, and facilitated co-operation from other Commission agencies. While Moravcik argues that business groups had little direct influence on the creation of the single market programme,[48] there was undoubtedly intense support for the inter-governmental initiatives and for an effective competition policy to ensure that they were enforced.

The second set of factors concerns political leadership. The significance of leadership from the Commissioner was established by Peter Sutherland, whose success was built upon by Leon Brittan, who became arguably the most forceful Commissioner in the history of DG IV, and a most effective member of the 1989–92 Commission. Before Sutherland departed in 1988 the press tended to attach much of the prominence of DG IV to his personal role, and there is no doubt that Sutherland seized, and symbolized, the moment. He was a dynamic, charismatic character portrayed as a young, tough Irishman (only 42 when he left office), who combined the legal flair of the barrister with the aggression of the rugby captain.[49] But it would be wrong to regard his influence as one of direct leadership. To a surprising degree there is within the Commission a disjuncture between the Commissioner and his Cabinet on the one hand, and the Directorate General on the other. Rather than the integration of the minister with his department so typical of Britain the European model is conducted in terms of 'us' and 'them'.

Contrary to early misgivings, Sir Leon Brittan proved just as effective as Sutherland and threw himself with ill-concealed relish into his Commission responsibilities. Also relatively young (49 when entering office), Brittan was impeccably well qualified for the job. Not only was he a weighty national politician from one of the larger Member States (his immediate predecessors were from Ireland, Holland, and two from Luxembourg), he shared the self-defined mission of DG IV, the pursuit of free competition, and was hence ideologically in tune with his officials. Living up to the reputation he acquired at the DTI, Brittan proved to be a sophisticated operator on the Brussels scene. Although notorious for intellectual arrogance, he became a decisive and determined administrator able to inspire loyalty, to impose priorities, and to provide strategic leadership. More surprisingly, he and his Cabinet became adept in the vital Brussels processes of negotiation and compromise. To a greater degree than Sutherland he was willing to lobby and to cut deals, sometimes to the frustration of DG IV officials who would have preferred tougher decisions.[50] Above all, Brittan put an end to any sense of drift in DG IV. He had his own priorities which he propounded in a torrent of speeches extending well beyond the competition brief. Both Sutherland and Brittan found DG IV to be a productive political platform and both were tipped as possible Commission presidents. Both continued to be prominent international figures in the field, Brittan as European Commissioner for International Economic Relations, Sutherland as acting Director General of the World Trade Organization (WTO).

Under Brittan DG IV underwent a process often described as 'maturation'[51] which involved a maturing both of legal powers and staff competence. The legal maturation involved the familiar accumulation of innovation, challenge, and adjudication which by the end of the decade had established a body of law enshrined in precedent. Indeed, lawyers in DG IV would remark that in thirty years European law had consolidated a body of doctrine that had taken one hundred years in the United States. The maturation of staff is more intangible but, as we have argued elsewhere,[52] the calibre of staff appeared to be one of DG IV's advantages. During the 1980s a 'third generation' of well-qualified, well-motivated, and self-confident staff were in place. They combined professional competence (as qualified lawyers or economists) with a commitment to the European ideal. Their work involves a high level of responsibility from the beginning, and they have a very well-developed sense of the sheer power at their disposal. As emphasized earlier, a rapporteur has a considerable influence in deciding (say) the acceptability of a large programme of regional aid, the conditions under which credit cards can be used across Europe, or the practical operation of patent protections which govern innovation activity within the pharmaceutical industry. Such weighty responsibility can be daunting, but it can also be immensely stimulating, and many officials are enthusiasts. The overall impression was of an organization which had a strong departmental 'culture', which was in turn becoming more positive and self-reinforcing, to produce an *esprit de corps* across most divisions. Hence both morale and self-confidence were at a high point. This was terribly important. If, as can be argued, DG IV moved from a reactive, rather negative mode of administration to one that is proactive, more managerially aware, positive, and innovatory, then this metamorphosis rests on staff attitudes. Staff must work confidently, be willing to be decisive and then to pursue cases with imagination and a dogged determination. In the field of science policy much has been made of the role of 'project champions' in successful processes of innovation; so DG IV relies on its officials to become 'case champions' if it is to expand its standing and jurisdiction. This combination of prioritized integration, effective leadership, and socio-legal maturation produced an organization that was engaged in major innovation in all areas of activity. It was active in article 85 and 86 but had also embarked on its successful mission to establish control over state aid. It was beginning to address the issues of public companies and national utility monopolies and to make progress in hitherto protected areas such as air transport. The whole spirit of the moment was symbolized by the successful negotiation of the Merger Regulation which had always been regarded as the jewel in the crown. The self-confident creation and outstandingly successful initial operation of the Merger Task Force completed the picture of a robust and impressive institution which was making policy as well as enforcing law, and which was acting as a model of successful supra-national governance. Jacob's 'federal agency' had come of age.

It has subsequently been argued that this very success contained the seeds of its own downfall.[53] Perhaps this is too strong a formulation, but there is no concealing the fact that European competition policy is on the retreat. We can take each of the factors which were conducive to success and identify a more negative influence post-1992. In particular the very successes of integration and of merger control have generated counteracting forces which have put DG IV on the defensive. As far as much popular opinion and official declarations are concerned, by 1 January 1993 the Single Market had been achieved and economic integration was an operational reality. What then was the purpose of DG IV? It could be likened to a poverty agency that actually succeeds in eliminating poverty; it is redundant. Of course this is a partial and superficial view, but it has enough force to undermine the pre-eminence given to DG IV and its mission. Gerber thus argues that, far from now being a mature and self-confident agency, 'The system is more convincingly portrayed as featuring an understaffed and somewhat uncertain Commission facing new problems, pressures, and demands with diminishing guidance from the Court and increasingly tentative support for its mission. The competition law system thus faces what can aptly be described as an "identity crisis".'[54] In order to evaluate the depths of this crisis, the nature of the criticisms of European competition policy, and the likely direction of reforms, we go on to review the current operation of policy.

CURRENT PERFORMANCE OF POLICY

From early 1993 a coincidence of events added to the volatility of European policy. These included the appointment of a new Competition Commissioner; the controversy over the review of the merger thresholds; the Commission's Notice to give national courts greater influence over articles 85 and 86; the creation of the European Economic Area; and the creation of the North American Free Trade Association (NAFTA), increasing the pressure for some degree of international rules on competition policy. The primary policy concerns and criticisms can be classified into two categories; minor procedural issues which are mostly of interest to the legal community, such as access to the file and comfort letters,[55] and major policy defects. In the latter category five problem areas can be identified which impinge on DG IV's effectiveness; namely, questions of efficiency, concentration of powers, failure of subsidiarity to appease national authorities, the degree of politicization, and a lack of accountability and transparency in the decision-making process. How the Commission is seen to tackle these issues in the context of responses to the rapid process of market globalization, and the pressures for competitiveness, will ultimately determine its future position and the role of competition policy.

The issue of efficiency: A lack of resources

In the first edition of his excellent study of competition law Goyder observed that, 'the chief continuing weakness of DG IV . . . in the enforcement of competition policy is that its inadequate resources both in financial terms and in numbers of officials, have prevented it from ever completely digesting the workload'. In 1993 he noted the continuing problem which was aggravated by the expansion of responsibilities.

As DG IV assumed ever more significance the pressure on its limited resources multiplied. So too did criticisms of the time it

TABLE 8.3. *Articles 85 and 86: cases outstanding*

Year	New cases	Formal decisions	Cases outstanding
1981	293	21	4,365
1985	304	18	3,313
1990	375	12	2,734
1991	388	17	2,287
1992	399	30	1,682
1993	390	12	1,231

Sources: Memorandum by Dr Claus-Dieter Ehlermann, in House of Lords, *Enforcement of Community Competition Rules 1993–94*, HL 7 (London: HMSO, 1993), 121; *XXIIIrd Report on Competition Policy, 1993* (Brussels: CEC, 1994), 120–1.

took to reach decisions. Various reasons can be cited to explain delay, including the backlog, the complexity of the cases, the necessity to provide greater economic evidence, the administrative complexity and the heavy burden involved in translating decisions and conducting investigations in the eleven official languages of the EU. When dealing with the 'efficiency' aspect it is absolutely vital to differentiate between merger cases and those antitrust cases under articles 85 and 86, for it is the latter that pose the problem. Indeed, DG IV has become a victim of its own success. Under the merger regulation 90 per cent of the cases are dealt with within one month and the remainder within four, so contrasts are drawn with DG IV's poor record with regards to antitrust and monopoly cases. In fact the backlog problem has been much reduced, as indicated in Table 8.3. The Commission declare the backlog to be cleared; outstanding cases are unlikely to fall further. None the less, individual large cases still take a prolonged period. *Woodpulp* demonstrated the worst excesses of the inefficiency issue, taking twelve years before a decision was reached,[56] and lawyers commonly regard the time delays in clearing cases as intolerable. The outcome is a lack of credibility and problems with compliance. Goyder also notes 'a widespread cynicism in business circles about the efficacy of the exemption process for all individual agreements unable for any reason to benefit from group exemption'.[57] This leads to a temptation not to notify.

Attempts to accelerate the procedure in antitrust cases, first targeted in the 1983 Competition Policy report, even when pushed vociferously in 1991 and 1992 by a forceful Commissioner such as Sir Leon Brittan, encountered such strong resistance from the various DG IV division directors, that he unilaterally imposed tighter timetables. Van Miert and Ehlermann are equally appreciative of the need for procedural improvement, but, as both readily admit, DG IV requires greater resources and a more even-handed sharing of responsibilities. Indeed, an imbalance in staffing levels exists within DG IV for the MTF, the most 'glamorous and exciting' part of the competition directorate is actually overstaffed. Individuals within the MTF deal with 2.4 cases simultaneously, while those investigating articles 85 and 86 are engaged in 16 cases.[58] The current drive for procedural improvement involves strict time limits for 'structural' co-operative joint ventures where business planning demands a rapid decision. More recently Mr Van Miert has announced a reorganization of the article 85/86 directorates to create a new Cartel Task Force aimed at the major complex cartels and reporting to the Director General.[59] This, of course, has substantive as well as procedural implications.

The refusal to grant additional staff numbers is extraordinary and ambiguous. It is unclear whether the Commission or the Member States operate a veto. Certainly the Commission has an inadequate policy on staff deployment and has been criticized for 'the apparently large number of under-employed staff in the Commission, the clear lack of staff in key areas of emerging policy responsibility, the inability ... to decide a rational redeployment policy ...'[60]

The effect is to undermine confidence in DG IV, to inhibit promotion, undermine morale, encourage the resort to unsatisfactory administrative short cuts, and to limit the scope for 'own-initiative' cases, sectoral studies, and measures to encourage compliance. Perhaps some member states feel they have an interest in limiting Commission activism. Certainly one further effect is to encourage moves to real subsidiarity with cases devolved to the national authorities and national courts. Thus, since the *Automec II* case, which indicated that the Commission had discretion to reject complaints, DG IV has begun to refer complainants to national authorities. As with other areas of the Commission, shortage of resources is the midwife to subsidiarity.

DG IV—undue concentration of powers?

Sir Sydney Lipworth, whilst still Chairman of the British Monopolies and Mergers Commission, encapsulated criticism of DG IV in his observation that 'because it is simultaneously detective, prosecutor, judge and executioner, it is structurally weak. Being one body may be administratively convenient, possibly efficient, but it gives rise to actual or potential conflicts of interest.'[61]

Some of DG IV's harshest critics, such as the Brussels-based lawyer Ivo van Bael, argue that this situation is immensely serious because in practice, most decisions are adopted without adequate scrutiny and debate. This is seen to raise issues of accountability and equity which are virtually constitutional. The view is shared by business associations, such as the European Round Table of Industrialists, who are generally discontented with this state of affairs and support a separation of powers to allow a basis for appeal.[62] DG IV officials are quick to repudiate any assertions of malpractice and point to the system of checks and safeguards designed to prevent partisan decisions or any rubber stamping exercise: safeguards in the form of internal procedures, the Commissioner and his cabinet, the role of the Legal Service, and especially the role of the Advisory Committee and the Courts. But are they adequate? In the course of the last five years the courts have become far more stringent but it is doubtful that this will placate the lawyers. It is true that the extensive exercise of discretion by DG IV officials could be abused and, indeed, it opens up possibilities of 'industry capture'. At the extreme, DG IV procedures are felt by some to display a 'lack of respect for natural justice and the rights of defence'.[63] This viewpoint has taken on a profound immediacy with the ruling by the Court of First Instance that Commission procedures are bound by the European Convention on Human Rights and particularly by article 6 which sustains the right to a fair trial. But although there is a high moral tone to the procedural critique there is also a strong strand of self-interest on the part of legal practitioners.

Subsidiarity and centralization of powers

The pressure for effective subsidiarity in the enforcement of European competition policy is now becoming acute. The issue came to the fore in 1992 in the wake of the Danish referendum (which endorsed Maastricht with the thinnest of majorities—50.7 per cent). Many member states pressed for real subsidiarity and the Commission backed away from new legislation and controversial deployment of its powers. In this atmosphere DG IV began to look for ways to subcontract enforcement to the national authorities and adjudication to the national courts. It has issued an important notice on co-operation with the national courts,[64] and is making every appearance of adopting a less expansive interpretation of its article 85 and 86 powers, but without supporting an amendment of Regulation 17.[65]

The key conflict is, however, over merger control. The merger regulation installed a dual control mechanism based on the high thresholds of world turnover of 5 billion ECU and Community turnover of 250 million ECU. In order to dispel further reservations, particularly from Germany, article 9, the so-called 'German clause', introduced an early practical example of subsidiarity. National authorities are able to request permission from the Commission to deal with cases that would otherwise fall within EU jurisdiction, if they feel that they have serious implications for competition within the domestic market. Subsidiarity was designed to alleviate national scepticism but, ironically, the reverse has occurred in the German case. The transfer of responsibility from Brussels has been grudging, and of the six requests to date under article 9, five from the BKartA and one from the Office of Fair Trading, only the British request has been granted for jurisdiction by the national authority.[66] Of the five requests made by the BKartA four were immediately rejected—*Varta/Bosch*, *Siemens/Philips*, *Alcatel/AEG*, and *Mannesmann/Hoesch*. This would certainly have been the fate of the fifth and most recent case, that of *CPC/ McCormick/Rabobank/Ostmann*, if the Commission had not miscalculated the precise time spans of action laid down under the Merger Regulation and thus forfeited the right to initiate further proceedings. Consequently, the case was passed to Berlin through a process of default, a grudging outcome which hardly placated the BKartA.[67] The German competition authorities are very concerned about the merger issue, to the extent that, with the British authorities, they blocked the lowering of the merger thresholds during 1993. This failure to lower the thresholds came as a shock to DG IV and has served as a highly symbolic setback. It provides the national authorities with a powerful bargaining counter in the debate over reform.

Politicization

In his confirmation hearings before the European Parliament, Mr Van Miert indicated opposition to the idea of an independent European Cartel Office, observing that 'Competition policy is not something neutral, it is "politics".'[68] Mr Van Miert was clearly right, and many would applaud his realism, but others would regard it as a heretical view, one which the Germans in particular find hard to accept.

Competition policy is politicized in its detailed operation, which necessitates the exercise of discretion and negotiation in a process aptly described by Peters as 'bureaucratic politics'.[69] It is also politicized in a cruder and highly visible way through the high politics of the College of Commissioners. Political influence at this level constitutes a major concern for the BKartA, for it is neither the Competition Commissioner nor DG IV that has the ultimate decision on competition matters, but the twenty-member European Commission. At the final stage of a controversial decision the Commission may be forced to a vote and commissioners, intent on protecting their own policies and national interests, can overrule the Competition Commissioner. Thus competition policy may have to become subordinated to industrial, regional, and employment interests or be neutralized by extreme national pressure. Wolfgang Kartte, a former BKartA president, therefore regards the EU merger regulation as suffering from a congenital defect (*Geburtsfehler*), because 'in critical cases the prohibition of a merger that would culminate in a dominant market position, is not decided by DG IV, but by all 17 Commissioners. Thus, the politicization of the European merger control has been guaranteed.'[70] He is not alone in expressing such trenchant views. German criticism has been remarkably outspoken.[71]

Transparency

One of the most striking aspects for the academic visitor to Brussels is the willingness of DG IV staff to engage in discussion. The doors in the Avenue de Cortenberg are freely opened and DG IV officials are eager to preach the competition gospel. In contrast, the policy-making process remains far from open. The non-core competition actors call for greater involvement and consultation in Commission plans and for the Commission to make more use of issuing Green Papers to test external responses and to give them the opportunity to play a role in policy creation.

DG IV is very aware of the virtues of transparency. It is to do with far more than image or accountability, because without transparency it is very difficult to establish credibility, legitimacy, and the ultimate goal of all regulatory agencies—willing compliance. As DG IV concedes, competition policy will be fully supported by business, policy-makers, and the general public only if it is widely understood.[72]

Efforts include speeches, press releases, legal and academic publications, and a new Information Unit which publishes a helpful quarterly Newsletter. None the less, DG IV is reluctant to fetter its discretion and has, for instance, resisted 'tariffication' (the preparation of a scale of fines for given infringements). Equally there is the practical problem of the confidentiality of business information which is particularly sensitive in merger decisions and precludes full discussion of many cases.

This raft of problems and criticisms has given rise to a series of proposals for reform but, before we briefly review those proposals, we consider one further issue that is becoming more salient in the competition policy of the 1990s: the relationship between competition policy and industrial policy.

THE COMPROMISE BETWEEN COMPETITION POLICY AND INDUSTRIAL POLICY

The concept of integration as a motive force behind competition policy has lost its pre-eminence as '1992' has come and gone. The next challenge facing the European Union, and the main candidate for the 'European vision' of the 1990s, is the concept of competitiveness. The relationship between competition and competitiveness is ambiguous and variable. The neo-classical theory of competition would suggest that competition is an essential prerequisite for competitiveness, and it is neo-classical concepts—because they are so familiar—that underlie European competition policy. But several alternative conceptualizations of competitiveness draw on alternative theories of competition—dynamic and institutional theories are but two examples.[73] In practice, therefore, policy-makers seldom regard competition policy as a direct instrument for the promotion of competitiveness. Indeed, industrial policy-makers have periodically regarded competition policy as a positive impediment to the creation of European companies and industries likely to be competitive on the world stage.

It might therefore be argued that if the institution of European competition policy is to retain its prestige and influence it will have to compromise with the requirements of competitiveness and will have to align itself with an emergent European industrial policy. Sir Leon Brittan was a genuine neo-liberal and quite opposed to any compromise with industrial policy. In this, as in many other areas, he and Jacques Delors were at odds. Delors was a persistent and active advocate of industrial policy which led him to criticize DG IV at large as well as Sir Leon. Ross cites an extraordinary meeting of Director Generals in 1991 at which Delors declared that 'it will not do to make light of industrial policy. The Community is not, and will not be, a free-trade zone. It is up to us to make a European organized space . . . There are some of you who seem to have barely progressed beyond the stage of elementary school. DG III and DG IV are worse here than the others.'[74]

Delors gave substance to this vision in his last major initiative, the White Paper on *Growth, Competitiveness, Employment* published in 1993.[75] This is a subtle paper which is centred on the issue of unemployment and embraces social and environmental issues. At its heart, however, is a bid to prepare the ground for a revival of sectorally based industrial policy. Rather alarmingly for DG IV, the White Paper says almost nothing about competition policy and certainly gives it no salience in its repertoire of possible ways forward.

Under Karel Van Miert DG IV has softened its attitude to industrial policy. A constant refrain in Van Miert's speeches has been the need for competition policy to work in sympathy with other Commission policy areas. On its first page the 1993 Competition Report asserts that 'It is inconceivable that competition policy could be applied without reference to the priorities fixed by the Community'. It goes on to review 'some of the ways in which competition policy may be adapted to meet the new Community priorities'.

These priorities include industrial policy and the environment. Later DG IV declared that 'far from being the direct opposite of industrial policy, competition policy is an essential instrument, with clear complementarity between the two policies'.[76] The form that such complementarity might take is illustrated in the fresh emphasis on prosecuting long-standing, large, horizontal cartels, the continued 'flexible' operation of the merger regulation, and the actions against governments in respect of state aid and utility infrastructure.

In more detail, the specific role envisaged for competition policy is elaborated in the recent important paper from DG III, *An Industrial Competitiveness Policy for the European Union*.[77] Here the competition rules receive some prominence. The emphasis is on international competition rules, on creating workable European-wide utility markets, and, above all, on state aid.[78] These aims seem to reinforce the bias already noted above towards applying competition law to governments rather than to companies. The paper also underlines the need for DG IV to look outside the Union and to press for stringent international competition rules. To this extent the Competition authorities are acting as economic diplomats, seeking to project a European model of market integration into an international arena. Europe can be expected to be highly active within the World Trade Organization, and Karel Van Miert recently observed that 'I believe the time has now come to ask whether an international body of rules on competition law ought not to be drawn up.'[79] European competition policy appears, then, to be moving towards a less puristly legalistic interpretation of its role to become explicitly instrumental. This is a very delicate shift of emphasis which Mr Van Miert is handling with some success. He has adopted a more conciliatory style than Sir Leon Brittan. Relations between his Cabinet and the staff of DG IV are said to be closer and co-operative, and the traditional antagonism between DG III (Industry) and DG IV has been moderated. There are now more, and more effective, inter-service groups, although the inherent incompatibilities between the two DGs mean that tensions persist.

Mr Van Miert was 53 in 1994 and has spent his whole career in close association with the European Communities, including periods in the private offices of commissioners and a spell as an MEP (Member of the European Parliament, 1979–85). His political roots are as a Flemish Socialist, a background which naturally raised expectations that he might be less rigorous and more *dirigiste* in his interpretation of the competition brief. In fact he has been seen as continuing the strict line of his predecessor, especially in the areas of cartel enforcement where he has, if anything, been stricter. Equally he has pressed hard for utility liberalization but has had also to accept the prevailing flexibility of merger control. The word associated with Mr Van Miert has been 'pragmatic'. This has applied especially to his dealings with state-aid cases which have escalated in size and sensitivity during the European recession of 1993–5. Criticism of the permissive stance over state aid in cases such as Bull, Hualon, and the steel industry has been quite intense.[80] He has just been confirmed as Competition Commissioner for a further four-year term from January 1995 in the Commission of Jacques Santer. It will be difficult to tread the narrow line between enforcing the competition rules as independent, objective parameters of the European market; and enforcing them in support of other Union priorities, such as competitiveness or environmental protection. As regards the former the German authorities have already launched a forceful defence of a fully independent competition jurisdiction in their call for an ECO. As regards the latter, Mr Van Miert will have a truly challenging task in applying the economic analysis of competitiveness to competition cases being decided through a juridical logic of legal process.

CONCLUSION

There are profound ambiguities running through 'the institution' of competition policy. Although the policy itself is conventionally justified in terms of economic welfare, its creation has, in most countries, been prompted by concerns of economic equity (even 'democracy'). This motive has been clearest in the cases of the United States and Japan, where protection of the 'little man' from the trusts, and protection of Japanese democracy from the *zaibatsu* were formative influences. In Europe the competition rules are as much designed to allow equality of participation in the common market, as they are to maximize the efficiency of the market.

It is one of the arguments of this chapter that both these goals, of efficiency and equity, have been displaced in favour of a goal of legality. This reflects the German influence on European practice (and legalism is an even more serious pathology in the German system) and is perhaps the price paid for the pact with the European Court. It is a legalism which has virtues and is biased towards considerations of equity, towards the freedom to compete in the market, and towards consumer protection, but in the core areas of articles 85 and 86 the dominant norm is one of legal defensibility. Neither the Commission nor the Court present a considered economic reasoning of decisions and the paucity of economic analysis has widely been noted.[81] This bias against the specific use of economic reasoning and the general pursuit of efficiency is under serious challenge. The challenge comes not from the dissatisfaction of economists, although that is manifest, but from the aspirations of business and political leaders to increase Europe's competitiveness.

In current Commission thinking competitiveness policy is a portmanteau term which includes industrial policy. For DG IV its contribution to industrial policy lies in establishing a framework of rules, enforcing policy in a fashion which privileges certain interests (e.g. small and medium-sized enterprises and R&D), and liberalizing utilities. These priorities might be acceptable to the main defenders of competition policy—Britain and Germany—but they are fearful of a more discriminatory and interventionist policy which judges individual cases by industrial policy criteria. This might even be regarded as more objectionable than the way in which cases are influenced by pressure and lobbying from industrial firms or groupings. Lobbying is inevitable and is perhaps tolerable to 'industry-friendly' governments in Britain and Germany.

Competition policy in most regimes is sensitive to the preferences of industry both in the design of the system and in its operation. This is, to a degree, unavoidable. A successful competition policy requires uncoerced compliance and therefore reasonable concession to industrial needs. In the European (and British) systems, however, business influence appears to be rapidly on the increase. The strength of the business lobby was noted above. In a sensitive treatment of merger control Nevens *et al.* emphasize the combination of national and industrial 'capture' which, they observe, may lead to 'excessive tolerance of market power'.[82] Mergers pose the problem in stark terms but so also do large state-aid cases. It is this trend which has caused the German authorities to press for substantial administrative reforms, a call echoed by financial journalists (but by no other governments).

An element of reform is unavoidable and the need to adapt has been accepted by Karel Van Miert and Claus-Dieter Ehlermann. Reform proposals vary from simple but important procedural changes, such as improving notification forms and publishing draft decisions; to the more fundamental, such as revising Regulation 17, creating an independent cartel authority, or—a new and provocative proposal from DG IV—strengthening the power of the Competition Commissioner by giving him substantial independence from the College of Commissioners.[83] Space prohibits an extensive examination of these possibilities, which we have discussed elsewhere. The key areas of institutional development will be the creation of effective subsidiarity and the possible creation of an independent cartel office.

Like all modes of decentralization, subsidiarity has both advantages and disadvantages. Apart from the obvious disadvantages of divergent criteria, variable enforcement and incompatible legal doctrines, the great uncertainty about subsidiarity is whether member states will encourage or permit their national authorities to act stringently. Scepticism is indicated. As the chapters on Germany and the UK in this volume reveal, the Brussels regime is the most effective in Europe. Subsidiarity is likely to lead to submergence.

The debate over an independent cartel office is already intense and will dominate European policy-making up to the Inter-Governmental Conference on Europe's political arrangements to be held in 1996. The strongest version of the proposal would consist of taking the enforcement of law on articles 85 and 86, mergers and state aids, out of DG IV and entrusting it to a new independent competition agency. Decisions would be subject to review by the courts and could perhaps be overturned in a process of public review by the Commission (although the German advisory body, the Monopolkommission, is against even this vestigial political override). The ECO would apply the law strictly and objectively just as the Bundeskartellamt now does in Germany. Views on this proposal are widely and deeply felt. What should be emphasized is the institutional perspective on these reform proposals. Our argument is that institutions and organizational configurations affect policy-making and policy criteria as well as administration. The success of DG IV rests in large part on a benign conjunction of effective leadership, a coherent ideology, a dedicated staff, and a decisive strategy; all imbued with a mission-ary zeal which generated a confident, proactive organizational culture, and established the authority of the institution. All these socio-political gains which are so important but so intangible could be threatened by the extremes of subsidiarity or fragmentation which fundamental reform proposals imply.

The focus of this chapter has been on the institution of Euro-pean competition policy. It embraces an ideational system as well as an organizational structure which centres on DG IV of the European Commission. We have argued that during the 1980s DG IV mobilized its latent powers to become the most influential anti-trust agency in the world and the most effective of the administra-tive units of the European Commission. It developed substantial autonomy and became a potent environmental, and sometimes direct, influence on the corporate strategies of large companies operating in Europe; on the form of the single market; on the industrial (and regional, and technology . . .) policies of the mem-ber states; and on the shape of utility liberalization. This is a formidable competence which follows from the extensive degree of discretion which DG IV and its officials managed to carve out for themselves. In fact, if not in name, DG IV has become an European federal agency. Current proposals would complete that process to create a legally independent agency which would be the world's first supranational competition agency. We have also argued, however, that the nature of DG IV has changed since 1991. It has become more 'political', more concerned with the activities of member states, more vulnerable and less self-confident in using its discretion and extending its jurisdiction. DG IV is in transition and European competition policy with it. The internal norms are being rebalanced, the major tension being between the norms of legality and competitiveness. At present it is difficult to determine whether the road will lead towards legal certainty, an ECO, and a marginalization of policy; or towards competitive advantage, co-ordinated policy, and controversial activism.

NOTES

1. Sir Leon Brittan, *European Competition Policy* (London: Brasseys, 1992), 18.

2. Valentine Korah, *An Introductory Guide to EC Competition Law and Practice* (5th edn., London: Sweet and Maxwell, 1994), 4. Note, however, that some authorities do stress an 'efficiency' goal; see Francis Snyder, *New Directions in European Community Law* (London: Weidenfeld & Nicolson, 1990), 92–3.

3. This possible legal doctrine rests on interpretation of article 3(f) of the Rome Treaty (now 3(g) of the Maastricht Treaty), which asserts the need to sustain competition; see Snyder, *New Directions*, 61–4.

4. The literature suddenly blossomed over the early 1990s. Particularly helpful are R. Keohane and S. Hoffman (eds.), *The New European Community: Decision Making and Institutional Change* (Oxford: Westview, 1991); Alberta Sbragia, 'Thinking about the European Future: The Uses of Comparison', in A. Sbragia (ed.), *Euro Politics* (Washington, DC: Brookings Institution, 1992); Sonia Mazey and Jeremy Richardson (eds.), *Lobbying in the European Community* (Oxford: Oxford University Press, 1993). Two of these studies are by Americans, but for a cross-section of good European work the *Journal of Common Market Studies* and the *Journal of European Public Policy* are to be recommended.

5. See the skilled arguments advanced by Andrew Moravcsik in e.g. 'A Liberal Intergovernmentalist Approach to the EC', *Journal of Common Market Studies*, 31/4 (Dec. 1993). A subtle exploration of a related theme can be found in the work of Alan Milward, e.g. *The European Rescue of the Nation State* (London: Routledge, 1992).

6. See e.g. Dan Goyder, *EC Competition Law* (2nd edn., Oxford: Clarendon Press, 1993); Richard Whish, *Competition Law* (3rd edn., London: Butterworths, 1993); and the *European Competition Law Review* (*ECLR*), now in its 16th volume (1995).

7. See Whish, *Competition Law*, 263, or Korah, *An Introductory Guide*, 105–6, both of whom express concern about the legalistic definitions of 'dominance' and the paucity of economic analysis typical of Commission decisions.

8. See Ethan Schwartz, 'Politics as Usual: The History of European Community Merger Control', *Yale Journal of International Law*, 18 (1993).

9. Article 2(3) of the Merger Regulation No. 4064/89 of 21 Dec. 1989, which entered into force on 21 Sept. 1990.

10. Commission of the European Communities (CEC), *20th Report on Competition Policy, 1990* (Luxembourg: European Communities, 1991), 50.

11. David Gerber, 'The Transformation of European Community Competition Law?', *Harvard International Law Journal*, 35/1 (winter 1994), 137.

12. Goyder, *EC Competition Law*, 34.

13. Ibid. 38.
14. See e.g. Korah, *An Introductory Guide*, ch. 5, which is devoted to Regulation 17.
15. For explorations of these ideas, see James March and Johan Olsen, *Rediscovering Institutions: The Organizational Basis of Politics* (New York: Free Press, 1989); Stephen Wilks and Maurice Wright, 'The Comparative Context of Japanese Political Economy', in Wilks and Wright (eds.), *The Promotion and Regulation of Industry in Japan* (London: Macmillan, 1991); and Mark Granovetter, 'Economic Action and Social Structures: The Problem of Embeddedness', *American Journal of Sociology*, 91 (Nov. 1985), repr. in Granovetter and R. Swedberg (eds.), *The Sociology of Economic Life* (Boulder, Colo.: Westview, 1992).
16. Snyder, *New Directions*, 93–7.
17. For an extended treatment, see Martin Donnelly and Ella Ritchie, 'The College of Commissioners and their *Cabinets*', in Geoffrey Edwards and David Spence (eds.), *The European Commission* (Harlow: Longman, 1994).
18. George Ross, *Jacques Delors and European Integration* (Cambridge: Polity, 1995), 119; this study offers a remarkable insight into the political workings of the Commission.
19. Ibid. 130–5, 178.
20. Sir Leon Brittan, 'The Principles and Practice of Merger Policy in the European Community', address at the Centre for European Policy Studies, Brussels, Sept. 1990.
21. 'Memorandum by the Joint Working Party on Competition Law', evidence to the Select Committee on the European Communities, *Enforcement of Community Competition Rules*, First Report, 1993–4, HL Paper 7 (London: HMSO, Dec. 1993), cited in Main Report, 23.
22. See the criticisms about the under-utilization of economic analysis in merger control by Damien Neven, Robin Nuttall, and Paul Seabright, *Merger in Daylight* (London: Centre for Economic Policy Research, 1993), chs. 2 and 3, and p. 241. The problem is felt to be greater under articles 85–6; see Korah, *An Introductory Guide*, 267, and several points of evidence to the Select Committee on the European Communities, *Enforcement of Community Competition Rules*, summarized in the Main Report, 24.
23. See e.g. Martin Shapiro, 'The European Court of Justice', in Sbragia (ed.), *Euro Politics*, but note that he virtually ignores the area of competition policy. Studies which suggest that the European Court may have become less innovatory include Hjalte Rasmussen, *On Law and Policy in the European Court of Justice: A Comparative Study in Judicial Policy Making* (Dordrecht: Martinus Nijhoff, 1986).

24. For an interesting discussion, see Goyder, *EC Competition Law*, 126–8.

25. See Rasmussen, *On Law and Policy*; and Gerber, 'The Transformation of European Community Competition Law', 126–8.

26. See the fascinating review by the Competition Law Association in evidence to the Select Committee on the European Communities, *Enforcement of Community Competition Rules*, Minutes of Evidence, 177–84.

27. The OECD publishes a helpful annual review of competition policy jurisdictions which include legislative and institutional changes, *Competition Policy in OECD Countries 1991–92* (Paris: OECD, 1994). There are reports on all the EU countries.

28. CEC, *Community Merger Control: Report from the Commission to the Council on the Implementation of the Merger Regulation*, COM (93) 385 final (Brussels, 28 July 1993), 12.

29. The Reports of the Parliament and the Economic and Social Committee are published as appendices to the annual Competition report. See *22nd Report on Competition Policy 1992* (Luxembourg: European Communities, 1993), annex I.

30. Interviews with Mel Read, UK MEP for Leicester and competition policy rapporteur; and Christian Benmer, Dutch MEP, Chair, Committee for Economic and Monetary Affairs, Feb. 1994.

31. See e.g. Lynn Collie, 'Business Lobbying in the European Community: The Union of Industrial and Employers' Confederation of Europe', in Mazey and Richardson (eds.), *Lobbying*.

32. For approaches see Wilks and Wright, 'The Comparative Context'; Maurice Wright, 'The Comparative Analysis of Industrial Policies: Policy Network and Sectoral Governance Structures in Britain and France', *Staatswissenschaften und Staatspraxis*, 4 (1991), 503–33; John Peterson, *High Technology and the Competition State: An Analysis of the Eureka Paradox* (London: Routledge, 1993); John Peterson, 'Decision-making in the European Union: Towards a Framework for Analysis', *Journal of European Public Policy*, 2/1 (Mar. 1995).

33. See P. M. Haas, 'Introduction: Epistemic Communities and International Policy Coordination', *International Organisation*, 46/1 (1992).

34. See the classic H. Heclo and A. Wildavsky, *The Private Government of Public Money* (London: Macmillan, 1974); and developments of those themes in e.g. Stephen Wilks and Maurice Wright, 'Conclusion: Comparing Government–Industry Relations: States, Sectors and Networks', in Wilks and Wright (eds.), *Comparative Government–Industry Relations* (Oxford: The Clarendon Press, 1987).

35. Sonia Mazey and Jeremy Richardson, 'The Commission and the Lobby', in Edwards and Spence (eds.), *The European Commission*, 170.

36. The Daimler Benz representative in Brussels, Dr. Hanns Glatz, was

sufficiently respected to be invited to give evidence to the House of Lords Select Committee on the European Communities. See *A Single Market for Cars*, 1989–90, HL 76 (London: HMSO, 1990), 25–35.
37. The influence of firms is stressed in Alan Cawson *et al.*, *Hostile Brothers: Competition and Closure in the European Electronics Industry* (Oxford: The Clarendon Press, 1990), see esp. ch. 13 for comment on Philips.
38. Sonia Mazey and Jeremy Richardson, 'Introduction: Transference of Power, Decision Rules and Rules of the Game', in Mazey and Richardson (eds.), *Lobbying*, 7.
39. Cawson *et al.*, *Hostile Brothers*, 183.
40. Collie, 'Business Lobbying', 218.
41. Address by Dr Claus-Dieter Ehlermann, 'Priorities of Competition Policy', to European Council on Legal Affairs, Conference Board Europe (1 Apr. 1993), photocopy, 3.
42. Confederation of British Industry, *Refocusing the Competition Rules*, and *Controlling State Aids* (London: CBI, Feb. 1994).
43. Select Committee on the European Communities, *Enforcement of Community Competition Rules*.
44. The outburst was aimed at national competition authorities, especially the Bundeskartellamt, every bit as much as at DG IV. See Andrew Hill, 'Bangemann Hits Out at Competition "Ayatollahs"', *Financial Times*, 11 Feb. 1992.
45. Karel Van Miert, speech reported in *International Bar News*, Jan./Feb. 1994, 15.
46. F. Jacobs, 'Jurisdiction and Enforcement in EEC Competition Cases', in D. Rowe, F. Jacobs, and P. Jackson (eds.), *Enterprise Law of the Eighties* (London: ABA, 1981), 205.
47. See Stephen Wilks, *The Metamorphosis of European Competition Policy*, RUSEL Working Paper 9, University of Exeter, 1992; repr. in F. Snyder (ed.), *European Law in Context: A Reader* (London: Dartmouth, 1992); see also D. Allen, 'Policing and Policy Making? Competition Policy in the European Communities', in H. Wallace *et al.* (eds.), *Policy Making in the European Communities* (London: Wiley, 1977), for a downbeat, critical survey.
48. Andrew Moravcsik, 'Negotiating the Single European Act', in Keohane and Hoffman (eds.), *The New European Community*, 65, 73.
49. William Dawkins, 'A Skilful Run for the Line' (profile of Sutherland), *Financial Times*, 28 Sept. 1987.
50. Lucy Kellaway, 'Tough Act of an EC Deal Maker' (profile of Brittan), *Financial Times*, 9 July 1990.
51. Jonathan Faull, 'The Enforcement of Competition Policy in the European Community: A Mature System', *Fordham International Law Journal*, 219 (1992).

52. Wilks, 'The Metamorphosis of European Competition Policy', 9–10.
53. An argument persuasively advanced by Gerber, 'The Transformation of European Community Competition Law', 135.
54. Ibid. 141.
55. These concerns are nicely summarized in the Select Committee on the European Communities, *Enforcement of Community Competition Rules*, Main Report, 'Recommendations Not Requiring Amendment of Regulation 17', 48.
56. See Alison Jones, 'Woodpulp: Concerted Practice and/or Concerted Parallelism', *European Competition Law Review*, 14/6 (1993), 273–8.
57. Goyder, *EC Competition Law* (2nd edn.), 501.
58. Detail given by Dr Ehlermann in a lecture entitled 'The Commission Standpoint' to a Conference on EC Competition Law, London, Kings College, 11 Feb. 1994.
59. DG IV, Cellule Information, *Competition Policy Newsletter*, 1/3 (autumn/winter 1994), 6.
60. David Spence, 'Structure, Functions and Procedures in the Commission', in Edwards and Spence (eds.), *The European Commission*, 100.
61. Sir Sydney Lipworth, 'EC Merger Control', in Diana Rowen (ed.), *Competition Policy in the Community* (London: European Policy Forum, 1992), 45.
62. See ERT paper, *Freedom to Compete: Competition Policy Issues for European Business* (Brussels: ERT, Dec. 1993).
63. See also, Joint Working Party on Competition Law of the Bars and Law Societies of the UK, Select Committee on the EC, *Enforcement of Community Competition Rules*, 59 and 67; Sir Sydney Lipworth, 'EC Merger Control', 45.
64. See Ivo Van Bael, 'The Role of the National Courts', editorial in *ECLR*, 15/1 (Jan/Feb. 1994), for a sceptical treatment of the notice; and Richard Whish, 'The Enforcement of EC Competition Law in the Domestic Courts of Member States', *ECLR*, 15/2 (Mar./Apr. 1994), for a balanced view.
65. See discussion in *23rd Report on Competition Policy 1993*, 107–8.
66. The *Steetley/Tarmac* case.
67. See *23rd Report on Competition Policy 1993*, 186.
68. Karel Van Miert, quoted in *Agence Europe*, 6 Jan. 1995.
69. See B. Guy Peters, 'Bureaucratic Politics and the Institutions of the European Community', in Sbragia (ed.), *Europolitics*; and Stephen Wilks and Lee McGowan, 'Discretion in European Merger Control: The German Regime in Context', *Journal of European Public Policy*, 2/1 (Mar. 1995).
70. Wolfgang Kartte, 'Die Politisierung der Europäischen Fusionkontrolle ist Programmiert', *Die Welt*, 31 Dec. 1990.
71. For a summary of German criticisms see the important article by Dr

Ehlermann, 'Reflections on a European Cartel Office', *Common Market Law Review*, 32/2 (Apr. 1995), 471–86, n. 3.

72. *23rd Report on Competition Policy 1993*, 103.
73. For a discussion of relevant theories see Chapter 1; a basic introduction in the European context can be found in David Young and Stan Metcalfe, 'Competition Policy', in Mike Artis and Norman Lee (eds.), *The Economics of the European Union* (Oxford: Oxford University Press, 1994); a stimulating review is to be found in chapter 2 of Neven *et al.*, *Merger in Daylight*; while a fuller, abstract treatment is provided in Paul Auerbach, *Competition: The Economics of Industrial Change* (Oxford: Blackwell, 1989).
74. Ross, *Jacques Delors*, 120–1.
75. Commission of the EC, *Growth, Competitiveness, Employment: The Challenges and Ways Forward into the 21st Century*, Bulletin of the EC, 6/93 (Luxembourg, 1993).
76. *23rd Report on Competition Policy 1993*, 13, 14, 90–1.
77. Commission of the EC, Communication of the Commission to the Council, *An Industrial Competitiveness Policy for the European Union*, COM (94) 319 final (Brussels, 14 Sept. 1994).
78. Ibid. 6, 30–6.
79. Karel Van Miert, speech at the Second EU/JAPAN Seminar on Competition, Sept. 1994, in *Competition Policy Newsletter*, 1/3, 3.
80. See, for instance, Emma Tucker, 'Feisty Fighter for a Level Playing Field', *Financial Times*, 5 Dec. 1994. The huge aid package proposed for Crédit Lyonnais will focus discontents; see *Financial Times*, 6 Mar. 1995.
81. This is a theme stressed by Korah, *An Introductory Guide*, ch. 14.
82. Nevens *et al.*, *Merger in Daylight*, 224.
83. A proposal advanced in Ehlermann, 'Reflections on the European Cartel Office'; for a fuller analysis see Stephen Wilks, 'Options for Reform of EC Competition Policy', in Aad van Mourik (ed.), *Developments in European Competition Policy* (Maastricht: EIPA, 1995); and Stephen Wilks and Lee McGowan, 'Disarming the Commission: The Debate Over a European Cartel Office', *Journal of Common Market Studies*, 32/2 (1995), 259–73.

9

Reconciling Competition Laws and Trade Policies: A New Challenge to International Co-operation

MICHAEL J. TREBILCOCK

INTRODUCTION

In a Trade Committee Symposium of the OECD in November 1991 on 'The OECD and New Trade Policy Challenges for the 1990s', the major conclusion reached was that, together with environmental laws and regulations, competition policy is likely to be the next major new issue on the international trade policy agenda of the 1990s.[1] A recent study by the Canadian Bureau of Competition Policy concludes that, 'The new focus on environmental regulation and competition law reflects a broader trend which is seeing the internationalization of a wide range of policies which, up to now, have been considered domestic in nature.'[2] According to Dr Sylvia Ostry in a recent paper 'Beyond the Border: The New International Policy Arena'[3]: 'The new arena for international policy cooperation is moving beyond the border, to domestic policies. The basic reason for this shift lies in changes in the extent and nature of the international linkages among countries which have produced a new type of friction I have called system friction.'[4] Ostry notes three phases of growing international linkage amongst countries since the Second World War. The first was driven by trade during the 1950s and 1960s and launched by the dismantling of protectionist barriers in successive GATT rounds. Over the decade of the 1970s, three massive commodity and oil shocks initiated the second phase, which was financial integration, via the recycling of the OPEC surplus, a process which accelerated in the 1980s, fuelled by the Reagan–Thatcher revolution of deregulation and privatization and the emergence of the Japanese current-account surplus. The third and most recent phase Ostry calls globalization, which is characterized by a dramatic surge in foreign direct investment which is centred principally on capital and technology flows. Growing levels of intra-industry and intra-enterprise trade increasingly dominate inter-sectoral trade, and international capital flows vastly exceed international trade flows. In her view, a globalizing world has a low tolerance for system divergence and requires a new approach to mitigating system friction by undertaking an international policy process to promote the convergence of those government policies which are most relevant to the process of innovation. According to Ostry, the prime agent of this third stage is the multinational enterprise, and an important factor driving globalization today is the increased research and development costs required in the race for the technological frontier and leading-edge sectors. This has stimulated not only a wave of international mergers and acquisitions (now the major form of FDI rather than greenfield investment), but also spawned an array of new forms of international networking among the MNEs including R&D and technology alliances.

Tensions between the objectives and application of domestic competition laws, and international trade policy have a long genesis. Competition laws were enacted in Canada and the USA late in the last century at the same time as their governments were adopting high tariff policies. Thus, for a good part of the ensuing century, competition laws in these two countries were interpreted and applied in a deep 'second-best' world, where domestic competition was promoted in contexts where foreign competition was often severely restrained by self-imposed protectionist trade policies.[5] While the trade liberalization that has occurred in the post-war period under GATT and under various regional trading arrangements—such as the EC, the FTA (Free Trade Agreement), and now NAFTA (North American Free Trade Agreement)—has mitigated these tensions, many trade restrictions still remain. Such restrictions are now less likely to be in the form of tariffs, and instead take the form of quantitative restrictions and the increasing utilization of trade remedy laws, in particular anti-dumping laws, with many countries adopting anti-dumping regimes for the first time during the 1980s, and utilization rates world-wide growing dramatically during the 1990s. While some have argued that completely unrestricted international trade largely obviates the need for domestic competition laws, there are reasons for scepticism about this claim, even if this ideal could be realized. First, even in the traded goods sector, depreciated exchange rates and transportation costs may often attenuate the impact of import competition, and in the non-traded goods sector, especially the service sector which is an increasingly important element in many domestic economies, import competition will often not be an effective competitive threat, and restrictions on foreign investment (an effective market presence rather than effective market access) may be more salient impediments to offshore competition.

Even if it is accepted that an unqualifiedly liberal international trade policy is not a complete substitute for effective domestic competition law, the question remains to be resolved of what form effective domestic competition laws should take in a liberal international trade policy environment. Here the concern increasingly voiced is that while liberal international trade policies will remove *public* (state-imposed) impediments to foreign competition, such policies will leave unaddressed *private* restrictions on competition, including foreign competition. In this respect, inadequately framed or enforced domestic competition laws are seen as an impediment to foreign competition and international trade to the extent that they permit private market restrictions that preclude effective market access or an effective market presence by foreign competitors. Thus, reflecting the converse of the tensions between competition policy and trade policy manifested a century ago, at the time of the initial enactment of competition laws in Canada and the USA, adequate domestic competition laws are seen as an increasingly important non-tariff barrier to trade.

This chapter first reviews international efforts at harmonization. The second part of the chapter analyses outstanding issues with respect to the interface between domestic competition policy and international trade policy, and the third section briefly evaluates some of the institutional implications that other countries are likely to face in the future if progress is to be made in the international co-ordination of the relationship between competition policy and trade policy.

INTERNATIONAL EFFORTS AT RECONCILIATION OF COMPETITION AND TRADE POLICIES

Multilateral forums

In the 1940s the precursor to the GATT—the Havana Charter and the International Trade Organization that it contemplated—envisaged multilateral regulation and review of restrictive business practices, but could not survive opposition in the US Congress motivated by concerns over international incursions into US domestic political sovereignty.[6] In 1953 the USA, Canada, and others, through the Economic and Social Council of the United Nations, prepared a draft agreement which envisaged the formation of an international co-ordinating agency which would receive, investigate, and recommend remedial action relating to complaints about restrictive business practices in international trade. Five years later, at the instance of Norway, the GATT created a committee to study the extent to which, and how, they should undertake to deal with restrictive business practices in international trade. These early attempts to reach international agreements yielded no practical result, differences in national policies at the time being too great to move beyond general recommendations.[7]

In 1980, the United Nations Conference on Trade and Development (UNCTAD) adopted a Code on Restrictive Business Practices.[8] However, the Code takes the form of recommendations which lack binding legal force, and has had negligible impact. Similarly, the UN Commission on Transnational Corporations has encountered severe difficulties in attracting legal endorsement by industrialized countries of a proposed Code of Conduct for TNC's, which would include provisions on restrictive business practices similar to those contained in the UNCTAD Code.[9] The OECD Agreement on Restrictive Practices Affecting International Trade of 1986 (dating back to more modest OECD initiatives beginning in 1959) is endorsed by all OECD members but imposes only modest obligations (i.e. member states commit themselves to notifying other member states where enforcement action is contemplated that may affect important interests of the latter, and to providing an opportunity for consultations).[10] Conciliation provisions, including use of the good offices of the OECD Committee on Competition Law and Policy, in the event of members being unable to reach agreement, have rarely, if ever, been invoked. The successful negotiation of an International Sale of Goods Law (the Vienna Sales Convention, 1980) under the auspices of the United Nations Commission on International Trade Law (UNCITRAL), which is presently being ratified by many countries, perhaps provides a basis for greater optimism, but the ability of private parties to contract out of this law creates a much less exacting set of political dynamics than the negotiation of a multilateral mandatory competition law.

Bilateral agreements

The USA has negotiated formal bilateral competition protocols with Canada,[11] Australia,[12] Germany,[13] and most recently the EC.[14] While important variations exist among these protocols, all are roughly patterned on a model of co-operation recommended by the OECD.[15] They do not extend for the most part beyond requiring the parties to notify each other of pending enforcement actions that may impact on important interests of the other party and to take account of the views of the latter in deciding whether to proceed.[16] The recent US–EC protocol goes somewhat further in article 6 in identifying a set of comity principles (similar to those embodied in the US Department of Justice International Guidelines and including positive comity)[17] by which the parties will be guided in deciding whether to exercise or forgo jurisdiction.

Regional trading blocs

The European Community, under articles 85 and 86 of the Treaty of Rome, has been successful in adopting a unified competition policy for all member states with respect to transactions that have a Community dimension. Moreover, with respect to transactions covered by the Treaty, enforcement is unified in the European Commission and ultimate adjudicative authority resides with the European Court of Justice. With respect to the interface between competition laws and international trade policies, the European Community in trade between member states has also abrogated anti-dumping and countervailing duty laws and remitted issues previously dealt with under these laws to the competition authority (DG IV) of the European Commission. In the case of matters previously dealt with under anti-dumping laws, these are now dealt with under predatory pricing and price discrimination rules of the Community's competition law. In the case of issues that were previously dealt with under countervailing duty laws, the competition authority has now formulated and administers a complex set of rules on subsidies that are designed to prevent member states from adopting subsidies that are competitively prejudicial to producer interests in other member states.

Australia and New Zealand, under the Australian–New Zealand Closer Economic Relations Trade Agreement (ANZCERTA), while not attempting the ambitious integration of their respective competition laws that has occurred in the European Community, nevertheless by a Protocol executed in 1988 and given effect in 1991 agreed to abolish anti-dumping actions between the two countries, to suspend all existing anti-dumping duties, and to harmonize their respective misuse of dominant-position provisions in their competition statutes, so as to permit producers in one country to initiate legal actions against abusive behaviour by producers in the other country, with courts in the first country being authorized to conduct hearings in the second country and to compel the production of evidence in the second country, with resulting orders being enforceable in the second country. To date, there have been no formal proceedings relating to cross-Tarman alleged abuses of dominant positions, suggesting that the former anti-dumping laws were protecting competitors, rather than the competitive process.

Under the Canada–US Free Trade Agreement no provisions were included that specifically entailed the harmonization of the two countries' competition laws or their integrated administration and enforcement. However, under articles 1906 and 1907, the Agreement contemplated the creation of a Working Group to develop a substitute system of rules in both countries for anti-dumping and countervailing duties as applied to their bilateral trade within a period of five to seven years after the entry into force of the Agreement. In the event of failure to implement a new regime at the end of this period, either country would be entitled to terminate the entire Agreement on six months' notice. In the preface to chapter 19, in the Canadian government's official version of the Agreement, it is stated that 'the goal of any new regime will be to obviate the need for border remedies, as are now sanctioned by the GATT anti-dumping and subsidies code, for example, by developing new rules on subsidy practices and relying on domestic competition law.' Little or no progress has been made to date on these negotiations.

The North American Free Trade Agreement (NAFTA), which in 1993 largely superceded the FTA, contains somewhat weaker commitments in this respect. Under article 1504, the Trilateral Trade Commission shall establish a working group on trade and competition to make recommendations to the Commission within five years of the date of entry into force of the Agreement on relevant issues concerning the relationship between competition laws and policies and trade in the free-trade area. Under article 1907(2), the Parties further agree to consult on *a)* the potential to develop more effective rules and disciplines concerning the use of government subsidies; and *b)* the potential for reliance on a substitute system of rules for dealing with unfair transborder or pricing practices in government subsidization. Under a side accord to NAFTA signed by the three parties in December 1993, following the election of the new federal government in Canada, the Working Group commitment under articles 1906 and 1907 of the FTA has been reinstated, with the Group to report within two years of the coming into force of NAFTA.

Beyond these provisions, NAFTA contains a short chapter (chapter 15) on competition policy, monopolies and state enterprises. Under this chapter, each party commits itself to adopting and maintaining measures to proscribe anti-competitive business conduct and to take appropriate action with respect thereto. Pursuant to this commitment, Mexico has recently enacted a comprehensive competition law. The parties also commit themselves to co-operating on issues of competition law enforcement policy, including mutual legal assistance, notification, consultation, and exchange of information relating to the enforcement of competition laws in the free-trade area. However, no party may have recourse to dispute settlement under the Agreement in the foregoing matters. In the case of monopolies and state enterprises, each party commits itself to ensuring that state-sanctioned monopolies will minimize or eliminate any nullification or impairment of benefits anticipated under the Agreement and that in the case of both privately owned and government-owned monopolies they will act solely in accordance with commercial consideration in the purchase or sale of goods or services in the relevant market and provide non-discriminatory treatment to investments of investors, and to goods and service providers, of another party.

OUTSTANDING ISSUES IN THE INTERFACE BETWEEN COMPETITION AND TRADE POLICIES: THE SOURCES OF SYSTEM FRICTION

Extra-territorial application of competition laws

A major source of system friction in the interface between competition and trade laws relates to different views of the appropriate scope of the extra-territorial application of competition laws. A brief review of the distinctive approaches taken by Canada, the USA, and the EC illustrates the resulting potential for multi-jurisdictional conflict.[18]

The Canadian approach

Canada has not historically applied its competition laws in an extra-territorial manner.[19] Merger pre-notification is triggered only by transactions involving an 'operating business' with Canadian assets.[20] Although the substantive merger provisions do not contain equally specific language, it seems clear that such reviews will focus exclusively on reductions of competition within Canada and that Tribunal orders will be limited to the Canadian operations of merging parties.[21]

The United States approach

The United States, in contrast, has for many decades attempted to impose 'respect for its antitrust laws on the entire world in order to serve national interests and to promote its economic ethics'.[22] Several countries have responded with 'blocking', 'gag', and 'clawback' statutes designed to frustrate the extra-territorial application of such laws.[23] The 'effects' test enunciated in Alcoa extends the jurisdiction of US courts to conduct having allegedly anti-competitive effects in any part of the United States.[24] The

Third Restatement of the Foreign Relations Law of the United States (the *Restatement*) asserts that a state may proscribe 'conduct outside its territory that has or is likely to have substantial effects within its territory'.[25] The DOJ's *International Antitrust Guidelines* define the extra-territorial reach of the Sherman Act as limited to foreign activities which have a 'direct, substantial and reasonably foreseeable effect on US commerce,'[26] but this apparently restricted interpretation is offset by the fact that the phrase 'US commerce' has been interpreted broadly to include both interstate and foreign trade. Thus, a merger or cartel involving foreign companies would satisfy this test if it allegedly caused anti-competitive effects on imports into the United States.

The effects test can be justified on the basis that the less intrusive territoriality principle[27] cannot alone meet the legitimate interest of a state in protecting elements of its economic order, an interest based on the right of each state to self-determination.[28] Even though the effects test is considered by many to be 'sound in principle', it errs in the direction of allocating jurisdiction too generously.[29] As markets become more interdependent and transactions more frequently cross national borders, it can be expected that governments will increasingly seek to claim concurrent and possibly conflicting jurisdiction.

Faced with mounting international opposition to extra-territorial application of antitrust legislation, US courts have made some attempts to limit the operation of the effects principle by requiring a consideration of the interests of foreign states. A 'jurisdictional rule of reason' was enunciated in the *Timberlane*[30] decision and elaborated in *Mannington Mills*[31] to deal with situations where the enforcement interests of the USA are outweighed by prejudice to considerations of foreign comity which may result from an extra-territorial assertion of jurisdiction.[32]

The DOJ has responded favourably to this approach and in its *International Antitrust Guidelines* identifies a range of factors that it will balance in exercising its enforcement powers in an international context:[33]

1) the relative significance, to the violation alleged, of conduct within the United States as compared to conduct abroad;
2) the nationality of the persons involved in or affected by the conduct;

3) the presence or absence of a purpose to affect United States consumers or competitors;
4) the relative significance and foreseeability of the effects of the conduct on the United States as compared to the effects abroad;
5) the existence of reasonable expectations that would be furthered or defeated by the action; and
6) the degree of conflict with foreign law or articulated foreign economic policies.

Apart from these general factors that attempt to weigh the extent of each state's interest in a transaction, Case 4 in the *Guidelines* indicates also that remedial efficacy should be considered.[34] In this example, two foreign firms exporting into the USA merge, giving them 60 per cent of the US market. However, neither has significant assets in the USA. In such a case, the DOJ suggests that it would normally be inappropriate to take enforcement action. However, in the *Institut Merieux/Connaught*[35] case a majority of the FTC (Federal Trade Commission) commissioners were prepared to assume jurisdiction on similar facts.

Interest-balancing tests have been developed by the courts under the rubrics of 'comity' or 'reasonableness'. The balancing factors employed by the courts when comity issues have been raised include: the degree of conflict with foreign law and policy; the nationality and principal place of business of the parties; the extent to which enforcement by a particular state would likely achieve compliance; the relative significance of effects in each jurisdiction; and any explicit purpose to harm United States commerce.[36] The various factors of comity considered in the leading cases are codified in the *Restatement* as a principle of 'reasonableness' which the drafters elevate to a rule of international law. It asserts that: 'each state is required to evaluate both its interests in exercising jurisdiction and those of the other state. When possible, the two states should consult with each other. If one state has a clearly greater interest, the other should defer.'[37]

The impact of the new doctrine has, however, fallen far short of expectations. The primary complaint against the interest-balancing approach stems from the failure of comity arguments to result in a US court declining jurisdiction.[38] For example, in a recent merger prosecution under the Clayton Act, a district court exercised jurisdiction despite a diplomatic note from the government of the acquiring party opposing intervention by the US government.[39]

Many recent US cases involving extra-territoriality have been private actions.[40] Government authorities cannot force the abandonment or settlement of such litigation. Since successful antitrust litigants are awarded treble damages, private parties have a strong incentive to bring suits and to seek a broad application of US laws regardless of international political ramifications.[41]

Clearly, the United States does not accept a legal obligation to consider the effect of its assumption of jurisdiction or the imposition of a remedy on the policies or sovereignty of another state.[42] Comity therefore remains a discretionary basis for the consideration of foreign interests. In *Laker Airways*, the court pointed out that there is no evidence that interest balancing represents a rule of international law or that there exists a 'rule of international law holding that a "more reasonable" assertion of jurisdiction displaces a "less reasonable" assertion of jurisdiction as long as both are . . . consistent with the limitations of jurisdiction imposed by international law'.[43] Moreover, the flexibility provided by the *Timberlane* case has probably been considerably restricted by the recent majority decision of the US Supreme Court in *Hartford Fire Insurance* v. *California*,[44] where the majority held that principles of international comity would only militate against exercising jurisdiction in cases where the defendants were required by foreign law to act in a fashion prohibited by the USA, or where compliance with the laws of both countries was otherwise impossible. Thus, although most states do value sensitivity to foreign interests, they generally regard themselves as politically, as opposed to legally, obligated to respect the interests of other states and to exercise moderation and restraint accordingly.[45]

Most recently, the USA has unilaterally attempted to impose its antitrust laws on US subsidiaries of foreign companies (principally Japanese) that are allegedly engaging in anti-competitive practices in their home markets which impair export opportunities for domestic firms.[46] The recent suit by the USA against Pilkington Glass alleging restrictive distribution arrangements in Europe that impede effective market access by US competitors is a current example. These initiatives represent a particularly expansive application of the effects doctrine, since jurisdiction is asserted where there are adverse effects on US activities in foreign markets even though no effects occur inside US territory.[47]

The European Community approach

The application of the EC's competition rules is clearly not limited to the territory of the Member States. In the *Wood Pulp* case, the Court of Justice adopted a modified version of the territoriality principle in holding that articles 85 and 86 of the *Treaty of Rome* are applicable where a conspiracy ('concerted practice') has the object or effect of restricting competition within the EC, and is 'implemented' within the EC.[48] As well, in the *Dyestuffs* case, the Court employed an 'economic unit doctrine' to impute liability to foreign companies operating subsidiaries within the Community.[49] It remains to be seen whether the Court will embrace an effects test comparable to that found in US jurisprudence if an appropriate case arises.

Under the EC Merger Regulation, the Commission has jurisdiction over mergers taking place outside the Community where the aggregate world-wide turnover of all the undertakings concerned exceeds ECU 5 billion and the Community-wide turnover of each of at least two of the parties exceeds ECU 250 million.[50] Since actual presence (i.e. a subsidiary) is not required, foreign firms which simply sell or distribute products in the Community may be embraced by the Regulation. In exercising its jurisdiction, the Commission may well seek to avoid conflicts, consider foreign states' interests wherever possible, and limit the scope of any divestiture decision to the removal of anti-competitive effects within the Community, but it is not legally obliged to do so.[51]

Horizontal arrangements

Historically, US antitrust law has adopted a strongly prohibitory approach to horizontal arrangements amongst competitors or potential competitors, applying a *per se* rule of criminal liability in the case of price-fixing and market allocation arrangements. The Canadian competition law does not adopt a *per se* prohibition of any horizontal arrangements (except for bid-rigging and agreements among banks on interest rates on loans and deposits), but otherwise only prohibits horizontal arrangements where they lessen competition 'unduly' (characterized recently by Mr Justice Gonthier in the Supreme Court of Canada's decision in the *PANS* case[52] as a 'partial rule of reason'). The European Community competition law that has developed under article 85 is somewhat more permissive again, relative to the Canadian and US law, and domestic competition laws in Germany, France, and Britain are more permissive yet again.[53] Most domestic competition laws, including those of the USA and Canada, include an explicit exemption for export cartels and for joint R&D ventures. Both Canada and the EC have a further exemption for specialization agreements. Japan has the most permissive laws relating to horizontal arrangements amongst competitors, and exempts a wide range of co-operative arrangements from the application of its competition laws.[54]

The exemption of export cartels seems explicable only on a 'beggar thy neighbour' principle, where the extraction of foreign surplus is weighted less heavily than domestic surplus.[55] The USA has complained that Japan also implicitly exempts import cartels from the application of its competition laws, thus prejudicing US and other countries' exports into Japan through group boycotts or monopsonization of import prices. Differing treatments of joint R&D ventures, joint production ventures, recession or rationalization cartels, and specialization agreements in different jurisdictions reflect divergent thinking on appropriate domestic industrial policies and are likely to prove difficult to resolve. Government-sponsored research consortia that are open only to domestic firms and not foreign subsidiaries are inconsistent with the National Treatment principle in international trade law and also carry the potential for conflict. A wide array of strategic alliances, especially amongst multinational enterprises operating in the high-technology sectors, some of which are viewed very differently under various countries' domestic competition laws, also carry the potential for significant conflict.[56] Privately negotiated voluntary export restraint agreements (VERs)—in effect, international market allocation cartels—also raise contentious jurisdictional issues.

Vertical arrangements

Historically, US antitrust law has adopted a strongly prohibitory approach to various kinds of vertical arrangements, such as resale price maintenance, exclusive dealing, exclusive territories, and tying arrangements, although the economic wisdom of these rules has been the subject of intense controversy among US anti-trust scholars over the past twenty years.[57] With the exception of resale price maintenance, Canadian competition law has adopted a rule-of-reason approach to all of these practices. European Community law permits block and individual exemptions for many of these arrangements, while Japanese competition law has historically taken a benign view of such arrangements, attracting allegations, from the USA in particular, that this constitutes condonation by the Japanese government of non-tariff barriers. A consistent allegation for the United States has been that US and other countries' exports into Japan are blocked by vertical tie-ups in the Japanese domestic distribution system co-ordinated by vertical production or distribution *keiretsu* or exclusive dealing arrangements.[58] Using the threat of unilateral trade sanctions under section 301 of the *Omnibus Trade and Competitiveness Act* of 1988 in the course of the US–Japan Structural Impediments Initiative (SII) talks, the USA sought commitments from Japan to strengthen antitrust scrutiny of these practices.

International mergers[59]

The number of mergers and acquisitions in many industrialized countries over the last decade has dramatically escalated, as has the number of foreign acquisitions.[60] At the same time, many countries have adopted effective merger regimes for the first time, although the procedural and substantive requirements in these regimes vary significantly from one country to another.[61] A number of recent high-profile international mergers have engaged the investigative and enforcement attention of antitrust authorities in several countries, not only raising transaction costs for merging parties in meeting multiple compliance requirements, but also raising the serious risk of divergent determinations by these authorities.[62] The potential for multi-jurisdictional conflict is particularly acute in the following scenarios. First, a multinational enterprise based in country A acquires another multinational enterprise based in country B. Both firms have subsidiaries producing similar lines of products in various domestic markets throughout the world. Here the impact of the merger would presumably have to be assessed market by market in the light of alternative sources of domestic or import competition in each market. Second, a foreign firm based in country A acquires a firm based in country B where the relevant products produced by the two firms are traded freely in a regional market, for example Canada and the USA, or member countries of the European Community. Given that the relevant geographic market for the product is supranational, domestic antitrust authorities throughout the larger or supranational regional market are likely to view their jurisdiction as legitimately engaged by the merger. Third, a foreign firm in country A acquires a competitor in country B producing a similar product line, but here the geographic market is neither national nor regional but global (e.g. the commercial airline manufacturing industry), and the merged entity will hold a large share of the global market for the product in question. Here, at least in theory, domestic competition authorities in all countries throughout the world where the product is or might potentially be sold, may be interested in reviewing the transaction.

An exploration of alternative models for reducing multi-jurisdictional conflict in international merger review is instructive not only as to the institutional possibilities in this context, but also with respect to the broader challenges of harmonizing domestic competition laws more generally. We can review briefly three basic models for reducing multi-jurisdictional conflict in international merger review. Each of these models in turn contains more and less ambitious variants.

Harmonization of domestic competition laws

Harmonization efforts might be directed to procedural harmonization or substantive harmonization or both. Clearly the more modest ambition would be to seek to achieve only some measure of procedural harmonization.

Procedural harmonization

A number of issues might be addressed from this perspective which could significantly reduce transaction costs.[63] First, some effort might be made to harmonize pre-merger notification requirements.

First, at present major discrepancies among the three jurisdictions exist as to information requirements that merging parties must meet. Some standardization of initial information requirements would seem desirable. The ABA recommends a relatively light initial filing with the possibility of a subsequent detailed request for information, but in the latter respect suggests that US authorities might focus their Second Requests more narrowly.[64] Whish and Wood would also require parties to notify domestic competition agencies of other agencies that have been notified of the merger.[65] Second, differences in the waiting periods before a transaction may be consummated might usefully be eliminated. Third, there would seem to be much value in the EC approach of specifying fixed time limits within which reviewing agencies must reach decisions. If all major jurisdictions agreed on a common set of time limits, uncertainty for merging parties would be considerably reduced. Fourth, standardization of rules for when discovery can be obtained for evidence located abroad would minimize potential for conflicts in this area.[66] Finally, confidentiality rules applicable to review agencies and their staff might be relaxed in order to permit exchanges of information between the various agencies investigating a single transaction.[67]

Harmonized requirements in these various areas would clearly be a useful advance, and would presumably reduce the transaction costs and uncertainty facing merging parties when multiple agencies review a merger. However, whatever the value of these gains, it must be acknowledged that they do not go to the heart of concerns over potential multi-jurisdictional conflicts in merger review. Specifically, they do little to reduce the likelihood of divergent determinations where mergers engage the jurisdiction of more than one agency. This severe limitation on the benefits available from procedural harmonization naturally leads to proposals for substantive harmonization.

Substantive harmonization

A preliminary question is whether international mergers possess special characteristics which would require different treatment from that given to domestic mergers. The OECD has concluded that there is no need for a separate set of substantive standards: the basic economic theory regarding pro-competitive and anti-competitive mergers is equally applicable in both the domestic and international contexts.[68]

The American Bar Association Special Committee on International Antitrust (the ABA Committee) express scepticism as to the prospects of serious substantive harmonization in the foreseeable future.[69] There are major substantive differences between the Canadian, US, and EC merger regimes,[70] and these differences multiply as further jurisdictions are examined. For example, in the ten OECD jurisdictions it reviewed, the ABA found that merger law in Canada, Germany, Japan, and the USA is motivated primarily by competition concerns, whereas in other jurisdictions (particularly Ireland, France, Spain, and the UK) industrial and public policy concerns play a significant role. However, in the USA, Canada, and the EC this diversity of objectives seems to pose less of a problem. The ABA also points out that political, as opposed to administrative, determinations of the acceptability of a merger play an important role in France, the UK, Germany, Spain, and Ireland.[71] Again, in the USA, Canada, and the EC, this is not a major problem. The ABA Committee concluded that 'it would be both unrealistic and presumptuous for this Committee to come forward with recommendations for a common substantive approach to international merger control at this time'.[72] In a subsequent chapter reviewing the advantages, disadvantages, and prospects for a World Competition Code, the Committee stated that 'perhaps the nations could reach agreement on a code, but it would either be agreement to principles so general that the rules would have no clear meaning, or the agreement would be the result of a process of bargaining in which each representative had to trade away something of value'.[73] This conclusion is a rather gloomy one, in that it leaves the prospects for serious multi-jurisdictional conflict essentially unresolved, even if some degree of procedural harmonization is achieved.

Perhaps the conclusion is excessively gloomy. As the ABA Committee itself proposes,[74] a modest move in the direction of substantive harmonization would be for all OECD merger review agencies to commit themselves to promulgating non-binding merger enforcement guidelines, which in draft form would be subject to prior comment by other review agencies. This proposal might usefully be taken a step further and agreement sought on a detailed check-list of issues that each set of guidelines would be required to address. By inducing this degree of articulation and transparency of merger review criteria, it seems plausible that some significant degree of convergence over time is likely to be achieved. The example of the recent Canadian *Merger Enforcement Guidelines*, which closely follow in many respects the US Merger Guidelines,[75] offers substantial encouragement in this respect.

Another strategy worthy of consideration would be to charge an international body of experts (e.g. under the aegis of the OECD Committee on Competition Law and Policy) to formulate and promulgate a non-binding Model Merger Review Law. Because it would not be binding on member countries of the OECD, and because it would be formulated by acknowledged experts in the competition law field rather than political or diplomatic representatives, the dangers identified by the ABA in countries attempting to negotiate a World Competition Code could largely be avoided. A Model Merger Review Law, like the US 'Restatements' promulgated by the American Law Institute, or Uniform Commercial and other laws promulgated by the US Uniform Law Commission, may well exert substantial exemplary or exhortatory influence on policy-makers, enforcement authorities, courts, and tribunals in member countries.

However, as with procedural harmonization, it must be acknowledged that even if major substantive harmonization is achieved, at the end of the day the potential still exists for divergent rulings by national competition authorities on international mergers. No degree of procedural and substantive harmonization can eliminate the qualitative judgements entailed in merger review nor the possibility that different agencies will reach different judgements, albeit within a common legal framework. Thus one is led to consider other models for reducing multi–jurisdictional conflict.

Designation of a lead review jurisdiction

Again, as with harmonization strategies, more and less modest options present themselves within this broad model. However, it is crucial to stress that any variant of the lead jurisdiction model is necessarily premised on the assumption that any international merger that might appropriately attract this institutional response implicates a supranational geographic market.

With any lead jurisdiction model, a threshold question arises as to the institutional forum within which the rules governing the designation of a lead jurisdiction should be negotiated. One option is to encourage bilateral negotiation of such rules. The main problem with the bilateral model is that geographic markets may often not break down cleanly along bilateral lines. To anticipate this problem a web of such agreements presumably would need to be negotiated, but this suggests a case for a multilateral sponsor.

The Co-ordinating agency model

Building on analogies with multi-jurisdictional filing regimes for new securities issues that have evolved in Canada and the USA, one could readily contemplate the designation of a lead jurisdiction to play the role of co-ordinating agency in the case of an international merger potentially impacting on a supranational geographic market. Such an agency could play a centralized information gathering function following initial notification to national review agencies, solicit comments from those review agencies whose markets are potentially impacted by the merger, and undertake an initial assessment of the likely competitive effects of the merger in the relevant geographic market. This assessment would be binding within the lead jurisdiction but operate merely as a recommendation to national enforcement agencies in other implicated jurisdictions, with presumably some kind of de facto presumption operating in favour of the recommendation.

The main difficulty raised by this model is: how does one go about identifying the lead jurisdiction? As the ABA Committee points out in its report, the 'effects' test now favoured by many jurisdictions (i.e. the presence of substantial direct and foreseeable effects within a jurisdiction) satisfies the requirements of international law as a jurisdictional test, although it allocates jurisdiction too generously.[76] In the case of an international merger impacting a supranational geographic market, obviously more than one jurisdiction can legitimately claim to be affected by the merger. As noted above, the US *International Antitrust Enforcement Guidelines* adopt a balancing test for deciding whether to take enforcement action that affects a foreign party. The recent US–EC Agreement also contemplates the application of a similar test.

The ABA Committee endorses the application of this kind of jurisdictional 'rule of reason' approach but suggests that the enforcement agency go on to ask a second question: which agency is appropriately equipped to fashion a remedy if one is felt to be required?[77] The ABA Committee recommends that when a merger has been notified to more than one jurisdiction, immediate consultation should take place among the agencies notified. A frank discussion of the relative interests involved and the location of assets ought to persuade all but the truly interested jurisdictions to defer. A three-week time frame, following initial notification of a merger to more than one national review authority, is contemplated for these consultations. The remaining jurisdictions, if more than one, should consult throughout the course of the review to minimize conflicting or duplicative requirements on the parties; and at the end of the process use best efforts to avoid imposing a remedy that conflicts with the policy of the other state or states.[78]

This proposal has some obvious virtues in that it moves beyond existing bilateral and OECD notification and comment obligations[79] to require genuine consultation with a view to narrowing down the number of jurisdictions engaging in independent review of a merger. However, significant problems remain. First, the kind of criteria adopted by the US Department of Justice in its 1988 *International Guidelines* and the US–EC in their recent Agreement are far from self-executing and leave room for a good deal of potential conflict and divergence of opinion as to how they should be applied in particular cases. Moreover, even if there is agreement as to how they should be applied in particular cases, the ABA acknowledges that this still leaves open the possibility of more than one jurisdiction legitimately remaining involved in a merger review, and thus also leaves open the possibility at the end of the day of divergent determinations. Finally, even if the USA decides to defer to foreign enforcement agencies in particular cases, there is still the prospect of private actions or enforcement initiatives by state attorneys general which, by virtue of the US Supreme Court decision in *American Stores*, are not barred simply by virtue of the fact that US antitrust authorities have cleared a merger.[80]

A further barrier to the adoption of a co-ordinating agency model is confidentiality. The OECD recommends that communications between enforcement agencies be treated as confidential by the recipients,[81] and most bilateral co-operation agreements contain such a provision. However, the ABA has noted that many domestic confidentiality provisions preclude such communications in the first place, and has recommended that legislative amendments need to be made to overcome such restrictions.[82]

In any event, the co-ordinating agency model does not prevent divergent outcomes from multi-jurisdictional merger reviews. The most that can be hoped for would be a reduction in transaction costs for international mergers falling into the three scenarios described above. Elimination of conflicting decisions would require a lead jurisdiction with more than co-ordinating powers, to which I now turn.

A lead jurisdiction with dispositive power

Going beyond the model identified above, but otherwise subject to most of the same considerations, one might contemplate multilateral agreement on a set of rules which would identify a lead jurisdiction where supranational relevant geographic markets are involved, which would not only perform the role of co-ordinating agency but would also be given dispositive power over mergers within its mandate. Unless dispositive power is assigned to a single lead jurisdiction over a merger that impacts on a supranational geographic market, as well as access to effective remedies, the potential for multi-jurisdictional conflict remains.

However, the ABA's suggestion that every enforcement agency notified of an international merger consider not only comity factors of the kind set out in the 1988 *International Guidelines* but also the issue of efficacy of remedy raises a serious dilemma. In some circumstances (e.g. where a local subsidiary exists) it may be possible to provide for a partial divestiture which avoids interjurisdictional conflict.[83] However, it will often be the case that the merging entities will be based outside the jurisdiction in which the principal competitive effects of the merger will be felt. This will obviously be true where the merging parties were previously exporters into this state's market. As Caves points out, national competition authorities will face considerable political pressure to allow mergers which have minimal effects in their own jurisdiction but enhance the appropriation of rents from foreign consumers.[84] In other words, as Caves notes, there will be a tendency for national competition authorities to take decisions that maximize national income, even at the expense of world income. However, this is not a tendency to be encouraged by multilateral efforts to harmonize merger review policies or competition law more generally. Thus, while the decision of the majority of the Federal Trade Commission in the *Institut Merieux/Connaught* case has been widely criticized,[85] if one accepts, for the sake of argument, that the principal anti-competitive effects of the merger in question were likely to be felt in the US market, it is not clear why a coherent multilateral merger review process would disqualify the US from effective opposition to this merger. This, in turn, raises the question of whether comity obligations of the kind referred to in the *International Guidelines* need to be extended to cover the case where national competition authorities should accept an affirmative obligation to take, or collaborate in implementing, effective remedial action in cases where mergers have substantial anti-competitive effects in another country. This far from trivial issue has received less attention than it deserves in discussions of international merger review regimes.

Under both lead jurisdiction models, another problem that has so far received little discussion in the literature would need to be addressed. As has already been emphasized, the lead jurisdiction response is only appropriate where the merger potentially impacts a regional or global geographic market. However, it is easy to imagine circumstances where various national competition authorities who have been notified or otherwise learn of the merger disagree as to whether a single supranational geographic market exists. This suggests that in addition to formulating some set of multilaterally agreed upon comity rules for identifying a lead jurisdiction and dealing with the question of access to effective remedies, agreement would be needed as to some methodology for determining whether the relevant geographic market is supranational or not.[86] In the event of disagreement on this issue, presumably there would not be the necessary consensus to appoint a lead jurisdiction to play either the co-ordinating agency role or *a fortiori* the dispositive decision–maker role.

Given the potential for disagreement among national authorities in identifying a single lead jurisdiction—perhaps because of disagreement over the scope of the geographic market, or concerning where the most substantial effects of the merger are likely to be felt, or regarding access to effective remedies—one is then led to consider a further variant of the lead jurisdiction approach.

Jurisdictional dispute resolution mechanisms

In cases where international mergers are notified to more than one national authority and where it is claimed either by the merging parties or by any of the national enforcement agencies that a supranational geographic market is entailed, and the consultation process proposed by the ABA Committee fails to yield a single lead jurisdiction on either of the lead jurisdiction models can-vassed above, one might consider vesting in the merging parties and any national enforcement agency the right to appeal the issue to a specialized supranational panel.[87] The Panel's function would not entail a review of the merger on the merits but assuming some prior agreement on comity rules and methodology for defining geographic markets, the Panel would apply these jurisdictional rules in identifying *ex ante* the lead jurisdiction.[88] A tight time frame would need to be imposed on this appeal process (e.g. four weeks from the expiration of the consultative process) to prevent excessive delay which could undermine potentially beneficial busi-ness transactions. Under the dispositive lead jurisdiction model, this would be the end of the matter, as all parties to this jurisdic-tional set of ground rules would have agreed in advance to accept the determination of the appeal Panel.

In the event that the weaker version of the lead jurisdiction model (i.e. the co-ordinating agency model) were to be adopted, the Panel could still resolve disputes in identifying *ex ante* this agency, although disputes are less likely to arise at this stage given that the agency's determinations are not binding but merely have presumptive weight with other enforcement agencies. However, the further possibility would then have to be addressed of diver-gent determinations by these agencies at the end of the review process—that is to say, a national enforcement agency refusing to accept the recommendations of the co-ordinating lead agency. In this event, one would need to contemplate a further (*ex post*) review process available both to the merging parties and other national enforcement agencies by appealing to a specialized supranational Panel to resolve the conflict, again not by reviewing the merger on the merits, but determining which jurisdiction is most substantially affected by the merger in terms of its competitive effects.

If this issue is to be rendered tractable in any of the lead jurisdiction models there would need to be agreement on the principles to be applied in evaluating the relative effects of merger in different jurisdictions. Effectively what is required is a 'primary effects' doctrine. The relevant principles would need to move beyond the present rather vague comity rules and should focus primarily on the relative, potential anti-competitive or consumer-welfare effects of an international merger (e.g. by examining relative allocation of market shares of output by jurisdiction), and not on other factors such as job maintenance or industrial policy considerations. A total welfare test of the kind adopted in Canadian merger law, while theoretically more correct, raises some problems in this respect. Even if an efficiency defence would rule out many job maintenance and industrial policy considerations, there are still likely to be cases where reductions in consumer welfare occur in one jurisdiction but real efficiency gains are realized in another (such as the *de Havilland* case). In identifying the jurisdiction most impacted by such a merger, how should these trade-offs be evaluated?

Whether multilateral agreement amongst major OECD countries could be achieved on a set of jurisdictional ground rules with respect to the application of which a specialized supranational Panel would be the ultimate arbiter would seem a daunting but nevertheless important challenge.

A supranational substantive merger review authority

This model is, of course, exemplified by the European Commission in the role now assigned to it by the EC Merger Regulation. This is a strong-form version of a supranational merger authority in that mergers over a certain size threshold are reviewed on their merits from the outset by the European Commission against its own legal norms, with national authorities ceding jurisdiction, in most circumstances, to the Commission, and with the Commission being vested with final dispositive power over all mergers within its mandate. However, as a number of commentators have pointed out,[89] there is serious room for doubt as to the generalizability of this model to jurisdictions beyond Europe. The EC case seem *sui generis* in many respects in the degree to which member states have been prepared to cede sovereignty to the central organs of the community. Moreover, it bears recalling that it took the member states 16 years to negotiate the EC merger review regime. The American Bar Association in its report reviewed the prospects for a World Competition Code that might be administered by a supranational authority, such as a specialized branch of the International Court of Justice or a specialized committee of the OECD, but, for reasons earlier noted, was sceptical as to both the prospects and wisdom of such a course of action.[90]

A more modest variant on the EC model of *ab initio* review of transnational mergers might contemplate a multilateral appeal or dispute resolution process in the event of divergent determinations by national authorities, but unlike the jurisdictional dispute resolution model canvassed above, provide for substantive review on the merits of a disputed merger. However, experience with multilateral dispute resolution under the GATT strongly suggests that in the absence of a multilaterally agreed code embodying well-specified governing substantive norms, such a mechanism is likely to prove ineffective (as in the case of GATT disputes over agricultural subsidies).

CONCLUSION: FUTURE INTERNATIONAL INSTITUTIONAL CHALLENGES

A number of options might be contemplated for promoting greater international co-operation in the harmonization and enforcement of domestic competition laws. First, one might contemplate a more ambitious set of bilateral agreements of the kind that the USA has negotiated with a number of countries, including Canada. The weakness with this approach is that it has realized relatively modest gains to date and that even if more ambitious agreements were to prove feasible, they run the risk of promoting trade arrangements that are inherently discriminatory and thus inconsistent with the Most Favoured Nation principle that is the cornerstone of the multilateral trading system. Second, one might contemplate more ambitious regional arrangements, like that in place in the EC, with harmonized laws and supranational enforcement and adjudicatory agencies. At present, the most likely candidates are NAFTA and ANZCERTA. However, given that these arrangements capture a relatively limited proportion of the trade of a number of the member states, system frictions with external trading partners are likely to remain a significant problem (as is also true of the EC). Third, a more ambitious multilateral harmonization initiative might be contemplated. Here, there appear to be two major sub-options in terms of choice of institutional forum. Some commentators favour the OECD Competition Law and Policy Committee as the natural forum, given its substantial history of involvement in this area, although at a later juncture agreed common codes might be transferred to the World Trade Organization (WTO) created in the recent Uruguay Round of the GATT for broader application. While the likelihood of agreement on a common set of competition norms may well be higher in the OECD, given its limited membership, even then substantial difficulties are likely to be encountered in achieving agreement amongst members of the Triad on sensitive issues noted above, for example with respect to various kinds of horizontal arrangements amongst competitors and with respect to vertical arrangements. However, even if agreement could be reached, it would lack legitimacy with developing countries and countries in transition from command to market economies who are not members of the OECD and who would have no reason to accept any legal norms agreed to, or to abide by the determinations of any adjudicative or dispute resolution process set up under the aegis of the OECD.

These limitations then naturally suggest the other sub-option in a multilateral context: reviving the original aspirations of the GATT and in the next round of multilateral negotiations seeking multilateral agreement on a minimum set of competition law standards and an appropriate dispute resolution process for adjudicating complaints about non-compliance with these standards. The adoption of a set of minimum standards for domestic intellectual property regimes in the recent Uruguay Round GATT Agreement provides some impetus for this approach.

For example, the *Draft International Antitrust Code* published by the International Antitrust Code Working Group (primarily a group of German competition scholars) on 10 July 1993, proposes minimum substantive standards for national antitrust laws that would address horizontal arrangements, vertical restrictions, mergers, and abuse of dominant position, and the establishment of an International Antitrust Authority under the auspices of the WTO.[91] Concentrations with international dimensions would be notified to all national antitrust enforcement agencies affected, as well as to the International Antitrust Authority.[92] The International Antitrust Authority would be an independent body established within the institutional framework of the WTO. Its powers would include the power to request actions in individual antitrust cases or groups of cases to be instituted by a national antitrust enforcement agency; to bring actions against national enforcement agencies if such agencies should refuse to take appropriate measures against individual restraints of competition; to sue private persons or undertakings before national law courts seeking injunctions against anti-competitive restraints of competition; to appeal from decisions of the national courts even when it was not a party in the trial, but under the same conditions as the parties to the case; to sue a party to the agreement for violations of the agreement; and to assist parties to the agreement to promulgate antitrust laws and to institute efficient antitrust administration.[93]

The *Draft Code* also envisages the establishment of a permanent International Antitrust Panel to operate in the framework of the new GATT dispute settlement mechanism under the WTO. Provided consultations were first tried but failed, this permanent six-member body would be authorized to adjudicate disputes between the parties to the agreement with respect to alleged violations of the agreement. The Panel would decide whether obligations under the agreement had been violated. If a national judicial decision was found to be inconsistent with the obligations under the agreement, the competent national law court or other authorities would have to reconsider their decisions to ensure conformity with the findings of the Panel.[94]

The GATT option has the obvious appeal of being comprehensive in coverage and non-discriminatory in application, but also carries the obvious difficulties of securing agreement among over 100 countries in very different stages of economic development and with very different philosophies of the relative roles of the state and the market in their economies. Opposing risks are presented by this option. Either, in order to achieve agreement, the norms adopted will be so general, so minimal, or so compromised as to mean next to nothing or to be productive of enormous uncertainty and conflict; or more meaningful agreement on a set of operational norms is achieved, but this 'freezes' competition law in a complex international treaty that precludes ready adaptability to new industrial organization phenomena or new learning.[95]

Rather than embarking on a multilateral enterprise nearly as ambitious as the *Draft International Antitrust Code*, a series of more modest multilateral initiatives might usefully be contemplated. These would focus on potentially anti-competitive practices that impact directly on international trade. For example, member states of the new World Trade Organization might agree to ensure that their domestic competition laws adopt prohibitions against both export and import cartels. With respect to merger law, as this might impact on international mergers, various forms of procedural harmonization, discussed earlier in this paper, might be contemplated. With respect to substantive harmonization, member states with merger laws might commit themselves, in the interests of transparency, to publishing a set of non-binding merger enforcement guidelines that indicate how these merger laws are likely to be enforced with respect to a checklist of issues that the guidelines would be required to address (but without a commitment to a common position on these issues). With respect to the contentious issue of vertical foreclosure of effective access to foreign markets, controversy here is likely to be particularly intense given widely differing industrial organization traditions in different countries, widely different antitrust traditions, and substantial theoretical controversies as to the appropriate form that laws should take with respect to vertical restrictions. In this area, it is difficult to contemplate ready multilateral consensus on an appropriate set of legal norms. Perhaps the most that might be hoped for is that member countries would agree that, as a baseline, vertical restrictions should be included in domestic competition laws as reviewable practices, without any common commitment to the legal norms governing the process of review. Again, as with merger review, it may be possible to reach agreement on a commitment for each member state to publish a set of non-binding vertical restraint enforcement guidelines that address a common checklist of issues. A bolder step would be to build on the chapter 19 binational panel experience under the FTA and NAFTA, relating to the application of domestic trade remedy laws, by providing a GATT panel procedure whereby aggrieved foreign parties (states or firms) could complain to a supranational panel in cases where it is alleged that member states are not faithfully interpreting or enforcing their own domestic competition laws (which they would remain free to change). In the meantime, it may be useful for the OECD to convene a group of internationally recognized competition law experts to work on a non-binding model international antitrust code that, over time, may exert an exemplary or exhortatory influence over the evolution of domestic competition law regimes.

However daunting the challenges, until we have achieved a basic reconciliation between trade and competition policy, we will have failed to complete a task that has eluded policy-makers for more than a century—the achievement of two economically coherent and consistent framework policies that are major policy determinants of the competitive health of every industrialized economy.

NOTES

1. See Derek Ireland, Discussion Paper, *Interactions Between Competition and Trade Policies: Challenges and Opportunities* (Canadian Bureau of Competition Policy, Nov. 1992), 1–2.
2. Ibid. 2.
3. In E. Kantzenbach, F. Scharrer, and L. Waverman (eds.), *Competition Policy in an Interdependent World* (Baden-Baden: Nomos, 1993).
4. Ibid. 261.
5. See M. Trebilcock, 'Competition Policy, Trade Policy and the Problem of Second Best', in R. S. Khemani and W. T. Stanbury (eds.), *Competition Law and Policy of the Centenary* (Halifax: Institute for Research on Public Policy, 1991), ch. 4.
6. See e.g. Olivier Long, *Law and its Limits in the GATT Multilateral Trade System* (London: Graham and Trotman–Martinus Nijhoff, 1987), 1–2; Kenneth Dam, *The GATT* (Chicago: University of Chicago Press, 1970), ch. 2; Frank Stone, *Canada, GATT, and the International Trade System* (Montreal: Institute for Research on Public Policy, 1987), 52–3; and John Jackson, *The World Trading System* (Cambridge, Mass.: MIT Press, 1989), ch. 2.
7. See George N. Addy, 'International Coordination of Competition Policy', in Kantzenbach *et al.* (eds.), *Competition Policy in an Interdependent World*, 292.
8. *The Set of Multilaterally Agreed Principles and Rules for the Control of Restrictive Business Practices*, UNCTAD Doc TD/RBP/Conf. 10/Rev.1, 5 Dec. 1980.

9. See P. Ebow Bondzai Simpson, *Legal Relationships Between Transnational Corporations and Host States* (New York: Quorum Books, 1990), ch. 5.
10. See Edward Glynn, 'International Agreements to Allocate Jurisdiction Over Mergers', in Barry Hawk (ed.), *International Mergers and Joint Ventures* (New York: Fordham Corporate Law Institute, 1991), 38–9. Addy, 'International Coordination of Competition Policies', 292–4; also 'International Agreements to Allocate Jurisdiction Over Mergers', in Hawk (ed.), *International Mergers and Joint Ventures*, 39–43.
11. *Memorandum of Understanding Between the Government of Canada and the Government of the United States of America as to Notification, Consultation and Cooperation with Respect to the Application of National Antitrust Laws* (1984), 23 I.L.M. 275; see Lawson Hunter and Susan Hutton, 'Where There is a Will There is a Way: Cooperation in Canada–U.S. Antitrust Relations', Paper presented in the American Conference Institute on Multinational Antitrust Enforcement, New York, 7 Mar. 1994.
12. *Agreement Between the Government of the United States of America and the Government of Australia Relating to Cooperation on Antitrust Matters* (1982), 20 I.L.M. 702.
13. *Agreement Between the Government of the United States of America and the Government of the Federal Republic of Germany Relating to Mutual Cooperation Regarding Restrictive Business Practices* (1976).
14. *Agreement Between the Commission of the European Communities and the Government of the United States of America Regarding the Application of their Competition Laws*, Washington, 23 Sept. 1991.
15. See Organization of Economic Co-operation and Development, *Revised Recommendation of the Council Concerning Co-operation between Member Countries on Restrictive Business Practices Affecting International Trade* (1986) [C(86)44(Final)]; and predecessor versions referenced therein.
16. See Glynn, 'International Agreements to Allocate Jurisdiction Over Mergers', 39–43.
17. US Department of Justice, *Antitrust Enforcement Guidelines for International Operations* (1988), discussed further below.
18. This discussion is drawn from Neil Campbell and Michael Trebilcock, 'International Merger Review: Problems of Multi-Jurisdictional Conflict', in Kantzenbach *et al.* (eds.), *Competition Policy in an Interdependent World*; see also Greg Tereposky, *Extraterritoriality in the 1990s* (Ottawa: Investment Canada, June 1993).
19. Indeed, the extension of the power to order production of corporate records in 1986 to affiliates, whether located inside or outside of Canada, was the first attempt to achieve extra-territorial jurisdiction:

298   *Michael J. Trebilcock*

see Lawson A. W. Hunter and John F. Blakeney, 'The Changing Canadian Competition Law Environment: Implications for International Business', *Review of International Business Law*, 21 (1987), 256.
20. Competition Act, R.S.C. 1985, c. C-34, as amended, s. 110.
21. John Clifford, John Kazanjian, and William Rowley, 'Canada', in Donald Baker and William Rowley (eds.), *International Mergers: The Antitrust Process* (London: Sweet and Maxwell, 1991), 630.
22. Deepa Rishikesh, 'Extraterritoriality versus Sovereignty in International Antitrust Jurisdiction', *World Competition,* 14/3 (1991), 36.
23. Joseph P. Griffin, 'United States Antitrust Laws and Transnational Business Transactions', 21 *International Lawyer* 307 (1987), 308–9.
24. *United States* v. *Aluminum Co. of America,* 148 F. 2d 416 (2d Cir., 1945).
25. American Law Institute, *Restatement of the Law, Foreign Relations Law of the United States (Third)* (1987), s. 402(1)(c).
26. United States Department of Justice, *Antitrust Enforcement Guidelines for International Operations* (1988), 21.
27. The territoriality principle holds that a state in whose territory an offence is committed has jurisdiction over such offence. It is the state where an act or conduct takes place that decides whether the act or conduct is an offence: J.-G. Castel, *Extraterritoriality in International Trade* (Toronto: Butterworths, 1988), 10.
28. Rishikesh, 'Extraterritoriality versus Sovereignty', 37.
29. American Bar Association Antitrust Section, *Report of the Special Committee on International Antitrust* (June 1991), 234–6.
30. *Timberlane Lumber Co.* v. *Bank of America,* 549 F. 2d 597 (9th Cir., 1976).
31. *Mannington Mills, Inc.* v. *Congoleum Corp.,* 595 F. 2d 1287 (3rd Cir., 1979).
32. Mark R. Joelson, 'Harmonization: A Doctrine for the Next Decade', 10 *Journal of International Law and Business* 133 (1990), 135.
33. U.S. Department of Justice, *Antitrust Enforcement Guidelines for International Operations* (1988), 32 n. 170.
34. Ibid. 45–6.
35. *Institut Merieux S.A.,* no. 891-0098, 55 Fed. Reg. 1614 (17 Jan. 1990).
36. Donald Baker, 'United States', in Baker and Rowley (eds.), *International Mergers,* 449.
37. American Law Institute, *Restatement,* s. 403, comment *e.*
38. Baker, 'United States', 449.
39. *United States* v. *Baker Hughes Inc.,* 731 F. Supp. 3 (D.D.C.), aff'd 908 F. 2d 981 (D.C. Cir., 1990). Since the State Department had considered the position of the foreign government before the DOJ

proceeded, the court declined to second-guess the decision of the executive branch to go ahead with the case.

40. See, for example, *Consolidated Gold Fields PLC* v. *Minorco S.A.*, 871 F. 2d 252 (2nd Cir., 1989).
41. Rishikesh, 'Extraterritoriality versus Sovereignty', 39.
42. American Bar Association Antitrust Section, *Report*, 237.
43. *Laker Airways Ltd.* v. *Sabena Belgian World Airlines*, 731 F. 2d 909 (D.C. Cir., 1984), at pp. 950 and 952. See also Castel, *Extraterritoriality in International Trade*, 61.
44. *Hartford Fire Insurance* v. *California* (June 28, 1993, 65: 1621 ATRR 30).
45. American Bar Association Antitrust Division, *Report*, 240.
46. See Rishikesh, 'Extraterritoriality versus Sovereignty', 60; and J. Rill, 'The Recent Structural Impediment Initiative (SII) Talks with Japan' (Justice Department briefing, 9 Apr. 1990).
47. Rishikesh, 'Extraterritoriality versus Sovereignty', 61.
48. *See Ahlstrom Osakeyhtio and Others* v. *EC Commission* (Joined Cases 89, 104, 114, 116, 117, and 125 to 129/85); [1988] 4 CMLR 901.
49. *ICI Ltd., J.R. Geigy AG, and Sandoz AG* v. *EC Commission* (Joined Cases 48, 52, and 53/69), [1972] E.C.R. 619, 787, and 845 respectively; [1972] CMLR 557.
50. *Council Regulation 4064/89 on the Control of Concentrations Between Undertakings*, O.J. L257/13 (1990), art. 1(2).
51. Michael Reynolds and Elizabeth Weightman, 'European Economic Community', in Baker and Rowley (eds.), *International Mergers*, 9.
52. *R.* v. *Nova Scotia Pharmaceutical Society* [1992] 2 S.C.R. 606.
53. See Presley Warner and Michael Trebilcock, 'Rethinking Price-Fixing Law', (1993) 38 *McGill Law Journal*, 679.
54. See Donald McFetridge, 'Globalization and Competition Policy', in Thomas Courchene and Douglas Purvis (eds.), *Productivity and Growth and Canada's International Competitiveness* (The Bell Canada Papers on Economic and Public Policy, 133) (Canada: John Deutsch Institute for the Study of Economic Policy, Queen's University, Canada, 1993), 150.
55. Ibid. 139.
56. See Discussion Paper, 'Strategic Alliances and Their Implications for Canadian Competition Policy', Canadian Competition Policy Bureau, Feb. 1993.
57. See e.g. Shyam Khemani and Mark Dutz, 'The Instruments of Competition Policy and their Relevance for Economic Development', in Claudio Frischtak (ed.), *Regulatory Policies and Reform in Industrializing Countries* (forthcoming, 1995).
58. See Michael Gerlach, *Alliance Capitalism: The Social Organization of*

Japanese Business (Berkeley and Los Angeles: University of California Press, 1992).
59. This section of the paper is drawn from Campbell and Trebilcock, 'International Merger Review'.
60. Ibid.
61. See Baker and Rowley, *International Mergers*.
62. A number of these cases are reviewed in Richard Whish and Diane Wood, *Merger Cases in the Real World: A Study of Control Procedures* (OECD: Paris, 1994).
63. Ibid. ch. 4.
64. American Bar Association Antitrust Division, *Report*, ch. 7. While the ABA considered a common notification form to be unrealistic at this time, they propose that agreement might at least be reached as to the categories or types of information to be provided on an initial notification.
65. Whish and Wood, *Merger Cases in the Real World*, 107.
66. American Bar Association Antitrust Section, *Report*, 267.
67. Ibid. 250.
68. OECD, *International Mergers and Competition Policy* (OECD: Paris, 1988), 14–15.
69. American Bar Association Antitrust Section, *Report*, 294.
70. See Neil Campbell and Michael Trebilcock, 'A Comparative Analysis of Merger Law: Canada, the United States, and the European Community', *World Competition*, 15/5 (1992); see more generally Donald Baker and William Rowley (eds.), *International Mergers: The Antitrust Process* (London: Sweet & Maxwell, 1991).
71. American Bar Association Antitrust Section, *Report*, 293.
72. Ibid. 294.
73. Ibid. 531.
74. Ibid. 295.
75. Director of Investigation and Research, *Merger Enforcement Guidelines* (Ottawa: Consumer and Corporate Affairs Canada, 1991).
76. American Bar Association Antitrust Section, *Report*, 236.
77. Ibid. 243.
78. Ibid. 249.
79. See Glynn, 'International Agreements'.
80. *California* v. *American Stores*, 110 S.Ct. 1853 (1990). The ABA Committee proposed that a court seized of such an action should solicit an opinion from the executive branch of the US government as to why government enforcement action was not thought appropriate: American Bar Association Antitrust Section, *Report*, 267.
81. OECD, *Revised Recommendation*, appendix, para. 7.
82. American Bar Association Antitrust Section, *Report*, 250, 266; see also Whish and Wood, *Merger Cases in the Real World*, 86–90, 105–7.

83. See OECD, *International Mergers* (1988), 37, which reviews several cases where this occurred.
84. Richard Caves, *Multinational Enterprises and Economic Analysis* (Cambridge: Cambridge University Press: 1982), 129. This situation is well-exemplified in the divergent positions taken by Canadian and EC competition authorities in the proposed acquisition by a European consortium of the Canadian de Havilland division of Boeing: see Addy, 'International Coordination of Competition Policy', 298.
85. See e.g. Deborah Owen and John Parisi, 'International Mergers and Joint Ventures: A Federal Trade Commission Perspective', and Douglas Rosenthal, 'The Potential for Jurisdictional Conflicts in Multistate International Merger Transactions', both in Hawk (ed.), *International Mergers and Joint Ventures*; and American Bar Association Antitrust Division, *Report*, 246.
86. For a review of some of the issues that would require resolution, see George Hay, John Hilke, and Philip Nelson, 'Geographic Market Definition in an International Context', in Hawk, *International Mergers and Joint Ventures*.
87. Sir Leon Brittan, the EC Competition Commissioner, has suggested the possibility of an 'arbitration' procedure in the event of jurisdictional disputes, at least in the context of a US–EC bilateral agreement: see Glynn, 'International Agreements', 43–4.
88. In some respects, such a Panel would bear analogies to the chapter 19 panels provided for under the Canada–US Free Trade Agreement to rule on anti-dumping and countervailing duty disputes between the two countries by determining whether either country has abused its jurisdiction in particular cases.
89. See e.g. Wernhard Moschel, 'International Restraints of Competition: A Regulatory Outline', 10 *Journal of International Law and Business* 76 (1990) 77.
90. American Bar Association Antitrust Committee, *Report*, ch. 12; see also Whish and Wood, *Merger Cases in the Real World*, 115.
91. Special Supplement (19 Aug. 1993), 64: 1628 ATRR; see Hunter and Hutton, 'Where There is a Will There is a Way', from whom the following summary is taken.
92. Ibid. art. 10.
93. Ibid. art. 19.
94. Ibid. art. 20.
95. See Ireland, *Interactions Between Competition and Trade Policies*, appendix H.

10

The Internationalization of Competition Policy

G. BRUCE DOERN

INTRODUCTION

To complement the substantive trade-competition policy linkages examined in Chapter 9, this chapter examines two political factors that are contributing to the greater internationalization of competition policy. These are the political power of nation-states and business, and the influence of international organizations and inter-agency relations within states. More specifically, it analyses whether internationalizing forces are likely to transform existing international arrangements in competition policy matters from those of a loose regime to that of a fully fledged international institutional system. Such an analysis can only be begun in this chapter since more than international political factors are at play. In Chapter 11, we add two further contributing variables, tensions in contemporary competition policy ideas, and concerns about accountability, representation, and transparency. These further factors are both international and domestic in nature and will allow us to deal more completely with the full interplay of factors that are likely to affect patterns of overall institutional reform in competition policy among and within countries.

This overall task in turn requires the bridging of two solitudes within the disciplines of political science and political economy. The solitudes arise from the tendency of international relations specialists to deal with the larger world of international relations and international integration but to downplay or oversimplify domestic politics and domestic institutions and decision processes, and for domestic political and policy specialists to engage in the reverse set of sins inherent in specialization.[1]

The chapter is organized into three sections. It begins with a brief conceptual map of key terms inherent in dealing with the internationalization of competition policy: internationalization; regimes; and institutions. The next two sections explore, in turn, the two political variables. Thus, we look explicitly at the power relations and stances of nation-states and business groups, many of these forged in the context of international geopolitics rather than just in competition policy terms, though with the latter looming larger in the post-cold war era. The chapter then zeroes in on existing international institutional players and agencies, and how they are responding to, dealing with, and are a part of the international pressures. This involves a look at how agencies and arenas such as the OECD, UNCTAD, EU, NAFTA, and APEC are facilitating co-operation, as Chapter 9 has shown, but also possess a bureaucratic stake in alternative outcomes. Some sense of the inter-agency dynamics within key countries is also presented because it cannot be assumed in any *political* analysis of competition policy that each national government, or international institution, is responding as a single, rational, purposeful, actor. In short, bureaucratic or inter-agency politics is involved.

KEY DEFINITIONAL AND CONCEPTUAL ISSUES

The notion of 'internationalizing' competition policy is intended to evoke a process that is propelled by, but goes beyond, globalization.[2] The latter is usually seen as a technological-economic phenomenon, but internationalizing processes, for the purposes of this chapter, refer to the actual penetration of international pressures into the concrete functioning of heretofore relatively free-standing domestic or national governmental institutions. While this implies a one-way set of interventions from the international realm to the domestic one, it may also include the reverse, the need to accommodate many more domestic interests and decision processes into how new international institutions are designed and politically justified.[3]

The definitional gray area of 'regimes versus institutions' is also central to the analysis. As later sections show, the political science and political economy of public policy literature, both by international and domestic specialists, uses these terms in somewhat different ways, but their joint use is devoted to the difficult practical task of capturing a subtle array of collective behaviour and public arrangements.[4] In the study of international relations, 'regimes'

evoke an array of informal co-operative relationships that are typically not centred on specific formal organizations and do not involve binding rules and dispute settlement processes.[5] A standard
definition of an international regime is that it is 'a set of principles,
norms, rules and decision making procedures around which actor
expectations converge in a given issue area' of international relations.[6] It is thus a term that conveys, at first glance, a focus on
micro or particular areas of policy (e.g. regimes for whaling or
Arctic pollution) in which competition policy may or may not fit,
since competition policy is usually seen as a quite broad frame-
work-oriented kind of policy in its domestic settings. In the study
of international relations, regime theory is also intimately con-
nected with the problem of studying a world where co-operative
rules and decisions must somehow be enforced without there being a world government.

The concept of regimes is also used in the study of domestic
public policy and regulation for a related but somewhat different
set of reasons. Thus, one speaks of regulatory regimes to cover not
only the formal regulatory body or agency in any given field of
regulation, but also the softer array of informal arrangements that
help achieve compliance.[7] Regimes in this domestic policy analysis
do involve organizations *per se*.

'Institutions' in an international setting, on the other hand, usually
refer to more entrenched systems of values, rules, and relationships more often than not centred around major organizations
(such as GATT). Political institutions in domestic settings also
typically suggest a macro-level of analysis and thus can range from
examples such as parliamentary government to federalism.[8] Alas,
discussion of issues such as 'degrees of institutionalization' or of
movement along a continuum from regime to institution can never
be fully precise, but it can be helpful.

The issue of the *degree* of institutionalization of competition
policy at the international level is bound up in these definitional
conundrums. Moreover, important political issues are involved in
regime as against institutional arrangements, even though, in the
end, both exist in some degree in most mature policy fields. For
example, if left totally as a set of regimes, competition policy may
be arranged to an excessive degree in the interests of business
power or in the interests of one or more dominant countries.
Greater institutionalization, depending on its form, may increase
the influence of the public interest or consumers, or of smaller or

middle-sized countries, depending, of course, upon exactly how institutions are designed and how open and transparent their dispute settlement processes are.

Dealing analytically with possible future paths in competition policy at the international level is not a simple task. One should be aware from the outset of several inherent arenas of policy, administration, and institutional development that may or may not potentially converge or have to be accommodated. Figure 10.1 supplies an initial analytical glimpse of four main arenas for thinking about the actual or potential internationalizing of competition policy in the 1990s (see p. 322).

On the vertical axis, the figure shows a rough 'policy versus administration' division. The horizontal axis suggests a rough division into regimes (where the majority of international competition policy currently resides) versus actual or potential international institutions. The two quadrants on the left thus refer, in effect, to current policy and to law enforcement and administrative discretion on cases. They indicate a set of general policy relationships involving co-operation and some harmonization (comity principles, memoranda of understanding, etc.) and co-operative enforcement actions (in cases, regulated situations; limited institutional exchanges of information). The two quadrants on the right of the chart suggest current or emerging policy and institutional conflicts and areas of convergence. One set deals with international framework policy areas such a trade, investment, and the environment. These also include regional and bilateral forms of institutionalization such as the EU's competition policy system. The other set deals with micro-economic decisions and cases that range from innovation policy (strategic alliances, R&D, and other joint ventures), to sectoral deregulation and regulatory initiatives and sectoral or other subsidies. Institutionally, these involve many formerly relatively sheltered domestic regulatory agencies and departments catering to domestic industry needs.

This chapter ultimately focuses more on the upper-right quadrant than on the other arenas, though all are examined or commented upon here and in the conclusions to the book presented in Chapter 11. The reason for the greater focus on the upper-right quadrant is that competition policy is moving into an international realm where, as Chapter 9 implies, it is intrinsically necessary to assess the degree of international institutionalization that exists in the adjacent fields of trade, investment, and environmental policy.

This is necessary in order to understand where competition policy may find its international institutional and political niche or resting place in the rest of the 1990s and beyond.[9]

POLITICAL POWER AND THE INTERESTS OF STATES AND BUSINESS

It is scarcely credible in considering the possible future directions of a more internationalized competition policy to ignore the basic forces of international political power and the interests of nation-states and business. In the mainstream literature on competition policy this is a variable that is rarely fully considered, in part because the internationalization process is more recent, but also because lawyers and economists tend not to focus on such factors.

Before attempting to discuss these important aspects of political power, it is essential to deal with pivotal analytical debates within political science in the study of international relations. International political economy essentially concerns itself with the study of the interacting effects of power, security, and the pursuit of wealth among nations.[10] Moreover, many international relations specialists adopt a realist-school approach which essentially argues that calculations about relative power and security are central to foreign policy-making and that this produces an unpredictable *'real politik'* quality in international relations. Such approaches to analysis suggest that security and economic issues are empirically and symbolically linked and that power is centrally involved.[11] Particular analyses have also focused on so-called hegemonic power which in part argues that only when an overwhelmingly dominant country, such as the USA in the post-Second World War era, holds such power can free-trade approaches remain stable.[12] The central role of business or capital as an overall interest are also central features of international and comparative political economy (as seen below).[13]

Nation-states and power

The approaches reviewed above tend to analyse power by assuming that nation-states are single, purposeful, unitary actors. Other approaches, including interest-group theory and public-choice theory, have begun to relax such assumptions with the result that the more specific influences of domestic politics writ large are more systematically included. But even these latter approaches do not penetrate too deeply into actual domestic decision-making institutions. They even downplay international agencies because the nation-state is the dominant unit of analysis and the focus is on political conflict.[14]

A further but definitely a sub-strand of international relations theory is that which studies realms of international cooperation including the existence of regimes, relations among and within international institutions, and, more recently, the existence of international coalitions of diverse interest groups and policy communities that extend well beyond business interests to include labour, human rights, environmental groups and aboriginal peoples, to name only a few.

Much like practitioners in the real world, students of international relations do not know quite what to make of the so-called post-cold war era that began in the 1990s. Discussions of a new international order are confounded by the stark emergence of newly released surges of nationalism and regional wars. With the reduction of the Soviet communist military and security threat, foreign policy attention in many Western countries has increasingly turned to economic definitions of security. Hence one hears in political rhetoric, the military-style metaphors of 'who's bashing whom', and even the identification of environmental issues as matters of national security.[15]

Further complicating the picture in the mid-1990s is the issue of how to factor in, first, the political reaction to the relative triumph, in the 1980s and early 1990s, of free trade and globalization, and secondly, the emergence of trading blocs or the triad of the European Union, North America, and Japan–Pacific, each anchored by one or more dominant countries. However, a sample of the basic postures of some key countries can already be gleaned from earlier chapters and from other sources.

Emerging views on competition policy and power

The US view

The United States, for example, has already given ample indication of its desire to export its competition policy system elsewhere, such as to APEC countries and Eastern Europe. US spokespersons ardently believe that their system is the best and most effectively implemented. This was most evident in the US–Japan Structural Initiative process.[16] But it has an added, more overt, high-tech industrial policy zest to it under the Clinton administration. The changes in approach are evident in the eyes of EU officials. For example, following the failure of the February 1994 US–Japan summit meeting, the EU's Sir Leon Brittan stated that 'our concern about the American approach has been that there is an element of managed trade' and that 'if you believe in a market economy that causes real problems'.[17] Following Clinton's personal role in winning a US$ 6 billion sale of airplanes with Saudi Arabia, these concerns were palpable. Images of the President as the 'chief salesman' leading the 'march to industrial policy' were quickly evoked.[18]

However, the US approach to an internationalized competition policy also has a sense of limits.[19] For example, the Americans know that their own competition policy institutions favouring the use of private legal action are not likely to be accepted in most countries, and thus the US does not push hard on this point. Moreover, if there was ever any enthusiasm by US competition officials for stronger international institutions for antitrust, it has been cooled in recent years by a latent fear that such institutions may be shaped more in the image of US *trade* authorities than their own *competition* experts. Thus, as discussed further below, there are intra-bureaucratic politics interwoven with national postures.

Selected EU country views

Within the EU, key countries articulate positions which partly are based on historic postures, but also partly measured by new or recent EU realities. For example, France is still far more overly supportive of industrial policy being a part of competition policy, especially *vis-à-vis* the USA. Britain is opposed to competition policy that contains too much industrial policy room, but at the same time insists on there being ample room for the continuation of ministerial discretion. Germany's international competition policy statements show a strong preference for a 'uniform European competition law incorporating national competition orders'.[20] German policy-makers see as both inevitable and desirable a more independent EU competition agency than DG IV is at present. It sees such an institution as being non-political, partly out of genuine belief, but also partly out of an assumption that Germany itself will have decisive power in shaping what the new institution is allowed to do. German policy statements seek an EU competition authority that is more centralized than present but they also stress that it does not 'presuppose a single Eureopean superauthority operating in a centralized way'. Citing the EU's principle of subsidiarity, Germany still sees a role for national authorities as well (see the concluding comments of Chapter 8).

Canada and Australia

As for smaller countries on the world stage such as Canada or Australia, the chief concern is to ensure that the international competition policy system is not designed only to meet the economic needs of the major powers, global or regional. Accordingly, as befits their traditional trade policy stances, they seek multilateral solutions wherever possible and bilateral ones where necessary.[21]

Business interests and power

As emphasized above, the interests of capital and business interests in general are central elements in the study of both international political economy and domestic policy formation. But, how will business power manifest itself on competition policy *per se*? Business power, as countless analyses have shown, is always twofold in nature. First, business interests exercise power in a profound functional sense simply and directly because governments in capitalist systems are fundamentally dependent upon business for economic prosperity and jobs for their citizens. Second, business interests have power that arises out of their great lobbying capacity. The first base of business power generally results in continuous pressure, in principle at least, in favour of free markets, free trade, and free investment flows. But the second basis undoubtedly generates divisions among business interests (national and international) since both corporate winners and losers arise from particular decisions by governments, or from the result of competitive market forces or the introduction of new technologies.

Clearly, the multinational corporation in a globalizing system of production and capital flows adds an even more compelling reality to business power, and thus multinational firms are a crucial variable in determining the extent to which competition policy is internationalized. As we have seen in each country case study, big business has always been a central player in the domestic processes of forging competition policy laws, but such laws contain provisions that are also (nominally at least) there to protect or placate small business as well, usually in the name of fair competition.

However, internationally it is not yet clear, which particular industrial sectors or key multinationals will lead or resist the move towards a greater internationalization of *competition* policies, practices, and institutions as distinct from trade and other policies. Business advisory groups are a part of the OECD and EU competition policy network, and thus general business influence is present. Among sectors, there is the presumption that the 'high-tech' sector (which often is in fact many sectors) will be especially interested in new competition rules at the international level. The service sector, or parts of it, were among the key interests that pressed for free trade in the 1980s and 1990s but these may or may not be a uniform set of interests when it comes to internationalized competition policy *per se*.[22]

Perhaps the best that can be said, is that much more needs to be known about business coalitions for and against the further internationalization of competition policy as distinct from past trade policy. It is clear that views are energetically being formulated by business groups and are projected in forums such as OECD Round Tables.[23] None the less, this is without doubt largely a non-topic among the economic and legal scholars of competition policy.

INTERNATIONAL AGENCIES AND INTER-AGENCY RELATIONS WITHIN STATES

The second political variable in the internationalization of competition policy is in one sense the most obvious and yet in other respects is the most subtle and least studied. This is the role that international agencies play in the process of international learning and in advancing or slowing new or emerging policy or institutional ideas. In this chapter, we are interested in the agencies with competition policy facilitating roles. However, of necessity, we must also deal with the agencies (or other parts of the same international body) that deal with closely related fields such as trade and investment policy. All these agencies are political bureaucracies in their own right, but they and their committees and discussion forums are composed of officials from individual member nation-states. The member states' positions and tactics are in turn the product of increasingly complex negotiations among agencies within the nation's home bureaucracy (see more below).

In traditional foreign policy, a nation's position is usually forged by the foreign affairs ministry, the president's or prime minister's office, and, where appropriate, defence departments. But where foreign policy begins to involve, as it increasingly does, heretofore largely domestic policy fields, then a more intense and complex array of bureaucratic players joins the fray both to advance ideas and interests, and to protect organizational turf. This is certainly happening in the trade–competition–investment policy nexus as well.[24] Within each country, the precise nature of these relations varies with the actual structure of government as well as with the influence of individual leaders in these agencies.

A full account of all the factors reviewed above is well beyond the bounds of this chapter. It is, however, essential to offer a selective glimpse of this political variable. First, I set out the way some key international agencies and forums have been handling and advancing competition policy, focusing especially on the OECD. Second, I look briefly at the comparative degree of international institutionalization that is present in the adjacent or nominally converging international fields of trade, investment, and environmental policy. Third, a sample of inter-agency relationships within nation-states is given, especially in the context of the point stressed by Ostry and others that a significant blurring of policy fields is occurring.

International agencies

With respect to international agencies and forums, it is evident that competition policy issues are looming larger but also proceeding quite tentatively. The international competition policy community functions in several organizations and settings. The most recent is the Asia Pacific Economic Council (APEC), whose benchmark meetings in Seattle in November 1993 included a discussion of competition policy. APEC includes countries without competition laws at all as well as countries with well-established competition laws. The United States in particular was anxious to put the issue on the Seattle agenda, in part to ensure that fast-growing APEC countries did not repeat the Japanese practice of having weakly enforced competition policy systems. The late 1980s early 1990s/ US–Japan Structural Impediments Initiative had itself been the major bilateral instance where international competition policy issues had been negotiated and where Japan undertook to toughen its enforcement practices.[25]

In North America, competition policy issues arose in both the Canada–US free-trade negotitiations and later in NAFTA. In the former, Canada proposed that competition laws fully replace anti-dumping legislation, but these proposals went astray because of the inability to get agreement on the politically related question of subsidy rules. Under NAFTA, chapter 15's provisions give an explicit mention of competition policy, but action is limited to the establishment of a Working Group on Trade and Competition.[26]

The above regional arenas join an international competition policy realm that otherwise has been centred nominally in the United Nations Conference on Trade and Development (UNCTAD) and the OECD. The UNCTAD involvement is a direct result of the failure in the late 1940s to establish an International Trade Organization that was supposed to have a mandate on restrictive business practices. GATT had tried to deal with these issues but its preoccupations were elsewhere, with tariffs and traditional trade matters. UNCTAD eventually moved into the vacuum. A UN Conference on Restrictive Trade Practices was held in 1979 and led to the adoption by the UN General Assembly of the Set of Mutually Agreed Equitable Principles and Rules for the Control of Restrictive Business Practices.[27]

These principles reflected the broad political spectrum of the United Nations. Restrictive practices were defined quite broadly and the general principles were tied to exhortations on mutually reinforcing action, the exchange and dissemination of information, and study and consultation. The principles also recognized the need for preferential or differential treatment for developing countries.[28] Interestingly, principles of good conduct were also enunciated for enterprises, including trans-national corporations. To provide some institutional backing for the principles an Intergovernmental Group of Experts on Restrictive Business Practices was established and has since met annually as a forum for study and consultation. In general, UNCTAD has confined itself to efforts to persuade all states to adopt competition laws in the first place, both through dialogue and through some technical assistance. It has not been involved in examining the newer concerns about competition and trade policy links.

No discussion of international competition policy agencies would be complete without including the EU. The EU's DG IV is itself an international entity *vis-à-vis* its member countries and constitutes a regional supranational structure. The international dimension of its work is receiving increasing salience, not least through advice and exhortation to the new member states and the aspirant East European members who have already joined the European Economic Area. These countries, such as Poland and Hungary, have all created competition regimes in the knowledge that this will be a condition of accession. The EU gives priority also to co-operation with other regimes, particularly that of the United States, and it does its best to support the FTC within Japan. For its part, DG IV is careful to co-ordinate its competition policies with those of the US, Japan, and other countries, and with other directorates within the EU Commission dealing with trade policy and industrial policy (see Chapter 8). Here it is perhaps sufficient to express agreement with Jacquemin's recent analysis of the EU's international dimensions when he concludes that, outside of comity arrangements, 'harmonization appears to be a possible objective but a difficult one: there is no clear consensus about the best standards in competition policy (including in economics); there is a danger that the strongest nations will impose their standards, good or bad, and finally, the degree of feasibility and practicality of harmonization is not clear'.[29]

OECD initiatives

It is the OECD which is, without doubt, the main international arena of exchange on competition policy matters.[30] The OECD is primarily a research and consultative body for the rich Western countries, but a key to understanding its competition policy role is to understand its committee structure. The OECD's Council and Executive Committee is supported by ten sectoral committees, one of which is the committee on Financial, Fiscal and Enterprise Affairs. Within this sector is a Committee on Competition Law and Policy whose work began in 1961. While undoubtedly a valuable focus for the exchange of ideas and the publication of a series of reports, a reading of speeches commemorating its first twenty-five years of work in 1987 shows that international relations in this field were very much in the soft, quasi-regime end of the spectrum of international arrangements. The speeches are congratulatory about the exchanges held, but can point to only generalized achievements rather than more concrete ones. This was in large part because competition law was largely domestic and seen to be domestic.[31] The OECD did establish a voluntary code of instruments in 1986, the OECD 1986 Recommendation, to facilitate better co-operation among countries. Much of this arose out of the need to defuse problems arising from the extra-territorial application of US antitrust laws and decisions.

In the late 1980s and early 1990s, the pace and breadth of OECD activity on competition policy picked up considerably, in part because of the intellectual influence of the Chicago School. It is important to stress that such activity, lock-step with similar happenings inside member state governments, now began to include several OECD sectoral committees. For example, Sylvia Ostry's discussion of system frictions referred to earlier is related by her directly to the OECD's early 1990s project on Technology and the Economy.[32] This work identified the need to focus on competition policy in relation to problems of market access in leading-edge high-tech sectors. Similarly, as I discuss further below, the OECD's Trade Committee established its own trade and competition policy committee.

Within the OECD's Committee on Competition Law and Policy, the more urgent pace of work is reflected in the activities of two working parties. One is on Competition and International Trade. Its work is very much concerned with a series of potential trade–competition policy linkages. Another working party on Co-operation Between Member Countries on Restrictive Business Practices Affecting International Trade is presently involved in two key studies, one on Merger Process Convergence, and another on Information Sharing.

The project on merger process convergence included a study by Professors Richard Whish and Diane Wood, distinguished competition policy lawyers in the UK and US respectively.[33] Indeed Wood is now a Deputy Assistant Attorney General in the Antitrust Division of the US Department of Justice. Whish and Wood examined in some detail nine case studies of mergers that involved the merger review processes of several countries or jurisdictions. Their recommendations focused on possible soft harmonization changes that might be adopted in the processes of review. The study regarded the formation of any supra-international merger authority as extremely premature.

The caution of countries regarding international competition policy matters is also evident in the reaction to the Whish–Wood study. The key problem here is that even some of the soft harmonization suggestions would involve changes to domestic law. And often the mere thought of the politics that might be unleashed if laws had to be changed is itself enough to prevent change. There are also serious concerns that the business community has yet to be seriously consulted on the Whish–Wood study recommendations.

The OECD study on information sharing is dealing with the extremely difficult issues of business confidentiality on the one hand and the need for transparency on the other, a topic to which we return in the final section of the paper. None the less, the hope in this realm of soft harmonization is that OECD experience from other similar areas such as taxation and securities can lead to better practices in competition policy as well.

Also at work under the Committee on Competition Law and Policy is the Convergence Steering Group. Formed in December 1992, this group is attempting to develop an OECD consensus statement on where convergence in laws and practices (with the emphasis on the latter) is already present or close at hand, where future progress is probable or likely, and where convergence is unlikely or undesirable. The Convergence Steering Group can already point to areas of progress in soft harmonization. Much of this centres on the past activities of the OECD itself, but it also includes the previously mentioned arenas of APEC, NAFTA, and EU developments. Soft harmonization can also be seen in the form of some mutual learning that is evident in recent legal changes or guidelines developed under EU, Canadian, US, and Australian competition policy.[34]

The OECD convergence exercise is also likely to stress key themes which the organization believes are directionally appropriate for the rest of the 1990s. These are likely to include items such as: the need for all countries to have competition framework laws; the need for transparent processes and politically independent enforcement; common analytical approaches; greater behaviourial versus structural approaches for determining anti-competitive practices; and positive as well as negative comity.

It is evident that the OECD's work on convergence is staying well clear of any implication that uniformity among nations is the goal. It is also extremely careful in avoiding any mention of a world competition policy agency. An independent study presented in July 1993 at the Max Planck Institute in Munich advocated a draft international antitrust code including provisions for an International Antitrust Authority and dispute settlement panels.[35] This radical proposal for a supra-world agency was roundly criticized by OECD representatives when it was presented at an OECD meeting in December 1993. It was presented by a private group of mainly German professors and other experts in antitrust law which called themselves the International Antitrust Code Working Group. The draft, as we see further below, was cast as a code which could have been incorporated into the GATT Uruguay Round negotiations but which of course was not. While working-group members clearly wanted to go much further along the international institutional continuum than OECD spokespersons, it is also instructive to point out that there were divisions among the working-group members as well. There was agreement among them about the international antitrust code but not about the institutions. Although this proposal was perhaps premature, many other specialists are thinking along similar lines. Thus F. M. Scherer, former chief economist at the FTC, has advocated the creation of an International Competition Policy Office within the WTO. He envisages that it would develop enforcement capabilities and, indeed, this sort of possibility is likely to be canvassed with increasing frequency.[36]

Internationalization in trade, investment, and environment policy fields

While the above discussion of international agencies is central, it must be set against a brief portrait of the degree of international institutionalization present in the adjacent or converging policy fields such as trade, investment, and the environment. Any such account of nominally separate policy fields must include: a sense of the basic evolution of each field's international system; the actual organizations in place (if any); and its approaches to, and processes for, dispute settlement. Harkening back to our differentiation of regimes from institutions, it will basically be argued that international policy fields that have both central organizations and recognized dispute settlement processes will be considered to be fully institutionalized.

When compared to trade, investment, and environment policy, competition policy at the international level must be viewed to be at the regime rather than the institutional end of the continuum. In this regard, it is similar to investment policy. Without doubt, trade policy, through GATT, is the most institutionalized, with environmental policy somewhere in between.

The softer notion of 'regimes' is used advisedly in the case of investment policy. Along with competition policy, it is arguably the least institutionalized of the four policy fields, though, as we will see, not without significant activity in recent years, especially in the wake of the growth of capitalism in Russia and Eastern Europe. There is no single or obvious international institutional or organizational home base for investment matters. Rather what exists are an array of codes, draft codes, and bilateral treaties and arrangements, in short, a loose regime of guides to conduct.[37]

If investment has a relatively loose international regime, then trade is the polar opposite. Real institutionalization has emerged centred around the GATT. Though the GATT is still formally based on an 'interim' 1947 agreement reached when more ambitious ideas for a true International Trade Organization failed, it has none the less established a solid set of principles, rules, and dispute-settlement methods encompassing well over 100 countries.[38] Through several 'rounds' of negotiations, including the recent Uruguay Round, the GATT has sought to promote liberalized trade, reduce protectionist practices, and in general promote economic growth and development. Arguably the most institutionalized feature of GATT is its dispute-settlement procedures. Articles 22 and 23 place emphasis first on bilateral consultations between countries, a process which resolves most disputes. Failing this the GATT panel system is invoked, an action taken about ten times annually in recent years.

The panel typically consists of three experts drawn from countries which have no interest in the dispute. The panels hear the views of both countries and of other interested parties, they then report findings and recommendations to the Council, usually within about a six-month period. If adopted by the Council, again by consensus, then there is a duty on the parties concerned to act according to the panel's findings. Where the offending party does not comply, the injured party may then seek authority from the other members of GATT to take some form of retaliatory action. This has happened only once. Compliance usually, though at times slowly, occurs because countries need to preserve their own credibility as reliable negotiators in other future disputes when the shoe may be on the other foot.

With respect to international environmental arrangements, it is necessary to revert to the language of regimes. The international environmental arena has been historically less centrally institutionalized than the trade arena, but more than the competition and investment arena. Accordingly, it must be seen as a *mélange* of agencies, a series of conventions and protocols, and an emerging typical decision process for conventions and protocols.[39] Strictly speaking, it is environmental conventions and protocols that are the closest parallel to GATT in that they set out international obligations, albeit in many such agreements rather than in one overarching agreement.

Inter-agency relations within nation-states

While the discussion in this section has been mainly about international agencies and arenas, its is essential to point out the degree to which policy, and likely future institutional options, are influenced by inter-agency relations within nation-states. The first obvious point to stress is simply that there are different departmental configurations in each country. In the UK, the trade function is within a Department of Trade and Industry. In Canada, trade is a part of the foreign policy ministry, Foreign Affairs, and International Trade Canada. Secondly, the inherent number of agencies in a given country varies quite widely and of course broadens enormously as soon as competition policy is seen to involve, as it increasingly does, regulated sectors within each nation-state, and hence their array of agencies (the regulatory commissions of the USA and Canada, and the regulatory offices of the UK).

A third feature of these inter-agency relations is that foreign policy ministries are, on the one hand, extremely tenacious in seeking to maintain their pre-eminence in foreign policy, but, on the other hand, are dependent on these previously largely 'domestic' departments for their expertise. This dependence is of no small import in areas such as competition, investment, and environment. Thus there exists in every national government a struggle over the lead foreign policy role. Indeed, a cascade of contending functional versus expertise-based relationships exists. For example, in the UK, the Office of Fair Trading has strong views about international issues but can be constrained from expressing them first by the DTI, which is jealous of its overall competition policy role, and the Foreign Office, which asserts overall foreign policy hegemony.

A related issue which emerges out of policy convergence and attendant inter-agency battles within governments is the simple recognition that they involve an intense mutual penetration of international and national policies and institutions into each other's realms. There is simultaneously a process of internationalizing domestic policy and the domesticization of international policy. This has always been true to some degree, but its scope and intensity is now increasing rapidly. Trade policy, as Chapter 9 has shown, was once primarily about border measures and tariffs, and hence about 'international' trade. National treatment, and other issues, brings it unambiguously over the border and into the heart of domestic policy in the sense that national governments have less room to discriminate in favour of their own industries and also in the sense that many policy fields heretofore thought to be 'domestic' are now affected by trade policy rules or processes.

What this maze of interlocking process means is that one cannot speak any more of purely international policies or institutions. This does not mean that discipline or knowledge experts will not protect their own turf as international specialists or domestic practitioners, but it does mean that the very question of what is international will assume a different shape, in part because domestic political interests will mobilize, and indeed already are, in both national and international arenas simultaneously.[40]

A recognition of this issue also means that selling or communicating policy change will be more difficult and conflictual, not only for normal nationalist and sovereignty reasons, but also because each policy change simply involves a more dense array of players both within and outside national boundaries. National policies will be more difficult to forge and various national interest groups will use international rules, and the argued inevitability or desirability of such rules, to 'discipline' domestic groups against the practice of some previously or currently allowed policy practice. This pattern has already become well established in Japan where *gaiatsu* (foreign pressure) is a familiar element in economic debates.

It is but a small step to move from the above point regarding an international–national maze to a related recognition that the very notion of there being 'trade', 'investment', 'environment' (and competition?) policy fields is increasingly a misnomer. Trade policy used to be made in most Western countries by a tiny club of officials in part because it was international, had multi-partisan support, and because it was more readily compartmentalized since it dealt mainly with tariffs at the border.[41] But trade policy now is a partial misnomer precisely because, in the name of non-discrimination, and the elimination of 'barriers' (read: previously exclusive domestic policy), it enters virtually every policy realm that has domestic policy departments and interest-group constituencies.

In a similar way, investment policy, if defined as policies that affect capital flows, plant location, and production decisions, also suffers from bouts of misplaced nomenclature. For example, 'trade' agreements such as the Uruguay agreement, now include 'trade-related investment measures', or TRIMS, thus implying that there are investment policy realms even beyond trade-related investment measures as indeed there are. This world 'outside' currently defined TRIMS is in fact the sum of all remaining domestic or internal policies that affect investment choices.

Finally, consider the evolution of environmental policy. As long as environmental policy was focused on an 'after the fact', 'clean-up', or curative approach, it could be compartmentalized and even marginalized, as indeed it was for most of the period from the mid-1970s to the late-1980s in most Western governments.[42] But as soon as it seeks to be cast as 'sustainable development' policy, which means in essence being 'before the fact' and preventative, then the old environmental terminology also becomes a misnomer.[43]

None of the above is intended to argue that countries do not still have to put their policy wine in appropriate accountable departmental and ministerial bottles. Nor does it suggest that the custodians of these 'fields' do not defend their realms. What it does suggest is that each is knowingly dealing with, to switch metaphors, a definitional sieve that will be important in the battle over new or evolving 'international' institutions and policies. In short, it is hard both to debate policy and to craft policies if one's policy area comes to mean 'everything'. All policy fields have imperialistic tendencies, and this is especially true of the converging ones being considered in this chapter.

CONCLUSIONS

This chapter has examined two key political factors in the internationalization of competition policy: the political power of nation-states and business, and the positions of, and interplay among, international agencies. It has also examined the need to differentiate regimes from institutions at the international level and the need to appreciate differences and complementarities between how international relations specialists and domestic policy specialists examine policies and institutions.

The chapter shows that the internationalization of competition policy is affected by the traditional characteristics of international politics where issues and judgements of relative power among states (and recently trading blocs as well) are continuously present. Such political calculations may well intensify around the new competition–trade–investment policy nexus, for the additional reason that nationalist sentiment will create pressures on governments not to be seen ceding more (or remaining) powers of sovereignty such as those that involve competition policy. Domestic and international political calculus will also depend greatly on the precise nature of business coalitions that form around the new 'system frictions' sketched out in Chapters 2 and 9.

With respect to international agencies and inter-agency relations among states, the analysis shows differing possibilities. On the one hand, international agencies such as the OECD and UNCTAD have sensibly generated regimes and arrangements in recognition of the international aspects of competition policy. But there is also some sense already of competition among international agencies

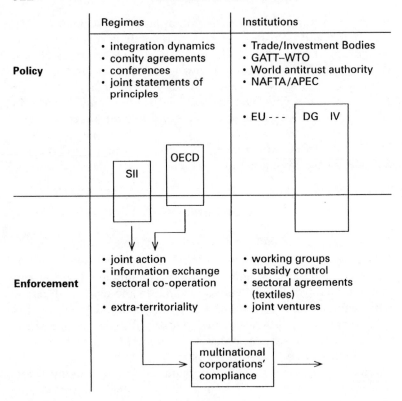

Fig. 10.1 Actual and potential internationalizing dimensions of competition policy

as to which will occupy the high ground or leading role in the new nexus of policies seeking new institutional forms. This competition also exists among agencies within national governments.

While both of the political variables are important for a full appreciation of the new internationalizing dynamics, the more specific conclusions that they suggest vary for each of the analytical quadrants sketched out in Figure 10.1. The quadrants on the left side of Figure 10.1, dealing with current law and case discretion, suggest that several kinds of regime-building activities are already sensibly present. These developments reflect practical experimentation and are appropriately characterized in the language of 'comity', 'positive comity', 'soft harmonization', harmonization, and exchange.

With respect to the upper right-hand quadrant, the analysis indicates that some institutionalization is occurring at the regional level, most specifically in the EU, but that the more radical (i.e. more institutionalized) notion of a supra-international antitrust authority is seen as being at best premature and at worst almost unthinkable. This is because discussions of such institutional forms are inevitably bound up in the full trade–investment–competition policy nexus that is now hovering around the WTO and the next GATT round.

All of the above suggests that the road to the possible 'GATT-ifying' of competition policy will be difficult and contentious. But before passing further concluding judgement on this question we need to look further and more comparatively at national competition policy institutions, and the constraints and opportunities they present, as competition policies are debated and as concerns about democratic accountability, representation, and transparency increase in the rest of the 1990s.

NOTES

1. See John S. Odell and Thomas D. Willet (eds.), *International Trade Policies: Gains from Exchange Between Economics and Political Science* (Ann Arbour: University of Michigan Press, 1993); Geraint Parry, 'The Interweaving of Foreign and Domestic Policy-Making', *Government and Opposition*, Special Issue on Globalization, 28/2 (spring 1993), 143–52; and Joseph A. Camilleri and Jim Falk, *The End of Sovereignty?* (Aldershot: Edward Elgar, 1992).
2. See David Held and Anthony McGrew, 'Globalization and the Liberal Democratic State', *Government and Opposition*, 28/2 (spring 1993), 261–88.
3. See Camilleri and Falk, *The End of Sovereignty?*, chs. 4 and 5; Susan Strange and John Stopford, *Rival States, Rival Firms: Competition for World Market Shares* (Cambridge: Cambridge University Press, 1991).
4. See John Francis, *The Politics of Regulation* (Oxford: Blackwell, 1993), ch. 2.
5. See Volker Rittberger (ed.), *Regime Theory and International Relations* (Oxford: The Clarendon Press, 1993); Oran R. Young, *International*

324   *G. Bruce Doern*

Cooperation (Ithaca, NY: Cornell University Press, 1989); and Stephen
D. Krasner (ed.), *International Regimes* (Ithaca, NY: Cornell University Press, 1983).
6. See Krasner, *International Regimes*, 1.
7. See Francis, *The Politics of Regulation*.
8. See e.g. James March and Johan Olsen, 'The New Institutionalism:
Organizational Factors in Political Life', *American Political Science
Review*, 78 (1984), 734–50.
9. See G. Bruce Doern, 'International Institutional and Policy Issues in
the Convergence of Investment, Trade and Environmental Policies',
in J. Benedickson (ed.), *Investment and Environment* (Toronto: C. D.
Howe Institute, 1994); and Kym Anderson and R. Blackhurst (eds.),
The Greening of World Trade Issues (London: Harvester Wheatsheaf,
1992).
10. See Stephen Gill and David Law, *The Global Political Economy*
(Baltimore: Johns Hopkins University Press, 1988); and Robert Walters
and David Blake, *The Politics of Global Economic Relations* (Engle-
wood Cliffs, NJ: Prentice-Hall, 1992).
11. See Odell and Willet, *International Trade Policies*.
12. See Robert Gilpin, *The Political Economy of International Relations*
(Princeton: Princeton University Press, 1987); and Edward D. Mans-
field, 'Effects of International Politics on Regionalism in International
Trade', in Kym Anderson and Richard Blackhurst (eds.), *Regional
Integration and the Global Trading System* (London: Harvester
Wheatsheaf, 1993), 199–217.
13. See e.g. Jan-Erik Lane and Svante Ersson, *Comparative Political
Economy* (London: Pinter, 1990); Stephen Wilks and Maurice Wright
(eds.), *Comparative Government–Industry Relations* (Oxford: The
Clarendon Press, 1987); and Charles Lindblom, *Democracy and the
Market System* (Oslo: Norwegian University Press, 1988).
14. See Camilleri and Falk, *The End of Sovereignty?*; Young, *International Cooperation*; and Krasner, *International Regimes*.
15. See J. T. Mathews, 'Redefining Security', *Foreign Affairs*, 68 (spring
1989).
16. See S. Anwar, 'The Impact of the Structural Impediments Initiative on
US–Japan Trade', *World Competition Law and Economics Review*,
16/2 (Dec. 1992), 53–66; and Robert Anderson, 'Competition Policy
Aspects of the US–Japan Structural Impediments Initiative: Implications For Canada', *Canadian Competition Policy Record*, 12/2 (June
1991), 39–49.
17. As Quoted in *The Independent*, 19 Feb. 1994, 33.
18. See *International Herald Tribune*, 22 Feb. 1994, 6.
19. See 'Interview: Anne K. Bingaman', *Antitrust* (fall 1993), 8–12; Charles
S. Starks, 'Internation Antitrust: Looking Ahead', Remarks before the

Antitrust and International Sections of the American Bar Association, New York, 9 Aug. 1993; and United States, *Economic Report of the President* (Washington, DC US Government Printing Office, 1994), 239–40.

20. See Dieter Wolf, 'Statement on German International Competition Policy', Presented to OECD Competition Law and Policy Committee, 3 Dec. 1992, 3.
21. See Government of Australia, *National Competition Policy: Report of the Independent Committee of Inquiry* (Canberra, 1993), and Derek Ireland, *Interactions Between Competition and Trade Policies: Challenges and Opportunities* (Ottawa: Bureau of Competition Policy, 1992).
22. For analyses of business interests in trade policies, see G. Bruce Doern and Brian Tomlin, *Faith and Fear: The Free Trade Story* (Toronto: Stoddart, 1991); I. M. Destler, *American Trade Politics: System Under Stress* (Washington, DC: Institute for International Economics, 1986); and Helen Milner, *Resisting Protectionism: Global Industries and the Politics of International Trade* (Princeton: Princeton University Press, 1988).
23. See Kym Anderson and Richard Blackhurst (eds.), *Regional Integration and the Global Trading System* (London: Harvester Wheatsheaf, 1993).
24. See Doern, 'International Institutional and Policy Issues'; *Green Diplomacy* (Toronto: C. D. Howe Institute, 1993).
25. See Stephen Wilks, *The Revival of Japanese Competition Policy and its Importance for EU–Japan relations* (London: Royal Institute for International Affairs, 1994).
26. See Derek Ireland, Zulfi Sadeque, and Don Partridge, 'Globalization, The Canadian Competition Act, and the Future Policy Agenda', Paper prepared for Conference on Trade, Investment and Competition Policies: Conflict or Convergence?, Ottawa, Centre for Trade Policy, May 1993; and Derek Ireland, *Interactions Between Competition and Trade Policies: Challenges and Opportunities* (Ottawa: Bureau of Competition Policy, 1992).
27. See United Nations Conference on Trade and Development, *The Set of Multilaterally Agreed Equitable Principles and Rules for the Control of Restrictive Business Practices* (Geneva: United Nations, 1981).
28. Ibid. 8–9.
29. See Alexis Jacquemin, 'The International Dimension of European Competition Policy', *Journal of Common Market Studies*, 31/1 (Mar. 1993), 99. See also Sir Leon Brittan, 'Competition Policy and International Relations', Address to Centre for European Policy Studies, 17 Mar. 1992; and C. D. Ehlermann, 'The International Dimension of Competition Policy', paper presented to Japan–EC Competition Seminar, Tokyo, 4 Nov. 1993.

326 G. Bruce Doern

30. See OECD, *Competition Law Enforcement* (Paris: OECD, 1983); OECD, *Competition Policy and International Trade: OECD Instruments of Cooperation* (Paris: OECD, 1987); OECD, *Competition and Economic Development* (Paris: OECD, 1991).
31. See OECD, *Twenty-Five Years of Competition Policy: Achievements and Challenges* (Paris: OECD, 1987).
32. Sylvia Ostry, 'Globalization, Domestic Policies and the Need For Harmonization', Paper presented to Workshop on Competition Policy in a Global Economy, University of California, Jan. 1993, 1.
33. See Richard Whish and Diane Wood, *Merger Cases in the Real World: A Study of Control Procedures* (Paris: OECD, 1994).
34. See Government of Australia, *National Competition Policy: Report of the Independent Committee of Inquiry* (Canberra, 1993).
35. See International Antitrust Code Working Group, *Draft International Antitrust Code* (Munich: July 1993).
36. See F. M. Schever, *Competition Policies for an Integrated World Economy* (Washington, DC: the Brookings Institution, 1994).
37. See Bruce Doern, 'International and Policy Issues in the Convergence of Investment, Trade and Environmental Policies'.
38. See Alan Oakley, *The Challenge of Free Trade* (London: Harvester Wheatsheaf, 1990), and Michael M. Hart and Debra P. Steger (eds.), *In Whose Interest: Due Process and Transparency in International Trade* (Ottawa: Centre for Trade Policy and Law, 1992).
39. See Doern, *Green Diplomacy*; and Andrew Hurrell and Benedict Kingsbury (eds.), *The International Politics of the Environment* (Oxford: The Clarendon Press, 1992).
40. See Camilleri and Falk, *The End of Sovereignty*.
41. See G. Bruce Doern and Brian Tomlin, *Faith and Fear*.
42. See G. Bruce Doern and Tom Conway, *The Greening of Canada: Federal Institutions and Decisions* (Toronto: University of Toronto Press, 1994), and Albert Weale, *The New Politics of Pollution* (Manchester: Manchester University Press, 1992).
43. See Michael Jacobs, *The Green Economy* (London: Pluto Press, 1991); and G. Bruce Doern, 'From Sectoral to Macro Green Governance: The Canadian Department of the Environment as an Aspiring Central Agency', *Governance*, 6/2 (Apr. 1993), 172–93.

11

Conclusions: International Convergence and National Contrasts

G. BRUCE DOERN AND STEPHEN WILKS

The purpose of this book has been to produce a comparative political and institutional examination of national competition policies and institutions, a focus given insufficient attention in the dominant legal and economic literature on this important area of economic policy. The main components of the analysis have now been completed. In Chapter 1, we made the general case for a political and institutional focus, including its inevitable links to globalized markets and to the need for comparative study. In Chapter 2, we looked at boundary issues, levels of analysis, and problems of analysing competition policy in comparison with other policy fields studied by political scientists. Chapters 3 to 8 then presented detailed jurisdictional analyses which mainly covered macro- and meso-levels of analysis, though with some elements of the micro-politics of implementation as well. Our focus in these chapters became much more institutional not only with respect to the core competition agencies involved in each jurisdiction but also with respect to institutions such as business. In Chapters 9 and 10, our attention shifted to the growing international elements of competition policy, both in substantive economic terms in its links with trade policy and with regard to two of the main political factors contributing to the internationalization of competition policy: the political power of states and business, and the role of international organizations.

In this chapter, we present conclusions on the analysis as a whole. To this end, the chapter is organized into four sections. In the first two sections we examine two political variables which are part of the pressures for institutional change but which are also simultaneously international and domestic in content. They are also inherently uncertain and speculative, in part because they are entwined with a nexus of trade and investment policy realms. These variables are: tensions among competition policy ideas; and democratic political concerns and values regarding accountability, representation, and transparency. The third section then offers concluding observations on international institutional reform options at both the multilateral and regional levels of global capitalism. The probability of these reforms producing a major transformation of international competition policy from a regime-based system to a more institutionalized one is then related to our final, overall comparative assessment of competition policy institutions in the six jurisdictions examined.

COMPETITION POLICY IDEAS AND TENSIONS

With the new-found attention given to competition policy and its close nexus with trade, industrial, investment, and other policies, the mid- to late 1990s ideas regarding competition policy have moved beyond those of the 1980s. The ideas now in dispute are occurring within a strong consensus that competitive market systems are superior to any contending approach. But despite this fact, there is considerable dispute about what competition policy is or ought to be.

The core intellectual debate about competition policy ideas is still largely among economists but, as we see in the discussion below, law, business administration, and other disciplines are also engaged. The debate is engaged at several related levels. Here we consider recently emergent questions of 'system frictions'; the actual versus the theoretical potential for practising 'managed trade' or neo-industrial policies; and the prospects for viable policy towards the strategic alliances and other modes of co-operation which have begun to develop among firms and across countries, especially in the realm of R&D or innovation.

System friction

System friction, as Sylvia Ostry argued in 1990, is much broader than protectionism.[1] The term 'underlined that there were several different market models, the differences stemming from both historical and cultural legacies as well as divergence in a range of domestic policies'.[2] These system differences influenced the international competitiveness of a firm, which was essentially the product of an 'interaction between the firm's own capabilities and the broad institutional context of its home country'.[3] These frictions had to be reduced through harmonization of those policies that affected a firm's innovative capability. Ostry went on to argue that a key area of focus would have to be on the issue of 'effective market access', a concept which she acknowledged to be 'soft and even slippery' and which had, at its core, the blurred boundaries of competition, trade, investment, and 'high tech industrial policy'. As an experienced economist and public servant, Ostry is careful to cast her arguments in the context of political realities among 'the Triad' of trading blocs, the EU, North America, and Japan–Pacific.

In stressing system friction Ostry has emphasized the practical manifestations of contrasting national institutions. It is clear that these institutions present firms with radically different mixes of pressures and opportunities (consider, for instance, the variations in systems of industrial relations[4]). But these institutions also embody differing national conceptions—sets of ideas—about how much competition is desirable, what modes of competition are acceptable, and the societally sanctioned trade-offs between competition and co-operation. It is evident from our country chapters that, although economic theory offers universal ideas about how economies work, there are strong national variations. The chapters on Japan and the United States present the contrast in stark terms and emphasize the fact that conflicts over competition policies are magnified by incompatible ideas about how systems should operate. The trade policy lierature is replete with examples of negotiators 'talking past each other'.[5] Something similar happens in the competition policy field, in ways whose foundations are increasingly being analysed through studies of 'comparative capitalism'. Albert's contrasts between Anglo-Saxon, Rhineland, and East Asian forms of capitalism have profound implications for attempts to harmonize competition policies.[6]

Managed trade

Other areas of the debate among economists are often cast in the more confined but similar debate about managed or strategic trade policy. Begun by authors such as Brander and Spencer, and Krugman, but also heavily criticized by mainline classical economists, this debate has focused for the last decade on whether countries could obtain welfare gains by subsidizing their producers in the development of new technology products launched for export in situations of imperfect competition where monopoly rents could be earned.[7] Krugman pointed out situations where this could happen, namely where there exist static scale economies involving declining marginal cost, opportunities to apply R&D to reduce costs, and the presence of learning-curve economies.[8]

The criticisms of this theory centre on the exact presence of these conditions, the assumptions it makes about the strategies and expectations of firms, and the levels of detailed knowledge that governments would have to possess, and what is more, act precisely on.[9] These criticisms, moreover, occurred in a period when 'industrial policy' was in political disrepute, especially in the Anglo-American democracies ruled by neo-conservative governments. None the less the managed-trade thesis became a part of the basis on which trade in high-technolgy industries, expecially by the Japanese, came to be partially analysed.[10]

It is at this point that it is important to stress how the debate about competition, competition policy, and competitiveness (which are clearly not all the same thing) moves out of the strict realm of economists and engages other disciplines, including business-school-based theorists and authors who look less at markets defined in neo-classical terms, and more at the nature of firms, the innovation process, and high technology.[11] These also include some authors who have reached the status of popular gurus because they write in such a way as to attract the attention of politicians and the media.

Authors such as Porter, Thurow, and Reich are in the latter class and thus are often seen (but also envied?) by economists almost as ex-economists or 'never were' economists whose work is seen as less rigorous, but who articulate concepts that strike a political resonance.[12] Thus Porter's 'diamond', including his stout defence of the importance of effective competition policy, drew politically effective attention to 'competitiveness' issues in ways that traditional economists' 'growth theory' often could not. Similarly, Thurow's *Head to Head* analogy of triad trading-bloc battles and Reich's 'who is us' queries about who really owns a nation's firms found a timely audience among political leaders and the media.

Also contained within this non-mainstream economics literature are other views of competition which are, in essence, more Schumpeterian in nature. This is because they deal with the underlying nature of innovation and change in markets, and hence with larger dynamic rather than static notions of efficiency. Some examples of this work are instructive regarding the conflicts of ideas about the nature of competition.

Laura Tyson's book for the otherwise mainstream Institute for International Economics is provocatively titled *Who's Bashing Whom?*.[13] Now a key Clinton adviser in her capacity as Chair of the Council of Economic Advisers, Tyson makes the case for what she calls, in agreement with Krugman, a 'cautious activism' in trade policy.[14] This is a position which she argues is '*not* synonymous with protectionism'. She argues that the several case studies in her book confirm the overall view that 'technology-intensive industries violate the assumptions of free trade theory and the static concepts that are the traditional basis for US trade policy. In such industries, costs fall and product quality improves as the scale of production increases, the returns to technological advance create beneficial spillovers for other economic activities, and barriers to entry generate market structures rife with first-mover advantages and strategic behaviour. A nation's competitive position in industries with these characteristics is less a function of its national factor endowments and more a function of strategic interactions between its firms and government and between them and the firms and governments of other nations.'[15] Krugman has pointedly distanced himself from Tyson and related arguments of this kind, regarding such quasi-popularized views as a 'dangerous obsession'.[16]

The managed-trade debate illustrates how reappraisals of competition processes, undertaken by economists concerned with the impact of technology on competitiveness, feed through into ideas about competition. The managed-trade debate sends mixed messages about the desirability of intense domestic competition and about technological collaboration. More particularly, it generates scepticism about allowing overseas competitors free access to the home market. This would increase competition, which might be regarded as desirable under a neo-classical approach, but is regarded as highly undesirable from a managed-trade perspective. How should competition policy-makers treat such conflicting prescriptions?

Co-operation or competition

Another even broader reinterpretation of the nature of competition is advanced by authors such as Jorde and Teece.[17] They maintain that 'new intellectual arguments are necessary to understand how competition takes place in many industries today'.[18] In work focusing on the role of economic thinking in antitrust analysis, Jorde and Teece argue that 'legal scholarship and judicial action [in the US] have been slow to recognize the primary importance of innovation to the competitive process'.[19] In particular, mainstream law and economics have failed to appreciate the role of co-operation among many firms and institutions in the overall innovation process, as well as the organizational requirements of innovation (for earlier comment on the competing economic views see Chapter 1).

In a similar vein, Michael Best speaks simply of the need to see the emergence of a 'new competition' centred much more on what he refers to as a Schumpeterian 'entrepreneurial firm' which, while market based and continuously sensitive to improvement in methods, products, and processes, is inherently a more flexible, social, and co-operative entity.[20] His analysis of co-ordinating mechanisms, from Japanese production to small Italian firms and regional co-operative ventures, points to something other than Fordite industrial firms that have dominated the last seventy or so years of capitalist competition and industrial structure.[21]

It is not difficult to see why competition policy ideas struggle for a new appropriate language. How does one reconcile new with old competition, and dynamic with static competition? How does one promote managed or strategic trade with cautious defensiveness, and yet not call it the previously debunked protectionist 'industrial' policy? How can Porter-like 'competitiveness' policy be distinguished in political rhetoric and practical actions from the narrower notions of traditional competition policy?

Some of this struggle, and hence its politics, is also found in the more particular debates among economists about strategic alliances among firms, and policies toward co-operation in research and development. The key question is whether such alliances are a threat to competition or a key manifestation of its socio-economic nature. Khemani and Waverman's analysis of strategic alliances as a competition policy issue shows the difficulties.[22] Before one even gets to assessing their competitive or anti-competitive effects, there are real problems of definition and information. In definitional terms, the problem is one of knowing which 'sub-set of . . . interfirm agreements are meant by "strategic" alliances?'. Khemani and Waverman settle on a definition which sees strategic alliances as 'forms of inter-firm agreements or arrangements between independent firms which involve knowledge production or sharing activities aimed at developing products or processes and forms of production. In this regard, the alliance may entail exchange of R&D and or transfer of various information.'[23] Two implications flow from this definition. One is that joint ventures are a subset of such alliances. The second is that they are not confined to some arbitrarily defined stage of 'pre-competitive R&D' but rather involve downstream production and marketing. This is a vital point because, to the extent that some OECD countries still admit that they practice industrial policy, it is precisely this R&D realm that provides a rationale.

The literature on investment policy suggests that such alliances are growing faster than mergers but that it is difficult to know not only because of definitional issues but also because they do not need to be announced or registered.[24] Competition policy authorities do not single out these alliances as they do with mergers. Some do have procedures for joint ventures and others have singled out exemptions for R&D agreements, even though many experts would agree that R&D activity cannot be separated from production processes.

The key economic puzzle, and the reason for case by case approaches, is identifying what kind of spillovers are occuring from alliance activity.[25] On the one hand, if alliances result in eliminating the socially wasteful duplication of efforts, then dynamic efficiency gains may occur and competition can be enhanced. On the other hand, especially if alliances are horizontal in nature, competition may be reduced by leading firms through forms of collusion or market power. The issue of R&D co-operative agreements is a variant of the above discussion.[26] There is considerable empirical dispute as to the actual causal relationship between inter-firm co-operation and technological innovation. Thus everything from simple R&D agreements to complex Japanese *keiretsu* are bound up in dispute at both conceptual and empirical levels.[27]

A recent study by economists Graham and Richardson has

characterized the new overall competitition–trade policy puzzles as being characterized by 'polymorphous economics' (a political scientist would simply call this 'politics').[28] This term not only meant that there was conflict in economic ideas about competition but also, as Graham and Richardson put it, that 'there is a perceptions–analysis' gap that may have important implications for policy. They observe that 'some of these practices—especially vertical agreements and deference to structures and arrangements aimed at facilitating innovation—are not clearly (*per se*) anticompetitive or "unfair", at least not in any presumptive way. Yet they are perceived to be inequitable.'[29]

It cannot be said that the ideas traced above are politically or economically in dispute only in an international context. Dispute on some of these areas is also domestic. But equally, significant international elements are present, particularly in high-technology, managed-trade policies where countries or trading blocs vie for advantage and supremacy.

The key concluding point about this brief survey of ideas about competition policy is that ideas are indeed in dispute. Hence they have political consequences and create political openings. But, equally, it must be stressed that these disputes are still largely within, not outside, the overall liberal economic paradigm.[30]

ACCOUNTABILITY, REPRESENTATION, AND TRANSPARENCY

The further political variable that is influencing the institutional reform debate, internationally and within countries, centres on the linked democratic issues of accountability, representation on or before decision-making bodies, and overall transparency and openness.[31] While there are clearly variations among countries regarding the exact meaning of each of these elements, they do raise a set of political concerns and values regarding potential new institutional forms. *Accountability* refers to the arrangements for reporting to, and receiving political direction from, political authorities. More broadly, accountability also relates to electorates and pluralist interests, especially consumers. The role of the courts and modes of legal redress are also vital in the overall system of accountability. *Representation* involves the issue of which groups (big and small business, consumers, labour) have representation either on the competition body itself or in its processes and appeal mechanisms. *Transparency* involves openness as to decision-making and the exercise of discretion. It is a vital ingredient in systems of accountability, and important in ensuring acceptance and compliance. It does, however, involve a partial collision between transparency and the vexing issue of confidential commercial information.

For the purposes of this quite conjectural part of our conclusions, the key puzzle is to try to project what might happen as current international competition policy arrangements evolve towards full-fledged international or regional institutions. This, in turn, requires some basic comparisons with international trade, investment, and environment institutions. In the case of trade and investment, there is a very direct economic link for reasons already examined. The environment nexus is added, partly because there are also economic links, but more particularly because it is our judgement that in the next international trade round environmental interests and processes will not be easily separated from the politics of establishing or strengthening integrated institutions. Indeed, among the first steps taken by the new World Trade Organization was the expression of its environmental responsibilities in the form of a senior Trade and Environment Committee created at the beginning of 1995.

With respect to a head-to-head 'competition versus trade' institutional comparison, several points are central. First, trade policy is primarily about controlling the behaviour of governments whereas competition policy is largely about regulating the behaviour of firms and businesses. Only in the case of state aid in the EU's DG IV mandate, or in the case of state-run enterprises, do competition institutions deal with the anti-competitive sins of governments. Second, as a logical result of the first point, trade policy has less of an enforceable legal base than competition policy. Hence both trade and competition policy specialists tend to agree that trade policy is decided through more political processes than through legal processes.[32] In short, trade policy is more political and competition policy is considerably de-politicized. Third, as Geza Feketekuty, the head of the OECD's Trade Committee, argues, 'trade policy has to be based on the political consent of those who lose as well as those who gain from the expansion of trade',[33] and hence greater weight is given to 'producer interests'. But competition policy 'tends to give greater weight to consumer interests than trade policy'[34]. The latter point is amply brought out in several recent studies of anti-dumping policy which conclude that such systems exist to protect competitors rather than to support the dynamics of competition.[35]

Each of the above points are broadly true, but with regard to the issue of the degree of politicization, we would argue that competition policy is in some ways simply politicized 'differently' rather than 'less' than trade policy. The evidence for this is found in the accountability–representation–transparency variable. First, it must be said that both trade and competition policy systems function under the stated or unstated assumption that markets (international and national) broadly function well and that policy and institutional systems are intended to deal with abuses that exist at the edges of normal behaviour. Second, competition policy is political often not because of which interests it includes, but those it excludes. Competition statutes tip their symbolic hats to small business as a political interest, but vary widely as to whether small business is in fact represented in its deliberations. Consumer interests are presumably central to competition law but, as always, it is difficult to know who or what processes supply the concrete mechanisms of such interest representation. Exempt industrial sectors still abound in competition legislation, a significant testimony to a politicized process at the time when legislation is being forged.

With respect to accountability, competition authorities often point with pride to the fact that ministers cannot interfere with cases. One can understand such views. But in the same breath, they often curiously view this as non-political, when in fact the exercise of discretion by case officers or by quasi-ministerial unelected heads of the agency is indeed political in the sense that they exercise administrative power and decide upon winners and losers. Similarly, when dealing with transparency, competition policy reveals decidedly mixed tendencies. Administration is typically centralized and, while agencies are often quite open with respect to developing policy guidelines, they can be very closed when it comes to revealing how comfort letters and confidential guidance mechanisms work and are decided.[36]

In all of the above issues, it is also important to stress the presence of interests other than business and the state, or even consumers. The political interests also include knowledge professions such as lawyers and economists who are the articulators of important procedural and analytical values but who are also the beneficiaries of competition enforcement and related regulatory activities. The chief example of this set of political interests resides in the United States with its massive trade and competition bar, but it clearly has its equivalents in other Western countries as well.

INTERNATIONAL REGIME AND INSTITUTIONAL REFORM ALTERNATIVES

From the vantage point of the mid-1990s, and in the light of the above tensions in ideas and concerns about accountability, what can be said about the actual options for international institutional reform? For the purposes of final, and necessarily speculative, commentary, two institutional arenas of reform are examined: multilateral; and regional (EU and North America). In each case our concern is with overall political and institutional constraints and issues.

As we look at this set of reform possibilities, it is essential to remind ourselves what it means to analyse institutions as political entities. Institutions are bundles of laws, agencies, values, and traditions, as well as relationships between political-economic stakeholders and citizens. In the realm of international institutions, what is at stake is not only national interests but also national sets of institutions which have policy, bureaucratic, and political concerns of their own to defend. Thus, as stressed in Chapter 10, one cannot speak of national governments as a single, unitary actor.

If one is to change the set of internationally involved institutions immersed in the merging realm of competition–trade–investment–industrial policies, then the first step at the institutional level within a country is to enumerate the potential institutions involved. For example, a minimum list for the USA or Canada would involve at least ten departments and regulators.

A further element of any international or domestic institutional redesign is that each of the existing policy and institutional mixes must be understood in terms of exactly what kinds of behaviours (by private and public actors) each is intended to change or produce.

For example, competition law may be adequate to replace some aspects of dumping law but not others. Some policies may emphasize price controls, cartel abuses, or be more concerned with minimizing compliance costs. All policy and institutional mixes are intended to induce people to 'behave' in desired ways but the behaviours are numerous.

The set of reform options runs from a single international competition agency, to modest co-operation based on a series of bilateral agreements. We already, of course, have an example of international co-ordination in the case of the European competition rules, but we can explore further possibilities at both the global and the regional levels.

Multilateral regimes and institutional reform

Multilateral arena changes could involve three possible scenarios: harmonization and mutual learning; a more institutionalized OECD-led process; and a world antitrust authority.[37] Harmonization and mutual adaptation would be the changes closest to the *status quo*. They would involve the separate gradual improvement and adaptation of each of the main functional areas of current competition law (criminal, mergers, abuse of dominant position; marketing practices, etc.).

A more institutionalized OECD-led option is one which could potentially go beyond its current information exchange and facilitative role. It could be endowed with some of the 'lead jurisdiction determining' modes of which Trebilcock spoke in Chapter 9 regarding merger cases, or it could issue reports on the extent to which countries adhere to the standards of a sample antitrust code. The difficulty here is the OECD itself. It is under pressure to become something other than the rich countries' economic research agency. Not only is it almost obliged to enlarge its membership to Eastern European countries, but it is also the object of political battles for control of its agenda between the USA and the EU, a process brought out into the open by the battle to choose a new head of the OECD in 1994. Moreover, as Chapter 10 showed, there are also contests for policy ideas and supremacy among the various trade, competition, and technology directorates of the OECD.

Moreover, the larger the OECD becomes, the more tensions will occur between developed and developing countries, and hence many of the conflicts telegraphed by the early 1970s UNCTAD experience are likely to surface in a 1990s context. In addition, the larger the OECD becomes, the more it would become an unwieldy, almost UN-like agency, stretched to its accommodative limits.

As for the supranational competition-led agency, this is probably, as Chapter 10 showed, a non-starter. The limited chances of this option are not only due to the size of the step that must be taken or contemplated. It is also because there are some inherent limits in the symbolic and real politics of sovereignty in all the key countries. The cummulative political effects of EU integration, and the FTA and NAFTA, however much they may be sold as pooled sovereignty, or as involving no losses of sovereignty, augur against further hasty reform. Politicians can only be seen ceding so much sovereignty in any given period, even when they are convinced that there are gains in national policy capacity from new international arrangements.

Indeed, it must be recognized that a kind of paradox exists between the general issues of trade–competition–investment policy convergence and the politics it produces. The convergence comes from a policy desire to make competition and liberalized markets the norm both between and within national markets. This means depoliticizing markets at the micro-level. But the more that this occurs, the more the new macro or supranational institutions have to be repoliticized in new replacement ways through proper representation, opportunities to participate, and the time to do both. If the three overlapping policy areas are depoliticized or eliminated, then the new integrated one has to meet an even more difficult macro-political test as to its legitimacy, procedures, and ways of accommodating political interests.

On this latter point we also draw attention to environmental policy matters. As the above trade–competition–investment policy nexus is dealt with in and around the next GATT–WTO round, environmental values and interests will also be present. The history of domestic environmental policy in all Western countries shows that environmental interest groups bring to the political arena a high level of tenacity and an insistence that decision processes be more transparent and involve a broad set of interest groups.[38] This is already apparent at the international level not

only in recent protocol decision-making situations but also in the
Rio Summit process itself.[39] The pressures to open the process are
also inherent because of very deep North–South divisions. Thus
there is little doubt that there will be intense pressure to broaden
the representation of interests in any overall merged institution
that also includes environmental policy criteria.

Regional institutional reform

The second arena of reform would seek a closer regional harmonization of all of the above trade and competition policy areas,
including some movement towards integrating institutions, for
example, by eliminating anti-dumping law and replacing it with
changes to competition or antitrust laws and practices. The EU
and NAFTA are the obvious focal points in this regard.

In the case of the European Union, an integrated institution in
the form of DG IV already exists and dumping laws no longer
operate among EU member states. However, as Chapters 6, 7, and
8 have shown, there are pressures for further EU institutional
reform.[40] The most radical alternative on the EU competition policy
reform agenda would be to turn DG IV into an independent agency.
This is the German proposal but it also has supporters in Spain
and the UK. The new agency would embrace the merger task force
and the article 85/86 enforcement divisions of DG IV, but all
legislative responsibility and development of policy would remain
with a Competition Commissioner and a rump DG IV. The resulting European Cartel Office (ECO) would apply the law strictly
and be concerned only with the economic impact of its actions.
Other public-interest criteria would be applied by the Commission
when it decided whether or not to support ECO decisions. According to its advocates, this separation of functions would address
issues related to current problems of consistency, politicization,
and transparency.

Other reform ideas are also on the EU agenda, including delegation to national authorities, greater integration with public-interest
criteria, and increased staffing in DG IV to overcome case back-
logs. As always, the mere opening up of the discussion for reform
creates severe political problems about the capacity to control the
agenda, all the more so because the EU membership has been

enlarged to fifteen with further new members in prospect and new presidential leadership in the shape of Jacques Santer.

With respect to North America in the wake of NAFTA, institutional reform debates are necessarily one step behind the EU agenda. This is because no equivalent step for dealing with anti-dumping and state aids has been taken. On the other hand, quite direct US–Canada co-operation does occur. As Chapter 9 showed, one of these instruments of co-operation is the 1984 bilateral Memorandum of Understanding between the Canadian and the United States competition policy authorities. Canada–US contacts and consultations on competition policy matters have since evolved into a series of regular meetings and much day-to-day professional interaction. Competition enforcement has also been facilitated in criminal matters by a Mutual Legal Assistance Treaty which allows action when the laws of only one country have been violated. Thus the special compulsory powers available within one country (such as search warrants) can be executed within the territory of the other.

A further specific impetus for more institutionalized competition policy relations came in the processes of negotiating the FTA in 1986–7 and the NAFTA in 1992. In the FTA negotiations, Canada pressed the US for overall changes in trade remedy laws (anti-dumping and subsidies) which envisaged a partial competition policy replacement of anti-dumping regimes. This pressure got nowhere. In the NAFTA negotiations which led to chapter 15 provisions calling for further discussions on competition law practices, Canada failed to secure reform. A competition chapter was put into NAFTA mainly as a symbolic measure to keep the pressure on the Americans who in almost all respects consider their full arsenal of trade remedy laws and competition laws as virtually sacrosanct.[41]

All of the above points suggest that when political criteria are applied to North American regional institutional reform options, the first best, second best, and third best choices suggested by Boddez and Trebilcock in their analysis of NAFTA trade and competition policy linkages would probably be reversed.[42] For Boddez and Trebilcock the best option is a supranational competition agency. The second best option is quite rapid harmonization of laws and practices within and among existing national authorities. The third best option is *ad hoc* change. Boddez and Trebilcock acknowledge the reverse ranking to some extent, but are unprepared to give it much positive credence because their approach is to treat political incursions as always being 'barriers'. For many politicians and governments, not to mention industrial and other interests, such institutional mixes are elements in the calculus of political acceptability and pluralist democracy.

According to this alternative set of criteria, the best and most likely alternative regionally is to reform each of the sets of competition trade and industrial policy institutions in each country and among member countries carefully and gradually, recognizing their new convergence, but also recognizing the many discrete behaviours involved. Some of this kind of reform activity is already underway.

Most models of a moderate regional institutional reform package involve a focus on replacing anti-dumping law with competition laws and institutions. While full harmonization of this part of the reform package seems to be implied, it is not clear that it has to be totally harmonized. For example, Canada–US harmonization need not have to include Canada adopting the right of private action in a new harmonized regime. But there may have to be more parallel rules of discovery to follow cases and obtain evidence in the other country. Even this moderate model of reform seems remote in the medium term because there appears to be no constituency in the United States, and probably not in Canada either, for disarming on the anti-dumping front without satisfaction being achieved simultaneously on the very difficult subsidies front.

CROSS-NATIONAL COMPARISONS OF COMPETITION POLICY

The interested student of comparative competition policy will search long and hard to find any systematic comparison of policy processes, institutions, and effectiveness. The search for an analytic institutional comparison is likely to be fruitless. There are available some excellent partial comparisons,[43] some good national treatments which do not attempt an explicit comparison,[44] and some comparisons by economists that whet the appetite but do not seize the comparative opportunity.[45] There is, of course, a wealth of descriptive material, such as that provided by the OECD,[46] and some outstanding legal texts,[47] but the comparative nettle has seemed hard to grasp.

The chapters presented above provide an analysis of six jurisdictions, and hence open up the opportunity for comparative analysis. As noted by Doern in Chapter 2, this volume constitutes the first attempt at competition policy comparison and, as also reviewed by Doern, it presents the ubiquitous problems of public policy comparison. Should we analyse the substance of policy or the function that it performs within society? Is policy an output or is it an independant variable which actually determines political processes?[48] Can one offer meaningful comparisons of countries as culturally diverse as Canada, Germany, and Japan? How much context can be allowed, are policies comprehensible when isolated to the degree undertaken here? Some of these points can be accommodated within the following discussion, but they are sufficiently complex to demand an extensive treatment. In the space available it is more productive to concentrate on mid-range comparison of such national variations as the relative independence of the national agencies; the intensity of enforcement; the relative balance between law and economics; the variations in legal doctrines; and the relative legitimacy and compliance levels of the various jurisdictions. Such comparison should yield important insights. For academics it serves to prepare the ground for future comparative study; for practitioners the comparison serves to highlight the many vexing incompatibilities between institutions and processes which place such difficulties in the path of the current efforts towards policy convergence.

Moving from the general to the specific, the first comparative feature, which also provides a context, is the variable salience of competition policy between the six political economies. In the United States competition policy has been prominent in political discourse, and in the mix of industrial policies, since the 1880s. Scherer notes 'that antitrust legislation was a child of the prairie frontier',[49] (also in Canada and Australia), but it was not until the post-war era that it became significant elsewhere. It entered into the crucial debate on the German social market economy in the 1950s;[50] into the British debate on monopoly and concentration in the 1960s; into Japanese industrial policy reappraisals in the 1970s; and into European economic integration in the 1980s. Doern notes that in Canada competition policy was insignificant until the mid-1980s (see Chapter 4), but was then brought into economic policy-making for reasons linked to economic efficiency.

There is a greater contemporary interest in competition policy in all these economies; an interest which is, of course, shared by other important states such as France and Italy, both of whom have also embarked on programmes of competition policy reform.[51] As noted in Chapter 1, that interest is provoked by liberalization, but is fuelled by a widespread concern to address issues of economic efficiency and to promote markets which employ competition to enhance efficiency. The popular and influential work of Porter simply underlines this concern. He observes that 'a strong antitrust policy . . . is essential to the rate of upgrading in an economy'.[52] This concern with competition as the prerequisite for efficiency is contentious, and there is an alternative school which stresses the benefits of economic co-operation (see above and Chapter 2). Neither, of course, was efficiency the original motive for the introduction of competition policy in any of these settings. It is striking that, while vigorous enforcement of competition policy is advocated for efficiency reasons, the creation of competition policies was in each case due to political rather than economic motives. Thus, in each of the six cases, competition policy was introduced for different political reasons, and serves a distinctive role within each society.

In Chapter 3 Peters points out that American antitrust was a reaction to 'robber-baron capitalism', and in the United States antitrust has always had a populist, moral, and evangelical tone which, while accepting the virtues of market capitalism, is all too aware of the excesses of greed and exploitation which an unregulated market can permit. This populism has never been a significant factor in Canada, argues Doern (see Chapter 4), although shared suspicion of United States capitalists perhaps gave an equivalent impetus to trade policy. Neither has populism been a significant factor in Britain or Japan, although this may be changing. In Britain there are indeed strong anxieties about concentration of economic power, and the need to sustain democracy, but these have traditionally been channelled through the Labour Party and have given rise to policies of nationalization, industrial planning, and a strengthened labour movement. As the 'new' Labour Party takes on a social democratic ideology, and as the excesses of privatized companies attract increased criticism, so the pressure to control through competition legislation is likely to increase. British competition policy has thus been pragmatic and moderate, responding to consumer pressures and to the rather inconsistent voices of industry pressing for workable rules to discipline the more unscrupulous opportunists within the market.

In Japan competition policy was, of course, imposed by the United States, but it has taken on an important, quasi-constitutional status as a symbol of the workings of the market system, and as a last line of defence against excessive economic concentration. In Germany too, it has a quasi-constitutional standing although, in this case, the Cartel Law reflects a more genuinely indigenous debate about the importance of liberalism, and of government framework regulation in creating the successful compromise of the social market economy. It could also be suggested that competition policy has a quasi-constitutional significance within the European Union. It acts as a vital guarantor of the single market, and is an economic bulwark for a community that has put ecomomics first. The origins of the European competition rules also, however, owe something to a fear of a resurgent German capitalism, and a reaction to pre-war cartelization, although they have been adapted to a role serving economic integration. Chapter 8 argues that the design and enforcement of European competition policy is thus imbued with the goal of integration rather than efficiency.

These variations in the timing of, and the motives for, the introduction of competition policy have affected the extent of the various jurisdictions; the fashion in which policy has been inserted into the institutional structure of the state; and the stringency of enforcement. We can consider each of these factors in turn.

Jurisdictions vary symbolically as well as substantively. Even where the reality may be one of gross market distortion, it is important for government and oligopolists to sustain faith in the market, and confidence that market freedoms are ultimately available.[53] It can thus be argued that the Sherman Act had a mainly symbolic impact (see Peters, Chapter 3 above), as did the earlier Canadian legislation of 1889. Similar arguments can, of course, be made for Japanese legislation, in this case providing symbolic reassurance to foreigners as well as to the Japanese. Just as the Japanese legislation has been used to counter criticism, so Sturm observes that German cartel legislation was employed to deflect criticism from the left (see Chapter 7). But, although the symbolic role is powerful, it can raise expectations and, over the longer run, may create serious problems for governments where the gap between enforcement and aspiration becomes too glaring. This is perhaps what has happened in Japan, and in Britain, where Chapters 5 and 6 indicate spectacular shortcomings in policy enforcement, and an extreme pressure for reform. In Japan pressure comes mainly from outside, in Britain it comes from lawyers and from both business and consumer groups. In each case the antidote to empty symbolism would seem to be well-informed and well-supported consumer groups. Such groups vary in their structure and in their access to levers of pressure. Here the legal system may be decisive. Complaints to agencies can be diverted with relative ease, but challenges through the legal system are harder to avoid. In this setting the United States system of private action, resting on the incentive of treble damages, stands out. It is interesting to note that private actions are also possible in the Japanese, Canadian, and European systems (through the national courts), and in each case the earlier chapters indicate some stirring of activity.

Substantive jurisdictions display considerable variation in ways that reflect the distinctive features of the six cases. One of the more intriguing variations lies in the extent to which detailed matters of generic consumer protection are integrated into competition policy administration. Although consumer welfare is an idealized end goal of much competition policy, it is pursued by abstract means through faith in the systemic virtues of competition. In addition, however, most states protect individual consumers through laws against fraud, deception, and manipulative trading. Consumer protection in this sense is outside the 'boundaries' which we set for the policy area in Chapter 2, but it is integrated to some extent with the competition policy jurisdiction in the UK, the USA, Canada, and Japan. The UK goes furthest in this respect so that two-thirds of the staff of the OFT (Office of Fair Trading) devote their efforts to trading standards and such consumer protection issues as regulation of consumer credit and of estate agents. This is perhaps a distraction for policy-makers, but it has been taken seriously and it may have the benign effect of directing attention towards the consumer interest and countering a powerful producer bias.

A second major jurisdictional exception is seen in the ability of the European Commission, as a supranational jurisdiction, to control the potentially anti-competitive behaviour of public authorities. Chapter 8 indicates that enforcement aimed at state aid, and at restrictive sectoral regulation, has constituted a major redirection in the focus of European policy over the past five years. This priority has biased the work of DG IV, and preoccupied its policy-makers, but it does also underline the intra-governmental role that competition policy authorities could be expected to play in national settings. The ability of the national authorities to argue their case within the core machinery of government is variable, depending on the 'core actors' defined in each of the chapters. What is clear is that the ability to influence other governmental interests is becoming more important if 'competition' is to become a generic policy concern across a series of related policy areas. Thus, for instance, the ability of the Japanese FTC to engage in Japanese debates about deregulation may be central in establishing its future credibility. In a more modest vein, of course, competition policy can be affected by federal systems. In both Germany and Canada the enforcement of policy is effectively centralized, but in the United States Peters points out that the fragmentation of administration extends to a growing state-level interest in antitrust.

Beyond these major divergencies all the six jurisdictions have established the full range of conventional competencies to create a mature set of institutions. Those competencies embrace the four areas of: control of monopoly power; control of horizontal restraints (mainly cartels); control of vertical restraints and restrictive practices; and merger control. In virtually all of these jurisdictions, and certainly in the European ones, merger control was the last area of competence to be added. In each of them, however, mergers have become the most important area of activity in terms of work-load, political attention, and likely impact on industrial sectors. Doern notes the attention given to mergers in Canada in the late 1980s (see Chapter 4), as does Sturm in the German setting. The work of the EC Merger Task Force has similarly come to dominate the European debate, while, even in Japan, the increased volume of mergers and the tendency of the FTC to secure modifications has begun to expand this area of activity. This trend reflects a general decline in the level of cartelization in most economies, and an intensifying of international economic activity which has produced a secular increase in the level of competition. The growth in the importance of merger control does, however, increase the political salience of competition policy and has the potential to increase the scope of administrative discretion, and reduce the influence of the courts. Wilks and McGowan certainly identify such a trend at the European level (see Chapter 8).

The discussion of the political salience of competition policy, its original rationale, and extent of jurisdiction provides a context for the analysis of institutions and processes. But this is a context of ideas as well as of legal powers. It would be myopic not to recognize, and to stress, that the very idea of competition has a very variable reception in the societies analysed, which takes us back to the issues of 'systems friction' explored above. The degree to which competition generates societal approval naturally affects the legitimacy of competition policy and the environment of co-operation within which the competition policy institutions operate. The polar opposites here are Japan and the United States. The risk of cultural caricaturing is ever present, but it is true to say that while 'competition' is regarded as a natural and desirable process in the United States it was regarded as incomprehensible and dangerous in post-war Japan. By the same token, monopoly (really oligopoly) is a term of abuse in the United States but has been regarded as a hierarchical inevitability in Japan.[54] It is no coincidence that antitrust is most activist in the United States and marginalized in Japan. The remaining countries lie between these two polar cases. German society has traditionally been sceptical of the virtue of competition, and even views in the United Kingdom are ambiguous. Canada is closer ideologically to the United States but has a far greater tolerance for protectionism and planning.

The effectiveness and credibility of competition policy is affected by the general societal reception of the principle, and it is simultaneously conditiitoned to a fundamental degree by the particular reception of competition policy by business. Each contributor has addressed the influence of business on the shape of competition policy. Doern observes that this influence is both structural and pluralist (in Chapter 10). The structural influence of business in market societies is widely accepted,[55] but does not necessarily translate into enthusiastic support for competition policy. Curiously, a neo-classical market would yield only small 'powerless' companies, whereas the reality in contemporary society is of huge and powerful companies represented in some countries by equally powerful business associations whose importance makes them into 'governing institutions'.[56] Many such companies are decidedly ambiguous about the active enforcement of competition policy. Sturm notes the hostility shown by German business to the proposed cartel law in the 1950s; and, even now, business regards the Bundeskartellamt with mixed feelings. In Chapter 6 Wilks speculates that British business is currently supporting the relaxation in British competition policy, while Peters comments on the worries experienced by US business over the Clinton team's activist policy. Again, Japan provides a polar case where business hostility to antimonopoly has historically marginalized the FTC.

The tendency is for business to be rather schizophrenic about competition policy. In a capitalist world of 'hostile brothers',[57] companies seek the protection of competition laws whilst worrying about the stringency of their enforcement. Doern describes the divided nature of the Canadian business lobby (see Chapter 4) but business is typically united in wanting stability and predictability in the legal framework. In every regime the competition authorities make strenuous efforts to consult with business and to appear reasonable and flexible. As Peters points out, the most effective competition policy relies on 'self-enforcement', a point echoed by Wilks in his discussion of compliance (see Chapter 6). It is also notable that in most jurisdictions, Germany being a possible exception, new laws, regulations, and guidelines are designed only after extensive discussion with business interests. Doern is clear that such interests have had a decisive influence in shaping legislation in the Canadian case, while the same argument can be applied to UK reform of monopoly control, the design of the European Merger Regulation, and the production of guidelines in Japan. Given the influence of business it can sometimes appear that competition policy may not be the application of laws by government to the private sector, but rather the state acting to formalize business self-regulation. At the most basic level of self-interest all enterprises show a concern to protect the values of the market system. Competition policy is a reliable tool in achieving just that.

It has been a consistent theme of this volume that politics makes a difference, and that political differences are embodied in varying institutional arrangements. As noted in Chapter 1, this argument is finding increasingly wide acceptance, especially among 'institutional economists' who speculate that comparative institutional endowments are a factor in the relative economic sucess of firms and states.

In fact there are some notable organizational consistencies in the way in which competition policy has been institutionalized. In all the regimes reviewed it has been entrusted to a legally independent agency with quasi-judicial powers. An assessment of the spectrum of operational, as opposed to legal, independence would put at the pole of extreme independence the Canadian Director of Investigation followed by the German Bundeskartellamt, the EC's Directorate General IV, perhaps bracketed with the twin US institutions of the FTC and the Antitrust Division of the Justice Department. Towards the 'dependent' end of the spectrum would be found the UK's OFT and the Japanese FTC. Both of these have a high level of formal independence but are in practice highly constrained by their political and institutional milieux.

The analyses of the practical autonomy, the internal procedures, the morale, resources, and discretionary powers of these bodies constitute a rich and original body of material in the earlier chapters. A series of comparisons can be drawn out of the discussions but it does not do justice to the range of comparative possibilities. Four areas that should be stressed concern the scope for policy initiatives; the contrasts in administrative entrepreneurship; the variations in organizational fragmentation; and the variations in legal process and appeal.

As regards policy initiatives, the heads of the competition agencies in Canada, Germany, and the EC clearly regard themselves as policy spokespersons and as policy innovators. This is particularly true of the EC, where a series of active Competition Commissioners have changed the face of European Competition Policy in a mere decade. Sturm emphasizes the independent initiative of the Bundeskartellamt and in both Japan and the UK the Chairman of the FTC and the Director General of Fair Trading have an independent role, but have not been able to translate this into substantial policy innovation. The picture varies somewhat when it comes to an assessment of the use of administrative discretion and the extent to which an entrepreneurial organizational culture has allowed a more expansive use of enforcement powers. Here the EC again stands out with self-confident officials achieving substantial expansion of jurisdiction. In the USA, Canada, and Japan too, although on a more modest scale, well-motivated officials have been creative in *de facto* policy innovation. The contrast here is with Germany, locked into an introverted circle of legally circumscribed enforcement, and the UK, where officials are saddled with irrelevant or inadequate legal powers.

Organizationally the UK stands out as the most fragmented regime. The multiple agencies contrast starkly with all the other cases; even the split US system seems to work adequately with a complementary approach rather than the series of vetoes which, as Wilks makes clear, the British system allows (see Chapter 6). It is, perhaps, little wonder that the solution of a single British authority has gained wide support. Each of the other agencies is bound to a lesser extent by political or legal constraints although each has an appeals procedure. The Japanese FTC is perhaps the most constrained by the multiple processes of linkage with other ministries and consensus building through consultation which Sanekata outlines as essential in the Japanese setting (see Chapter 5).

Legal process and appeal provides a fourth institutional comparison. A distinction is conventionally drawn between 'public-interest' regimes in which administrative discretion is pre-eminent, and 'effects on competition' regimes in which strict legal tests and prohibitions are applied and adjudicated at law. Britain provides the public-interest example in which ministerial discretion based on political and administrative judgements is the central principle. British legislation allows the minister and his advisers to take account of virtually anything (see the discussion of section 84 in Chapter 6). Germany is the contrasting 'effects' system in which legal tests are applied and are adjudicated by the civil courts. The EC follows the German model while the regimes of Japan, the USA, and Canada have more similarities with the German than the British model. It is not, however, clear that this contrast is particularly helpful. In reality all regimes have very high levels of administative discretion and informal bargaining. Some use tribunals, some courts, some both. But in all regimes litigation is only the tip of the iceberg. The more revealing comparison is in the processes and philosophies of enforcement and it is to these that we can turn last.

It is, of course, the variability of enforcement which so markedly distinguishes the various regimes under review. In modern, highly organized economies there are a huge number of potential breaches of strict competition principles. Some breaches are so hard to justify that *per se* rules can be made against them, but it could be argued that every contractual agreement is, it its way, a breach of the competition principle. A recognition that this was an unreasonable way to apply the law gave rise to the United States 'rule of reason' doctrine, but what this really illustrates is the challenge presented to all competition authorities to establish a threshold of illegality.

The way in which that threshold has been defined has varied over time, especially in the United States where distinct cycles of antitrust enforcement can be discerned. The threshold of illegality depends not only on political guidance but on administrative self-restraint, legal constraints, and the requirements of a workable compliance policy. It is clear that these various factors have combined to produce extremely low levels of enforcement in some regimes and very forceful levels in others. The constant complaint against Japan has not been against the competition laws, but against the way they are enforced. In contrast, European rules have been enforced with quite extraordinary creativity since the 1970s to extend the enforcement agenda. In the Japanese case administrative self-restraint was the main culprit, in the European case Wilks and McGowan argue that activism rested on a remarkable partnership with the European Court (see Chapter 8). Quite the contrary can be seen in the German case where the Courts have acted as a brake and almost as an opponent of strict enforcement (see, for instance, the example of retailing in Chapter 7).

The difficult threshold decisions about negotiation and prosecution are nicely illustrated by the Canadian screening list discussed in Chapter 4. It illustrates the difficult practical decisions that face competition officials who have to balance the availability of evidence, staff, legal support, political support, impact, and reasonableness. It is hardly surprising that large numbers of cases in every regime are settled informally. As Doern points out in Chapter 2, a low level of prosecutions may be a sign of success rather than failure.

The factor that has always tempered any inclination to engage in adverserial enforcement, and which has received greater emphasis in the contemporary era of liberalization, is the requirement of compliance. As noted above, enforcement has to be reasonable, flexible, and 'fair'; if it is otherwise criticisms from business will tend to mobilize effective opposition. Systematic attention to compliance has traditionally been a feature of US practice where a sub-discipline of 'regulatory politics' has evolved to study the ways in which pragmatic independent regulators engage with their clientele. These approaches are belatedly receiving more attention in Europe as forms of agency regulation become more widespread.[58] DG IV is making more deliberate attempts to encourage companies to set up compliance programmes, with some modest success. The Japanese FTC is taking a similar approach with its guidelines and has been following this programme of 'preventative law' since the early 1980s (as outlined in Chapter 5). In Canada also this emphasis on compliance has come to the fore, with a new Division within the Competition Bureau and direct support from the Director of Investigation (see Chapter 4). The emphasis on compliance represents an important cross-national trend. It seems to indicate a thorough compromise with industry on the US model and may hold out the risk of capture. Competition policy officials already have to tread a difficult line between legal stipulations, efficiency tests, and administrative reasonableness. Their credibility may become hard to sustain.

In the introductory chapter the ideas of institutionalism were briefly reviewed and Peters revisited the theory briefly in Chapter 3. We conceive of institutions as sets of rules and values and we share the views of the 'historical institutionalist' school which emphasizes the early choices about policy and institutions. In this view policies are possessed with a degree of inertia, they are embedded in institutional settings and become, to a degree, 'path dependent'.[59] We observe this process at work in all our six cases. The chapters on Japan and on the EC describe this syndrome but it reaches its apogee in the German case. Sturm presents a fascinating picture of an agency marked by great continuity and self-confidence but adapting badly to its challenging environment. The other self-confident regime is that of the United States where antitrust is part of the national culture and is almost a service industry sub-sector, embracing academics, lawyers, and lobbyists, as well as officials.

These two self-confident regimes, the US and the German, are the two contenders for national 'models' of antitrust. The US model is, of course, the real parent of the Japanese and, much less directly, of the German and European regimes, but the German cartel authorities are keen to impose their variant of the model on European institutions. What does emerge from this discussion, however, is the proposition that no one model of reform offers itself. Each regime has adapted to national circumstances. The European model has been the most effective in recent years but that is itself under challenge and its basic dynamic force, that of European integration, has been greatly attenuated.

If comparison of national and regional competition policy institutions does not provide a clear model for future international arrangements at least it reveals a number of relevant observations with which we can conclude. The first is that the creation of institutions is a political process. For all the earnest work on technical convergence in the OECD, and the constructive bilateral agreements, the creation of an international set of institutions will require a major political initiative. The second trend is one that was emphasized in the Europe chapter as well as in the discussion of efficiency above. Despite the purism of competition lawyers and economists, competition policy must engage with other policy areas and create policy linkages. The linkage with industrial policy is already well developed but the international linkage will have to extend to environmental and perhaps even human rights policy. With her facility for phrase-creation Sylvia Ostry has noted that these policy areas are built on '"transformational coalitions" who are dedicated to fundamental change in economic and political behaviour'.[60] These coalitions are opposed to a new world order built on the unrestricted freedom of business which is escaping the regulatory grasp of the national state.[61] Our third observation is therefore that competition policies, which were introduced to sustain competitive markets and to curb excesses of market power, have come dangerously close to a role transformation and are working to support companies powerful in the market. This is a model of policy that will commend itself to the representatives of multinational enterprises but which should generate strong reservations elsewhere. Any design for new international competition policy institutions should ground itself in a critical view of international corporate concentration and look to the radical and crusading roots of the competition policy tradition.

NOTES

1. See Sylvia Ostry, *Governments and Corporations in a Shrinking World: Trade and Innovation Policies in The United States, Europe, and*

Japan (New York: Council on Foreign Relations, 1990). See also Ostry, 'Globalization, Domestic Policies and the Need For Harmonization', paper presented to a Workshop on Competition Policy in a Global Economy, University of California, Jan. 1993.

2. Ibid. 2.
3. Ibid. 2.
4. See the comparative institutional studies of industrial relations systems by Colin Crouch, *Industrial Relations and European State Traditions* (Oxford: The Clarendon Press, 1992); and Wolfgang Streeck, *Social Institutions and Economic Performance: Studies of Industrial Relations in Advanced Capitalist Economies* (London: Sage, 1992).
5. One of the best treatments of this theme is by Clyde Prestowitz, *Trading Places: How America Allowed Japan to Take the Lead* (Tokyo: Tuttle, 1988).
6. Michel Albert, *Capitalism Against Capitalism* (London: Whurr, 1993).
7. See J. A. Brander and B. J. Spencer, 'International R&D Strategy and Industrial Rivalry', *Review of Economic Studies*, 50 (1983), 707–22, and Paul Krugman (ed.), *Strategic Trade Policy and the New International Economics* (Cambridge, Mass.: MIT Press, 1986), introd.
8. See Donald Hay, 'International Aspects of Competition Policy in the United Kingdom', Oxford, Institute of Economics and Statistics, unpublished paper, Nov. 1993.
9. See J. David Richardson, 'Empirical Research on Trade Liberalization with Imperfect Competition: A Survey', *OECD Economic Studies*, 12 (Paris: OECD, spring 1989).
10. See Laura D'Andrea Tyson, *Who's Bashing Whom? Trade Conflict in High Technology Industries* (Washington, DC: Institute for International Economics, 1992), and Akira Goto and Kotaro Suzumura, 'Keiretsu-Interfirm Relationships in Japan', paper presented to a Workshop on Competition Policy in a Global Economy, University of California, Jan. 1993.
11. See Richard R. Nelson (ed.), *National Innovation Systems: A Comparative Analysis* (Oxford: Oxford University Press, 1993).
12. See Michael Porter, *The Competitive Advantage of Nations* (New York: Free Press, 1990); Lester Thurow, *Head To Head* (London: Nicholas Brealy, 1993); and Robert Reich, *The Work of Nations* (New York: Knopf, 1991).
13. Tyson, *Who's Bashing Whom?*.
14. Ibid. 13.
15. Ibid. 3.
16. See Paul Krugman, 'Competitiveness: A Dangerous Obsession', *Foreign Affairs*, Mar./Apr. 1994, 28–44.
17. The authors are law and business specialists respectively, Thomas M. Jorde and David J. Teece, 'Rule of Reason Analysis of Horizontal

356   G. *Bruce Doern and Stephen Wilks*

Arrangements: Agreements Designed to Advance Innovation and Commercialize Technology', *Antitrust Law Journal*, 61/2 (1992), 579–620.
18. Ibid. 579.
19. Ibid. 579.
20. See Michael Best, *The New Competition* (Cambridge: Polity Press, 1990).
21. See also Albert, *Capitalism Against Capitalism*.
22. See L. Waverman and S. Khemani, 'Strategic Alliances: A Threat To Competition?', paper presented at a Workshop on Competition Policy in a Global Economy, University of California, Jan. 1993.
23. Ibid. 2.
24. See A. E. Safarian, 'Foreign Direct Investment and International Cooperative Agreements: Trends and Issues', paper presented at a Workshop on Competition Policy in a Global Economy, University of California, Jan. 1993.
25. See Rainer Markl and Werner Meissner, 'Strategic Alliances and Joint Ventures: The European Case', paper presented to a Workshop on Competition Policy in a Global Economy, University of California, Jan. 1993.
26. See Stephen Martin, 'Public Policies Toward Cooperation in Research and Development: The European Community, Japan, and the United States', paper presented to a Workshop on Competition Policy in a Global Economy, University of California, Jan. 1993; and Kotaro Suzumura and Akira Goto, 'Collaborative Research and Development: Economic Analysis in the Light of Japanese Experience', paper presented to a Workshop as above.
27. See Donald G. McFetridge, 'Competition Policy and Market Access', paper presented to a Conference on Canada and International Trade, University of Ottawa, May 1993.
28. See Edward M. Graham and J. David Richardson, 'Global Competition Policies: Issues in Trade and Industrial Economics', manuscript (Washington, DC: Institute for International Economics, 1993).
29. See J. David Richardson, 'Remarks for Reconciliation or Adjudication Panel', Conference on Trade, Investment and Competition Policies: Conflict or Convergence, Centre for Trade Policy and Law, University of Ottawa, May 1993, 4.
30. See Robert D. Anderson and S. Dev Khosla, *Competition Policy as a Dimension of Economic Policy: A Comparative Perspective and Agenda for the Future*, revised draft (Ottawa: Bureau of Competition Policy, 1994).
31. For further discussion, see G. Bruce Doern, *Competition Policy Decision Processes in the European Community and United Kingdom* (Ottawa: Bureau of Competition Policy, 1992); see also the discussion of these issues in Chapter 8 above.

32. They disagree on much else. For a provocative assertion of the pre-eminence of trade policy see B. Hoeckman and P. Mavroidis, *Competition, Competition Policy, and the GATT*, Policy Research Working Paper 1228 (Washington, DC: World Bank, 1993).
33. See Geza Feketekuty, 'Reflections on the Interaction Between Trade Policy and Competition Policy: A Contribution to the Development of a Conceptual Framework' (Paris: OECD, Feb. 1993), 11.
34. Ibid. 15.
35. See J. Michael Finger (ed.), *Antidumping: How It Works and Who Gets Hurt* (Ann Arbour: University of Michigan Press, 1993), and Thomas Boddez and M. Trebilcock, *Unfinished Business: Reforming Trade Remedy Laws in North America* (Toronto: C. D. Howe Institute, 1993).
36. See G. Bruce Doern, 'A Political-Institutional Framework for the Analysis of Competition Policy Institutions', *Governance*, 8/2 (Apr. 1995), 195–214.
37. See James Mathis, 'International Cooperation: Has the Time Come for the Integration of Competition Policies?', paper presented to the Workshop on Developments in European Competition Policy, Maastricht, July 1994.
38. See Glen Toner, 'The Canadian Environmental Movement: A Conceptual Map', unpublished paper, Carleton University, 1991; and Albert Weale, *The New Politics of Pollution* (Manchester: Manchester University Press, 1992).
39. See, Barbara J. Bramble and Gareth Porter, 'Non-Governmental Organizations and the Making of US International Environmental Policy', in Andrew Hurrell and B. Kingsbury (eds.), *The International Politics of the Environment* (Oxford: The Clarendon Press, 1992), 313–53, and Andrew Simms, 'If Not Then, When? Non-Governmental Organizations and the Earth Summit Process', *Environmental Politics*, 2/1 (spring, 1993), 94–101.
40. See also Stephen Wilks, 'Options for Reform of EC Competition Policy', in Aad Van Mourik (ed.), *The Reform of EU Competition Policy* (Maastricht: EIPA, 1995), forthcoming.
41. For a discussion of NAFTA and trade bloc issues see T. D. Mason and A. M. Turay (eds.), *Japan, NAFTA and Europe* (London: Macmillan, 1994).
42. Boddez and Trebilcock, *Unfinished Business*.
43. For instance, Tony Freyer, *Regulating Big Business: Antitrust in Great Britain and America 1880–1990* (Cambridge: Cambridge University Press, 1992).
44. For instance, David Audretsch, *The Market and the State: Government Policy Towards Business in Europe, Japan and the USA* (London: Harvester Wheatsheaf, 1989).

45. For instance F. M. Scherer, *Competition Policies for an Integrated World Economy* (Washington, DC: The Brookings Institution, 1994); or W. S. Comanor *et al.*, *Competition Policy in Europe and North America: Economic Issues and Institutions* (London: Harwood, 1990).

46. See the annual OECD reports on competition policy; their *ad hoc* competition policy publications; and the various papers released by the Competition Law and Policy Committee (also discussed by Trebilcock in Chapter 9).

47. Recent studies are summarized in the standard texts such as Richard Whish, *Competition Law* (3rd edn., London: Butterworths, 1993). A very helpful earlier text is Corwin Edwards, *Trade Regulations Overseas: The National Laws* (Dobbs Ferry: Oceana, 1966).

48. See an earlier effort at grappling with these issues in Stephen Wilks and Maurice Wright, 'The Comparative Context of Japanese Political Economy', in Wilks and Wright (eds.), *The Promotion and Regulation of Industry in Japan* (London: Macmillan, 1991), 11–31.

49. Scherer, *Competition Policies*, 18.

50. See the outstanding historical work by David Gerber, e.g. 'Constitutionalising the Economy: German Neo-liberalism, Competition Law and the "New" Europe', *American Journal of Comparative Law*, 42 (1994), 25–84.

51. See F. Jenny, 'French Competition Policy in Perspective', in Comanor *et al.*, *Competition Policy*, 146–88; and for current Italian reforms various issues of the *European Competition Law Review*.

52. Porter, *The Competitive Advantage*, 117 n. 11.

53. A point regularly made, even by economists; see C. Green, 'Industrial Organization Paradigms, Empirical Evidence and the Economic Case for Competition Policy', *Canadian Journal of Economics*, 20/3 (Aug. 1987), 482–505.

54. See the standard work, by Eleanor Hadley, *Antitrust in Japan* (Princeton: Princeton University Press, 1970), 13.

55. The essential work is Charles Lindblom, *Politics and Markets* (New York: Basic Books, 1977), but the literature is now very extensive.

56. The phrase is used by Keith Middlemas in his *Politics in Industrial Society* (London: André Deutsch, 1979).

57. An expressive term used by Alan Cawson and his colleagues in A. Cawson, K. Morgan, D. Webber, P. Holmes, and Anne Stevens, *Hostile Brothers: Competition and Closure in the European Electronics Industry* (Oxford: The Clarendon Press, 1990).

58. There is a rapidly developing literature on comparative regulation. For a flavour see Giandomenico Majone, 'Paradoxes of Privatization and Deregulation', *Journal of European Public Policy*, 1/1 (June 1994), 53–69; or Stephen Wilks, review, *Political Studies*, 42/4 (1995), 721–2.

59. For further recent exploration of these themes see Elinor Ostrom, 'New Horizons in Institutional Analysis', *American Political Science Review*, 89/1 (Mar. 1995), review article, 174–8.

60. Sylvia Ostry, 'New Dimensions of Market Access', paper presented to an OECD Round Table on Market Access in a Globalizing World Economy (Paris: OECD, July 1994), 11.

61. An idea explored in Vivien Schmidt, 'The New World Order Incorporated: The Rise of Business and the Decline of the Nation-State', *Daedalus*, spring, 1995, 75–106.

SELECT BIBLIOGRAPHY

We have selected basic economic and legal references on competition policy from the earlier chapters but, in particular, we have included sources which deal with the political and institutional aspects of competition policy. English language references only.

American Bar Association, *Report of the American Bar Association Section of Antitrust Task Force on the Antitrust Division of the U.S. Department of Justice* (Chicago: American Bar Association, 1989).

ANDERSON, ROBERT D. and KHOSLA, S. DEV, *Competition Policy as a Dimension of Economic Policy: A Comparative Dimension* (Ottawa: Bureau of Competition Policy, 1993).

AUERBACH, PAUL, *The Economics of Industrial Change* (Oxford: Blackwell, 1988).

Australian Government, *National Competition Policy: Report of the Independent Committee of Inquiry* (Canberra, 1993).

AYRES, IAN and BRAITHWAITE, JOHN, *Responsive Regulation: Transcending the Deregulation Debate* (Oxford: Oxford University Press, 1992).

BALDWIN, R. and McCRUDDEN, C., *Regulation and Public Law* (London: Weidenfeld and Nicolson, 1987).

BAUMOL, W. J., PANZAR, J. C. and WILLIG, R. D., *Contestable Markets and the Theory of Industry Structure* (New York: Harcourt, Brace, Jovanovitch, 1988).

BEST, MICHAEL H., *The New Competition: Institutions of Industrial Restructuring* (Cambridge: Polity Press, 1990).

BICKEL, D. R., 'The Antitrust Division's Adoption of the Chicago School Economic Policy Calls for Some Reorganization: But is the Division's New Policy Here to Stay?', *Houston Law Review*, 20 (1982), 1083–127.

BISHOP, M. and KAY, J. (eds.), *European Mergers and Merger Policy* (Oxford: Oxford University Press, 1993).

BLAISDELL, T. C., *The Federal Trade Commission: An Experiment in the Regulation of American Business* (New York: Columbia University Press, 1932).

BODDEZ, THOMAS M. and TREBILCOCK, MICHAEL, *Unfinished Business: Reforming Trade Remedy Laws in North America* (Toronto: C. D. Howe Institute, 1993).

BORRIE, SIR GORDON, 'Merger Policy: Current Policy Concerns'. In James A. Fairburn and John Kay (eds.), *Mergers and Merger Policy* (Oxford: Oxford University Press, 1989), 246–63.

BURKE, TERRY A., GENN-BASH, A. and HAINES, B., *Competition in Theory and Practice* (rev.edn., London: Routledge, 1991).

CAMILLERI, JOSEPH A. and FALK, JIM, *The End of Sovereignty?* (Aldershot: Edward Elgar, 1992).

CARLETON, DENNIS W. and PERLOFF, JEFFREY M., *Modern Industrial Organization* (Glenview, Ill.: Scott, Foresman, 1990).

COMANOR, W. S., GEORGE, K., JAQUEMIN, A., JENNY, F., KANTZENBACH, E., ORDOVER, J. and WAVERMAN, L., *Competition Policy in Europe and North America: Economic Issues and Institutions* (London: Harwood, 1990).

COWLING, K. and TOMANN, HORST (eds.), *Industrial Policy after 1992: An Anglo-German Perpsective* (London: Anglo-German Foundation, 1990).

CRAMPTON, PAUL S., *Mergers and the Competition Act* (Toronto: Carswell, 1990).

DAVIDSON, ROY M., 'When Merger Guidelines Fail to Guide', *Canadian Competition Policy Record*, 12 (Dec. 1991), 44–51.

Director of Investigation and Research, *Submission to the National Transportation Act Review Commission* (Ottawa: Bureau of Competition Policy, 1992).

DOERN, G. BRUCE, *Fairer Play: Canadian Competition Policy Institutions in a Global Market* (Toronto: C. D. Howe Institute, 1995).

—— 'A Political-Institutional Framework for the Analysis of Competition Policy Institutions', *Governance*, Apr. 1995.

—— *Modernizing Economic Framework Legislation: A Discussion Paper* (Ottawa: Consumer and Corporate Affairs Canada, 1987).

—— and TOMLIN, BRIAN W., *Faith and Fear: The Free Trade Story* (Toronto: Stoddart, 1991).

EISNER, M. A., *Antitrust and the Triumph of Economics* (Chapel Hill: University of North Carolina Press, 1991).

—— 'Bureaucratic Professionalism and the Limits of the Political Control Thesis: The Case of the Federal Trade Commission', *Governance*, 6 (1993), 127–53.

FAIRBURN, JAMES A. and KAY, JOHN, (eds.), *Mergers and Merger Policy* (Oxford: Oxford University Press, 1989).

FIRST, HARRY, FOX, ELEANOR, and PITOFSKY, ROBERT, *Revitalizing Antitrust in its Second Century* (New York: Quorum Books, 1991).

FRANCIS, JOHN, *The Politics of Regulation: A Comparative Perspective* (Oxford: Blackwell, 1993).

FRAZER, TIM, *Monopoly, Competition and the Law* (Brighton: Wheatsheaf, 1988).

FREYER, TONY, *Regulating Big Business: Antitrust in Great Britain and America 1880–1990* (Cambridge: Cambridge University Press, 1992).

GERBER, DAVID J., 'The Transformation of European Community Competition Law', *Harvard International Law Journal*, 35 (1994), 97–147.

GORECKI, PAUL K. and STANBURY, W. T., *The Objectives of Canadian Competition Policy 1888–1983* (Montreal: Institute for Research on Public Policy, 1984).

GOYDER, D., *EC Competition Law* (2nd edn., Oxford: The Clarendon Press, 1993).

HADLEY, ELEANOR, *Antitrust in Japan* (Princeton: Princeton University Press, 1970).

HARRIS, R. A. and MILKIS, S. M., *The Politics of Regulatory Change* (New York: Oxford University Press, 1989).

HAY, DONALD, 'The Assessment: Competition Policy', *Oxford Review of Economic Policy*, Special Issue on Competition Policy, 9/2 (summer 1993), 1–26.

HOOD, CHRISTOPHER, *Administrative Analysis* (London: Harvester Wheatsheaf, 1986).

House of Lords, Select Committee on the European Communities, *Enforcement of Community Competition Rules*, Report with evidence, 1993–4, HL 7 (London: HMSO, 1993).

International Antitrust Code Working Group, *Draft International Antitrust Code* (Munich, July 1993).

IRELAND, DEREK, *Interactions Between Competition and Trade Policies: Challenges and Opportunities* (Ottawa: Bureau of Competition Policy, 1992).

IYORI, H. and UESUGI, A., *The Antimonopoly Laws of Japan* (New York: Federal Legal Publications Inc., 1994).

JACQUEMIN, ALEXIS, 'The International Dimension of European Competition Policy', *Journal of Common Market Studies*, 31 (Mar. 1993), 91–101.

JORDE, THOMAS M. and TEECE, DAVID J., (eds.), *Antitrust, Innovation and Competitiveness* (Oxford: Oxford University Press, 1992).

KATZMANN, R. A., *Regulatory Bureaucracy: The Federal Trade Commission and Antitrust Policy* (Cambridge, Mass.: MIT Press, 1980).

KAUPER, T. E., 'The Role of Economic Analysis in the Antitrust Division Before and After the Establishment of the Economic Policy Office', *Antitrust Bulletin*, 29 (1984), 111–32.

KHEMANI, R. S. and STANBURY, W. T. (eds.), *Canadian Competition Law and Policy at the Centenary* (Montreal: Institute for Research on Public Policy, 1991).

KHOSLA, D., *et al.*, *Reference Document on Abuse of Dominance* (Ottawa: Bureau of Competition Policy, 1991).

KORAH, VALENTINE, *An Introductory Guide to EC Competition Law and Practice* (5th edn., London: Sweet and Maxwell, 1994).

KWOKA, J. and WHITE, L. J. (eds.), *The Antitrust Revolution* (New York: Harper Collins, 1989; 2nd edn., 1994).

Law Reform Commission, *Policy Implementation, Compliance and Administrative Law* (Ottawa: Law Reform Commission, 1986).

MARCH, J. G. and OLSEN, J. P. *Rediscovering Institutions* (New York: Free Press, 1989).

MATHESON, FRANK, TREBILCOCK, M. and WALKER, MICHAEL (eds.), *The Law and Economics of Competition Policy* (Vancouver: Fraser Institute, 1990).

McCHESNEY, FRED S. and SHUGART, WILLIAM F. II (eds.), *The Causes and Consequences of Antitrust: The Public-Choice Perspective* (Chicago: University of Chicago Press, 1995).

MATSUSHITA, MITSUO, *International Trade and Competition Law in Japan* (Oxford: Oxford University Press, 1993).

MEIER, K. J., *Regulation: Politics, Bureaucracy, Economics* (New York: St Martins, 1985).

MONTAGNON, PETER (ed.), *European Competition Policy* (London: Pinter, 1990).

NEVEN, DAMIEN, NUTTALL, ROBIN, and SEABRIGHT, PAUL, *Mergers in Daylight: The Economics and Politics of European Merger Control* (London: Centre for Economic Policy Research, 1993).

NEWBORN, STEPHEN A. and SNIDER, VIRGINIA, 'The Growing Judicial Acceptance of the Merger Guidelines', *Antitrust Law Journal*, 60 (1992), 849–65.

OECD, *Competition Law Enforcement* (Paris: OECD, 1983).

—— *Competition Policy and International Trade: OECD Instruments of Cooperation* (Paris: OECD, 1987).

—— *Twenty-Five Years of Competition Policy: Achievements and Challenges* (Paris: OECD, 1987).

—— *Competition and Economic Development* (Paris: OECD, 1991).

—— Committee on Competition Policy. *Annual Report on Developments in Germany* (Paris: OECD, 1991).

OSTRY, SYLVIA, *Governments and Corporations in a Shrinking World: Trade and Innovation Policies in the United States, Europe and Japan* (New York: Council on Foreign Relations, 1990).

PINDER, JOHN, *European Community* (Oxford: Oxford University Press, 1991).

PORTER, MICHAEL, *The Competitive Advantage of Nations* (New York: Free Press, 1992).

POSNER, R. A., 'The Chicago School of Antitrust Analysis', *University of Pennsylvania Law Review*, 127 (1979), 925–48.

PRATT, JOHN, 'Changes in UK Competition Policy: A Wasted Opportunity', *European Competition Law Review*, 2 (1994).

RAMSAY, IAN, 'The Office of Fair Trading'. In R. Baldwin and C. McCrudden (eds.), *Regulation and Public Law* (London: Weidenfeld and Nicolson, 1987).

RAMSEYER, J. MARK, 'The Costs of the Consensual Myth: Antitrust Enforcement and Institutional Barriers to Litigation in Japan', *Yale Law Journal*, 94/1–3 (1984–5), 604–45.

REASONER, H. M., 'Antitrust Policy', in M. Feldstein (ed.), *American Economic Policy in the 1980s* (Chicago: Chicago University Press, 1994).

SALOP, S. C. and WHITE, L. J., 'Private Antitrust Litigation: Introduction and Framework for Analysis', in White (ed.), *Private Antitrust Litigation* (Cambridge, Mass.: MIT Press, 1988).

SANEKATA, KENJI, 'Antitrust in Japan: Recent Trends and Their Sociopolitical Background', *University of British Columbia Law Review*, 20/2 (1986), 380–96.

SCHERER, F. M., *Competition Policies for an Integrated World Economy* (Washington, DC: the Brookings Institution, 1994).

—— and ROSS, D., *Industrial Market Structure and Economic Performance* (3rd edn., Boston: Houghton Mifflin, 1990).

SHUGHART, WILLIAM F., 'Private Antitrust Enforcement: Compensation, Deterrence or Extortion', *Regulation*, fall, 1990, 53–61.

—— *Antitrust Policy and Interest Group Politics* (New York: Quorum Books, 1990).

STANBURY, W. T., *Business Interests and the Reform of Canadian Competition Policy, 1971–1975* (Toronto: Carswell Methuen, 1977).

—— 'An Assessment of the Merger Review Process under the Competition Act', *Canadian Business Law Journal*, 20 (Aug. 1992), 422–63.

THORELLI, H., *Federal Antitrust Policy: Origins of an American Tradition* (Baltimore: Johns Hopkins University Press, 1954).

TREBILCOCK, MICHAEL, 'The Evolution of Competition Policy: A Comparative Perspective'. In Frank Matheson *et al.*, *The Law and Economics of Competition Policy* (Vancouver: Fraser Institute, 1990), 1–26.

WEAVER, R. K. and ROCKMAN, B. A., *Do Institutions Matter? Government Capabilities in the United States and Abroad* (Washington, DC: Brookings Institution, 1993).

WEISS, J. 'The Structure-Conduct Performance Paradigm and Antitrust', *University of Pennsylvania Law Review*, 127 (1979), 1104–40.

WHISH, RICHARD, *Competition Law* (3rd edn., London: Butterworths, 1989).

—— and WOOD, DIANE P., *OECD Merger Process Convergence Project* (Paris: OECD, 1994).

WHITE, L. J. (ed.), *Private Antitrust Litigation: New Evidence New Learning* (New York, Free Press, 1988).

WILKS, STEPHEN, *The Metamorphosis of European Competition Policy* (Exeter: RUSEL Working Paper 9, 1992).

—— *The Office of Fair Trading in Administrative Context* (London: Centre for the Study of Regulated Industries, 1994).

—— *The Revival of Japanese Competition Policy and Its Importance For*

EU–Japan Relations (London: Royal Institute of International Affairs, 1994).

—— and MCGOWAN, LEE, 'Discretion in European Merger Control: The German Regime in Context', *European Journal of Public Policy*, 2/1 (1995), 41–68.

—— 'Disarming the Commission: The Debate over a European Cartel Office', *Journal of Common Market Studies*, 33/2 (1995), 259–73.

WILLIAMSON, O. E., *Markets and Hierarchies: Analysis and Anti-Trust Implications* (New York: Free Press, 1975).

—— *Antitrust Economics* (Oxford: Blackwell, 1987).

INDEX

Index compiled by Frank Pert